Acclaim for This Groundbreaking Biography

This book is much more than simply another biography about St. Faustina. Award-winning journalist and historian Ewa Czaczkowska researches the life of Faustina with a relentless drive to discover what made her tick. As a journalist, she knows that she's breaking the big story about the mystic whose life and mission have inspired the Divine Mercy movement. As a historian, Czaczkowska knows that she needs to place Faustina within the context of her times.

No armchair researcher, Czaczkowska leaves no stone unturned as she follows in the footsteps of Faustina the mystic, visiting each of the locations the saint called home throughout her life. At each location, not only does Czaczkowska give readers a grasp of how the times and Faustina's environment shaped her, the biographer also shares more personally the testimonies of those who knew Faustina best.

As a result, Czaczkowska helps you get to know Faustina as a living, breathing human being. Among other things, you discover this future saint had a temper, disappointed her father when she came home late one evening from a dance, and doubted at times whether her visions of the Lord were real. And many of the testimonies and photos that Czaczkowska presents are unique to this biography, the fruit of the author's passionate research.

Czaczkowska also delves into St. Faustina's rich interior life. For example, you can now follow the saint's visions of heaven, hell, and purgatory in a comprehensible way. Gaps in her inner life that are not clarified in the *Diary* are addressed, giving you a better sense of what was happening in her spiritual life as she received many of her revelations from Jesus.

To sum up, the biographer paints a compelling, fresh, and intimate portrait of Faustina. This great mystic emerges as a real person who struggled with her inadequacies and limitations even as she was blessed with extraordinary spiritual gifts and given a unique mission by Jesus Himself. That is why I highly recommend this groundbreaking biography.

— **From the Foreword by Fr. Kazimierz Chwałek, MIC**
Provincial Superior of the Marian Fathers in the U.S. and Argentina

Important saints should be brought closer to people in many ways. It is important to do so in an interesting manner and in language accessible to contemporary readers, while presenting the depth of the spirituality of the saint. All of these conditions are met in this biography about St. Faustina by Ewa Czaczkowska.

— **Cardinal Kazimierz Nycz**
Archbishop of Warsaw, Poland

FAUSTINA

the mystic
&
Her Message

Ewa K. Czaczkowska

MARIAN PRESS
STOCKBRIDGE
MA 01263

PRO CHRISTO ET ECCLESIA

2014

Available from:
Marian Helpers Center
Stockbridge, MA 01263

Prayerline: 1-800-804-3823
Orderline: 1-800-462-7426
www.marian.org
www.thedivinemercy.org

Library of Congress Catalog Number: 2014955011
ISBN: 978-1-59614-310-4

Design of Cover and Pages: Kathy Szpak
Cover Image: Celestial Sunrise image

Translation:
Orest Pawlak, Agata Rottkamp, Mrs. Margaret N. Stevens,
Karolina Socha-Duśko, and Zofia Szozda

Editing and Proofreading:
Chris Sparks, David Came, Andrew Leeco,
Br. Timothy Childers, MIC, and Maciej Talar

Imprimi Potest:
Very Rev. Kazimierz Chwałek, MIC
Provincial Superior
The Blessed Virgin Mary, Mother of Mercy Province
Congregation of Marian Fathers of the Immaculate Conception
November 1, 2014, All Saints Day

Note to Reader: Following the conventions of the *Diary of St. Maria Faustina Kowalska*,
the words of Jesus cited from the *Diary* in this book are in boldface and
the words of the Blessed Virgin Mary are in italics.

For texts from the English Edition of the *Diary of St. Maria Faustina Kowalska:
Divine Mercy in My Soul.* 1987 © Marian Fathers of the Immaculate
Conception of the B.V.M. All rights reserved. Used with permission.

Nihil Obstat:
Lector Officialis
Most Rev. George H. Pearce, SNM

Imprimatur:
Most Rev. Joseph F. Maguire
Bishop of Springfield, Mass.
January 29, 1988

Printed in the United States of America

CONTENTS

ACKNOWLEDGMENTS
FOR THE ENGLISH-LANGUAGE EDITION

MARIAN PRESS GRATEFULLY ACKNOWLEDGES the contributions of the following people who helped prepare *Faustina: The Mystic and Her Message* by Ewa Czaczkowska for publication. It is the English-language edition of the author's original book in Polish, which is titled *Siostra Faustyna: Biografia Świętej* (*Faustina: The Biography of a Saint*).

First of all, we acknowledge and thank Orest Pawlak of www.translatores.com and his team of translators who labored under very tight deadlines to ensure that our English-language edition could be published in 2014. They did the heavy lifting by translating the original Polish text into English with the popular American reader in mind. Along with Mr. Pawlak of Kraków, Poland, other members of the translation team were Agata Rottkamp of Silver Spring, Maryland; Mrs. Margaret N. Stevens of Malton, North Yorkshire, the United Kingdom; Karolina Socha-Duśko of Kraków, Poland; and Zofia Szozda of Tarnobrzeg, Poland.

Among the team, special mention goes to Ms. Rottkamp, who carefully edited and proofread the whole book, while other translators focused on particular sections or parts of the book. Ms. Rottkamp, in short, served as the "translation editor," making sure that the translation of the book as a whole was consistent and clear. Further, Mrs. Stevens was invaluable in coordinating the translation work and contributing to it in various ways, both large and small, from the very beginning.

The translators faced many challenges. Given the Polish text's focus on Roman Catholicism and the religious life during the time of St. Faustina in her native Poland, as well as on Christian mysticism in order to describe her rich inner life, many theological and religious terms had to be accurately rendered into English. Aspects of the culture, history, and geography of Poland, both before and after World War II, also had to be explained to the American reader. In many cases, the translators recommended that the editors provide clarification or further explanation of such matters in endnotes to the work. The editors usually agreed, and the endnotes to the book rapidly grew in number.

Further, working on behalf of the Marian Fathers, Fr. Seraphim Michalenko, MIC, and Maciej Talar painstakingly checked the English translation for accuracy, focusing especially on facts relevant to the life of St. Faustina and the history of the Divine Mercy movement. Father Michalenko was drawing upon his extensive background on the saint and the movement she inspired — including his more than 20 years as vice postulator for North America of Faustina's canonization cause and his crucial role in the publication of the original Polish edition of her *Diary* as well as various translations of it. Mr. Talar assisted him as the longtime editor of the Marian Fathers' Polish quarterly magazine, *Róże Maryi*.

The principal editor of the English-language edition for Marian Press was Chris Sparks, who worked closely with me on the final editing and proofreading of the text in English, based on any concerns and suggestions from both Mr. Pawlak's translation team and our own in-house fact checkers, Fr. Michalenko and Mr. Talar. He composed many of the endnotes. Mr. Sparks works for the Marians as an assistant editor and writer. Further, Andrew Leeco assisted with the proofreading and also worked on compiling and checking all of the page references for the Index of Names in the back of the book. Mr. Leeco works for the Marians as an associate editor and designer. Mr. Talar also assisted the editors with the final editing and proofreading.

Kathy Szpak, who works for the Marians as a graphic designer, was responsible for both the cover and page design of *Faustina: The Mystic and Her Message.*

Finally, Fr. Kazimierz Chwałek, MIC, provincial superior of the Blessed Virgin Mary, Mother of Mercy Province of the Marian Fathers of the Immaculate Conception, wrote the foreword.

Once again, on behalf of Marian Press, thank you for helping us make this book a reality. Saint Faustina, pray for us!

David Came
Executive Editor of Marian Press

FOREWORD

Here's the reason you have a very special book in your hands: A couple of years ago, I was eagerly reading the Polish original of this new biography of St. Faustina by Ewa Czaczkowska since the Marian Fathers in Stockbridge, Massachusetts, were interested in translating it into English. I found myself thrilled at the prospect because the more I read, the more I began to realize that this award-winning biographer, historian, and investigative journalist had broken new ground in her approach to understanding St. Faustina as a real person.

This is much more than simply another biography about the saint. Czaczkowska researches and writes about Faustina with a relentless drive and passion to discover what made her tick. As a journalist, she knows that she's breaking the big story about the mystic whose life and mission have inspired the Divine Mercy movement, one of the greatest grassroots movements in the history of the Catholic Church. As a historian, Czaczkowska knows that she needs to place Faustina within the context of her times, which includes an understanding of how she was shaped by the religious, cultural, political, and social aspects of her environment.

No armchair researcher, Czaczkowska leaves no stone unturned as she literally follows in the footsteps of Faustina the mystic, visiting each of the locations the saint called home throughout her life. As such, she visits the family home in the village where Helen Kowalska grew up, the homes of the families in nearby towns where she served briefly as a domestic servant before entering the convent, and, of course, the convents in the towns and cities where she served as a religious known as Sr. Faustina. At each location, not only does Czaczkowska give readers a grasp of how the times and Faustina's environment shaped her, but the biographer also shares more personally the testimonies of those who knew Faustina best: her family members, the families she worked for, her fellow religious in the convent, her spiritual directors and confessors, and the wards or girls the sisters were caring for (many of whom experienced conversions through Faustina's example and prayers).

A Living, Breathing Human Being

As a result, Czaczkowska helps you get to know Faustina as a living, breathing human being. Among other things, you discover that this future saint had a temper, disappointed her father when she came home late one evening from a dance, and doubted at times whether her visions of the Lord were real. And many of the testimonies and photos that Czaczkowska presents are unique to this biography, the fruit of the author's passionate research. For instance, in the chapter about Helen Kowalska's time as a domestic servant in Łódź, there is a rare photo of her before she entered the convent. She appears in secular dress walking down a city street with two of her blood sisters; the young women seem to be on their way to a religious festival. Czaczkowska confirmed with the aid of forensic science that there is a high degree of probability it really is Helen in the photo, the woman we're accustomed to only seeing in her religious habit as Sr. Faustina.

While the external aspects of St. Faustina's life are fascinating, Czaczkowska does not end there. She delves into St. Faustina's heart and soul and reconstructs the saint's rich interior life — the mystical experiences that are taking place in her soul even as she is fulfilling her external duties as a nun. Czaczkowska draws not only from Faustina's *Diary* but also from letters to her spiritual directors and superiors to give the reader a sense of her inner life.

With the popular reader in mind, the biographer uses simple and clear language in describing Faustina's interior life as a Christian mystic. For example, we follow St. Faustina's visions of heaven, hell, and purgatory in a comprehensible way. At her side, we learn the truth of the Incarnation and the saving Passion of the Lord Jesus during Holy Mass. While this kind of information is included in the *Diary*, Czaczkowska uses the explanations of scholars to help the reader understand it better.

This biography even fills in some of the gaps in Faustina's inner life that are not clarified in the *Diary* itself. For instance, we get a better sense of what was happening in her spiritual life as she received many of her revelations from Jesus. This is not surprising given Czaczkowska's relentless pursuit of the real Faustina and the fact that the *Diary*'s chronology is confusing at various points. In fact, one of the main reasons the chronology is confusing is that Faustina was tricked by the devil into destroying her *Diary* and then began to write it all over again.

In describing Faustina's life as a mystic, Czaczkowska displays her knowledge and ability to address the spiritual dimension of human experience, not well understood by our contemporary society that tends to stay on a superficial level. Thus, Czaczkowska helps us enter the world of the spiritual realities that were at the heart of Faustina's life and mission.

That is why the title and subtitle *Faustina: The Mystic and Her Message* are so apt. The reader realizes that with St. Faustina, we are dealing not only with a faithful follower of Christ in religious life but with a mystic, someone endowed by the Lord with extraordinary graces for the benefit of others. And in the case of Faustina, not only are we dealing with a mystic but with one of the greatest mystics of all time. Her mission is Christ's mission. Her life was a profound participation in Christ's life, and her message is Jesus, the merciful and loving Savior of the world, and the revelations He gave her about His mercy. It's ultimately all about Him and His mercy.

While everything I have said thus far about *Faustina: The Mystic and Her Message* would be enough to highly recommend it as a groundbreaking biography, there's even more. Marketers describe products with special features that set them off in the marketplace as "value-added." The term certainly applies here. Not only are there rare photos of Faustina, but there is a large photo insert in the back of the book with many color photos. And the much shorter second part of the book includes a concise history of the spread of the Divine Mercy message and devotion, covering all the way from the death of Faustina to Pope John Paul II's entrustment of the world to Divine Mercy in 2002.

In Part Two, you will learn of the rapid spread of the devotion during World War II and its aftermath. Then, you'll hear of the young movement's growing pains in the 1950s, especially the questions asked about various versions of the Divine Mercy image, with particular attention given to the image painted by Adolf Hyła. You will learn of the ban imposed by the Holy See by the late 1950s on the devotion and the reasons for it. Finally, you will discover the persons and events that prepared the path for the Church's recognition of the supernatural nature of Faustina's revelations. You'll hear of Cardinal Karol Wojtyła's role in advancing Sr. Faustina's canonization cause and helping to get the ban lifted, together with the Rev. Professor Ignatius Rożycki's brilliant analysis of the essential features of the *Diary*.

Divine Mercy Milestones

Building on what the author covers in Part Two, in this section I'll highlight the important contributions of my Marian province headquartered in Stockbridge in advancing Faustina's canonization cause, in publishing her *Diary*, and in promoting the Divine Mercy message and devotion worldwide. Further, while the author largely ends Part Two with Pope John Paul II's entrustment in 2002, I provide some personal reflections on St. John Paul II's beatification and canonization. These occasions were significant for both Faustina's and John Paul's legacies because the Divine Mercy devotion was prominent at both of them.

Our story starts with a Marian's miraculous escape from war-torn Europe to the United States of America during the early years of World War II.

Father Joseph Jarzębowski, MIC: Upon Faustina's death in 1938, her spiritual director, Blessed Michael Sopoćko, became the *de facto* bearer of her revelations. With the Nazis advancing from the west and the Soviets advancing from the east, Fr. Sopoćko made one of the most consequential decisions in Catholic history, giving key materials concerning Faustina's revelations to a Marian priest who was trying to get out of Europe. That priest, Fr. Joseph Jarzębowski, MIC (1897-1964), vowed that if he made it to America, he would promote Divine Mercy for the rest of his life.

In 1940, Fr. Jarzębowski embarked on a perilous journey from Poland to the United States. The fate of the Divine Mercy message in America was in his hands. Then that fall, Fr. Jarzębowski tried unsuccessfully to get his American visa renewed. By this time, he had the text of a Novena to Divine Mercy and a copy of the image of Divine Mercy with him. Despite the fact that his visa to America had expired, he went ahead and tried to get an exit permit from the Soviets. Miraculously, he received the permit. Travel across Siberia to Japan was arranged. Just before he left, he went to visit Fr. Sopoćko in Vilnius. Father Sopoćko told Fr. Jarzębowski to take a memorandum that he had written concerning the devotion to Divine Mercy. The next day, Fr. Jarzębowski celebrated a Holy Mass before the original Divine Mercy image, painted by Eugene Kazimirowski under Sr. Faustina's direction. Our Lord had asked St. Faustina to have it painted and then to spread its veneration throughout the world. Father Jarzębowski entrusted the journey ahead to the Divine Mercy.

He journeyed to Kaunas, Lithuania, overnight and was able to leave on a train on Ash Wednesday, February 26, 1941, at 3 p.m. — the Hour of Great Mercy. Every coach had two members of the NKVD (the old KGB); NKVD agents expressed concern to Fr. Jarzębowski about his not having a Japanese transit visa. He told them it was waiting for him in Vladivostok. He continued on. In Vladivostok, there was still the need to get a Japanese visa, and he would have to show them his expired American visa. Although the Japanese Consulate closed at 3 p.m. and they arrived after three, a Jewish lawyer named Białogórski successfully argued for the consulate to stay open for them. Father Jarzębowski prayed to the Merciful Jesus. The consulate decided to grant the visa. They inspected his expired visa (he didn't give them the part with the expiration date) and found it in order. The stamp was pressed for the Japanese visa.

When he was boarding the ship to Japan, he heard that customs was confiscating crosses and books. He prayed to Jesus to save his Divine Mercy materials. It was yet another tense moment. The officer took Father's breviary out of a bag and looked through it. He wasn't sure what to make of it, but he found the prayercards charming and decided to let it all go. The officer marked that bag with chalk and then marked a second bag containing Divine Mercy materials. He did not even bother to look inside!

The ship was greatly overcrowded. There were 500 people onboard and accommodations for only 80. It took two days and two nights to reach Japan. While in Japan, Fr. Jarzębowski gave a retreat to the Franciscans in Nagasaki. He arrived in Seattle in May 1941, seven months before the Japanese attack on Pearl Harbor, and from there made his way to Washington, D.C., firmly convinced that the Merciful Savior had brought him safely across the thousands of miles to his brothers in the U.S.

Father Walter Pelczynski, MIC: The Marians in the U.S., including a third-year seminarian named Br. Walter Pelczynski, MIC (1916-2000), became convinced that they should promote the devotion. By October 8, 1942, the Marians had received an imprimatur from Archbishop Michael J. Curley of Baltimore, Maryland, to print a Polish edition of the Divine Mercy Chaplet, Novena, Image, and an article by Fr. Jarzębowski. An English translation, called *Novena to the Mercy of God*, was published. In all, 50,000 copies were printed in 1943. With the help of the Felician Sisters in Michigan and Connecticut, the Marians began to spread the message.

While working with Fr. Jarzębowski as a seminarian in Washington, D.C., Br. Walter Pelczynski helped plant the seed that would become the Association of Marian Helpers. The seminarians would correspond with family members and others, asking them to help support their vocations. The men would also form friendships with people who had given their names at different parishes where brochures were distributed that included the message of Divine Mercy. The Marians had become promoters of the Divine Mercy message and devotion a mere four years after the death of St. Faustina. Known as "Fr. Pel," Fr. Walter Pelczynski would go on to serve as the founding director of the Association of Marian Helpers in Stockbridge, serving four terms altogether as director, spanning the 1940s to the early 1980s.

It's not hyperbole to say that because of Fr. Pel, millions of people around the world have come to know the Divine Mercy message and devotion through the Marians' publishing apostolate in Stockbridge, which has sent prayercards, newsletters, pamphlets, and magazines to thousands upon thousands of devotees. In fact, stepping out in faith, he purchased the first portion of the Marians' Eden Hill property in 1943 and then founded the Association there in Stockbridge in 1944. "I went there without a dollar in my pocket," Fr. Pel wrote in his memoirs. "Within two months, we had acquired the extensive property in Stockbridge that was to become our center of activities in the United States as well as for our missions abroad." He summed up his legacy, saying in his memoirs, "One can hardly doubt when I read so many beautiful accounts of graces received by people, conversions of souls, and special protection over homes and families where the image of Divine Mercy was venerated."

Several Marians helped Fr. Pel in this apostolic mission, including Fr. Julian Chróściechowski, MIC, and Fr. Seraphim Michalenko, MIC.

Father Seraphim Michalenko, MIC: Born in 1930, he has known the Marians of the Immaculate Conception — and Divine Mercy — from his earliest days growing up in Adams, Massachusetts. Father Seraphim also came from the same parish as Fr. Pel. During Fr. Seraphim's childhood, when Fr. Pel would come home on vacation, he would always visit the Michalenko family. Further, Fr. Jarzębowski would preach at the parish in Adams in the mid-1940s. After one occasion when Fr. Jarzębowski preached, Fr. Seraphim's pastor enshrined the Divine Mercy image in his church — the first such enshrinement in the Western Hemisphere. Inspired by these Marians, Seraphim joined their Congregation and became a priest.

Father Seraphim is a familiar face to viewers of the Eternal Word Television Network (EWTN) due to his hosting Divine Mercy Sunday telecasts from Stockbridge, as well as to his appearances on instructive and inspirational programs dealing with the Divine Mercy message and devotion. He has been involved in spreading this message for more than 50 years. Father Seraphim served as rector of the National Shrine of The Divine Mercy, two terms as director of the Association of Marian Helpers, and founding director of the John Paul II Institute of Divine Mercy, all three located in Stockbridge. For more than 20 years, he was vice-postulator for North America of the canonization cause of Sr. Maria Faustina Kowalska. He was a witness to the miracle attributed to St. Faustina's intercession that was recognized for her beatification in 1993.

In fact, with great faith, Bob Digan invited Fr. Seraphim to accompany him and his wife, Maureen, and son Bobby on a trip to Sr. Faustina's tomb to witness the healings of his wife and son! Maureen had an inoperable disease called lymphedema and Bobby was born brain-damaged and had a severe seizure disorder that left him unable to communicate well or move freely. Together, Maureen, Bobby, Bob, and Fr. Seraphim made their way to Poland. And, indeed, two healings occurred. Bobby suddenly became a playful child, energetic like he had never been before, and Maureen's incurable disease disappeared.

Father Seraphim was also involved in the 1995 case of Fr. Ron Pytel, the Baltimore, Maryland, priest who was miraculously healed from an inoperable heart defect through the intercession of then-Blessed Faustina. Father Seraphim helped guide the process of gathering medical records and witnesses' accounts connected with the healing. Together with Fr. Pytel, Fr. Seraphim presented the case to the Vatican.

In fact, I was present at the healing in Baltimore on October 5, 1995, the feast day of then-Blessed Faustina, when Fr. Pytel and some of his friends, parishioners, and fellow Divine Mercy devotees gathered for a day of prayer, Adoration, and conferences at Holy Rosary Church, the Baltimore archdiocesan Shrine of The Divine Mercy. After a time of prayer for the healing of his heart through Blessed Faustina's intercession, Fr. Pytel venerated a relic of the blessed and then collapsed. He felt paralyzed, but was completely at peace. A subsequent visit to his cardiologist showed that his heart had been healed.

It is significant that both of the miracles for St. Faustina involved an American, and a Marian witnessed each of the miracles. It is as though God in His Providence underscored the role He had given our Marian Congregation, especially here in the United States of America, in advancing Faustina's cause and her message of mercy.

But let's return to Fr. Seraphim, this time with the focus on his crucial role in publishing the *Diary*. In 1979, the Jesuits, chaplains of the Sisters of Our Lady of Mercy convent in Kraków, provided the proper equipment to photograph each *Diary* page on 35mm film. Father Seraphim, who was in Poland at the time, volunteered to get the photographic record out of Communist Poland. The atheistic regime in Poland had a strict ban on religious materials entering or leaving the country. For his return flight to America, Fr. Seraphim, in effect, became a smuggler for God and the cause of Divine Mercy. He packed the photographic pages into his suitcase, making no deliberate attempt to hide the material. The Communist authorities never checked his bags. But the job wasn't done.

The *Diary* now needed to be published, and I was among those whom Fr. Seraphim recruited to help with the proofreading. I had just returned from Poland in the summer of 1979 after studying Polish philology (the language, including its roots, history, and literature) for more than three years.

So during the 1980s, after the Holy See lifted the ban on the forms of devotions proposed by Sr. Faustina, Fr. Seraphim was called to head the Divine Mercy Department at the Marian Helpers headquarters in Stockbridge. First on the docket was preparing for publication the original Polish edition of the *Diary of Sr. Maria Faustina Kowalska*, which was published in 1981. I recall that as I got to know the *Diary* in my proofreading, I could not help but be profoundly affected by the words of Sr. Faustina and the spiritual content that flowed from them. Since Polish literature was familiar to me, I recognized the simplicity of her language. Yet amidst the simplicity was a depth of spiritual and theological insights.

Along with his work on the *Diary*, Fr. Seraphim supervised the production of various books, booklets, and pamphlets on the Divine Mercy message and devotion. In 1981, he wrote and published *The Divine Mercy Message and Devotion* booklet, which remains so popular that devotees refer to it as the handbook of Divine Mercy. He also oversaw various translations of the *Diary* for publication, including the English-language edition in 1987 and the Spanish-language edition in 1996.

Further, Fr. Seraphim served as theological advisor for *Divine Mercy — No Escape*, an award-winning docudrama on Faustina's life, and for the devotional film *Sister Faustina: The Promise of Mercy*. In addition, he played a significant role in the production and narration of a video released in 1992 called *Sister Faustina: The Apostle of Divine Mercy*. He also supervised the scripting and production of yet another film titled *Time for Mercy*, released in 1994 by the Marians in conjunction with Marian Communications Ltd., which won several prestigious awards.

Through his subsequent research, writings, and talks, Fr. Seraphim has become one of the most renowned experts on the Divine Mercy message and the life of St. Faustina in the world. He meticulously reviewed our English translation of this biography of St. Faustina as we prepared it for publication.

Kazimirowski Divine Mercy Image (Restored Vilnius Image): In Part Two, Czaczkowska mentions the restoration of the Divine Mercy image by Eugene Kazimirowski, which is the only image painted under Sr. Faustina's personal direction. The restoration of the image was funded by the Marian Fathers in Stockbridge and their Association of Marian Helpers. Cardinal Audrys Bačkis of Vilnius, Lithuania, had sought the urgent help of the Marians, so we appealed to our readers in an issue of *Marian Helper* magazine in 2001. Our Marian Helpers generously responded, so the Cardinal was able to fund the restoration.

Pope John Paul II's Beatification: Since Czaczkowska only briefly mentions John Paul II's beatification, I wanted to share some personal highlights of the beatification for Faustina and the Divine Mercy message and devotion. I personally attended the occasion and think the following points are worth mentioning: First, it was significant, as noted by then-Pope Benedict XVI, that John Paul II was being beatified on May 1, 2011, Divine Mercy Sunday. Here, Pope Benedict observed that John Paul named the Second Sunday of Easter as Divine Mercy Sunday when he canonized St. Faustina in 2000 and died on the vigil of the feast day in 2005. Second, before the liturgy of May 1, 2011, the Divine Mercy Chaplet was chanted in five languages before a large image of Divine Mercy which was displayed at the main outdoor altar. Further, Pope Benedict incensed the image during the liturgy. From the chaplet and the image to celebrating the feast day, all of these were important signs that Faustina's message was being recognized in St. Peter's, right at the heart of the Church.

Blessed John Paul II's Canonization: I also personally attended the canonization. Once again, as with John Paul's beatification, Divine Mercy Sunday itself was on prominent display. First, Pope Francis selected April 27, 2014, Divine Mercy Sunday, as the date for the joint canonization of Popes John XXIII and John Paul II. Second, the miracle recognized for John Paul II's canonization involving a Costa Rican woman actually occurred on May 1, 2011, Divine Mercy Sunday, and the very day of his beatification! It was striking as well that the Chaplet of Divine Mercy was recited before the liturgy, as it was at the beatification. There is something else that's worth highlighting: Along with recitation of the chaplet before the liturgy, an excerpt from John Paul II's homily at the canonization of St. Faustina in 2000 was read to the faithful — thus underscoring the integral link between Faustina's and John Paul's legacies as great apostles of Divine Mercy. Finally, I found it encouraging the way Pope Francis in his homily emphasized God's mercy in referring to both of the new saints, John Paul II and John XXIII: "May both of them teach us not to be scandalized by the wounds of Christ and to enter ever more deeply into the mystery of Divine Mercy, which always hopes and always forgives, because it always loves."

It's fascinating to see how the papacy of John Paul II and then his beatification and canonization have helped fulfill St. Faustina's prophecy about the devotion being given "a new splendor" in the Church (*Diary*, 378).

In closing, we're overjoyed to publish the English-language edition of the biography that you now have in your hands. *Faustina: The Mystic and Her Message* is a biography that you may read for greater understanding of this incredible, extraordinary woman of faith. You may want to read it to deepen your understanding of the *Diary* and grow in the spiritual life. But you can also read it to find inspiration every day of your life, especially in responding to the call to be merciful. Whichever aspect you are most interested in, you will not be disappointed. What makes it stand out from other biographies on Faustina that I have read is the compelling, fresh, and intimate portrait of Faustina that the biographer paints. As I've shown, Faustina emerges as a real person who struggled with her inadequacies and limitations even as she was blessed with extraordinary spiritual gifts and given a unique mission by Jesus Himself. That is why I highly recommend this groundbreaking biography.

How wonderful it is to read about St. Faustina and the extraordinary blessings and graces the Lord bestowed upon her. Yet we cannot forget that the Lord is also calling us to pass on the good news of His salvation and merciful love. He chose not only St. Faustina, St. John Paul II, and Blessed Michael Sopoćko, but also the Sisters of Our Lady of Mercy, the Marian Fathers of the Immaculate Conception, and the countless men and women who have proclaimed the message of Divine Mercy and lived it, ever since World War II. Consider how the Lord might be calling you, my dear reader, to join in sharing His message of Divine Mercy. May learning more about St. Faustina's life and her mission of mercy in our time inspire you to join the ranks of millions of souls who make up the Divine Mercy movement that is transforming the face of the Church, healing the world, and preparing it for the final coming of Christ.

Fr. Kazimierz Chwałek, MIC
Provincial Superior
The Blessed Virgin Mary, Mother of Mercy Province
October 5, 2014, the Feast Day of St. Faustina Kowalska

PART ONE

The Mystic
and the Message
from Jesus

INTRODUCTION

'Are You My God
or Some Kind of Phantom?'

"**A**LL THESE THINGS COULD STILL BE ENDURED. But when the Lord demanded that I should paint that picture, they began to speak openly about me and to regard me as a hysteric and a fantasist" (*Diary*, 125). Thus wrote Sr. Faustina in her *Diary* about her experiences in 1931. "Fantasist," or rather dreamer, but also a hysteric, visionary, eccentric, and wretch. How many other insults would she have to endure?

And all this because of the revelations of Jesus, who commanded her to paint the now-celebrated image of Divine Mercy with the signature *Jesus, I trust in You*. That command was also the beginning of her mission to proclaim the message of Divine Mercy to the world. For almost two years, Sr. Faustina did not meet a single person who affirmed her belief that the revelation of Jesus was not a figment of her imagination. This was a very difficult period for her — perhaps the most difficult time of her life.

It began on February 22, 1931. Sister Faustina, who at that time had been in the Congregation of the Sisters of Our Lady of Mercy for six years, had lived for nearly a year in their convent in Płock. It was the First Sunday of Lent.[1] It was evening. Faustina had just returned to her cell. Earlier, she had eaten supper and said her prayers in the convent chapel. She was preparing for bed. Suddenly, she saw Jesus in her cell. "One hand [was] raised in the gesture of blessing, the other was touching the garment at the breast. From beneath the garment, slightly drawn aside at the breast, there were emanating two large rays, one red, the other pale. In silence I kept my gaze fixed on the Lord; my soul was struck with awe, but also with great joy. After a while, Jesus said to me, **Paint an image according to the pattern you see, with the signature: Jesus, I trust in You. I desire that this image be venerated, first in your chapel, and [then] throughout the world. I promise that the soul that will venerate this image will not perish. I also promise victory over [its] enemies already here on earth, especially at the hour of death. I Myself will defend it as My own glory**" (*Diary*, 47-48).

"Sisters who were passing the building at that moment saw a light in the window, brighter than that of an oil lamp," says Sr. Clavera Wolska,[2] who was then the Superior of the Płock convent, repeating what has survived in the oral tradition of the sisters.

The encounter in her cell was no illusion. Sister Faustina was sure of this. She had seen the Lord a few times before. He had spoken to her before she joined the Congregation, urging her to take that step, and also during her time of formation in the convent as she progressed on the path of the mystical life. After the purification of her senses and spirit during her dark night of the soul, Faustina came to know about God's essence and experience a union of love with Him in the increasingly sudden moments of light that He granted to her soul. For Faustina, who previously knew nothing of the twists and turns of the mystical life, these experiences were as remarkable as they were difficult. As long, however, as everything was taking place inside her soul and applied solely to herself, it was the joy of her heart. However, that Sunday, February 22, 1931, everything changed. That day, Jesus entrusted her with the mission of proclaiming the message of Divine Mercy to the whole world. Painting the image was the first part of this mission.

Four years later, Jesus would tell Faustina that her task was to prepare the world for His final coming. Already in Płock, however, she was terrified by the enormity of the task that, with time, would merely take on greater proportions.

Her reaction should hardly be surprising. She could not paint the image herself, as she lacked the skill. Jesus commanded Faustina to convey all that He told her to her superiors. They, however, did not believe her words. Years later, she noted in her *Diary* that she silently complained to God that they "treated me with pity as though I were being deluded or were imagining things" (*Diary*, 38). She expected that the superiors (who, she believed, should have a better understanding of the spiritual life than she did) would offer their help.

The first person to whom Faustina spoke about Jesus' revelations was her confessor. Unfortunately, we do not know who this was. At the time, three priests would hear confessions in the Płock convent of the Congregation of the Sisters of Our Lady of Mercy: Adolf Modzelewski, Louis Wilkoński, and Wacław Jezusek. After World War II, Fr. Jezusek, who died in 1982, would speak extensively and enthusiastically of Sr. Faustina's revelations to the clergy at the Płock theological seminary. This does not mean, however, that he may not have been more skeptical of Faustina's experiences earlier on. It is known that the priest to whom Faustina first confessed the revelations she received from Jesus responded with considerable reserve. In fact, he countermanded the command from Jesus. He told Faustina, "That refers to your soul … paint God's image in your soul" (*Diary*, 49). When Sr. Faustina, calmed by such an interpretation, stepped away from the confessional, she heard Jesus say, "**My image already is in your soul**." After a while, Jesus added, "**I desire that there be a Feast of Mercy. I want this image, which you will paint with a brush, to be solemnly blessed on the first Sunday after Easter; that Sunday is to be the Feast of Mercy**" (*Diary*, 49). He also said that, on that day, priests should preach to the people about His "**great mercy … towards the souls of sinners**" (*Diary*, 50).

Thus, Jesus expressed yet another desire: the establishment of the Feast of Divine Mercy. The devotion to Jesus as represented in the Divine Mercy image and the Feast of Divine Mercy were the first two forms the new devotion to the Divine Mercy were to take, and Sr. Faustina, urged on by Christ Himself, persistently struggled to introduce them from that point onwards. Jesus, in the revelations that followed, would instruct her further about Divine Mercy.

Faustina, having met with no understanding from her confessor, confided her revelation from Jesus to the Superior of the Płock convent, Mother Rose Kłobukowska. However, she too expressed doubt. "When I spoke about this to Mother Superior … that God had asked this of me, she answered that Jesus should give some sign so that we could recognize Him more clearly. When I asked the Lord Jesus for a sign as a proof 'that You are truly my God and Lord and that this request comes from You,' I heard this interior voice, **I will make this all clear to the Superior by means of the graces which I will grant through this image**" (*Diary*, 51). Jesus demanded, but He did not make it easy for Faustina to complete her task. Only many years later did Faustina understand what it was that Jesus expressly told her: that difficulties were necessary to confirm the truth of the revelation. Moreover, the greatest value in the eyes of God does not lie in the effects of man's action, but, rather, in the intention with which the action is undertaken, and the suffering connected with it.

However, in 1931, Faustina was disoriented and confused. She wrote, "I would go from the superiors to the confessor and from the confessor to the superiors, and I found no peace" (*Diary,* 122).

The task of Faustina's superiors was not an easy one either. They must have been deeply surprised and troubled when one day a young sister from the lowly second choir[3] declared that Jesus had revealed Himself to her and asked her to make a new type of religious painting.[4] Moreover, He had commanded that the Church establish a new feast. What Faustina's superiors must have seen was probably a good and humble nun, united with Christ, but also a nun who was simple and uneducated, and not even fully professed yet. Why — they could have been thinking — would Jesus reveal Himself to *her*? Why choose her to proclaim His message? And what could she know about mysticism? Where could she have experienced these spiritual states? Behind the counter of the bakery, or at the kitchen stove where she worked?

Private revelations are challenging to deal with. They are not problematic as long as they are intended only for the individual who receives the revelation — that is, concerning only that person's conversion or the increase of his or her own faith. They become difficult when the visionary announces that he or she has received a mission to convey the words of God, the Blessed Virgin Mary, or the saints to the world. For the Church, the ultimate Revelation of God is Christ, the Son of God. This most important Revelation — referred to as Public Revelation — is contained in the Holy Scriptures and Sacred Tradition. The Church does not reject private revelation if she is able to ascertain, through a long and arduous process, that the revelation does not expand, exceed, or change Public Revelation, but only brings out some of its forgotten or neglected threads, which are of particular import in a given historical period. The second, no less important, factor is to make sure that the visionary does not proclaim the revelations for selfish reasons, such as seeking praise or satisfying his or her ambitions, and that he or she is leading a fully Christian life. In verifying the authenticity of revelations, it is extremely important to submit to the discipline of the Church and to the decisions of one's superiors, even at the cost of suffering.

"One of the greatest dangers of revelations arises from the fact that they take place in the realm of the senses. They affect the senses of sight, hearing, touch, or smell," emphasizes Fr. John Machniak, a professor of the theology of spirituality and the author of many books on Sr. Faustina's spirituality. "Anything that affects our senses can also be open to the activity of an evil spirit that can deceive the person," he explains. "That is why St. John of the Cross tells us to reject all revelations, even the ones that bring us closer to God, in order not to fall into the trap that an evil spirit can set for man."

But it was not just for these reasons that St. John of the Cross — one of the greatest mystics and a Doctor of the Church — accorded little value to visions. Revelations in the sphere of the senses are in fact only the beginning of the mystical path, which is fully realized in the union with God in love.

Faustina's superiors and confessors probably had even more reasons to remain distrustful toward what she was saying. In all probability, they had already encountered a number of people whose supposed revelations were no more than symptoms of mental illness.[5] Inner experiences can have a strong impact on an individual's psyche, and thus, at times, it may be difficult to distinguish a mystical experience from a mental affliction. This calls for considerable care and even psychiatric assessment. And so, a few years later in Vilnius, Fr. Michael Sopoćko — before he became Sr. Faustina's spiritual director and helper in preaching the message of Divine Mercy — requested that a psychiatrist examine the future saint.

There was a further reason for the objections to Faustina's revelations. The Jesuit Fr. Joseph Andrasz, who became Faustina's spiritual director near the end of her life, claimed that her Congregation was skeptical of unusual revelations since it simply did not expect them to take place. The Congregation of the Sisters of Our Lady of Mercy, "founded on the asceticism of St. Ignatius," founder of the Jesuit order, was "far from all exaltation," and had its established methods and approaches to work. "Through its rules, by its spiritual exercises through annual retreats, by conferences conducted by priests and superiors, the Congregation instills into its sisters a great respect not for the extraordinary, but for quiet, effective work, beginning with repentance and humility, and ending with a burning but also sacrificial love of God and souls."

"You can definitely say that the spiritual soil of the Congregation does not at all tend to develop mystical visions of an uncertain value," concluded Fr. Andrasz, who got to know the Congregation well in the 1930s.

Thus, Sr. Faustina was — to put it in human terms — left alone with revelations that were not intended only for herself but for the whole world. Her sole companion was Jesus, whose presence and love would give her strength to carry out the mission with which she had been entrusted until the end of her days. This does not imply that Faustina was not troubled by doubts and dilemmas. Her superiors, distrustful of her words, only made these doubts stronger and introduced confusion into her heart. This lasted until she met confessors who recognized the true nature of her spiritual life. During her time in Płock, Sr. Faustina, reprimanded by superiors, began to, as she put it, "grow a bit negligent," that is, to avoid interior inspirations: "I began to avoid encounters with the Lord in my soul because I did not want to fall prey to illusions." However, this was in vain, as "the word of God is clear, and nothing can stifle it," she wrote. The Lord pursued her with "His gifts" amid her struggles: "Truly I experienced, alternately, torture and joy" (*Diary*, 130). The more she attempted to run from Jesus' commands, the more He urged her to act. Sister Leocadia Drzazga remembered years afterwards that on one occasion in Płock, Sr. Faustina told her, "One should pray a lot for the souls who experience revelations and visions, as they experience doubt and feel so insecure that they could break down."

Once, Sr. Faustina, exhausted by this uncertainty, turned to Jesus. She wrote, "'Jesus, are You my God or some kind of phantom? Because my Superiors say that there are all sorts of illusions and phantoms. If You are my Lord, I beg You to bless me.' Then Jesus made a big sign of the cross over me and I, too, signed myself. When I asked pardon of Jesus for this question, He replied that I had in no way displeased Him by this question and that my confidence pleased Him very much" (*Diary*, 54). Months went by, however, and Faustina was unable to fulfill a single one of Jesus' requests. She once told Sr. Damiana Ziółek, whom she befriended in Płock, that "one of the sisters" had seen a "lovely Lord Jesus ... all gleaming in rays," and that she wanted "to paint Lord Jesus, but she could not." Although Damiana could see the delight with which she spoke, she did not guess that Faustina was speaking about herself. Faustina asked some of the other sisters for help, without revealing any details to them. Sister Bozenna Pniewska recalled, "I couldn't paint faces and I did not understand that she meant a new kind of picture, so I suggested that I could allow her to choose one from the many beautiful pictures I had in my possession. She thanked me but did not take me up on my offer."

In the fall of 1931, the Superior of the convent in Płock, Mother Rose Kłobukowska, informed Superior General Michael Moraczewska that, according to Sr. Faustina, Jesus had requested her to paint a picture.

Mother Michael Moraczewska recalled, "Although I treated her with a lot of kindness, involuntarily I must have added to her suffering. ... As long as her profound inner and mystical experiences did not go beyond the convent walls and remained a mystery between God, her soul, and the superiors, I was happy, seeing in all of these graces a great gift which God had bestowed on the Congregation. However, this was not the case when Sister's revelations began to seek to be known externally. Then I became afraid of introducing the slightest novelty, false devotions, etc. into the life of the Church and, because I was the Superior General, I felt that I was responsible for our Congregation as regards this matter."

She also admitted that she feared Faustina could be displaying "an underlying tendency of wild imagination or perhaps even hysteria because what she predicted did not always come to pass." Therefore, the Superior General admitted that she listened to Faustina "eagerly and with a joyful heart" as she spoke of her "deep and lovely thoughts and supernatural enlightenments" until she asked "for some outward action." Then, Mother Moraczewska approached Sr. Faustina's request "with considerable reservation."

It is unknown what Mother Moraczewska advised the Superior of the Płock community to do with Faustina's case. Perhaps she suggested remaining cautious and not yielding to Sr. Faustina's suggestions. When, in November 1932, Faustina arrived in Warsaw from Płock and told the Superior General about the command of Jesus in person, the Superior replied, "All right, Sister, I will provide you with paints and canvas. Please go ahead and paint!" Faustina left saddened.

Having found no understanding from anyone, she prayed heartily for a spiritual director who would help her understand what was happening in her soul and help her do as Jesus had commanded her.

Meanwhile, in the Płock convent, word started spreading that Faustina had supposedly seen Jesus. The sisters began to look at her with interest, carefully observing her. As she did not seem to stand out from the others in any other respect than her particular love of prayer, most did not believe these sensational stories. Some sisters would warn Faustina that she was falling prey to delusions, saying she was a fantasist and hysteric. Other sisters were more friendly to Faustina, including Damiana Ziółek. We do not know whether it was she, or another sister, who asked Faustina to defend herself from slander. Sister Faustina wrote, "She was a sincere soul, and she told me sincerely what she had heard. But I had to listen to such things every day" (*Diary*, 125). And although it tormented her interiorly, Faustina decided not to explain herself but to endure everything in silence and humility. "Some were irritated by my silence, especially those who were more curious. Others, who reflected more deeply, said, 'Sister Faustina must be very close to God if she has the strength to bear so much suffering.' It was as if I were facing two groups of judges. I strove after interior and exterior silence. I said nothing about myself, even though I was questioned directly by some sisters. My lips were sealed. I suffered like a dove, without complaint. But some sisters seemed to find pleasure in vexing me in whatever way they could. My patience irritated them. But God gave me so much inner strength that I endured it calmly" (*Diary*, 126). In the *Diary*, which she did not start until 1934, Faustina revisited this time in the Płock convent, which shows how difficult the episode was for her. After a period of interest in her, there was a momentary lull among the sisters, after which the interest returned with great intensity. This coincided with some kind of external problems that Faustina, however, did not describe in detail. "I could now see that everywhere I was being watched like a thief: in the chapel; while I was carrying out my duties; in my cell. I was now aware that, besides the presence of God, I had always close to me a human presence as well. And I must say that, more than once, this human presence bothered me greatly. There were times when I wondered whether I should undress to wash myself or not. Indeed, even that poor bed of mine was checked many times. More than once I was seized with laughter when I learned they would not even leave my bed alone. One of the sisters herself told me that she came to observe me in my cell every evening to see how I behave in it" (*Diary*, 128).

Sister Faustina, taunted with insinuations of hysteria, scrutinized by her superiors, confessors, and sisters, and at times disbelieving her very self, never ceased praying for a spiritual director. Her prayers were heard in 1933, when she met Fr. Michael Sopoćko (now Blessed) in Vilnius. A year later, the image of the Merciful Jesus was painted. However, it took more than half a century for acceptance of Sr. Faustina's private revelations to gain momentum within the Church.

Chapter One

Głogowiec-Świnice Warckie

1905-1921

She Desired to 'Never Bring Shame on Her Father Again'

MARIANNA KOWALSKA HAD BEEN FEARING THIS BIRTH. She had nearly paid with her life for the last two. On August 25, 1905, at eight o'clock in the morning, she gave birth to her third daughter, Helen. The labor was short, with no complications. It is not known who assisted with it. It could have been a neighbor from Głogowiec experienced in midwifery, or perhaps her stepmother, who arrived from nearby Dąbie on the Ner. That morning, Marianna's husband, Stanislaus, must have taken the cows out to pasture behind the house and fed the animals in the barn. There was no urgent work to be done in the fields. The sheaves had already been brought in, and the potatoes were to be dug up soon. Stanislaus may have been taking care of his daughters — 3-year-old Josephine and 2-year-old Eve, who was nicknamed "Jeannie" at home — or perhaps he was going about his woodworking. His workshop was close by, in the woodshed next to the stable. The weather that day promised to be warm and sunny. At four in the morning in Warsaw, thermometers registered 59 degrees Fahrenheit.

And yet, these times were very restless. Echoes of global conflicts were also reverberating in Głogowiec, a village that was then located at the western limits of the vast Russian Empire in the Kalisz Governorate. Poland, continually subject to partition by her three conquerors, was not to regain independence until 13 years later. Since January 1905, a bourgeois-democratic revolution had been underway in Tsarist Russia, embroiled as that country was in a political, social, and economic crisis. From St. Petersburg, the revolution quickly spread to the streets of Polish cities — mainly Warsaw and Częstochowa, and to Zagłębie Dąbrowskie and Łódź, which was just over 31 miles from Głogowiec. Factory workers were protesting against autocratic rule and demanding an improvement in economic conditions. In many locations, this led to bloody clashes with the imperial army and police. The dead and wounded numbered in the hundreds. Martial law was imposed in Łódź, where the workers' protests turned into a three-day long battle in the streets. On August 19, Tsar Nicholas II declared the convocation of the Duma as a representative body of the people, but only in an advisory capacity. This action alone was not able to pacify the situation. A new wave of mass strikes broke out. On the day of Helen Kowalska's birth — August 25, 1905 — martial law was declared in Warsaw, which was only about 100 miles away.

The *Warsaw Courier* published two pages of disciplinary rules which — by order of the Russian governor General Maximovich — were to be compulsory for city residents under penalty of severe punishment.

Youth, students, and teachers who had already been contesting the Russification of the educational system for the past year were also taking part in strikes in the Polish territories. Russian was the official language for government and schooling, and increasingly, Russian teachers were replacing their Polish counterparts. A strike also broke out in a teachers' college in the town of Łęczyca, situated a little over 12 miles east of Głogowiec. The movement against the Russification of education was so powerful that in June 1905, the authorities agreed to introduce the Polish language in private and public schools as the language of instruction in teaching religion and Polish.

Residents of the Kalisz Governorate also felt the aftereffects of Russia's defeat to far-off Japan in a recent war. One of the consequences of this defeat was to separate the Łódź textile industry from its eastern sources of raw materials and markets for its products, which, in turn, resulted in a swelling of the ranks of the unemployed, thereby decreasing demand for agricultural products supplied by peasants from the surrounding villages. Polish newspapers carefully reported, first, on the progress of the war, and then on the progress of the Russo-Japanese negotiations held at the American Portsmouth Naval Shipyard, where discussions begun on August 9 finally concluded with the signing of a peace treaty on September 5.

News from the rest of the world was slow to find its way to Głogowiec, a village tucked in among the plains overgrown with mixed forests. They arrived more quickly to Świnice Warckie, a larger neighboring village named after its founder, the Archbishop of Gniezno Jacob Świnka. At the beginning of the 20th century, Świnice Warckie was the crossroads for the major city centers of Łódź, Łęczyca, Łowicz, Warsaw, Kalisz, and Włocławek. Merchants and traders would stop over in Świnice for a rest. They would dine in the inns, let their horses out to pasture, and share the latest news from around the world with the locals. Some of these tidbits certainly also reached Stanislaus Kowalski while he did carpentry work for local residents, or while he walked along the country road to church in Świnice Warckie on Sunday.

The parish church, under the patronage of St. Casimir, stands in the center of the village. It is already the fourth church building on this spot. Earlier churches were destroyed, starting with the first, a wooden structure from circa 1300 funded by Archbishop Świnka. The present-day, modest, single-nave church dates back to the mid-19th century. Being too small to house the increasing numbers of pilgrims who flock here, it has been under expansion over the last several years. Since 2002, the church has held the title of a diocesan shrine dedicated to the birth and Baptism of St. Faustina.

The main part of the church looks today just as it would have on the afternoon of August 27, 1905, when Stanislaus Kowalski brought his daughter to the sanctuary two days after her birth, on a Sunday at one o'clock. The pastor of the parish, Fr. Joseph Chodyński, baptized the child in the same multi-colored wooden baptismal font found in the church today. He administered the Sacrament in Latin, but had to prepare the certificate of Baptism using the Cyrillic alphabet of Russian, the official language: "On this day, August 27, 1905, at one o'clock in the afternoon, the following took place. Stanislaus Kowalski, farmer, aged 40 years, of Głogowiec, having petitioned for Baptism in the presence of Francis Bednarek, aged 35 years, and Joseph Stasiak, aged 40 years, both farmers of Głogowiec, presented to us an infant of the female sex, born of his wedded wife Marianna née Babel, aged 30, at eight o'clock in the morning on August 25 of this year in the village of Głogowiec. The child received the name Helen in Holy Baptism, which was administered on this day, and the godparents were Constantine Bednarek and Marianna Szewczyk. This document has been signed by ourselves, having been read to the petitioner and to unlettered witnesses."

"By ourselves" denoted Fr. Chodyński and Stanislaus Kowalski, who was relatively uneducated and had signed the baptismal certificate by means of an "x," just like two years prior, when he had had Eve baptized. The document names two dates for the event, one according to the Gregorian calendar as used by the Poles, and the other according to the Julian calendar, which was obligatory in

Russia and was used in government offices in the parts of Poland under Russian partition. Next to the date of August 25 (Helen's birthday), there also appears a 12, and next to August 27 (the date of the Baptism), August 14. Moreover, due to an error in the baptismal act as well as erroneous translations of the document in literature, the age of Helen's father at the time is mistakenly given as 40 or even 45 years of age. In 1905, Stanislaus Kowalski was 37 years old.

There is something quite moving about the church in Świnice, humble and noble in its simplicity. It was here that Helen Kowalska, first as a child, then later as a teenager, had the first of her profound spiritual experiences. And it was here that, while praying in front of the Blessed Sacrament as a 7-year-old girl, Helen heard in her heart the invitation to live a more perfect life without yet understanding what that was to mean. As a 9-year-old, she received her First Holy Communion in this very church and made her first confession in the confessional, which is here to this day. She prayed to Our Lady of Częstochowa before the image of the Black Madonna over the main altar, where it hung until it was transferred to a side altar in 1983 to make way for the miraculous image of the Merciful Jesus. And it must have been here that she pondered in her heart the meaning of all of the extraordinary states she had experienced in her soul, and of the light that she had seen since childhood. Perhaps it was precisely in this church that she determined to become a "great saint." For 16 years, nearly half of St. Faustina's short life, the church in Świnice was the place of her prayer.

Helen's parents, Marianna and Stanislaus Kowalski, moved to Głogowiec in the parish of Świnice at the turn of the 20th century. Unfortunately, we do not know the exact date. They had already been married for several years, as they had wed in 1892. She was 17 at the time, and he, 24. Stanislaus was born on May 6, 1868, in the neighboring village of Kraski. Marianna née Babel (her maiden name is sometimes given as Bawej) was born on March 8, 1875, in the village of Mniewo near Koło. They met in 1891 in Dąbie on the Ner, where Marianna lived with her father and stepmother and Stanislaus worked as a carpenter in a brewery. They exchanged vows on November 9, 1892, in the Church of St. Nicholas, which can still be found in Dąbie today. After the wedding, Stanislaus continued to work at the brewery, while Marianna took care of their household. It is not known what prompted them to move to Głogowiec. There, they bought a little more than 12 acres of land, roughly five of which were pasture.

Their long, thin swath of land stretched from the road all the way back to the woods. The soil was barren and could support mainly rye and potatoes. The house was in great disrepair, so the Kowalskis decided to build a new one. They could afford only the cheapest building material — marl,[6] quarried in nearby Rożniatów. The light yellow stone was hewn into rectangular, somewhat uneven blocks and then bound with a clay mortar that crumbled quite easily. The building was covered with a thatched roof. Stanislaus Kowalski completed all of the carpentry work himself. It was not a large home and boasted a layout typical for peasant farmhouses of the day: two rooms separated by a large hall. On the right was a kitchen with a stove, where Stanislaus moved his carpentry workshop in winter, and on the left, a large room. In the rear of the house was a door leading to the backyard. Little remains of the original furnishings of the Kowalski home from the time when Helen lived there; just her father's carpentry bench and three paintings depicting the Sacred Heart of Jesus, the Holy Family, and St. Agatha. Other items that are on view in St. Faustina's family home are period pieces, but are not original to her family.

The home that pilgrims can visit nowadays is also somewhat changed. It supposedly looks just as it did in the photos from years ago, but at a second glance, it is clear that — after a complete renovation finished in 2003 — the current building is a quite different, improved version of the original. The restored light-yellow walls gleam, and there is no trace of the dents in the clay mortar that are clearly visible in the neighboring houses. New windows and doors have been installed. The roof has been covered with new tiles. The farmyard also looks different. The old ramshackle barn on the right was torn down, and former stables have been adapted to meet the needs of pilgrims. The fruit trees in the garden, visible in the photograph taken in 1935 when Sr. Faustina made her one and only visit to her parents, are no longer there. In front of the house, however, rose bushes bloom in the exact same place where Helen once planted them.

Until quite recently, Faustina's family still lived in the house where the future saint was born. In the late 1980s, Miecislaus Kowalski, Helen's brother, moved to a large, two-story house built next door. Several years later, the first major renovation of St. Faustina's family home was undertaken by the parish. The building was in such disrepair that it would have fallen into complete ruin without quick intervention.

When the Kowalskis finished building their house circa 1900, they never supposed that it would soon become too cramped. In the first 10 years of their marriage, they had no children. Marianna suffered, and prayed with her husband for offspring. Their first child was born in 1902, and another child came a year later. Helen, who was the third, "seemed to bring good luck," her mother recalled, as from then on her successive pregnancies and births became easier. Natalia came into the world in 1908, Stanislaus in 1912, Miecislaus in 1915, Lucy in 1916, and Wanda in 1920. Two daughters — Casimira and Bronislava — died in infancy. In sum, Marianna gave birth to 10 children in an 18-year period.

Feeding the growing brood on a little more than seven acres of poor land would demand little short of a miracle. The father's odd carpentry jobs could not cover other necessary costs, so it should come as no surprise that the family was poverty-stricken. This, indeed, was the reality for the majority of peasant families at the time. More than half of the farms in this part of the Russian partition (in what was previously the Kingdom of Poland) were even smaller than the Kowalskis' farmstead — this included the so-called "dwarf farms," which were comprised of up to about five acres, as well as small farms with no more than a little more than 12 acres of land. In 1910, 38 percent of land was in the hands of owners of large estates, such as Stanislaus Sempołowski, who owned nearly a thousand acres in Świnice.

Father was the head of the Kowalski household. "He was severe, unyielding and demanding of everyone at home," recall his sons Miecislaus, who inherited the farmstead from his father, and Stanislaus, who was organist in the Świnice church just after World War II. Years later, Stanislaus still remembered the spanking that his father gave him for tearing slender birch branches from the neighbor's tree. Mother Marianna took care of the home. She was "resourceful and hardworking, strong-willed, devoted to her family," and more gentle in manner than Helen's father. A photograph taken in 1935 in front of the Kowalski home shows Helen's parents: Stanislaus — slim and dark-haired, with a full moustache — and Marianna with a kerchief tied around her head. Stanislaus was devout and very hard-working. He would wake up at dawn to sing the *Little Office of the Blessed Virgin Mary*, the hymn "When the Morning Dawn Rises," and, during Lent, the *Lenten Lamentations*. Helen's father's chosen form of devotion was often trying for the whole family, since the house was cramped and several children slept in one bed. "He would get up first, when the family was still asleep and — without taking into consideration the children or our exhausted mother, worn out by taking care of the children day and night — would sing his *Hours* loudly and fervently, desiring foremost to honor the Virgin Mary. Mother, barely alive, would ask him not to, or even get angry at him for waking her. Nothing helped."

Thus Helen's siblings recalled years later. When asked about the Kowalski family after the war, Fr. Francis Jabłoński, pastor of the parish in Świnice from 1937 onwards, said that they "did not stand out from the other parishioners, who were themselves very average Catholics." But this was much later.

Very little is known about the early years of Helen Kowalska's life before she entered the convent. She writes very sparingly of this in her *Diary*, which she began in 1933. It's conceivable that more information was contained in the first version of the *Diary*, which she destroyed when she was misled by the deception of an evil spirit. But when she began to write the *Diary* afresh a year later, at the same time trying to recapture what she had already recorded earlier, it is likely that earlier events paled in comparison with the descriptions of her new, intense spiritual experiences. Unfortunately, the letters that Helen wrote to her family from her places of work as a domestic servant and then, later, from the convent, have been destroyed.

"We had her letters, a whole stack of them, but we burnt them," Helen's brother Stanislaus lamented many years later.

He recalled that the letters "were very beautiful." Helen would always write about the goodness of God, and she encouraged her family to trust in Him. Only three letters remain from the ample correspondence with her family. Her sister Jeannie burnt the rest during the Second World War because, she explained, "I was afraid that the letters might fall into the hands of our enemies during a search." In addition to family affairs, the letters also concerned religious matters.

The fact that the memories Sr. Faustina's closest family members have of her have been recorded and saved is, in large part, due to the work of Sr. Bernardine Wilczek, who came to Głogowiec in 1948 with this express purpose. Sister Wilczek undertook this task at the instruction of the superiors of her order and at the request of Fr. Joseph Andrasz, Sr. Faustina's first confessor, who wrote an unpublished manuscript about his extraordinary penitent. Sister Wilczek, who had known Sr. Faustina, gave witness to her own extraordinary courage by helping Jews to escape from the Warsaw ghetto during World War II. Sister Wilczek and Sr. Faustina had been in novitiate together.

The testimonies of Sr. Faustina's mother and siblings were compiled for a second time by Fr. Jabłoński in June of 1952 for the planned informative process, to be carried out in connection with her beatification cause. This time, the family gave testimony under oath. Marianna Kowalska, who was illiterate, bore witness to the truth of their accounts with her ink thumbprint on the signature line. Unfortunately, Sr. Faustina's father was no longer alive; he had died in July 1946 and was buried at the cemetery close to the church in Świnice. Marianna died in February 1965.

The Kowalski children began working at a young age. They took the cows out to pasture, looked after their younger siblings, and helped their parents in the fields. This was the typical lot of village children. All agricultural labor was done manually; grain was reaped with a sickle and threshed with a tool called a flail that consisted of a wooden staff with a short, heavy stick swinging from it. Fortunate was the family who owned a horse to help with the most burdensome tasks. When the Kowalski family had their horse confiscated by soldiers during the First World War, they couldn't afford to buy another one, so they harnessed their cow to the plow. Helen's brothers would help with the threshing when they were only 9 years old.

Helen, too, had responsibilities — not just in the house caring for the younger children, but also taking the cows out to pasture. A neighbor of the Kowalskis, Sophia Olejniczak, described how little Helen "would read books" while grazing the cows "and liked to talk about what she had read." Sister Faustina, on the other hand, recalled years later that she had helped harrow the fields using a plough-like implement — an arduous task for a teenage girl. Nonetheless, she followed all of her parents' instructions obediently, as attested by both her mother and siblings. "She was happy to do any task, and never refused anyone anything," recalled her mother. Helen's sister Natalia Grzelak (Olszyńska by her first marriage), three years her junior, confirms, "She was glad to do any type of work, and was cheerful and agreeable, and devout at the same time; our parents loved her perhaps the most of all the children, and pointed her out as an example."

Marianna Kowalska said that Helen was "the favorite and the best of the children." According to her siblings, she was lively and merry like her father, who favored her among the other children for that very reason. Stanislaus Kowalski, Helen's brother, claimed that his father liked her because she was the most obedient. "We didn't envy her for having won our father's heart, because we knew that that was only fair. Her advice to us was, 'Be obedient, too, and Father will love you just as much.'" Helen's mother, however, remembered things differently. "The children would hit and bully her because she was in Daddy and Mommy's good graces." Indeed, her father must have trusted Helen greatly, as she knew where he kept his shotgun, while neither his eldest daughter nor any of his sons did.

Sister Faustina's family home in Głogowiec, as seen from the yard.

Helen sometimes paid the piper for her siblings because when the children would play pranks, they would run off, while she stayed and didn't even try to make excuses. "She was good, always kind, cheerful and kindly disposed towards them; she never got angry," wrote Sr. Wilczek of Helen's relations with her siblings. Helen was a sensitive, intelligent child. "Oh, you merciful *baba* [old woman]!" the children would jest when Helen took pity on a suffering hen or dog. She once put on some of her mother's old clothes and went begging in the village, all the while saying her prayers; she gave what she collected to the parish priest so he could distribute it to the poor. This was also what she intended to do with the earnings from a raffle, for which she made toys out of paper and rags.

In 1917, Helen started attending the school that had just opened in Świnice. No traces of the school building remain. It stood near the church on the road to Łęczyca. Twelve-year-old Helen already knew how to read. Her father had taught her. "Only Father and Bereziński could read; they subscribed to magazines," remembered Natalia who, like the other children, was proud that her father was one of the only two people in Głogowiec who had mastered the art of reading. It is not known whether there were magazines at the Kowalskis' house during the horrendous years of wartime poverty, or whether they only appeared later. There were, however, religious books that Helen would read while grazing the cows in the meadow behind her house. Helen attended school for nearly three years. In 1919 or 1920, she left school just like the other older pupils. The school administration decided that she should cede her place to younger children. "Though she went to school for a short time ... she knew a whole lot and wanted to teach others," recalled Natalia about Helen. "She could tell us and the other village children about all sorts of things, but spoke most often about the lives of the saints, and she would also teach us our prayers."

Helen had both good and bad memories from school. One of the good memories, which was part of the Kowalski family lore, was when she received a prize for reciting a poem during the official visit of the school inspector. One of the bad ones was the humiliation she experienced at the hands of two school-girls who did not want to sit at the same school bench with her because of her shabby attire. The schoolteacher, a certain Mr. Łaziński, noticing Helen's tears, supposedly said, "It doesn't matter if you are more poorly dressed; you are still the better student." Marianna Kowalska remembered that the teacher praised her daughter with great enthusiasm, saying, "I should say that Mrs. Kowalski's child is the best. She never complains."

From early childhood, Helen had extraordinary spiritual experiences. She had visions. She told her siblings, for example, that the Mother of God appeared to her in her dreams. She saw her looking beautiful while walking in the garden of Eden. She also saw a brightness, an unparalleled radiance, the light of God. Marianna Kowalska recalled the conversation she had with 13-year-old Helen, who said she saw a light when she woke up at night. "Where's it at, then? Are you stupid? You're just seeing things and talking nonsense," her mother chided. But Helen would wake up with a start in the night and sit up in bed. She would pray. "You'll lose your mind from not sleeping and waking up so suddenly. Go to sleep!" her mother scolded her. "But no, Mommy, it's probably an angel that's waking me so that I don't sleep, so that I would pray," she responded.

This must have happened many times, because Marianna Kowalska recalls that Helen, who would be sleepy during the day, would ask whether she could take a nap, to which her mother did not always agree.

Helen was raised in unusually difficult and austere conditions and had her feet planted firmly on the ground. She was a realist. She knew that the radiance she saw was not the result of delusions or hallucinations. Neither her father nor her mother, however, was able to comprehend this, because what she experienced did not fit into their religious categories of thought, formed as they were by folk faith traditions. Not finding understanding among those closest to her, Helen began to hide her experiences away in her heart. She wouldn't talk about them at home. She also considered them irrelevant to conversations with the priest in confession. She was left alone with them. Yet she knew that these spiritual experiences were an invitation to a different life. As Sr. Faustina would write in her *Diary* many years later, she had felt a calling to the religious life from when she was 7 years old, when she heard "God's voice in [her] soul; that is, an invitation to a more perfect life" (*Diary*, 7). However, she didn't meet anyone at the time who could explain to her what she was going through. "When I was seven years old, at a Vespers Service conducted before the Lord Jesus in the monstrance, the love of God was imparted to me for the first time and filled my little heart; and the Lord gave me understanding of divine things" (*Diary*, 1404), she noted once again. Ludmilla Grygiel, describing the mystical life of Sr. Faustina, points out some elements of acquired contemplation at this particular moment in her life, but also a kind of "gleam of infused contemplation," or the imparting of the understanding of divine things.

As a child, Helen did not know how she could respond to Jesus' invitation. She didn't know that there was such a thing as religious life. However, with longing and fascination, she used to tell her parents and siblings stories about hermits who "ate only roots and honey from the forest." "Ever since she was little, she would tell us that she wasn't going to stay with us, that she would go away to be with the 'pilgrims,' because her father had once read about 'pilgrims' and she took that to heart," Natalia Grzelak recalls, "Who in our village would have known that there are different convents where girls like our Helen could go?"

As is already apparent, the future saint had some sense of her own destiny even then. She knew that she would leave home. This desire was fulfilled in spite of her parents' objections. "You're not going anywhere," her father or mother would respond when she spoke of the "pilgrims," and later, once she knew that her place was in the convent.

She would pray from her early childhood years on. In the evenings, she would kneel down to say her prayers together with her parents and siblings. During the day, she would invite her siblings to pray. She was the one who looked after the little family altar set up on the table in the main room, consisting of a little cross and two glazed pottery statuettes of Jesus and Mary, which her father had brought back from a pilgrimage to Częstochowa. When leaving home, she placed them in the custody of her younger sister Natalia, who donated them to the sisters in the convent in Łagiewniki before her death. The only authentic keepsakes that remain from the saint's family home are a simple metal crucifix, figurines that have been patched up with glue, and several letters written to her family. These are now in the care of the Congregation of the Sisters of Our Lady of Mercy.

Receiving her First Holy Communion was a tremendous experience for Helen. This took place in 1914. The First World War broke out at the end of July. That autumn saw the unleashing of one of the largest operations on the eastern front — the Battle of Łódź. Altogether, 800,000 soldiers from central Europe and Russia took part in the battle. In its wake, the Russians relinquished the Kalisz and Świnice territories, and the Germans began their occupation. This occupation lasted for four years until the end of the war, which finally brought with it long-desired independence for Poland after 123 years of partition. Helen must have remembered the years of Poland's national oppression. Perhaps that is why she continued to cultivate patriotic sentiments and prayed fervently for Poland until the very end of her life.

When the country was on the brink of war in 1914, Helen was 9. After Helen had received her First Holy Communion, Mrs. Berezińska, a neighbor from Głogowiec, asked her why she was returning from church alone and not with the other girls. Helen responded, "I am walking with the Lord Jesus." Marianna Kowalska recalls, "I remember that as she was returning home from Holy Communion, she asked her friend, 'Listen, are you filled with joy today? Because I feel something in my heart, because I have God in my soul.'"

"The little altar" from the family home of St. Faustina:
A crucifix and glazed pottery statuettes depicting the Sacred Heart of Jesus and the Immaculate Heart of Mary. From the collection of the museum in Kraków-Łagiewniki.

Starting that day, whenever she received Holy Communion, she enjoyed walking home alone. She avoided company. And she wanted to go to church daily. Her mother admitted she didn't always let her go, because there was always much to be done with all of the young kids at home. "But when Sunday came, she [Helen] got up at daybreak and, so as not to wake anyone, went out through the window, took the cows and led them out to pasture. When Father would get up to drive out the cows, he'd take a look in the barn — they weren't there. And so it was little Helen who grazed the cows up until it was time to go to church." Helen, obedient to her mother during the week, was obviously preempting possible tasks on Sunday so that nothing would get in the way of her being able to attend Mass, though sometimes she couldn't go to church even on a Sunday. The reason why must have been a very painful one for her: she didn't have anything to wear. The Kowalski sisters had one dress, which they took turns wearing. On the Sundays when one of her sisters wore the dress, Helen would take the prayer book and hole up in a corner or run to the garden to read the entire text of the Mass in peace and quiet. Sometimes her mother got angry at her for this because she would have preferred getting some help in the kitchen, but Helen would explain, "Mommy, don't be cross, because the Lord Jesus would have been more cross if I didn't do that." Natalia, a mere girl at the time, never forgot how Helen, who was three years older, once explained to her about what happens during different parts of the Mass.

"Pay attention to what the priest does. When he processes into the church, Christ is going to pray in the Garden of Olives, and He is sweating bloody sweat. When the priest opens the celebration of the Holy Mass, the Lord Jesus is praying. Now the priest kisses the altar: that's when Judas kisses the Lord and delivers Him into the hands of the Jews. The priest approaches the side of the altar — they are leading Jesus Christ to Annas. When he intones the 'Kyrie eleison,' they are slapping Him and spitting in His face; they lead Him to Caiaphas, and next, to Pontius Pilate. When the priest washes his hands, Pilate is washing his hands. When the priest uncovers the chalice on the altar, Pilate is having Jesus disrobed; when the priest stands still, they are flogging Him. The priest covers the chalice, and they are placing the crown of thorns on His head. When he raises the Host — Christ is being raised on the cross. When the priest breaks the Host and drops it into the chalice — Jesus dies."

Truly astonishing here is the way in which Helen, as a mere girl, having likely read an allegorical description of the Holy Mass, explained to her sister the Sacrifice of Jesus and its consummation during the celebration of the Holy Eucharist.

During the 16 years that Helen spent in Głogowiec, there was one event that left a deep imprint on the family's collective memory and also left its mark on the future saint. It was an ordinary country dance, one of many organized in Świnice Warckie. No one remembers the date. It might have taken place in 1919. The goal of the festivities was a noble one: the proceeds were earmarked for the needs of the parish. Josephine, the oldest daughter of the Kowalskis, was invited to the dance. From the family's varied accounts of the event, one might gather that either the parents sent Helen to accompany her sister, or Josephine convinced her to come along. Their father supposedly knew nothing about them going out, which seems unlikely. The girls enjoyed themselves for what must have been a long time. They came home late. In one version of the story it was ten o'clock, but according to another, it was after midnight. To add insult to injury, the girls were accompanied home by a certain Mr. Kociurski. Stanislaus Kowalski wasn't asleep; he was up waiting for his daughters. "Is this how I raised you, so you would bring shame and disgrace onto my house?" he reproached them, very upset.

For Helen, her father's reprimand was an earth-shaking experience. She knew that he was disappointed in her. He had gotten so angry at her, and this, supposedly, for the very first time. Thereafter, when she was asked to go to a dance, she would say that she had to ask her father. But that event had deeper repercussions. Helen said as much to Jeannie when she visited Helen in the convent in Warsaw. She admitted — as Jeannie recalled years later — that when her father got angry at her, she desired to "never bring shame on her Father again, but would try hard so as to give him a good reputation and solace, and not disgrace."

Was it then, indeed, that she decided to become a saint? Like one of the saints in the stories read aloud by her father at home? "I desired to become a great saint from my earliest years," she would write years later in her *Diary* (1372).

Helen wanted to be obedient to her father, but she defied him on one point — she entered the convent. The dictates of her heart and God's call were stronger than her parents' stubborn refusal.

Yet, before this took place, Helen left home to work in the city. On a little more than seven acres of arable land, Stanislaus Kowalski was not only unable to provide an education for his eight children or dowries for his daughters; he couldn't even feed or clothe them. For this reason, once the Kowalski daughters were old enough, they worked as maids to earn a living and to help their family. This was the typical course of events for children from large peasant families. From their overpopulated villages, where there was too little land and too many hands to work it, young people would venture out into the wide world to make a living, sometimes going as far as the New World across the Atlantic. In Polish cities and towns, men would hire themselves out as day laborers, and girls as housemaids. The Kowalski household must have been utterly poverty-stricken, since the parents agreed in 1916 to allow their 8-year-old daughter Natalia to leave home in order to work in the home of distant relatives, where she took care of the younger children.

Helen was older when she first left home to go work — she was 16. For one or two years, she had already been talking to her parents about going away for work. She argued that her father's work was arduous, and that she didn't have anything to wear on Sundays; she had the worst dress. Her parents agreed. It just so happened that an acquaintance of the Kowalskis, Jane Ługowska from the neighboring village of Rogów, had recently mentioned that her sister Leocadia Bryszewska was looking for a maid. She lived in Aleksandrów, near Łódź. Helen left. It was the year 1921. She returned to Głogowiec one year later. It was then that she first asked her parents' permission to enter the convent. Years later, Marianna Kowalska recalled the words of her daughter: "Mommy, I must enter the convent."

Both parents, however, flatly refused to give their permission. Her father argued that he was in debt and had no money to pay for the dowry required by various congregations at that time. Helen told her parents that she "didn't need any money," because "the Lord Jesus Himself will lead me to the convent." But she didn't get anywhere. Her parents were tough, and they didn't agree. Natalia recalled that it was probably then that their pastor, Fr. Roman Pawłowski, urged Helen's father to sell the family's cow to provide his daughter with a dowry and postulant's wardrobe, since she had such a great desire to enter the convent. Her father wouldn't hear of it because "how will we make a living with such a large family?" And, in any case, the cow was needed to pull the plow.

Since she couldn't enter the convent, Helen left once more to work as a servant. This time she worked in Łódź. It was probably during this period — from 1922 to 1924 — that she used to come to visit her parents. But from the moment she left Łódź for Warsaw in 1924 and entered the convent, she didn't visit Głogowiec again until 1935 — 11 years later. She returned as a nun named

Sr. Faustina. She had seen her parents only once since 1924, when they travelled to Kraków for Faustina's first profession of vows in 1928.

Sister Faustina came to Głogowiec from the convent in Vilnius after being alerted by her family to her mother's serious illness. Marianna Kowalska was having severe attacks of acute liver pain. Having received permission from her Sister Superior, Faustina boarded the train on February 15, 1935. She was in Warsaw by morning, and by eight in the evening, she had already arrived in Głogowiec. "She came to my room, praised God, and knelt down beside me, by the bed, and said at once, 'Mommy, you will get up yet.'" Thus, Marianna Kowalska recalled the words of her daughter after many years. To her own astonishment and that of the rest of the family, Marianna immediately sat up in bed on her own. "I saw her — already I got well. The next day was Sunday. She was getting ready for church. My husband harnessed the horse, and I went to church with them. And I have been healthy to this very day," said Marianna Kowalska in 1952.

Their meeting was very emotional. "What a joy it was for my parents and for the whole family!" wrote Sr. Faustina. "After greeting each other, we knelt down to thank God for the grace of being able to be together once again in this life" (*Diary*, 397). "When I saw how my father prayed, I was very much ashamed that, after so many years in the convent, I was not able to pray with such sincerity and fervor. And so I never cease thanking God for such parents" (*Diary*, 398). Sister Faustina looked on with astonishment at how much had changed at home. "The garden had been so small, and now I could not recognize it. My brothers and sisters had still been children, and now they were all grown up. I was surprised that I did not find them as they had been when we parted" (*Diary*, 399).

Everyone wanted to meet with Helen, whom they had not seen for a long time. "The days at home passed in much company, as everybody wanted to see me and talk with me. Often I could count as many as twenty-five people there," she wrote (*Diary*, 401). There are 14 people in the photo taken during Sr. Faustina's visit, a photo that has luckily been preserved. They are standing in the garden with trees in the background. The winter was obviously a mild one that year, and there are no traces of snow. Everyone, including the children, posed for the photograph without their coats. In their Sunday best, they surround Helen-Faustina, who sits in the place of honor in a chair in the very center of the group. Next to her on the right sits her mother with one of her granddaughters on her lap, and then her father. To the left sit Sr. Faustina's aunt and uncle on her father's side — Josephine and Joseph Kowalski. Two children are seated in front of her. The men are sporting white shirts and bowties, and the women are wearing dresses adorned with white collars or bows. The future saint did not get to see two of her sisters during this visit, which worried her. "I felt interiorly that their souls were in great danger. Pain gripped my heart at the thought of them. Once, when I felt very close to God, I fervently asked the Lord to grant them grace, and the Lord answered me, **I am granting them not only necessary graces, but special graces as well.** I understood that the Lord would call them to a greater union with Him" (*Diary*, 401).

During her stay in Głogowiec, Sr. Faustina spoke a lot about God and the lives of the saints. "It seemed to me that our house was truly the house of God, as each evening we talked about nothing but God. When, tired from these talks and yearning for solitude and silence, I quietly slipped out into the garden in the evening so I could converse with God alone, even in this I was unsuccessful; immediately my brothers and sisters came ... and, once again, I had to talk ... " (*Diary*, 401). She found moments for interior prayer when her brothers began to sing at her request. They had lovely voices. One played the violin and the other the mandolin. "I rejoice immensely that such great love reigns in our family," she noted.

It is not clear how much time Faustina spent with her family. However, it was not just relatives who visited the Kowalskis during her visit. Helen's neighbors, her old friends, also came by. Now, they were women in their thirties with husbands, children, and problems.

"What also cost me a lot was that I had to kiss the children. The women I knew came with their children and asked me to take them in my arms, at least for a moment, and kiss them. They regarded this as a great favor, and for me it was a chance to practice virtue, since many of the children were quite dirty. But in order to overcome my feelings and show no repugnance, I would kiss such a dirty child twice. One of these friends came with a child whose eyes were diseased and filled with pus. ... My nature recoiled, but not paying attention to anything, I took the child and kissed it twice, right on the infection, asking God to heal it. I had many opportunities to practice virtue. I listened to people pour out their grievances, and I saw that no heart was joyful, because no heart truly loved God; and this did not surprise me at all" (*Diary*, 401).

Sister Faustina attended church daily in Świnice Warckie, accompanied by her brother Stanislaus. She fondly recalled all that she had experienced in this church. "How easy it was to pray in that little church! I remembered all the graces that I had received there, and which I had not understood at the time and had so often abused. I wondered how I could have been so blind." Suddenly, the Lord Jesus appeared to her in these meditations and said, "**My chosen one, I will give you even greater graces that you may be the witness of My infinite mercy throughout all eternity**" (*Diary*, 400). These words of Jesus now stand inscribed inside the church in Świnice.

Sister Faustina spent a lot of time with her younger brother Stanislaus. "I felt that he was very pleasing to God," she wrote (*Diary*, 399). She went for walks with him through the fields, probably in the very places where she had once grazed the cows. When, at their parting, she spoke to him about the goodness of God, he burst out crying "like a little child, and I was not surprised, for this was a pure soul and, as such, more capable of recognizing God" (*Diary*, 402).

There were many tears at her parting. "My father, my mother, and my godmother blessed me with tears in their eyes, wished me the greatest faithfulness to God's graces, and begged me never to forget how many graces God had granted me in calling me to the religious life" (*Diary*, 402). Helen's parents — who initially had been opposed to her entering the convent — were not only overjoyed that Helen was a nun, but they gave her their blessing. "Although everyone was crying," continues Sr. Faustina, "I did not shed a single tear; I tried to be brave and comforted them as best I could, reminding them of heaven where there would be no more parting" (*Diary*, 402). It was only when she got into the car that she burst into tears. "I let my heart have its way, and I, too, cried like a baby, for joy that God was granting our family so many graces, and I became steeped in a prayer of thanksgiving" (*Diary*, 403).

This was her last visit to Głogowiec. She stopped off in Łódź on her return trip. She wanted to visit her sister Natalia, who had not known about her visit to their parents. Natalia and her husband then lived on 189 Piotrkowska Street. "The neighbor said she had waited a long time to see me, for me to return from work, but in the end, she wedged three roses behind the door handle as a sign that she had been there," Natalia recalled. By that evening, Sr. Faustina was already in Warsaw.

Chapter Two

Aleksandrów

1921-1922

'Why I'm Leaving I Cannot Say,
But I Can't Stay Any Longer'

THE CURRENT ONE-STORY ANNEX BUILDING, with its bright façade and white lace curtains in the windows, in no way resembles the former bakery of the Bryszewskis. Neither do its current inhabitants have anything in common with its previous history, dating back almost a century. Ninety-nine years ago, several bakers bustled about the place daily under the watchful eye of the owner, Casimir Bryszewski. Hot, freshly-baked bread immediately found its way from the oven to the storefront of the Bryszewski tenement house on 30 Parzęczewska Street, now No. 7 on May 1st Street. Casimir's wife, Leocadia, held sway in the store. Today, instead of the bakery sign, a granite plaque with this inscription graces the front of the building: "Helen Kowalska lived and worked in this house from 1921 to 1922."

Since then, the building has changed owners and was expanded into what was previously a garden area to the left of the entrance. But the main section of the building looks just as it did when Helen lived here. The same spacious hall is still there, from which she would enter the kitchen on the right, where she worked and slept under a window on a fold-out couch. A staircase leads up from the hall to the second floor, where the Bryszewskis occupied three rooms.

We do not know much about Helen's stay in Aleksandrów. It is not even exactly known when she arrived here, or how long she stayed. Various dates appear for Helen's departure for Aleksandrów in the memoirs of her mother, Marianna Kowalska, as recorded by Sr. Bernardine Wilczek in 1948. Her memory was clouded by the passage of time and manifold events, not to mention that Helen was one of several Kowalski daughters who left home to work as a servant. Helen's mother mentions the year 1920 several times and even mentions 1919 once. According to these dates, Helen would have been 14 or 15 years old when she began work as a housemaid. Consequently, in materials kept in the archives of the convent in Łagiewniki, Sr. Wilczek has dated the period of Helen's stay at the Bryszewskis to the years 1920-1921. But an important fact emerges in subsequent testimonies gathered four years later by Fr. Francis Jabłoński in Głogowiec. Marianna Kowalska testified under oath on June 6, 1952, that she "didn't remember exactly" the year when Helen left for Aleksandrów to work as a domestic servant. She did remember, however, that she stayed at home for "just a few days" after her return and then left for Łódź. The period of Helen's employment in Łódź is better documented. It is clear that she resided there from 1922 to 1924. In theory, her "few days'" stay at home could have fallen toward the end of 1921 and the beginning of 1922; if that were the case, it would be possible for Helen to have worked in Aleksandrów in 1920 to 1921. This is in keeping with what Sr. Wilczek heard during her first stint in Głogowiec.

However, this hypothesis is discredited by two other pieces of information. Firstly, Helen's mother claims that her daughter was at the Bryszewskis for "not even a year," which is affirmed by the testimony of other family members. And there is also another decisive argument. Before taking the veil and making her profession of temporary and perpetual vows, Sr. Faustina testified during her so-called canonical exam[7] that she had received the Sacrament of Confirmation in Aleksandrów in 1922. In relevant documents, the months of February and May 1922 appear once on each, and in another document, just the year is given. For all of these reasons, as one might guess, it is presumed that Helen Kowalska worked in Aleksandrów from 1921 to 1922. Therefore, she was 16 to 17 years old at the time.

One can say with certainty that this was a very important time for the sensitive and intelligent Helen. This was the first time that she had lived away from her family home. She was working and got to know city life. But most importantly, it was right after her return from Aleksandrów that she told her parents for the first time that she had to enter the convent. She did not say that she *wanted* to enter the convent, but that she *had* to. It was here, in Aleksandrów, that she had powerful interior experiences that permitted her to clearly delineate her future.

When Helen came to Aleksandrów in 1921, the town was still recovering from its wounds after the end of the Great War, three years prior. Textile factories that had produced mainly socks and stockings had not yet gathered full steam, having been cut off by Russia from eastern markets after Poland regained its independence. The town, which had its municipal rights restored in 1924, had a population of 8,000. Its mosaic of nationalities and cultures must have been a surprise for Helen. Her family's village and the neighboring town of Świnice Warckie were inhabited by Poles. In her village, she surely would have also met Polish Jews, as they were involved in minor trade and ran some of the local inns. Before the war, she might have seen Russian Tsarist officials in Świnice — then, after its outbreak, German soldiers. But these were occupying forces, not residents of Polish territories. In contrast, Aleksandrów's majority ethnic group was German, according to the 1921 census. They accounted for as much as 37 percent of the town's population; there were fewer Poles — 34 percent; and Polish Jews made up 29 percent of the population.

This type of ethnic distribution was unique in central Poland. The disproportionately high percentage of Germans in the population had its roots in the mid-19th century, when Raphael Bratoszewski founded a town on his land, bringing in settlers who were weavers from Prussia and Saxony. Their wooden houses remain to this day in the same neighborhood as the Bryszewski's tenement house — squat buildings, with a wide front and steep roofs.

In the 1920s, the Germans were the richest ethnic group in Aleksandrów. They owned the majority of the factories that produced stockings as well as many small-scale manufacturing businesses. Polish Jews, on the other hand, were heavily represented in the trades and commerce. As for the Poles in Aleksandrów, they were predominantly laborers and also owned smaller manufacturing and skilled labor businesses, including the Bryszewski's bakery.

Helen's employers belonged to the group of Polish Aleksandrów residents with a highly developed national and social consciousness. At the time, Casimir had been vice-president of the Volunteer Fire Corps for a year, a position he presumably received in honor of having led a group of Polish firemen in an operation to disarm the German forces occupying the town in 1918. He was also the co-founder of the Association of Christian Property Owners.

The Bryszewski's tenement building stands just a few blocks from the town center, which encompasses the broad Kościuszko Square and its English-style gardens. The gardens used to house an orangerie, a café, a gardener's house, the town weighing house, and busts of insurrection leaders. The most impressive building in Aleksandrów stands next to the square — the neoclassical town hall. Once, market stalls, whose wares were reminiscent of the town's entire socio-cultural make-up, used to line its outer walls. Today, offices and banks stand in their stead. Helen, too, must have come here, either alone or with Leocadia Bryszewska, who did the shopping. The sounds of Polish, German, Yiddish, and sometimes Russian intermingled here as well as at the weekly market days and monthly fairs, when local peasants rode in on horse-drawn carts filled with the fruits of their harvest.

Sister Bernardine Wilczek visited Helen's employer in Aleksandrów after the Second World War. But Leocadia Bryszewska was not able to say much about Helen. She didn't remember anything beyond the fact that Helen had been very nice to her, well behaved, and dutiful. Zenon Bryszewski — Leocadia and Casimir's only son, who was 6 years old when Helen came to work for his parents — recalled many years later what her responsibilities were: "She cleaned, helped with the cooking and had to wash the dishes, take out the garbage, bring in the water because there was no running water, serve meals to the bakery workers who were fed by my parents, and — when time allowed — she played with me." She had plenty to do. Helen sent the money she earned to her parents in Głogowiec.

The memoirs of Zenon Bryszewski (b. 1915) were recorded in August 1993; that is, four months after the beatification of Sr. Faustina. This 78-year-old man still remembered that he had liked Helen as a child. When she had a free moment, she would tell him fairytales and real-life stories, ones that had taken place back in her village. For example, there was one about a squire who came back after his death and was seen by people. He recalled, "Sometimes she would sit me on her lap, or I would sit in a small chair next to her, and we would talk; actually, she would talk, and I listened." He also remembered saying his evening prayers with Helen and his parents, and saying the Rosary in October.

Helen attended Mass at the only Catholic church in Aleksandrów at the time — St. Raphael's Church, just next to Kościuszko Square. She met only Poles there because, as a rule, the ethnic breakdown in Aleksandrów coincided with the denominational breakdown, as was the case in all of pre-war Poland. Germans worshiped in the Evangelical Church of the Augsburg Confession, a beautiful neoclassical church on the opposite corner of the square, which today appears to be in urgent need of repairs. Polish Jews met in one of their five houses of prayer or in the large synagogue, of which no trace remains today.

At the time, Aleksandrów was one of the most important centers for the Hasidim in Poland. It was here that the Hasidic Yeshiva of the Aleksander dynasty, which was well known throughout all of Europe, was located. To this day, Hasidic Jews from the world over flock to Aleksandrów to visit the grave of the late Jerahmeel Israel Isaac Danziger (d.1910), Jewish thinker and author of the tome *Jismach Israel*. Dressed in long *chalat*[8] robes, tall *spodik*[9] hats or fur-rimmed *shtreimels*[10] on their heads and with sidelocks, they elicit much greater interest today than they did a century earlier, when they were just one part of the multicultural mosaic that made up Aleksandrów.

Helen attended St. Raphael's Church (built in 1822), which at the time was a single-nave structure with a wooden belfry and significantly smaller than today's church building. The pastor, Fr. Sigmund Knapski, began to expand the church when Helen was employed there. It was precisely when Helen was working in Aleksandrów that the city was visited several times by the Bishop of Łódź, Vincent Tymieniecki, who conferred upon her the Sacrament of Confirmation. When? Sometime in 1921 or 1922, based on evidence from several sources.[11]

The expansion of St. Raphael's that commenced in 1922 was completed four years later. But the church's current appearance is the result of a later expansion that took place in the 1990s. The church building was widened and lengthened, its ceiling was raised, and it was "crowned" with another steeple.

We do not know if Helen's employers allowed her to attend daily Mass. Neither do we know if she took the tram for the roughly seven-and-a-half-mile stretch separating her from Łódź so she could visit her uncle Michael Rapacki, and possibly one of her sisters who worked there. The journey only lasted an hour, but the fare was not cheap for a housemaid's budget. Several years later, in 1937, the ticket cost 70 groszy, while about two pounds of bread cost just 30 groszy.[12] It's likely that the ratio was similar in the 1920s.

Helen's stay in Aleksandrów was an important experience for her. It took place before she set off for the city of Łódź, which had a population of several hundred thousand residents, and later for Warsaw. Despite this, however, she treats this period marginally in her *Diary*, as she does the entire period prior to entering the convent. And yet, something occurred in Aleksandrów that forced her to ask her parents' permission to enter religious life. Her family remembers that moment. Though their memories differ on the details, they are in agreement on the core issue. One day, Helen saw a great light in the Bryszewski's yard. Whether she noticed it from the kitchen window, as one version of the family story goes, or while going out to the yard with buckets in hand, according to another, is less significant. What is important is that the light was so bright that Helen was terrified. She thought it was a fire. She began shouting that "the yard was burning" (in one version of the story) or that the "shed" was on fire (in another). The baker's hired hands, who had just been putting the bread into the oven, ran out of the bakery. But they didn't see anything, which is no wonder, because it was "the Lord Jesus who had appeared" to Helen, as her sister Natalia explained years later.

It is not clear whether Helen had told her about this herself, which is rather unlikely, or if Natalia deduced it from other visions and apparitions described in the *Diary*, particularly the vision Helen had of Jesus in Łódź that prompted Helen to take a decisive step. In any case, it does seem certain that Helen saw more than just light. After all, she had already seen a radiance or bright light before, as a young girl in her family home in Głogowiec, and she had told her parents about it. This time the light must have been different, since it so shocked Helen. It must have been different, because it was "the Lord Jesus who appeared" to her — to recall Natalia's words.

Concerned about Helen's emotional state, the Bryszewskis called a doctor, who prescribed her some headache medicine. At the same time, her employers informed Helen's parents that she had gotten "all mixed up." In response, the Kowalskis sent their oldest daughter, Josephine, to Aleksandrów to check on what had happened. "I saw light. Tell Mommy not to worry. I'm not stupid, but I am not going to tell them any more about it. I am not going to stay here much longer." These were Helen's words, drawn out of her with difficulty, as Josephine well remembered.

Helen did not want to speak about what — or rather, whom — she had seen. She knew that no one would believe her words or understand her. She remained alone with her experience. She knew that it was no delusion or hallucination — she was too reasonable and pragmatic for that. Marianna Kowalska claims that Helen had more visions of light in Aleksandrów. This is what caused her to decide to quit her job as a domestic servant in favor of entering the convent, following the internal voice that had called her to a more perfect life when she was 7 years old. She was certain that the convent was the right place for her. And so she set off for Głogowiec to ask her parents for their consent.

"Why are you leaving? Stay!" Leocadia Bryszewska tried to convince her. But the only response she received was, "Why I am leaving I cannot say, but I can't stay any longer."

Chapter Three

Łódź

1922-1924

'How Long Will You Keep Putting Me Off?'

IT WAS A SUNDAY. A WARM JUNE AFTERNOON IN 1924. A fair was going on in Łódź's Venice Park on the outskirts of the city. Some were trying their luck at the raffle or gazing at the fireworks displays and magicians' tricks. Others strolled beneath the chestnut trees along ponds linked by canals supplied with water from the nearby Jasień River. Perhaps one of the young men decided to show off in front of the ladies and jump from a tall wooden pole through a ring of fire into one of the ponds. There was certainly no lack of those eager to shinny up the tall pole for the prize at the top — a bottle of vodka. Nor was there a lack of those happy to shoot with a bow and arrow at the bull's eye. As usual, the largest crowds were on the dance floor. Young men passed along secret notes to hitherto unknown girls. The orchestra was playing. The park was noisy and merry.

At some point, four girls came to the park: three Kowalski sisters — Jeannie, Natalia, and Helen — and their friend Lucy Strzelecka. Helen, her hair in a braid and dressed in a pleated pink cretonne[13] dress, did not feel quite at ease. She did not want to come to this fair. She had let her sisters persuade her. Jeannie even paid for her ticket. Some young man walked up to Helen. He asked her to dance. She excused herself, saying she really did not know how. He promised to lead. They began to dance. But this did not last long, scarcely a minute. Suddenly, she stopped dancing. She froze mid-step. She left the surprised young man and, after a while, abandoned her sisters and friend, saying she had a headache.

"As I began to dance I suddenly saw Jesus at my side," Sr. Faustina wrote several years later in her *Diary*. He looked as though He was on the Way of the Cross — "racked with pain, stripped of His clothing, all covered with wounds."

Like a jealous youth, He reproached her, saying, **"How long shall I put up with you and how long will you keep putting Me off?"** (*Diary*, 9).

Everything changed in that moment. Her meeting with Jesus Christ came as a great shock to her. It was not only totally unambiguous, but also probably just as unexpected. From that moment on, "there remained Jesus and I" (*Diary*, 9), she noted years later.

That boy from Venice Park probably never found out who the strangely-behaved girl was — nor did he probably ever learn the identity of the One to whom he had "lost" the dance.

Helen had been living in Łódź for two years. She came here in 1922 after a short stay in Głogowiec, during which her parents refused her request to enter a convent. She worked as a domestic servant. When she first arrived in Łódź, at the time a city of nearly five hundred thousand inhabitants and the second largest in Poland, she stayed with some relatives at 9 Nowo-Krótka Street (today Krośnieńska Street), just a few hundred yards from Venice Park. It was Michael Rapacki, Helen's father's cousin on his mother's side, who lived at that address — in a tenement building without running water or proper sanitation. He had left Świnice Warckie in 1919.

A granite plaque to the right of the entrance to the vine-covered two-story building commemorates Helen's stay here. Inside, there is a shabby stairwell. It looks as if it has not been renovated since Helen used these stairs. The wooden stairs are filthy. Looking through two tarnished ground-floor windows on the right, one can see the abandoned interior of what was once the Rapackis' apartment. The entrance from the stairwell is barred shut with crumbling chipboard. The Rapackis' apartment had at least two rooms and a hallway, which were occupied by Michael, his wife, Stanislava, and their daughter Sophie.

It is probably Michael Rapacki who helped Helen to find work. She hired herself out as help to three women tertiaries, members of the Third Order of St. Francis. It is not known where these women lived, but the Third Order ran the pharmacy on the intersection of Nowo-Pabianicka (today Sanocka) and Pabianicka Streets, not far from Michael Rapacki's home. Helen worked at the tertiaries' house, but stayed with her uncle.

Her family still remembers how — as conditions of her employment — she insisted on the right to attend daily Mass, receive the Sacrament of Confession with the tertiaries' regular confessor, and also visit the sick and dying. These were very mature requests for a 17-year-old girl. They indicated the direction and goal of her life. Not only was Helen sensitive to the physical suffering of the sick and dying, but she also sensed deep within how important the last moments of a human being's life are on a spiritual level. In the future, the Lord Jesus was to dictate the words of the Divine Mercy Chaplet to her. To anyone who would recite this prayer in trust, He made a promise to come to the aid of the dying. Helen also already sensed the importance of having regular spiritual direction and later wrote about this in her *Diary* (see 145, 680, 937-941). Father Joseph Andrasz notes that the regular confessor of the tertiaries was Fr. Wenceslaus Wyrzykowski, which means that he was also Helen's regular confessor in Łódź. It could be supposed that she also confessed to him after she no longer worked for the tertiaries. Father Wyrzykowski was the cathedral rector for many years and a known community organizer in Łódź; in fact, he was the founder of the Association of Christian Factory Workers.

Factory workers in Łódź accounted for 70 percent of the workforce. They posed an immense challenge to and task for the Church. In addition to spiritual guidance, they needed help organizing themselves in order to present their demands as a single entity to factory owners, and secondly, they needed welfare assistance. Only once — and only briefly — did employment in Łódź reach pre-World War I levels. That was in 1922, just as Helen arrived in the city. At that time, about one hundred thousand workers were employed in Łódź. The drop in production, and consequently in employment, was not just the result of the devastation caused by the war, but was also due to Russian policies that closed eastern textile markets to Poland after the latter regained its independence in November 1918. Before 1914, these markets absorbed 80 percent of what was manufactured in Łódź. Although industrial production rose over the next several years during the interwar period, it never reached 1914 levels. A major economic crisis added to the difficulties on the eastern markets. As a result, the city was prey to chronic unemployment throughout the entire interwar period, which led to immense poverty and homelessness. Tuberculosis proliferated and became a serious social and health problem.

Łódź had been the center of Poland's textile industry from the 19th century onwards. As the Nobel prize-winning author Ladislaus Reymont described in his novel *The Promised Land*, the city drew people hungry for big money as well as peasants from overpopulated villages seeking work. Those lacking a strong spiritual grounding tumbled to the depths of human squalor: to prostitution, alcoholism, and crime.

In the period between the two World Wars, Łódź was a city of great social contrasts: hopeless poverty and the massive fortunes of the factory owners — Israel

Poznański, Karol Scheibler, and Louis Grohmann, as well as dozens of other lesser and greater entrepreneurs. Remnants of their empires still remain today in the form of vast industrial-residential complexes comprised of factory buildings, workers' tenements, and immense owners' palaces. Among the most magnificent is the more than 74-acre complex of the Poznańskis on Ogrodowa Street, with a palace reminiscent of the Parisian Louvre. As for the renovated Poznański factory buildings, they currently house the "Manufaktura" retail and commercial center. The majority of factories, retail stores, and banks in Łódź were in the hands of ethnic minorities — nearly one-third of the residents of Łódź were Polish Jews, and Germans made up seven percent of the population. They had their own organizations and associations, political parties, schools, places of worship and cemeteries, shops, and newspapers.

Helen likely observed these contrasts during her two-year stay in Łódź, particularly after she changed jobs and moved closer to the city center. It is not known why she left the tertiaries. "She worked in several places in Łódź. If she didn't like the lifestyle or their way of running the household, she left for another place," explained Stanislava Rapacka. Unfortunately, Michael Rapacki, who was closer to Helen, did not live long enough to tell Sr. Bernardine Wilczek about her. He died in 1947, one year before Sr. Wilczek appeared at the Rapackis' to ask questions about Helen. Stanislava Rapacka, Michael's wife, did not know much about her, because she wasn't very interested in the girl's life. This is quite likely why she remembers Helen having worked as a servant at several houses in Łódź. In fact, she worked in two.

After leaving the tertiaries, Helen went to an employment office. It was there that she was given the address of Marcianna Wieczorek who lived on 29 Gubernatorska Street (now Abramowski Street). This mentally strong and resourceful 44-year-old woman lived with her family on the second floor of a three-story tenement building. She had once worked as a servant in the palace of Mr. Scheibler, one of the greatest of the Łódź factory owners, where she learned to speak German quite fluently. On the ground floor was a store that she ran herself. It was popularly called "Mrs. Sadowski's store," as that was the surname of her first husband, Adalbert, an expert stonemason. The Sadowskis had three children, but one of them died in infancy, and their teenage son was murdered. Adalbert Sadowski died not long after this tragedy, in October 1918.

The findings of journalist Agnes Jarocka indicate that six months after his death, in April 1919, Marcianna married Anthony Wieczorek, the widower of

Antonia née Kłosińska and six years her junior. Anthony had two children — Stanislava and Boleslaus. So when Helen showed up in February 1923 at the house on 29 Gubernatorska Street, there were three children there: 12-year-old Josephine (nicknamed Jutka) from Marcianna's first marriage and Anthony Wieczorek's two children.

Gubernatorska Street was located in the center of town. It was a stone's throw, a mere few hundred yards, from Piotrkowska Street, the main street in Łódź where commerce and culture thrived. To this very day, the wealthiest, most eclectic Vienna Secession-style townhouses and palaces of former residents of Łódź still stand on Piotrkowska Street. The most splendid of the townhouses belonged to Karol Scheibler near the palatial residences of Julius Heinzel and of the brothers Karol and Emil Steinert, to name a few. Helen Kowalska arrived at "Mrs. Sadowska's store" on Friday, February 2, 1923 — that is, on Candlemas.

Marcianna Wieczorek recalls, "At first I didn't want to take her on as a housemaid because she was so well dressed — much too elegant for a domestic servant. I offered her a much lower wage than she requested, because I wanted to get rid of her, but dear little Helen agreed to everything."

Indeed, Helen was dressed nicely. That was something new. The same girl who didn't have a dress to wear to church on Sunday a few years back finally had something to put on. From Marcianna Wieczorek's description, one could reckon that she was, if anything, dressed up — at least for a servant. When Helen was running away to the convent a year later, she asked her uncle to give her things away to family: the pink dress (the one that she wore to her neighbor's wedding in Głogowiec and to the dance in Venice Park) to her sister Jeannie, the black dress to her eldest (married) sister Josephine Jasińska, and the black skirt to her mother Marianna. She probably left something else for Natalia, who was also working as a servant in Łódź at the time. Perhaps her coat, which Mrs. Wieczorkowa first saw her wear in February.

This was her entire "wardrobe." It was everything that she had from home and that she bought as a servant. The rest fit into a small bundle, which she brought with her to Warsaw. "What I am wearing is enough for me; the Lord Jesus will provide me with everything," she told her uncle before she left for Warsaw.

Helen did not have much money for personal expenses. She sent most of what she earned to her parents in Głogowiec (and as a servant, she didn't earn much). One might assume that the pay rate was similar throughout Poland, but it is difficult to determine the exact amount, particularly in the first post-war years when inflation was raging. It reached the level of hyperinflation in

1923 when Helen began working at Mrs. Wieczorek's. After the treasury reform carried out in 1924, the monthly salary for a domestic servant ranged from 20 to 30 zloty. Helen earned little, as Marcianna Wieczorek herself admits that she lowered her wage. A domestic servant's earnings were at the bottom of the wage scale. After the currency reform, an unqualified factory worker earned 60 to 80 zloty, a qualified worker earned 150, a police officer 300, a government official from 180 to 420, and an accountant 600 zloty. According to contemporaneous calculations, a family of four would require 150 zloty per month to survive. Around two pounds of sugar cost one zloty; a quarter of a gallon of milk, a quarter zloty; about two pounds of pork, 1.20 zloty. In Łódź, owners demanded about 17 zloty a month in rent for a room with no kitchen or bath. Clearly, the salary of a domestic servant did not go far, even if one had free room and board like Helen did, having a bed to sleep on at her employer's. And yet — as Marcianna Wieczorek insists — Helen gave the impression of being a woman of fashion.

The photograph of a young woman in a checkered jacket appears in publications devoted to St. Faustina. It supposedly depicts Helen in 1923 or 1924, during the period when she was working for Marcianna Wieczorek. The Sisters of Our Lady of Mercy in Biała, near Płock, received this photograph from Natalia Grzelak, the sister of Helen-Faustina. This Community took care of Ms. Grzelak during the last years of her life (she died in Biała in 1997). There are three people in the photo: a smiling blonde and a brunette with sharply-defined features stand next to the girl in the checkered jacket.

Helen Kowalska in Łódź — first from the left. Next to her, most likely, is her oldest sister Josephine. Her older sister Eve (Jeannie) is on the right.

Most likely, these are Helen's sisters — Josephine and Jeannie Kowalska. Flags and banners can be seen in the background. It was a spring or early autumn day. Perhaps the girls were on their way to a religious festival in May. But is that really Helen Kowalska in the photograph?

The initial comparison of this photograph with an untouched photo of Sr. Faustina from her novitiate and with a photograph of her from 1935 (when she visited her family in Głogowiec) raises some doubts. The woman in the photograph taken in Łódź is good-looking. She has a pleasant expression and an open and honest smile, but she looks to be more mature and older than Helen, who was 18 years old at the time. Moreover, in the photograph the girl's hair is not as thick as her sister Natalia described Helen's hair to be, with "a braid as thick as my arm." Yet the girl's hair is done the way Helen did her hair — braided and pinned up high on her head in a so-called crown.

To be certain that these are indeed photos of the same person, I put them in the hands of experts from the Polish Forensic Association. Professor Bronislaus Młodziejowski, a legal anthropologist, carried out an expert appraisal. He conducted a detailed analysis of the morphological features of the head and face of the woman in the photograph from 1923 or 1924 as well as of the morphological features of Sr. Faustina in her religious habit in six photographs: three from her novitiate and one each from 1930, 1933, and 1935. Then, he compared them. The conclusion?

"The most significant features are common, and are characterized by a high degree of correspondence," he says. Professor Młodziejowski also stresses that several characteristics were impossible to compare because of Sr. Faustina's head being covered by her veil. He also recorded certain discrepancies between features due to Helen's wide smile on one of the photos, "which changes the clarity of features and their proportions." Not without significance is also the "passage of time, during which a subset of features undergoes intensification, while others maintain their shape, and while yet others emerge, documenting the characteristic ontogenesis of a given individual." In sum, the final result is positive: it can be said with a very high level of probability that the same person is depicted in the photo from 1923 or 1924 and the later photographs — Helen Kowalska.

What did she look like? Sister Faustina was described as follows on her identity card issued on March 2, 1931: "height: average; hair: blond; shape of face: oval; eye color: gray; identifying characteristics: none."

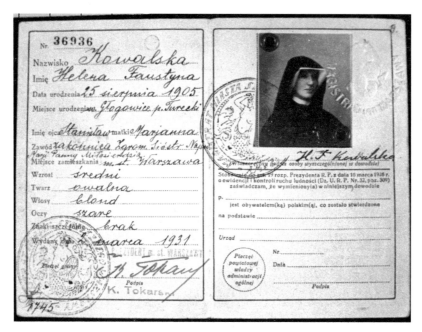

Sister Faustina's identity card, as issued in March 1931 in Warsaw.

People who knew Helen describe her in greater detail. Aldona Lipszyc, for whom Helen worked from 1924 to 1925, speaks of her having "smooth reddish hair, a thick braid, a friendly, open, peaceful face with some freckles."

Sister Borgia Tichy, her Superior in the convent in Vilnius, describes her thus: "She was auburn-haired with the complexion typical for red-heads, with many freckles in spring and summer, to the point where even the irises of her grey-green eyes had yellow flecks in them. The pupils of her eyes were often very large. When she was happy or excited in any way, they took on a particular radiance, which in effect gave the illusion of black eyes. Pupils that dilate easily are characteristic of excitable and high-strung people. An oblong face, regular features, a mouth that was quite wide, but proportional. ... She usually communicated her internal joy with a smile."

Natalia Grzelak recalls that Helen "was a very slender and happy girl, and could have been deemed attractive."

Sister Cajetan Bartkowiak speaks of her thus: "Sister Faustina was of medium height, slender, pretty. She had grey-green, always smiling eyes, which drew attention with their unusual radiance and lent her charm."

All that said, St. Faustina has been represented in a somewhat idealized way in numerous, more or less successful, portraits of her as a blessed and later as a saint. She appears to be an angelic, unearthly beauty in them and seems to be lacking any internal expression.

"She looked different," says Maria Nowicka with conviction. Today a 99-year-old with an unfailing memory, Maria was the eldest daughter of Aldona and Samuel Joseph Lipszyc. She sometimes gazes at the portrait of St. Faustina that hangs in her apartment in Żoliborz Warsaw, but claims that she can't pick out the resemblance to the girl who worked in her family home. Even if her memory is failing her, since she was only 5 or 6 years old at the time, the portrait still does not agree with what her mother Aldona said about Helen. When I showed Maria Nowicka copies of the black and white, pre-war untouched photos of Sr. Faustina that have been in publication for several years, she joyfully exclaimed, "Yes, that's our Helen!"

Very few photographs remain of Sr. Faustina. But in those that were taken during the first period of Helen Kowalska's stay in the convent, one can see her cheerfulness, her interior joy, and even a certain playfulness in her smile and eyes.

Portrait of Sr. Faustina from May 1, 1933.

Marcianna Wieczorek described her former housemaid as "agreeable and a bit of a jokester."

In a later photograph, taken in 1935 in her parents' home in Głogowiec, Sr. Faustina is different: serious, with her eyes fixed somewhere in the distance, as if beyond the here and now. Her face also appears changed. This photograph was taken three and a half years before her death. At this time, she was already seriously ill, although her tuberculosis had not yet been diagnosed.

Marcianna Wieczorek, put off at first by Helen's elegant appearance, which, in her opinion, was unsuitable for a domestic servant, was nonetheless very satisfied with her work. After the war, she told Sr. Bernardine Wilczek that Helen "was polite, kind, hard-working, immeasurably good. ... You could rely on her completely. However many times I left to go on a trip, I always was at ease, because I was not needed there. She did better in the house than I did. ... She was thoughtful and quick with her work; whatever I planned to do, she had already done." Helen worked in the house and possibly also in Mrs. Wieczorkowa's store. She also played with her employer's children. She told them stories. From Mrs. Wieczorek's account, we can conclude that Helen fasted very often: on Wednesdays, Fridays, and Saturdays, and daily during Lent. "On Ash Wednesday, she didn't drink anything. She ate dairy products only on Sundays, Mondays, Tuesdays, and Thursdays." This means that Helen did not eat meat or animal fats throughout the whole of Lent. She ate only dairy products, and then not on every day of the week during Lent. "I can't say anything bad about her at all. ... That little Helen, she really inspired me spiritually."

From that point on, Marcianna Wieczorek attended Mass more willingly, and she received the Sacraments of Confession and of the Eucharist more frequently. Helen, who had experienced great poverty at home, was sensitive to the lot of the poor. She also saw far too many poor people in Łódź. At the house where she worked, a lonely, sick man lived in the small space below the stairs.

Natalia Grzelak remembers that "Helen would take him something to eat, wash him, cheer him up, talk to him about the Lord God; and in the end, she brought a priest with her to hear his confession and give him Communion. I was there when the priest came; that man was in a very poor state, and Helen was happy that he had managed to be united with God, because he died the very next day. She always wanted to bring people to God."

Helen also saw the poorest of the poor behind the tenement houses on the odd-numbered side of Gubernatorska Street, that is, behind the building where she was working. The "catacombs" were located just a few yards away from the buildings. They made up a slum of sorts for the poorest. Entire families hunkered down in these outbuildings hastily put together with shabby materials, with no running water, no electricity, no plumbing, and with only 12 to 16 square yards at their disposal. Today, no trace remains of the so-called catacombs. They were demolished in the 1950s. In their place, residents of the tenement buildings dug deep trenches where they set up small cellar-like storage units for coal, wood, and potatoes.

The reason for trenches was so that the storage units wouldn't block the view of the park from the tenement windows. Residents don't use the below-ground storage units anymore, so the trenches stand empty, but the view that remains is still surreal.

In Łódź, Helen never stopped thinking about entering the convent. Sister Bernarda Wilczek claims that while the future saint was working for the tertiaries, she wrote a letter to her parents asking them to let her enter the convent. But once again, the Kowalskis flatly refused.

Soon afterwards, Helen left her position at the tertiaries and began working for Marcianna Wieczorek as a domestic servant. In the *Diary*, Sr. Faustina noted that she asked her parents for permission to enter the convent when she was 18. She came of age — that is, she turned 18 — on August 25, 1923. It is not clear, however, whether Helen had this particular date in mind, or 1923 in general. She may have asked once or even twice within the same year. Most likely, when she left the tertiaries at the turn of 1923, she asked her parents for permission to pursue her heart's desire. Because they refused, she sought employment with Mrs. Wieczorek. When Helen turned 18 in August, she may have asked them once more.

Her uncle Rapacki, whom she visited at his place on 9 Nowo-Krótka Street, sometimes made fun of her plans. He would also say that her parents wouldn't ever hear of it. "I'll give her a convent," scowled Helen's mother in a conversation with Mr. Rapacki.

The resolve of her parents is astonishing. The Kowalskis were faithful and pious people. They had eight living children, six of them daughters. Sister Wilczek once asked Helen's mother why they had been so opposed to their daughter's wishes: why "was she so stingy with the Lord God?" "With so many daughters, why did she not want to give that sole one to a convent?"

"Because she was the best child, the dearest … and so obedient and hard-working. The most loving," she heard in response.

Yet there were also additional reasons. Her parents did not want to give their consent because they knew that entering a convent required a dowry, which they could not guarantee their daughter. It was Helen, working as a housemaid in the city, who was helping her parents. She sent them money. Her entering the convent would mean they would lose badly needed financial support. Helen had five younger siblings. The youngest, Wanda, was born in 1920, and so the family's needs were great.

Despite her strong desire to follow God's call and enter the convent, she could not even conceive of going against her mother and father's will. That is why, when she heard her parents' adamant "no" yet again, she tried to stifle her calling to the religious life. "I turned myself over to the vain things of life, paying no attention to the call of grace, although my soul found no satisfaction in any of these things. The incessant call of grace caused me much anguish. I tried, however, to stifle it with amusements. Interiorly, I shunned God, turning with all my heart to creatures, " she wrote of this period in her life (*Diary*, 8). Those "vain things of life" and her "turning to creatures" were an attempt to live like other girls her age. Perhaps it was at that time — after her parents had refused her yet again — that she went and bought the new coat or dress that she was wearing when she first went to see Mrs. Wieczorek.

The Lord God gave Helen a strong calling, but He did not make it easy for her to follow Him. Similarly, after she entered the convent, Jesus gave her weighty tasks but apparently did not aid her in carrying them out. Helen had to fight for her own vocation, even at the price of defying her parents. But in 1924, discouraged by her mother and father's resistance, she decided to abide by their wishes, even though this gave her no satisfaction deep within.

It was in this state of mind that she agreed, though reluctantly, to go along with her sisters to the Venice Park dance. Her older sister Jeannie, who "enjoyed going out and having fun when she had time off," encouraged Helen, saying that maybe they would go dance a bit or win something in the raffle. She even bought a ticket for Helen, who was still unconvinced. On a servant's wages, the ticket was not cheap. In the 1920s, when the Kowalski daughters — who were then single — lived in Łódź, a ticket to Venice Park cost 50 groszy on days of performances and 20 groszy on regular days.

Today, no one checks tickets at the entrance to the park. There is no one selling them either. The park itself no longer calls to mind the former Venice Park, famous for its dances, concerts, and spectacles. There are no restaurants, dance halls, or theaters. Neither is there any trace of the ponds and canals, which have all been filled in. Even the park's name, no longer suitable to the locale, has been changed. Now, Julius Słowacki (the Polish Romantic poet) is the "patron" of the park and its visitors. Children frolic on the playground under the watchful eyes of their mothers. Elderly gentlemen leisurely deliberate their next move at the chess tables.

Only the chestnut trees blossom in May like they used to — just as abundantly, excessively even. One of them — exceptional in its size — must remember that dance of some 90 years ago and Jesus' appearance to the young girl. That tree has become an object of spontaneous reverence for the residents of Łódź. A cross, images of the Merciful Jesus, and St. Faustina are all affixed to its trunk. There are also flowers around it, and the flames of votive candles flicker at its roots. Nearby, a bit to the side, a huge boulder with a plaque on it informs visitors that it was here that Jesus appeared to Helen Kowalska, the mystic who was later to become St. Faustina.

After her vision of Jesus, Helen quickly left her companions. She ran straight to the nearest church — the huge Cathedral Basilica of St. Stanislaus Kostka, which was completed in 1912. Its steeple, at more than 320 feet high, is still the tallest building in the city. This church, which had been raised to the rank of cathedral just a few years prior, was well known to Helen. She had attended Mass here, either alone or with her sisters, while she was staying at her uncle's and at the Wieczorek's. The rector was the aforementioned Fr. Wenceslaus Wyrzykowski.

"It was almost twilight; there were only a few people in the cathedral. Paying no attention to what was happening around me, I fell prostrate before the Blessed Sacrament and begged the Lord to be good enough to give me to understand what I should do next," she related in her *Diary* (9). "Then I heard these words: **Go at once to Warsaw; you will enter a convent there**. I rose from prayer, came home, and took care of things that needed to be settled. As best I could, I confided to my sister what took place within my soul. I told her to say good-bye to our parents" (*Diary*, 10).

Helen then ran to Nowo-Krótka Street to say good-bye to her uncle. "For God's sake, Helen, what on earth are you doing? After all, your dear mother and father are going to weep and gnash their teeth," the troubled Michael Rapacki reportedly said.

"Oh, Uncle, don't tell my parents anything for now, only when you go to visit them," Helen responded, perhaps surprising even herself. Helen was decisive, but shaken at the same time. She was defying her mother and father's wishes. Although she was not leaving her actual family home, it seemed like she was running away from it — from her family.

She sobbed "until she shook," recalls Stanislava Rapacka. Helen asked her uncle to take her to the train station and bought "some vodka and cake" for him. Seated in the train compartment, she still cried so hard that "it was painful to watch. If the train had stopped, I probably would have taken her off it. But it didn't stop," he later told his wife. Is this at all surprising? Helen was 19 years old. She was on a train to the unknown. She was following the voice of Jesus, to whom she entrusted herself completely.

At the time, trains to Warsaw departed from the Łódź Industrial Station. The journey lasted two hours and 20 minutes. Since Helen immediately began her search for lodging when she arrived in the capital, we can assume that she left in the afternoon. What was the date? In the literature on the subject, Helen's departure from Łódź and arrival in the capital is given as July 1924. Sometimes there is even a more precise date: July 1. This is the date that Mrs. Wieczorek gave Sr. Wilczek in 1948. She also told her, "I don't know where she went off to. She was supposed to leave sooner, but she waited until my baby was born; that's how kind she was."

After nearly a quarter century, Mrs. Wieczorek remembered to the day both the beginning and the end of Helen's employment as a housemaid. This is somewhat strange. But there exist people with phenomenal memories. Perhaps she is one of them? Or perhaps she noted the date or associated it with other events that were engraved on her memory. The birth and death of a child would qualify as such events. Marcianna Wieczorek remembered that Helen stayed until her child's birth. Agnes Jarocka, the aforementioned journalist, found out that Marcianna and Anthony Wieczorek's son was born on Sunday, June 8, 1924. Unfortunately, he died just one hour later.

Marcianna Wieczorek also remembered that Helen was supposed to leave earlier, before Marcianna gave birth. Why that was — we don't know. Maybe there was some kind of misunderstanding in the house? Or perhaps the reasons were poor finances and living conditions? If she was supposed to leave earlier, but decided to stay especially for the birth, it could not have been due to what happened in Venice Park. When she was in the cathedral, Helen clearly heard the words in her heart, **"Go at once to Warsaw."** This was such a powerful experience that we have to assume she did just that. She left at once for Warsaw, without any delay.

That means that her earlier intention to change jobs must have been caused by something else. Trusting that Mrs. Wieczorek had an excellent memory, and that nothing would have kept Helen in Łódź after her vision of Jesus, we can assume that the apparition in Venice Park occurred after June 8. As a housemaid, Helen had some time off on Sundays. That is also when the dances took place in Venice Park. After June 8, the next Sundays in June 1924 were on the 15th, 22nd, and 29th of the month. The Rev. Professor Ignatius Różycki, one of the theological experts assisting with her cause of beatification, says that she immediately obeyed Jesus. Taking leave of her employer and sister, she left for Warsaw that very same day.

Alternate possible dates for Helen's arrival in Warsaw also crop up in people's memories. Mother Michael Moraczewska, then Mother Superior at the Warsaw convent of the Sisters of Our Lady of Mercy, was the one who agreed to accept Helen into the Congregation (on condition that she first work to pay for her postulant's wardrobe). Years later, she recalled that she spoke with Helen for the first time "one spring morning in 1924." But it is clear from other sources that Mother Michael had a poor memory. Once Helen had saved up enough for her first postulant's wardrobe payment and brought it to the convent door, Mother Superior could not recall who she was. Sister Wilczek, who in 1948 collected materials about Faustina for the period between her employment in Łódź and entry to the convent, noted as follows, "May 1924 – August 1, 1925 – domestic service for Mrs. Lipszyc in Ostrówek, Wołomin County." That was where the future saint earned money for her postulant's wardrobe. Elsewhere, she noted that Helen worked in the Lipszyc home "for 1 year and 3 months, and then, with the required postulant's wardrobe in hand, she entered the convent in Warsaw in 1925."

Yet Aldona Lipszyc, Helen's employer, remembered her showing up in the summer of 1924. But most importantly, Sr. Faustina herself wrote in her *Diary* that after finding a convent that would accept her, "for many reasons I still had to remain in the world for more than a year " (*Diary*, 15). What Faustina noted to be "more than a year" was in fact only a little over 12 months.

Whatever the exact dates of her travel to Warsaw and then her employment there, Helen definitely entered the convent on August 1, 1925.

Chapter Four

Warsaw

1924, 1925-1926, 1928,
1929, 1932-1933, 1935, 1936

'I Am Burdened, But I Sense the Great Divine Grace that Lets Me Bear It All'

WARSAW TERRIFIED HELEN. When she got off at the Warsaw-Vienna Train Station at the intersection of Jerozolimskie Avenue and Marszałkowska Street — now the location of the Centrum subway stop — she found herself in the center of a city of a million people. This was her first time in Warsaw, and she didn't know anyone.

"When I got off the train and saw that all were going their separate ways, I was overcome with fear. What am I to do? To whom should I turn, as I know no one?" she reflected years later in her *Diary* (11).

The main exit of the stately station building, designed by the famous architect Henry Marconi in the mid-19th century, led to Jerozolimskie Avenue. At that time, it was one of the most recognizable spots in Warsaw. Rows of tall Italian poplars lined both sides of the 130 feet wide avenue. A median with planters separated the two opposing lanes of tram, car, and horse-carriage traffic. Vienna Secession- and Modernist-style apartment buildings, each a few stories high, stood on the south side of Jerozolimskie Avenue. Across from the station was the Polonia Palace Hotel, built in the Parisian Beaux-Arts style. Station sidetracks and loading ramps were located on the other side of the street.

Helen had come to Warsaw because this was what Jesus had instructed her to do in the Łódź cathedral, to which she had run directly from Venice Park. Now, frozen in fear, not knowing what to do next, she turned with trust to Mary, the Mother of God. "Mary, lead me, guide me."

"Immediately I heard these words within me telling me to leave the town and to go to a certain nearby village where I would find a safe lodging for the night. I did so and found, in fact, that everything was just as the Mother of God told me" (*Diary*, 11).

Since Helen sought lodging immediately after her arrival, it can be surmised that she came to Warsaw in the afternoon. Perhaps she arrived at 5:35 p.m., because that is when the train arrived from Łódź, according to a 1924 train schedule. The name of the village where she spent the night is unknown. From the hints that she left in her *Diary*, however, one can guess the direction she went in, and how she got there.

Helen recorded that when she returned to Warsaw the next morning, she went into the first church that she saw. This was the Church of Our Lady of the Immaculate Conception in the Parish of St. James the Apostle, on Narutowicz Square in Warsaw's Ochota district, in the western part of the city. This means that she must have gone in this general direction the day before. But it is not true that Helen took the Local Electric Train (EKD), now commonly known as "Wukadka" (WKD), that links Warsaw with Grodzisk Mazowiecki. This cannot be true for the simple reason that this train line wasn't up and running until three years later, December 11, 1927.

So how and where did Helen travel in her search for a night's lodging? There are two possible explanations.

First, she could have gotten back on the train at the Vienna Station, the one travelling west toward Łowicz, and gotten off the train at a station beyond the city limits. This is unlikely, however, as it would have been very hard for her to get a glimpse of the church in Ochota from the train window. This would have been all the more difficult given that, in 1924, the Neo-Romanesque church did not yet have the tall four-sided steeple that it boasts now. Moreover, she would have had to work out the church's direction from the train window and then walk or take the tram for a few miles after returning to the station the next morning. Other churches in the center of the town would have been closer for her. So this explanation doesn't work.

That is why I offer a second explanation. After she arrived from Łódź, Helen got off the train and walked towards the tram stop. She must have asked someone how to get out of the city. According to a 1924 map of Warsaw, the stop for tram line No. 7 was close to the train station. The tram from Radzymińska Street in the city's Praga district ran to Ochota by way of Jerozolimskie Avenue. The route ran along Grójecka Street, where Narutowicz Square and the Church of the Immaculate Conception are located and continued until the intersection of Grójecka and Opaczewska Streets. This was the last stop on the No. 7 line, because in those days, this marked the city limit, and this is where suburban tramline A began. It had been opened a year earlier, and ran from the Grójecka and Opaczewska Streets intersection all the way to Okęcie, where the city council was planning to build an airport. The tram ran through the villages of Szczęśliwice, Zosin, Raków, and Okęcie. Today, they are all part of Warsaw.

Helen probably got off in one of these villages and found lodgings for the night. She returned to Warsaw early the next day. She travelled back on the same trams; they were the only ones on this route, anyway. Tram A brought her to the then-cobblestoned Grójecka Street, and then she took tram No. 7 to Gabriel Narutowicz Square. This square, constructed just a year earlier, was named after the first president of the Second Polish Republic, who was assassinated in 1922. Helen noticed the church on the square from the tram windows — perhaps even the day before. She got off here.

This version of events seems most likely. Her *Diary* reveals what happened next. She went into the church and began to pray. The Church of the Immaculate Conception of the Blessed Virgin Mary, begun in 1910, was still under construction. It is one the most striking works of Polish Modernism. To this very day, instead of the cupola that was initially planned to crown it, its steeple is covered over by a flat roof. A plaque in the nave of the main church and a portrait of St. Faustina remind visitors that this was the place where Helen prayed in 1924.

Helen asked Jesus for His advice as to what she should do next. "Holy Masses were being celebrated, one after another," she wrote years later. "During one of them I heard the words: **Go to that priest and tell him everything; he will tell you what to do next**" (*Diary*, 12). That priest was Fr. James Dąbrowski, the pastor of that parish for the last six years. Several years later, he died from gangrene resulting from a leg injury sustained during the bombing of his church in September 1939.

After Mass, Helen went to the sacristy. "I told the priest all that had taken place in my soul, and I asked him to advise me where to take the veil, in which religious order" (*Diary*, 12). You can imagine the surprise of the priest, which Helen herself mentions in her *Diary*. After all, he was 62, no longer all that young, and he must have seen a lot in his life. But this certainly was the first time something like this had happened to him — a young woman was standing in front of him, bundle in hand, and looking clearly lost. Instead of directing her to a convent, Fr. Dąbrowski gave her the address of "a pious lady" (*Diary*, 13) with whom she could stay, and encouraged her, saying that God would continue to lead her.

That "lady" was Aldona Lipszyc née Jastrzębska, the wife of Samuel Joseph Lipszyc, an agricultural engineer and central government official. Years later, she remembered well that Fr. Dąbrowski sent Helen Kowalska to her with a letter informing Mrs. Lipszyc that he "doesn't know her and hopes she will prove capable" as a domestic servant. That was in July 1924.

"Mother needed help. That is why my father asked the priest that if he met anyone worthy of recommendation, to send them to us," explained Maria Nowicka, the eldest daughter of Aldona and Samuel Lipszyc.

Father Dąbrowski knew Samuel, Maria's father, from the days when he was pastor of the parish in Klembów, a town more than 18 miles northeast of Warsaw. The village Ostrówek belonged to the parish where Meyer Lipszyc, Samuel's father, bought a wooden summer cottage in 1913. The cottage was a typical "dacha," one of those built by Russian Tsarist officials from the mid-19th century onward, when Russia was one of the three occupying forces of Polish lands.

"My father was a bachelor at the time and the only intellectual in Ostrówek," says Maria Nowicka, born in 1919 and gifted with both eloquence and a superb memory. "Every now and then, in the evenings, he would pay Fr. Dąbrowski a visit at the rectory. They would debate on theological and philosophical issues, and occasionally they sparred at chess. The two became friends."

In September 1918, Fr. Dąbrowski, who was already a pastor in Warsaw at the time, baptized the 28-year-old Samuel Joseph Lipszyc (a convert from Judaism), and then witnessed his marriage vows to 22-year-old Aldona Jastrzębska. After the wedding, the newlyweds moved into the wooden dacha in Ostrówek. Later on, Fr. Dąbrowski also baptized all of their children. In 1924, when Helen Kowalska arrived on their doorstep, there were five of them in the Lipszyc family: the twins Maria and Thaddeus (1919), Sophia (1921), Leopold (1923), and the newborn Nina (1924). Visna (1926) and Hedwig (1928) were born later.

"Whenever Mom was about to give birth to another baby, she would pack up all the kids, leave Ostrówek, and go to Warsaw. She would stay at her sister Veronica Jastrzębska's apartment on 30 Smolna Street. After a while, we would all go back home to Ostrówek," recalls Maria Nowicka.

That was also what happened in 1924. Aldona Lipszyc gave birth to her fifth child, Nina, in Warsaw on April 21. Maria Nowicka does not know how long her parents stayed in Warsaw after her sister's birth. It could have been several weeks, maybe months. The sisters Veronica and Aldona were very close. Their mother had died when Aldona was five years old. Veronica, 17 at the time and the eldest of the children, mothered her and their other siblings. Years later, she convinced three of them to move to Warsaw, including Aldona who moved in with her at the apartment on Smolna Street. This was close to the Kowalczykówna and Jaworkówna High School on Wiejska Street where she went to school. It took a bit longer for her to get to Vilnius Station in Warsaw's Prague, where later — as Mrs. Lipszyc — she would leave for Ostrówek.

The literature on Sr. Faustina mentions July 1, 1924, as the day when she began working for the Lipszyc family in Ostrówek. However, it is almost certain that Helen Kowalska first came to the apartment on Smolna Street with her recommendation from Fr. Dąbrowski. She made a good impression on Aldona, who describes Helen as "fair, healthy, cheerful, even merry." Aldona took her on immediately. Helen stayed with the Lipszyc family in Warsaw for some time. Maria Nowicka is sure that this is what happened.

"Helen would not have found her way to Ostrówek alone," she says firmly. This is almost certainly true; even today it is not easy to find the Lipszyc's former home by car, located as it is on the edge of a forest reserve. Finding it would have been even more difficult in 1924. In those days, people traveled by train on the Warsaw-Petersburg line to Tłuszcz (the Klembów stop was added later). From there, the Lipszyc dacha was nearly a four-mile walk, more than one mile of that through the woods. One might assume that Helen first went to Samuel Joseph Lipszyc with her recommendation from Fr. Dąbrowski, and then travelled on with him to Ostrówek. At the time, he was working either in the Ministry of Agriculture and Agricultural Reform, or in the Voivodship [District] Land Office — Maria Nowicka is not able to recall which. From Aldona Lipszyc's memories, however, it is clear that Helen brought the note to her.

There is also one more piece of evidence in favor of Helen having stayed with the Lipszyc family in Warsaw for a certain amount of time. Father Dąbrowski did not point Helen to a specific convent during their first conversation. She spent some time looking for one. Finding one was not easy, as girls without dowries were either very unwillingly accepted or refused. Faustina noted in her *Diary* that Aldona Lipszyc received her kindly. She does not give Aldona's last name in the *Diary*, a practice that she keeps for all those whom she mentions in her writings. Faustina noted, "During the time I stayed with her, I was looking for a convent, but at whatever convent door I knocked, I was turned away. Sorrow gripped my heart, and I said to the Lord Jesus, 'Help me, don't leave me alone.' At last I knocked on our door" — that is, the door of the Congregation of the Sisters of Our Lady of Mercy in Warsaw (*Diary*, 13).

"Helen could not have traveled by train from Ostrówek to Warsaw to find a convent. She worked as a servant for us, and she worked very hard," says Maria Nowicka. "Her help was also needed on Sundays."

In Maria's opinion, the only time Helen could have looked for a congregation to take her in was while she was living with the Lipszyc family in Warsaw.

There is also one more important piece of evidence that in 1924 the Lipszyc family, along with the children, was staying on Smolna Street in Warsaw and not, for example, on Koszykowa Street in the home of Samuel's parents, Meyer and Chaya Sura Lipszyc. (His parents built their house on Pilicka Street later.) Next to the entry for Nina's Baptism (which took place a year later, in May 1925) in the parish records of St. James's Church, Fr. Dąbrowski listed 30 Smolna Street as the parents' place of residence.

The house — or rather, massive complex — where Aldona Lipszyc's sister lived stands in the center of the city. Her large apartment, consisting of several rooms, was located on the sixth floor of the building that housed the all-boys secondary school of the Jan Zamoyski Association. It is the alma mater of many eminent people from Warsaw. In the spring of 1924, when Helen showed up at Veronica Jastrzębska's apartment, George Giedroyc[14] and Stanislaus Żeleński[15] were in the midst of their high school completion exams (Stanislaus lived across the street, at No. 13). Other Zamoyski graduates include Thaddeus Kotarbiński,[16] Melchior Wańkowicz,[17] Stephen Kieniewicz,[18] George Andrzejewski,[19] and Witold Małcużyński.[20] The building continues to house a middle school, high school, and school dormitory, but it does not look as it did in 1924. The complex went up in flames during the Warsaw Uprising. The building was rebuilt, but without the beautiful Vienna Secession-style façade, and without the sixth floor where Veronica Jastrzębska's apartment was located before the war.

One hundred years ago, Smolna Street was located in the center of Warsaw, much as it is today. After Poland regained its independence in 1918, the city once again became the seat of the highest authorities and central government offices of the Republic. Their main task was to create a unified state out of a country that, for 123 years, had been occupied by three neighboring empires: those of Russia, Germany, and Austria. Poland's newly-regained freedom was threatened once more only two years later, when the Bolshevik army advanced as far as Warsaw. In the great Battle of Radzymin, called the Miracle on the Vistula,

Soviet divisions were defeated on August 15, 1920. The Polish armed forces not only protected the country against Communism, but also ended the Red Army's march westward. The first years of Polish independence were politically unstable, a time of huge challenges and problems, but also of growth.

This was clearly evident in the center of the capital, which was pulsating with life in the 1920s. Wealthy residents lived there — the intelligentsia, the petit bourgeoisie, the bourgeoisie, and the artists. The Branickis owned several grand buildings, including the palace at the corner of Smolna and Nowy Świat Streets. In contrast to today, Smolna Street was completely built up on both sides with tall tenement buildings. The famous "Gastronomia" restaurant with its glass verandas was located at the junction of Nowy Świat Street and Jerozolimskie Avenue. (Today's locale of the same name is unaffiliated with it.) Nowy Świat Street was a place of commerce and entertainment. It boasted mostly Neoclassical apartment buildings and was also dotted with several aristocratic palaces. At street level, the apartment buildings housed stores, pastry shops, cafés, restaurants, and cabarets, which were fashionable at the time. In the clubs, patrons danced the immortal tango and learned the Charleston. Cinemas, operetta, and vaudeville theatres sprang up in the courtyards of the apartment buildings. Foksal Street, right next to Smolna, was famous before the war for its fantastic gardens, where theater groups performed in the summertime.

Residents of Warsaw, as elsewhere, were obviously very segregated socially and economically. Factory workers lived in close quarters in rental tenement buildings, which lacked any amenities, in the center of the city or on the outskirts. They poured into the capital from overpopulated villages in the Mazowsze and Podlasie regions. They were absorbed by Warsaw's industries — primarily metal and food industries — which prospered in the 1920s.

According to the general census of 1921, almost one-third of Warsaw's work force was employed in industry and the trades. Nearly 20 percent of the work force worked in commerce and finance, and eight percent worked, like Helen Kowalska, as domestic servants. As much as 16 percent of the work force was in the public service, including Samuel Joseph Lipszyc. One-third of the population of prewar Warsaw was made up of Jews — the biggest ethnic and religious minority — who lived in the northern districts of the city. It is not unlikely that Helen, while looking for a convent, passed by Jewish districts. She might have also caught a glimpse of the Great Synagogue in the distance, one of the greatest examples of the 19th-century architecture of Warsaw. It no longer exists today, having been blown up by the Germans during the Second World War.

It is not known which church Helen attended in Warsaw. Saint Alexander's Church on Three Crosses Square was the closest to Smolna Street. It was much larger and taller then than it is now. Helen must have noticed its cupola when she turned from Smolna Street onto Nowy Świat Street. But if she turned right, in the direction of the Old Town Market Square, the first church she would have passed is the Baroque-style Holy Cross Church. Sister Faustina does not record in her *Diary* which or how many convent doors she knocked on with her request to be allowed to enter. There must have been several, since she wrote, "At whatever convent door I knocked, I was turned away" (*Diary*, 13). It is not known if someone guided her as to where and what kind of congregations she might visit. Perhaps Fr. Dąbrowski helped her (as Fr. Michael Sopoćko reckoned), or maybe Mr. and Mrs. Lipszyc did. The reason why Helen was rejected was simple but painful for her: she had neither a dowry nor an education to offer. From a material point of view, she had nothing to contribute to a congregation. She was not a valuable candidate. "Nothing extraordinary," Mother Margaret Gimbutt summed her up after speaking to her for the first time.

Many congregations didn't even accept women of "lower birth," or those from the lowest rungs of society, with no education or dowry. One of these was the Congregation of Franciscan Sisters of the Family of Mary, dubbed the "Rodziniarki" [the Family Sisters], whose convent is located on Żytnia Street in Warsaw, next door to the Congregation of the Sisters of Our Lady of Mercy. It is highly likely that Helen also contacted them. To this day, so the story goes, the sisters still regret that they didn't recognize a future saint in Helen.

The Sisters of Our Lady of Mercy accepted young women of any social status, but required that they be divided up into choirs. The candidate's level of education determined which choir she belonged to. The Congregation's main task was to reintegrate girls into society by giving them an education and helping them to develop. For this reason, sisters who had graduated from school were greatly valued. As only girls from affluent homes used to receive a good education, the first choir belonged to the elite. Young women with an inferior education, or those who hadn't finished school at all, entered the second choir, which was connected with a "lower social status" and the lack of a dowry. The Holy See had the right to release a candidate from having to provide a dowry. That is what happened in the case of Helen Kowalska, who was accepted into the second choir — but not without some difficulties.

Most likely, Helen knocked at the convent door on 3/9 Żytnia Street in Warsaw's Wola district in July 1924. She showed up in the morning, according to the recollections of Mother Michael Moraczewska, but according to Mother Borgia Tichy, at about noon. It was either a spring day (according to Mother Michael) or a day in July (as Mother Borgia recalls). Sister Clara Himmer, the doorkeeper, announced the appearance of a "new vocation" to then-Mother General Leonard Cielecka. (This particular convent was the seat of the general administration of the entire Congregation at that time.) Mother General sent her to speak with Mother Margaret Gimbutt. Helen did not make the best impression on her. "Inconspicuous, slightly too old, fragile, a servant, by occupation a cook, and, what's more, having no dowry, and not even the least of any money for a postulant's wardrobe" — these are the words by which Mother Margaret described the candidate to the Superior, as Mother Borgia Tichy recalled years later.

Helen probably would have been rejected by this Congregation as well, if Mother Moraczewska had not walked in on the conversation. At the time, she was Mother Superior at the Żytnia convent, and would soon become, in 1928, Mother General of the entire Congregation. Later, Sr. Faustina described her as "permeated with divine light and very loving of God." She was very well-educated, spoke several languages, and was a graduate of the music conservatory. She wanted to see the candidate in person.

Years later, she admitted that Helen also failed to make a good first impression on her "because of her somewhat unkempt external appearance. I thought to myself: this is not for us." She intended to send her away immediately, but she thought, "It would be more in keeping with love for one's neighbor to ask the girl a few superficial questions first before bidding her farewell." During the conversation, she noticed that the "candidate gains in closer contact, she has a nice smile, an amiable expression, and great simplicity, honesty, and common sense in expressing herself." She changed her opinion, therefore, and wished to accept her. Mother Moraczewska didn't mention what Helen wrote in her *Diary*: "She told me, after a short conversation, to go to the Lord of the house and ask whether He would accept me. I understood at once that I was to ask this of the Lord Jesus. With great joy, I went to the chapel and asked Jesus, 'Lord of this house, do You accept me? This is how one of these sisters told me to put the question to You.'

"Immediately I heard this voice: **I do accept; you are in My Heart.** When I returned from the chapel, Mother Superior asked first of all, 'Well, has the Lord accepted you?' I answered, 'Yes.' 'If the Lord has accepted, [she said] then I also will accept'" (*Diary*, 14).

It is possible, as Maria Winowska notes in her book *The Right to Mercy*, that Mother Moraczewska sent Helen to the chapel to gain some time and think through her response. But one difficulty surfaced — Helen's poverty. "Not speaking of a dowry (from which the Holy See easily gives a dispensation), she did not have any money for her postulant's wardrobe, and we had no funds at all for that purpose," recalls Mother Moraczewska.

Consequently, Helen had to earn money for her postulant's wardrobe. She arranged with Mother Superior that she would bring the money she earned to the convent for them to keep. Mother Michael Moraczewska admits that she forgot about Helen after that conversation. That is why she was surprised when she was told several months later that "some little person brought 60 zloty for safekeeping, explaining that she had been instructed to do so." Only after thinking things through did I recall what that was all about," says Mother Moraczewska. "From then on, Helen's deposit continued to increase regularly so that in a year, she had amassed several hundred zloty, sufficient money at that time for a postulant's wardrobe."

When she first knocked at the doors of the convent on Żytnia Street, she probably didn't know anything about the Congregation that was housed within. It was a relatively new Congregation, established in the mid-19th century. Many congregations of women religious came into existence in Poland at this time. They were founded on the concept of the personal sanctification of nuns by means of addressing various social ills and, in this particular case, by assisting women who were — as we would say today — from the margins of society, mostly prostitutes, who wanted to change their lives. For this reason, members of the Congregation of the Sisters of Our Lady of Mercy were commonly called "Magdalenes," as in St. Mary Magdalene, the sinner and penitent, while their wards were referred to as "penitents."

In the 19th century, prostitution was a serious social problem in the Polish territories. Uneducated women from overpopulated villages escaped to cities, where they often had no chance of making a living by honest means. Eve Caroline, Teresa Antoinette from the line of the Sułkowski princes, also known as Countess Vladislava Potocka, desired to help women in these circumstances. She herself was a childless widow after a marriage of 17 years. She stayed with the religious community of Mother Thérèse Rondeau in Laval, France, for eight months, observing the sisters' methods of work in similar circumstances to those she would face back home. Mother Teresa Potocka — which is how she was called in her new role as foundress of a new congregation — borrowed the Constitution, the principal spiritual orientation, and apostolic charism from the French religious community.

For this reason, Mother Thérèse Rondeau is also considered a co-foundress of the Congregation. Both of the women, it should be noted, frequently made references to the work of the French aristocrat Thérèse de Lamourous. In 1801, after the French Revolution, this lady established a house in Bordeaux, called the "House of Mercy," for prostitutes who wanted to change their lives. Neither Mother Potocka in the Polish territories, nor Mother Rondeau in France, initially wanted to "establish a religious order, but rather desired to serve fallen women," explains Fr. Joachim R. Bar, the author of the most comprehensive study to date on the history of the Congregation of the Sisters of Our Lady of Mercy. Nevertheless, the conferral of an organizational structure to this initiative of several women friends united by noble goals and ideals was an unavoidable stage in the development of the Congregation.

The official date of the founding of the Congregation of the Sisters of Our Lady of Mercy is November 1, 1862, when Mother Potocka, along with her companions, opened her first House of Mercy on Żytnia Street in Warsaw. Thanks to an endowment from the Archbishop of Warsaw Sigmund Szczęsny Feliński (who has since been canonized), the house was established in the former summer cottage of the director of the National Theater, Adalbert Bogusławski, considered the "Father of Polish theater." The one-story cottage with dormer windows was quite run-down. Actually, one could say it was in ruins. Yet it was to be quite a while before the sisters erected a new convent house there.

Both religious communities were initially autonomous — Mother Thérèse Rondeau's in Laval and Mother Teresa Potocka's in Warsaw. It was not until 1878 that they were joined after the death of Mother Rondeau at the request of the sisters in France, who wanted to receive official recognition of the Congregation from the Holy See. Almost a half-century later, the Congregations separated again, returning complete autonomy to the convents of the Congregation in Poland, as approved by the Holy See in a decree in May 1922. In 1927, the Holy See accepted the Congregation's new Constitution, at first for a seven-year trial period, and then fully in 1935.

At first, the "Houses of Mercy" would only take in adult women who themselves sought assistance in their returning to an honest way of life. But the demand for the sister's services was broader than that. "Common prostitutes would come here, girls who sold flowers in the street, girls suspended from school, and those who had sought adventure. Sometimes parents or relatives would bring their adolescent girls when they could no longer handle them," writes Fr. Bar.

Helen was part of the Congregation during the interwar period, when it was broadening its scope of activity. In addition to accepting "fallen" women into their educational institutions, the sisters also began to take in girls who were minors and in need of moral renewal due to the poor social conditions of the day. There were also ever more girls referred to the sisters by the state educational system and the courts. Ultimately, the sisters began to take in women who were serving prison sentences. "The houses of our Congregation should be open to all fallen or uncared for girls and women, in whatever state of spiritual poverty they find themselves, as long as they promise to work to improve themselves and submit to the regulations of the institution," was one of the statutes of the Constitutions of the Congregation of the Sisters of Our Lady of Mercy.

In 1928, that is, three years after Sr. Faustina joined, the Congregation counted 221 sisters in its ranks, and in the year that the Second World War broke out, 306. According to Fr. Bar's estimates, there were many more wards than sisters. In 1928, 820 wards were living in all the convent houses, and in 1939, 1,032.

The Congregation of the Sisters of Our Lady of Mercy was not the only one that dealt with so-called "fallen" women at that time. Three other congregations that were founded on Polish lands in the 19th century had the same goal: the Congregation of the Sisters of Divine Providence, founded by Antoinette Mirska; the Congregation of the Sisters of the Good Shepherd of Divine Providence, or the "Pasterki," founded by Blessed Maria Karłowska; and the "Pasterzanki" (Good Shepherd Sisters) who wore no religious habit, that is, the Congregation of the Servants of the Mother of the Good Shepherd, founded by Blessed Fr. Honoratus Koźmiński, Margaret Moriconi, and Helen Bułharowska. Thus, these other Congregations — whose aim was also to help such women in need — were founded by likeminded holy and strong women in collaboration with the clergy, with sensitive hearts and a well-developed sense of moral and social responsibility.

Saturday, August 1, 1925, was a summery day. In Warsaw, the mercury on thermometers climbed up to 86 degrees Fahrenheit in the afternoon. The banks of the Vistula became the "most populated district of the capital," as the *Warsaw Courier* reported in its Sunday edition, illustrating the point copiously with photos of the women of Warsaw sporting the latest trends in swimwear. The city was reeling from the news of a train accident not far from Central Station and of the fatal crash of a Breguet XIV airplane, with two pilots at the controls — Flying Officers Karol Fijałkowski and Anthony Heidler.

This was one of the most important days in the life of Helen Kowalska. It was the vigil of the feast of Our Lady of the Angels. That evening, she stepped through the convent gate. After years of seeking her parents' approval to no avail, and after many sacrifices, her desire for the religious life was fulfilled. She entered the Congregation of the Sisters of Our Lady of Mercy. Three weeks later, on August 25, she turned 20. Years later, she wrote, "I felt immensely happy; it seemed to me that I had stepped into the life of Paradise. A single prayer was bursting forth from my heart, one of thanksgiving" (*Diary*, 17).

The convent stands in the same place to this day. The same goes for the chapel, which has functioned as a parish church for the last 30 years. And yet, after being rebuilt and renovated, the buildings, which were destroyed during the Warsaw Uprising, look different than they used to in 1925. The convent used to be in a one-story, red brick building with two wings. The chapel, like others belonging to the Congregation, was modest in size, with a single nave and an entrance from the courtyard. Some years later, in 1938, the sisters added another floor onto the convent building and expanded the chapel. They added a bell-tower and side nave to the chapel and enlarged the sanctuary. After World War II, the Communist authorities did not permit the reconstruction of the destroyed convent and chapel for a very long time, not until the 1970s. During this period, the sisters' property was divided up between the Congregation, the parish, and the Polish Episcopal Conference, which built its central office on the site.

The reconstructed convent — now a three-story building — is larger than it was before the war. Moreover, the chapel has become a parish church and is now under the patronage of the Divine Mercy and St. Faustina. An image of the Merciful Jesus hangs above the main altar, instead of the icon of Our Lady of Częstochowa that used to be there. In the side chapel there is a depiction of St. Faustina. The reconstruction and expansion of the church has been ongoing since 2003; earlier, it was only provisionally adapted for liturgical purposes. Unfortunately, all traces of the destruction wrought during the Warsaw Uprising were removed during the reconstruction, erasing a telling part of the church's history. This place is little known to Varsovians (residents of Warsaw). And this is not just because the church is hardly visible from the street, but for the simple reason that few people know this is where St. Faustina began her path in the religious life and that Jesus appeared to her here as well.

After stepping through the cloister gate of the convent on August 1, 1925, Helen Kowalska became what is known as an aspirant. She was examined "by two older sisters as to whether she was free of obstacles [to entering the convent], if she possessed the attributes of body and soul needed to bear the difficulties of religious life," wrote Fr. Joseph Andrasz, who got to know Helen several years later in Kraków, then as Sr. Faustina. Helen passed her first examination and became a postulant. She received a set of dark clothing, but not a habit yet, and on her head, she wore a small veil. She moved into a large room with many other sisters. At that time, all the sisters slept in such dormitories.

There was just one closet in the room, where the sisters hung up their habits. Narrow, metal-frame beds were separated by screens with white, stiffly-starched curtains gathered in small pleats. Behind each screen, in addition to a bed, there was a nightstand, a small table with a washbasin, and pitchers for warm and cold water. That was all. Sometimes, there was also a desk and chair, but it is doubtful that an aspirant would have had them, too. This space, set off by a screen, was called the sister's cell. A few years later, Sr. Faustina would write her *Diary* while sitting on her bed or at a little table in a cell, just like one of these in various convent houses.

The postulancy, which Helen began in August 1925, was one of several stages she needed to pass in order to become a "fully-fledged" sister. It lasted from three to six months, and could not be extended for more than six months. The next stage was a two-year novitiate, after which came a temporary profession, that is, the profession of vows for one year. Vows were renewed each year for five years, and only after that could a nun make her profession of perpetual vows. Only then did a sister receive the full rights and responsibilities of being a member of the Congregation. Helen-Faustina made her perpetual vows in 1933, that is, eight years after entering the convent. When Helen first joined the Congregation, the road before her would have seemed a long one.

For the time being, she was at the threshold of religious life. The postulancy was a time for both sides to get to know each other: the superiors needed to ensure that a candidate really had a vocation; and the candidate herself needed to confirm — or otherwise indicate — that she wanted to remain in the Congregation. And so Helen began to be acquainted with the spirituality of the Congregation, its customs, its rule of life, and its apostolic orientation, as well as the kind of work that she would be doing.

In the beginning, the superiors sent Helen to help in the kitchen. Sister Sabina Tronina recalls, "Helen would sometimes ask me during the course of the day, 'Sister, I would like to go to the chapel.' I didn't always allow her to go. I explained to her that she was not a professed sister yet and that she didn't need to say some of the prayers. It was enough for her to be in the chapel in the morning and evening."

Helen was disappointed with the amount of time that postulants and sisters were allotted for prayer. The Congregation's Constitutions, which carefully ordered the lives of the sisters, prescribed half an hour of meditation after waking, and then Holy Mass. During the day the sisters had time for spiritual reading (15 minutes), meditation (30 minutes), praying part of the Rosary, and the communal singing of the *Little Office of the Immaculate Conception of the Blessed Virgin Mary* in unison.

One of the hand-written notebooks of the *Diary* of St. Faustina, her rosary, and missal.

They also were expected to perform an examination of conscience twice daily, in the afternoon and evening. In addition, the sisters went to confession once a week, set aside a retreat day for contemplation and prayer once a month, and, twice yearly, made retreats which lasted eight and three days, respectively. The nuns were encouraged to pray individually as well, as long as their devotions didn't get in the way of their daily responsibilities.

And the sisters had much to do, particularly the ones in the second choir, of which Helen was a member. Their work was arduous and took almost the entire day. Helen had a contemplative heart, which was better suited to life in a cloistered order where nuns spend the majority of their time in prayer, cut off from the rest of the world. This is why Helen wondered if the Congregation she had joined was the right one for her. She would prefer, as she wrote, to be in a convent with a more demanding rule of life, where more time would be devoted to prayer than to physical activity. She was in a serious quandary: on the one hand, her Congregation had agreed to accept her and she had worked for a year to earn money for her postulant's wardrobe; but now she was coming to the realization that this was not the place where she had longed to be, after all.

Her inner conflict was heightened by the directress of the postulants, Jane Bartkiewicz, the former vicar general of the Congregation, an energetic, demanding woman who could also be despotic. "She knew how to be tender-hearted, but at the same time her method of disciplining the sisters created an atmosphere of fear," as endnote 9 to the *Diary* describes her. Helen must have also sensed this "atmosphere of fear."

Consequently, three weeks after entering the convent, Helen was determined to "definitely leave." She wanted to inform Mother Moraczewska, then Mother Superior at the convent house, of her decision, but circumstances never seemed conducive to having a conversation. One day in the evening, as Helen noted in her *Diary*, during prayer in the "little chapel" located on the second floor of the convent house, she firmly determined to inform her Superior of her decision the next morning.

"I came to my cell. The sisters were already in bed — the lights were out. I entered the cell full of anguish and discontent; I did not know what to do with myself. I threw myself headlong on the ground and began to pray fervently that I might come to know the will of God. ... After a while a brightness filled my cell, and on the curtain I saw the very sorrowful Face of Jesus. There were open wounds on His Face, and large tears were falling on my bedspread. Not knowing what all this meant, I asked Jesus, 'Jesus, who has hurt You so?' And Jesus said to me, **It is you who will cause Me this pain if you leave the convent. It is to this place that I called you and nowhere else; and I have prepared many graces for you**" (*Diary*, 19).

Helen immediately apologized to Jesus and changed her mind. In confession the next day, she told the priest about what had happened. He responded that "God's will is clear from this," saying that she shouldn't even think of another congregation. "From that moment on, I have always felt happy and content," Faustina wrote years later (*Diary*, 19). Towards the end of her life, a time would come when she would once more consider leaving this congregation, but for a completely different reason — because that is the way she interpreted Jesus' desire for the establishment of a new Congregation that, by prayer, would obtain Divine Mercy for the world.

Jesus' words "**It is to this place I have called you ... and I have prepared many graces for you**" are inscribed today on the walls of the Warsaw convent house of the Congregation of the Sisters of Our Lady of Mercy. Helen-Faustina, who longed for a life behind the grille of a contemplative order, learned, with time, to combine her work with continual prayer and even contemplation. She was able to reach the heights of the mystical life in her active religious community. From the moment she learned that her soul was the place where God was present and where she met with Him in the most profound way, she spent every moment of her life with Him, including while she was at work. She didn't need to go to the chapel and divide her time between prayer and work to be in constant contact with God. It must be emphasized that the Congregation that Jesus chose for Helen has mercy inscribed in its very name and spirituality. The Congregation bore witness to God's mercy daily, surrounding with merciful love the girls and women in their care who desired moral renewal. By choosing a religious of this Congregation to receive and spread His message of Divine Mercy, perhaps Jesus wanted for the sisters to embrace, not just their female wards, but all people and the entire world.

Helen remained in the Congregation, although it certainly was not easy for her. Her spiritual conflicts had an impact on her health. Consequently, her superiors sent her to the sisters' summer house in Skolimów near Warsaw for a while. Aldona Lipszyc visited her in the convent on Żytnia Street in the fall of 1925. "Helen was very happy that I had come ... she clearly wished to speak with me face to face," her former employer recalled years later. "Taking advantage of the momentary absence of the sister who was accompanying her, while walking me back to the gate, she told me that she was struggling, that the rules of convent life required her to keep silent, to walk slowly, and not defend herself when blamed for something unjustly. I remember her telling me about a situation where — in order to grow in the virtue of humility — she had to bear a painful, humiliating experience, although she was not guilty of whatever it was she was accused of. I found all of this depressing; I sensed that they were breaking her simple, joyful nature. I said, 'For God's sake, Helen, you went to serve God and now you can't be yourself or speak the whole truth. Leave it all and come back.' Then we couldn't talk anymore."

Perhaps the "painful situation that humiliated her in front of everyone" that Helen mentioned to Mrs. Lipszyc was the one described in her *Diary*. The cook, Sr. Marcianna Oświęcimska, told Helen to wash the dishes after dinner. When she returned, the work had not been completed. Helen didn't finish because she had to serve some sisters who were late for dinner. Sister Marcianna, dissatisfied with Helen, ordered her to sit on the table as a penance and began completing the assigned task herself. "The sisters came along and were astounded to find me sitting on the table, and each one had her say. One said that I was a loafer and another, 'What an eccentric!' ... Others said, 'What kind of a sister will she make?' ... Truly, God alone knows how many acts of self-denial it took. I thought I'd die of shame" (*Diary*, 151).

Helen-Faustina wrote these words about eight years later from a perspective that allowed her to see how God sometimes permitted such situations to come about for her "internal formation." After this incident, she noted, "He [Jesus] compensated me for this humiliation by a great consolation." Jesus appeared to Helen in the chapel "in great beauty," saying, "**My daughter, do not be afraid of sufferings; I am with you**" (*Diary*, 151). This was the second time that Helen had a vision of Jesus at the Warsaw convent.

"I am burdened, but I sense the great divine grace that lets me bear it all," she told Aldona Lipszyc during their last conversation. This was on January 23, 1926, just before Helen's departure for Kraków to complete her postulancy. Helen visited Aldona on her way back from the dentist, where she went accompanied by another nun, the sister who was responsible for social matters. At the time, the Lipszyc family was staying in Warsaw, on Rakowiecka Street in the apartment of Stanislaus Meller, newly-wedded to Veronica Jastrzębska (they moved to their own apartment in the Żoliborz district in 1928).

Aldona recalls of the visit, "Helen burst into our apartment and began to tell us about her experiences feverishly, hastily, happily, and freely.[21] ... I saw how much she had changed and how much she was struggling; I suggested she come back to us if she felt that this was not her path. ... She told me then that she was going to Kraków for her novitiate, and that if she didn't persevere she would leave and come back to me. She said that she was working in the kitchen, that she had learned a lot, and if she returned, she could make the children all sorts of tasty things."

Maria Nowicka was then little more than 6 years old, but she remembered that visit well.

"The sister accompanying Helen stayed with us in one room, and Mama and Helen locked themselves up in another," she recalls. "I remember that when they came out, both were in tears. Sweet little Helen said good-bye to us, and the two sisters left. And we children asked Mama why dear Helen didn't stay, why she didn't play with us, why she wasn't happy, why both of them had been crying? Mama told us in a few words that Helen was a little sad and that she wept a bit. But later, Mama kept on coming back to that meeting many times, that is why I remember it so clearly. She said that Helen was having a very difficult time in the convent. She told Mama no one understood her, but that she would persevere, because Jesus had told her to. She said that she would bear all of the suffering, and she would be obedient, because that was her greatest desire and goal in life."

As a second-choir religious (coadjutor), Helen was to play an auxiliary role in the Congregation by assisting those in the first choir in the principal mission of the community, which was to help wayward women straighten out their lives. Coadjutors ran the household, doing the cooking, the laundry, and the cleaning. They also tilled the soil, tended the garden, and took care of the animals. Sisters from the first choir, called directors, had the task of caring for and teaching their wards, in addition to managing the administration of the Congregation. But sisters in the second choir also had an influence on the wards' "re-socialization," since the wards helped them with housework and on the farm.

From the very beginning of the Congregation's existence — notes Fr. Joachim Bar — the sisters followed four rules in caring for their wards, as adopted from the house in Laval: isolate the girls from their bad environment, offer them shelter, instill good behavior into them, and protect them from returning to their former way of life.

Wards of the Sisters of Our Lady of Mercy in Łagiewniki.

Consequently, the "penitents" were banned from speaking about their past. This was an iron rule that the sisters rigorously observed. So that the girls would forget about their past experiences more quickly, they were given new names, just as in the religious life, as though the new name was to give each girl a new identity. Modern psychology considers the suppression of past experiences to one's subconscious as the worst method of dealing with problems, but at the time, the effectiveness of this kind of therapy was clearly endorsed. The sisters also made sure that their wards had no unsupervised contact with the outside world, so that any acquaintances from their past way of life would not lure them away from the institution. For this reason, convent chapels were built so as to be accessible from the courtyard and not from the street. They were, in effect, inaccessible to anyone on the outside. This did not change until World War II.

Instilling good behavior in the girls also meant accustoming them to prayer and undertaking various religious practices. All of the wards had to thoroughly learn the catechism. As for protecting them from returning to their old way of life, this was done by teaching them new skills that would allow them to earn a living by honest means. The sisters who directed the girls would therefore teach their wards to read, write, and do arithmetic, and would also teach them basic history, geography, and biology, as well as instructing them in drawing, needlework, and tailoring. With time, the sisters set up schools for the girls, where they taught the full set of courses offered in elementary or vocational schools.

Work was an important part of the wards' moral renewal. Girls and women were taught house and farm work, and they were trained to be systematic in it. The work of the wards in the convent laundries, sewing and needlework workshops (at least at the Warsaw convent), bakeries, gardens, and farms was also a source of income and help in the maintenance of the convent houses.

After studying the Congregation's archives, Fr. Bar estimated that about 75 percent of the wards "experienced a spiritual rebirth and persevered on a straight path." They usually spent three years in the sisters' institutions. Those who did not have any family and who had nowhere to go stayed longer. Sometimes, they remained for their whole lives, like Camilla (also known as Maria Olszewska) from Walendów who is now more than 90 years old and who came to the convent as an orphan. The sisters' iron rule was that their wards could not join the Congregation, even those who were the most capable, educated, and pious.

Helen completed her postulancy under the direction of Mother Bartkiewicz, who accurately assessed that she was "in very close communion with the Lord Jesus," "has her own interior life, which she keeps very much to herself," and has had "contact with the souls of the dead." When recalling the Warsaw period of Helen's postulancy, Mother Borgia Tichy stated that, while she was "superficially unattractive, in her behavior she exhibited a certain subtlety and sensitivity that was greater than that of the others."

Sister Faustina came to Warsaw several more times: in 1928, 1929, at the turn of 1932 to 1933, in 1935, and 1936 — that is to say, at various stages of her religious and spiritual life. She would spend several months, weeks, days, or sometimes just a single day at the convent on Żytnia Street, sometimes merely taking a break on her journey between the different convents of the Congregation where she was sent by her superiors. In sum, Helen-Faustina spent about two years in Warsaw.

It was nearly three years later — on October 31, 1928 — that she returned to the Żytnia Street convent for the first time after leaving in January 1926. She came from Łagiewniki. She had finished her postulancy, her novitiate, and had made her first temporary profession of vows six months earlier. So she was no longer "little Helen" but Sr. Faustina, and wore her habit and veil. She spent four months in Warsaw where she was assigned to work in the kitchen for the sisters' wards. There were more than 200 of them at the convent at that time, which meant that the work was not easy. The girls helped the cooks, which always gave Faustina an opportunity to talk with them about God and to encourage them to persevere in doing good. Mother Michael Moraczewska noted, "The children who worked with her there had great respect for her. ... As she worked, Sister inspired them and encouraged them to make small sacrifices for God."

As compared to 1926, Faustina had already advanced a long way on her path in the mystical life. This life — writes Fr. Stanislaus Urbański, a scholar, professor, and author of many books on mysticism, including one devoted to the spirituality of St. Faustina — consists of "uniting a person with the Triune God through love." In order to reach this kind of union — which is, in essence, "participating in the life of God" — a long road of development in the internal life is necessary, made possible thanks to God's grace.

Led by the Lord, Sr. Faustina — one of the greatest mystics of all time — reached the heights of the loving union of a soul with God. Her spiritual betrothal to God would be followed by the ultimate act of the marriage of hearts, where the soul is wedded to God in the fullest way possible on earth. But this would come about several years later. For the moment, in 1928, Sr. Faustina was still on her path toward the summit of union with God.

She came to Warsaw from the Łagiewniki convent, where she had experienced the dark night of the senses and soul for one and a half years. The dark night is one of the first stages in the mystical life, during which the soul is passively purified, as St. John of the Cross wrote, of everything but purity and love — that is, of everything that is not God — in order to better prepare the soul for a more intimate union with Him. God prepared Sr. Faustina for a more intimate union with Himself, so that she could come to know one of His attributes in particular: mercy, the proclamation of which became the future saint's mission. And although Sr. Faustina would experience a period of darkness again in the following years, at this point, after a time of great spiritual suffering and aridity, her soul finally experienced — as she called it — "a state of loving repose" (*Diary*, 115).

Faustina would experience infused contemplation and acts of union of her soul with God ever more frequently and intensively. Because now — after her soul had been "purified by God Himself" — it could speak to "God without the need of expressing itself through the senses," and He could fill her soul with His light. "The soul is most closely united to God; it is immersed in the Deity;

its knowledge is complete and perfect, not sporadic as before, but total and absolute," she wrote of this time in her *Diary* years later (115).

Faustina usually experienced union with God — or, as she called it, "drowning in God," "immersion in the Divinity," or "being steeped in God" — during the act of infused contemplation, when God gave her a deeper knowledge of herself in a single flash of light, allowing her to understand His essence to some extent. Infused contemplation, which is a gift from God, is defined in different ways in the relevant literature. Faustina called it "profound interior recollection" in which her intellect "learns more in one moment than during long years of thinking and meditation, both as regards the essence of God and as regards revealed truths, and also as regards the knowledge of my own misery" (*Diary*, 882).

This type of knowledge is not rational, although the intellect recognizes it clearly. Rather, it comes through love — it is in no way "earned" or acquired by a person, but received from God as a gift. An "earned" form of contemplation is known as acquired contemplation, that is, a higher form of prayer that follows mental prayer and emotional prayer. Acquired contemplation is within the reach of everyone who leads a deep spiritual life. Faustina experienced infused contemplation or some glimmers of it long before entering the convent. She most likely experienced it for the first time when she was just 7 years old, when she heard the invitation to a more perfect way of life in her soul. Now, after the dark night of the soul and senses, she experienced it often.

Sister Faustina did not know the theory of mysticism. She knew no more than what she herself experienced and what her spiritual directors (Fr. Michael Sopoćko and Fr. Joseph Andrasz) told her later. She had not read the writings of the great mystics, particularly the works of St. John of the Cross — who systematized and described individual stages of the mystical life — or of St. Teresa of Ávila. Consequently, she described the "encounters," as she called them, of her soul with God "at the moments of Your special visitations" (*Diary*, 6) in simple, uneducated language as best she could, often complaining at the same time that words could not describe what her soul experienced. But thanks to her lack of knowledge of the theory of the mystical life, her *Diary* takes on a unique value.

"Her lack of education and literary clumsiness become, in a certain sense, her trump card, because it makes it easier for us to notice the very essence of her mystical experience, described by her with unusual directness and simplicity, without any attempt to systematize or theorize. Faustina's lack of education enhances the specific nature of her mystical experiences and the knowledge acquired through them," notes Ludmilla Grygiel in her book *Zawierzyć Bożemu Miłosierdziu* (*Entrustment to Divine Mercy*).

Faustina at times complained in her *Diary* that it was impossible to describe events of the spiritual realm using the language of the senses. As difficult as it was for her to explain her mystical experiences, it is just as difficult for those who haven't had them, or have just had a small foretaste of them, to completely understand what lies behind the mystics' words. That is why it is easier for those who write about Sr. Faustina to focus on her external and internal visions and revelations, which relate to the realm of the senses, than to put into words what was the most profound essence of her spiritual life — that is, the loving union of her soul with God. Faustina not "only" saw Jesus, but she also was united to Him, united to Divine Love through love. Therefore, she existed in a realm where the bodily senses no longer functioned.

Sister Faustina's spiritual life was accompanied by many mystical phenomena (which are variously named in the literature on the subject): external and interior visions, including hearing words externally and interiorly. She also had many charisms — the gift of reading souls, the gift of prophecy, as well as the gift of "snuggling" her head up to the Hearts of Jesus and Mary (this last being a practice to which all mankind is called; see *Diary*, 104, 138, 960, 1074). She also experienced extraordinary phenomena in her person. For instance, she received invisible stigmata and the gift of bilocation. Faustina wrote of these, "Neither graces, nor revelations, nor raptures, nor gifts granted to a soul make it perfect, but rather the intimate union of the soul with God. These gifts are merely ornaments of the soul, but constitute neither its essence nor its perfection. My sanctity and perfection consist in the close union of my will with the will of God" (*Diary*, 1107).

But let us return to the few months at the turn of 1928 to 1929 that Sr. Faustina spent in Warsaw. In her spiritual life, after her "trials by fire" (the dark night of the spirit and the senses), this was a time of her "loving repose" in God. It was the time when — as she recalled years later — the soul "enjoys intimate union with God. It has many visions, both corporeal and intellectual. It hears many supernatural words and sometimes distinct orders" (*Diary*, 121). Saint John of the Cross claimed that these kinds of experiences in the realm of the senses occur particularly at the beginning of the path of the mystical life. As the holy mystic explains, God "brings man to perfection according to the way of man's own nature, working from what is lowest and most exterior up to what is most interior and highest" (*Ascent of Mount Carmel*, Ch. XVII). God does this gradually, depending on the degree of the soul's preparation.

Faustina knew this from her own experience. At the end of her life, she wrote that she had fewer external visions, that her "senses sleep" (*Diary*, 882), and that her communing with God was purely spiritual in nature. But Jesus appeared to her to the very end — He who was her Master and the One who had entrusted her with the proclamation of the message about Divine Mercy to the world.

During this stay in Warsaw, Sr. Faustina had several important visions that she described in her *Diary*. One of them foretold her being declared a saint. The scene that she saw took place in the "large" convent chapel, that is, in today's parish church. "Once," she describes, "I saw a big crowd of people in our chapel, in front of the chapel and in the street, because there was no room for them inside." When she was walking across the courtyard to the church, the crowd began throwing at her whatever was at hand, "mud, stones, sand, brooms, to such an extent that I at first hesitated to go forward. ... When I entered the chapel, the superiors, the sisters, the students, and even my parents started to hit me with whatever they could, and so whether I wanted to or not, I quickly took my place on the altar. As soon as I was there, the very same people, the students, the sisters, the superiors, and my parents all began to hold their arms out to me asking for graces. ... At the same time my soul was filled with ineffable happiness, and I heard these words: **Do whatever you wish, distribute graces as you will, to whom you will, and when you will**" (*Diary*, 31).

The path to the beatification of Sr. Faustina was a long and difficult one. Most likely, the blows that she experienced in her vision of being made a saint presaged these difficulties. John Paul II proclaimed Faustina blessed in 1993, and a saint in 2000. In this way, her childhood dream of becoming a great saint was fulfilled. She desired to love Jesus with a greater love, such as "no human soul has ever loved You before" (*Diary*, 283).[22]

In another vision, Faustina saw the annihilation of Warsaw. She didn't name the city in her *Diary*, but it is clear from the description that it was the capital city. At the end of her life, Faustina would foretell the eruption of a new, horrible war, but she didn't speak of it at this time. Instead, she wrote down Jesus' words: "that He would cause a chastisement to fall upon the most beautiful city in our country. This chastisement would be that with which God punished Sodom and

Gomorrah." Consequently, Faustina prayed for Warsaw and for Poland, as Jesus instructed her to: **"My child, unite yourself closely to Me during the Sacrifice and offer My Blood and My Wounds to My Father in expiation for the sins of that city"** (*Diary*, 39). In these words, which refer to Christ's sacrifice as an atonement for people's sins, we can hear the foreshadowing of the Divine Mercy Chaplet, which Jesus would dictate to Faustina several years later.

But at this point, in the chapel on Żytnia Street during the sacrifice of the Mass, Faustina offered "the blood and wounds" of Christ in atonement for the sins of the residents of Warsaw. She did this for seven consecutive days. On the seventh day of her prayers for her country, she had the following vision: "I saw Jesus in a bright cloud and began to beg Him to look upon the city and upon our whole country." She ardently pleaded for His blessing. "Immediately Jesus said, **For your sake I bless the entire country.** And He made a big sign of the cross over our country" (*Diary*, 39). That was in the fall of 1928. Neither then nor later, when she was bewailing the fate of Warsaw, would Faustina concretely name the sins committed in her motherland. But Fr. Sopoćko, her spiritual director whom she would meet in Vilnius, recalled that when he asked her once to tell him what kinds of sins God would punish people for, she said, "particularly the sin of killing unborn children, because that is the most grievous sin of all."

At this time, Faustina also had a vision that foretold her mission. That is, one day she was summoned interiorly to Divine Judgment. "Suddenly I saw the complete condition of my soul as God sees it. I could clearly see all that is displeasing to God. I did not know that even the smallest transgressions will have to be accounted for." Jesus said that she was "**guilty of one day of fire in purgatory.**" She immediately wanted to "throw [her]self ... into the flames of purgatory," but Jesus stopped her and asked, **"Which do you prefer, suffer now for one day in purgatory or for a short while on earth?"** Faustina was ready to suffer everything, but Jesus said, **"One** [of the two] **is enough; you will go back to earth, and there you will suffer much, but not for long; you will accomplish My will and My desires, and a faithful servant of Mine will help you to do this."** He then added, **"Know that you will have much, much to suffer, but don't let this frighten you; I am with you"** (*Diary*, 36). Faustina would hear the words **"I am with you"** from Jesus many times in the future during moments of suffering.

Faustina's suffering lasted from then until her death, that is, for 10 more years, until 1938. From a human point of view, this was a long time. From God's eternal perspective, it was certainly a "short time." Faustina noted that shortly after she had this vision, she fell ill. She didn't have tuberculosis yet, but she was experiencing general weakness and exhaustion.

Yet her suffering was not just of a physical nature. She also had to bear psychological torment from the sisters who did not believe in her physical ailments. They thought that since the doctor had not verified the illness, she was making it up in order to avoid her responsibilities in the kitchen. Who knows if that wasn't more painful? "Often my best intentions were misinterpreted by the sisters," she wrote (*Diary*, 38). But she also understood that these were the "instruments" that God was allowing in order to teach her humility and purify her soul from attachments to people. After all, Jesus had foretold that she would find neither "relief nor help nor comfort" anywhere else but in Him.

For a long time, Faustina could not understand one thing: Jesus told her to tell her superiors everything about her conversations with Him and about her inspirations, and yet her superiors did not believe what she said. Instead, she wrote, they "treated me with pity as though I were being deluded or were imagining things" (*Diary*, 38). Similarly, her confessor determined that, while all of her experiences could have their source in God, they could also be an illusion, or the work of an evil spirit. God was testing Faustina, training her in obedience. All the while, she met with much unpleasantness from the sisters. Sister Samuela Wasilewska remembered, "Once, after various tribulations she told me that she was leaving the kitchen for a moment, and she went to the chapel. Unbeknownst to her, I followed her to the chapel. She was kneeling with her hands clasped in prayer and sobbing loudly."

Another situation is also very telling. Sister Samuela, then a postulant in the kitchen alongside Faustina, was witness to the following: "One of the sisters came back from town and her boots had gotten very muddy. She was angry with Sr. Faustina about something. Agitated, she might not have even noticed that she had taken off the boots. Sister Faustina bent over, picked up the boots, and gave me one to wash while she washed the other in the sink. I asked her later why she did that for such a bothersome sister. She replied, 'It is for the love of the Lord Jesus.'"

Faustina aimed to fulfill all of Jesus' instructions. One of these was obedience to her superiors. And as they were suspicious of her visions, and even denied them, she was sometimes torn between obedience to Jesus and those He instructed her to obey. As a result, she tried to "avoid God interiorly." But when she avoided communing with God internally, she wrote, she experienced His presence even more.

It was the custom in the Congregation for the sisters to renew their vows of poverty, chastity, and obedience after completing a three- or eight-day retreat. It was just during this moment of renewing her vows, during Holy Mass in the Warsaw convent chapel in 1929, that Faustina had a vision: "Jesus appeared suddenly at my side clad in a white garment with a golden girdle around His waist, and He said to me, **I give you eternal love that your purity may be untarnished and as a sign that you will never be subject to temptations against purity**. Jesus took off his golden cincture and tied it around my waist." Sister Faustina, who was recording this several years later, declared, "Since then I have never experienced any attacks against this virtue, either in my heart or in my mind. I later understood that this was one of the greatest graces which the Most Holy Virgin Mary had obtained for me, as for many years I had been asking this grace of her" (*Diary*, 40).

It was probably during this stay in Warsaw that Faustina was showing Sr. Samuela Wasilewska, who was from the Suwałki region, several of the churches in the city during their free time. Faustina got to know them while she was living with the Lipszyc family on Smolna Street and looking for a convent, and possibly also during her postulancy. Sister Samuela remembers, "Among other places we went to an Orthodox church because she wanted to show me that as well. She knelt down and prayed. She later said that God is everywhere and that one should praise Him in every place. She also mentioned something about the unification of the Churches — that it was to take place in the future."

It is not known which of the three Warsaw Orthodox churches the sisters visited. A fourth — the great St. Alexander Nevski Cathedral on Saski Square, a symbol of the Russian occupation of Polish lands for 200 years — had been torn down two years earlier, in 1926. The nuns might have visited the Orthodox church of St. John Climacus in the Wola district, built to serve as a cemetery church at the turn of the 19th century. The small Holy Trinity Orthodox Church in the Podwale district was closer to the convent, right on the Old City Square. Or they might have crossed the Vistula River to the Praga district by tram. The magnificent Metropolitan Orthodox Church of St. Mary Magdalene is located there, the principal sanctuary for the Orthodox Christians of Warsaw, of whom there were about five thousand before the war. Faustina must have seen this Orthodox church when she travelled by train to Ostrówek from the neighboring Vilnius Station.

What is significant is what Faustina told Sr. Samuela inside the Orthodox church: "God is everywhere." This was many decades prior to the Second Vatican Council, when ecumenism was just being born. While she was living in Aleksandrów, Łódź, and Ostrówek before she entered the convent, Sr. Faustina came to know and respect people of various religions, confessions, and cultures. But her words about the unification of the Churches were perhaps something more than just the wish of her heart.

On February 21, 1929, Sr. Faustina left Warsaw for Vilnius. Just four months later — on June 11 — she found herself in the capital yet again. She came for a short while, because she was leaving for the convent in Kiekrz, near Poznań, on July 7. Instead of staying at the Żytnia Street convent, she spent that month in Warsaw at its affiliated house at 44 Hetmańska Street in the Grochów district. In 1929, this was in the distant outskirts of the capital. It was not difficult to get there, however: Hetmańska Street runs into one of the major arteries in the Praga district — Grochowska Street. Tram No. 24 travelled eastward along that street for the first time in November 1925. Grochów was incorporated into the capital city just several years earlier, in 1916. Hetmańska Street was a green part of Warsaw — with large gardens, arable fields, and fresh air.

That was why the sisters on Żytnia Street bought a five-acre-plus parcel of land there in 1926. One year later, in 1927, they erected a wooden house and a greenhouse and started a garden on their property. This green retreat became a place of relaxation in the summertime for the sisters and the wards of the Congregation. They called it — in honor of St. Joseph, one of the patron saints of the Congregation — "Józefinek." The nuns' plot of land was adjacent to the family home of the writer Jan Dobraczyński.[23] This still holds true today.

Sister Faustina went to "Józefinek" for the first time on Christmas 1928. She came by for a short while to visit the sisters there. She was no stranger to the house when she returned there half a year later, in June 1929. The wooden barracks that housed Faustina's cell stood there until 1975, when it was taken down. In 1929, only a few sisters lived on Hetmańska Street, and, consequently, the work in the kitchen certainly wasn't overly exhausting for Faustina. The large garden where she might also have worked was a good spot for recreation. Mother

Moraczewska recalled that Sr. Faustina had made such a good impression on the residents of the house that when she was leaving, the wards "packed up their belongings and declared that they would follow her."

Faustina came to Warsaw once more in 1929, in October. This time she stayed at the house on Żytnia Street. It is not known how long she stayed there — perhaps until May 1930, when she left for the convent in Płock.

At the time when Sr. Faustina belonged to it, the Congregation had 11 religious houses: in Warsaw, Kraków, Vilnius, Walendów near Warsaw, Płock, Częstochowa, Radom, Kalisz, Kiekrz, Lviv, and Supraśl. These convents also had affiliated houses: the Warsaw convent had a sister house in suburban Grochów; the Kraków convent's sister house was in Rabka-Zdrój; the Płock convent's, in Biała; and the Walendów convent's, in Derdy. Helen spent some time in most of these convent houses, as she was often transferred from one to another. Over the 13 years that she was in the Congregation, she spent time in 10 convents and affiliated houses. She spent more than one year in only four of them.

Sister Louise Gadzina once asked Mother Joseph Brzoza, then Mother Superior of the Warsaw convent, why Sr. Faustina was transferred so frequently. The response she received was that there were two kinds of transfers: some sisters were moved due to their personality, and others because of the needs of the Congregation. In the second instance, the transfers didn't always take place without complications, but Faustina never caused any problems.

This does not mean that moving was not difficult for Faustina. But she considered the will of the superiors to be sacred, and the final word. And precisely because she allowed herself to be moved wherever she was needed, without contesting it or complaining, some sisters called her a "pushover." "Generally that isn't a desirable label," wrote Fr. Joseph Andrasz. "She was not called that because she didn't do her job well, but because her conscientiousness and scrupulousness in performing her responsibilities set her apart." Father Andrasz rightly notes that more sisters got to know her thanks to the fact that Faustina lived in nearly all of the Congregation's houses. However, the frequent changes also had negative consequences for Faustina, not only because she had to adapt to a new house community and a new set of circumstances, which often meant learning to do a new job (each convent, she wrote, was like a little novitiate), but also because the frequent changes also meant a change of confessors. Consequently, Faustina had to reveal her spiritual life to yet another priest, which was neither easy for her nor for the priest, who often lacked the time to get to know her well.

From a letter that Sr. Faustina wrote to a kindred soul, Sr. Justine Gołofit, in October 1929, it is clear that she was very happy at the Warsaw convent during this period. She emphasized that this didn't mean that she wasn't suffering, but that she was happy all the same that she could serve Jesus. "The more I experience suffering, the greater my desire to suffer, and when we know that the suffering is sent to us by the One whom I love, then it is no longer suffering but rather delight and happiness," she wrote. She informed Justine that she was cooking for the sisters. "My dear little Sister knows well what it is like in the kitchen, always quick and one can never keep up." She used to prepare the meals together with a much older and more experienced nun, Sr. Hyacinth Mesjasz, and two postulants. She also had other duties. This letter was written at night when she was on watch duty, guarding the house against thieves.

Faustina came to the convent on Żytnia Street for another longer stay at the turn of 1932 to 1933. At that time, she was undergoing her third probation alongside four other sisters — that is, preparing to make her perpetual vows. The probation lasted for five months — from November 1932 to April 1933.

Mother Michael Moraczewska commented, "The period of preparation for perpetual vows was quite difficult ... for Sr. Faustina." There were several reasons for that. Faustina was feeling physically weak. She was so weak that Sr. Suzanne Tokarska, whom Faustina was supposed to help in the vestiary where the sisters' clothing was repaired, complained that she "couldn't use her for any of the more difficult work, because she had to lie down and couldn't do anything more, because she was ill." Sister Faustina already had tuberculosis, but it was still undiagnosed. After examining her in the house clinic, the Congregation's doctor, Jane Kozińska-Sobierajska, stated, "I cannot find anything in Sister's lungs." Sister Adalberta Banach recalled, "I noticed an expression of surprise on Sr. Faustina's face, as she was very pale and sickly, but she calmly replied, 'But it hurts all the same,' and left resignedly."

Many years later, Mother Michael Moraczewska admitted that Faustina's medical diagnosis was not accurate. But the sisters, including Suzanne Tokarska, reiterated that the analysis of Sr. Faustina's saliva had been negative. There can only be one explanation for this: her illness was still in a latent stage.

The second reason for Sr. Faustina's suffering at the time was spiritual. It had to do with Jesus' apparition to her two years earlier in 1931 in Płock, where He had expressed His wish that His image be painted with the signature "Jesus, I trust in You," and that a Feast of Divine Mercy be established. This information spread amongst the sisters in Płock, causing her great suffering, and it made its way to the Warsaw convent from there.

"Sister, you can get it out of your head that the Lord Jesus might be communing in such an intimate way with someone who is so miserable and imperfect! The Lord Jesus only communes with holy souls — remember that!" One of the older mothers sent these "fiery bolts" at Faustina, informing her that the Lord Jesus could not possibly appear to cooks from the second choir. The name of that mother is not given in the *Diary*. But it was no secret in the convent that this was Jane Bartkiewicz. "I acknowledged that she was right, because I am indeed a wretched person, but still I trust in God's mercy," wrote Sr. Faustina (*Diary*, 133). This was not the only time that she was humiliated by Mother Jane, who had also been Helen-Faustina's postulancy directress. At that time, she had approved of Helen, stating that she "must be a soul pleasing to the Lord Jesus." Mother Michael Moraczewska commented, "Sister Faustina was extremely sensitive and felt these admonitions very keenly."

They touched her soul so strongly that she recalled them three times in her *Diary*. That was also probably because Mother Bartkiewicz — the unnamed individual in Faustina's *Diary* — was strongly opposed to Faustina being admitted to the probation and to her attending the retreat in preparation for it. But there were other sisters at the Warsaw convent who understood the nature of the young nun's experiences well. Faustina had the support of the Directress of Probation, Mother Margaret Gimbutt, the same nun who spoke to Helen Kowalska in 1924 when she came to the convent door asking to be allowed to join the Congregation. "This holy mother," as Faustina called her, told her, "If you continue cooperating with God's grace in this way, Sister, you will be only one step away from close union with God. You understand what I mean by this. This means that your characteristic trait should be faithfulness to the grace of the Lord. God does not lead all souls along such a path" (*Diary*, 204).

Faustina tried to remain at peace throughout the entire probation period. She was in close communion with Jesus. It happened that, during a moment of infused contemplation, she understood what Jesus expected of her. "The Lord gave me to understand that I should offer myself to Him so that He could do with me as He pleased. I was to remain standing before Him as a victim offering," she noted. She was to become, in His likeness, a sacrifice to God for the sins of sinners. The following day, during another moment of infused contemplation, when "the presence of God penetrated" Faustina, her intellect was suddenly illuminated, and she came to know what this sacrifice would consist of. "A vision passed before the eyes of my soul; it was like the vision Jesus had in the Garden of Olives. First, the physical sufferings and all the circumstances that would increase them; [then] the full scope of the spiritual sufferings and those that no one would know about. Everything entered into the vision: false suspicions, loss of good name. I've summarized it here, but this knowledge was already so clear that what I went through later on was in no way different from what I had known at that moment. My name is to be: 'sacrifice.' When the vision ended, a cold sweat bathed my forehead," she confessed (*Diary*, 135).

When Sr. Faustina consented to make the sacrifice "with all my heart and all my will," stating, "Do with me as You please. I subject myself to Your will" (*Diary*, 136), then she experienced infused contemplation yet again. And at once, she experienced such a union of her soul with God that she couldn't express it in the language of the senses. "I felt that His Majesty was enveloping me. I was extraordinarily fused with God. I saw that God was well pleased with me and, reciprocally, my spirit drowned itself in Him. Aware of this union with God, I felt I was especially loved and, in turn, I loved with all my soul. A great mystery took place during that adoration, a mystery between the Lord and myself. It seemed to me that I would die of love [at the sight of] His glance. I spoke much with the Lord, without uttering a single word. And the Lord said to me, **You are the delight of My Heart**." Faustina admitted, "At that moment I felt transconsecrated [a sacrifice devoted to God through and through]. My earthly body was the same, but my soul was different; God was now living in it with the totality of His delight. This is not a feeling, but a conscious reality that nothing can obscure." She added, "A great mystery has been accomplished between God and me" (*Diary*, 137-138).

Sister Faustina sensed that she was consecrated to God. "I want to be transformed into Jesus in order to be able to give myself completely to souls. ... I absorb God into myself in order to give Him to souls" (*Diary*, 193). In her book on Sr. Faustina, Maria Tarnawska notes that the turning point in her mystical life was the moment when she agreed to become a sacrifice, and God received her consent to join with Him in sacrifice for sinners. From this moment, God would lead her "ever deeper into the essence of this relationship" and develop "in her the ability to devote herself without reservation." Sister Faustina would offer all of her physical and moral suffering in sacrifice for the sins of others. She would learn to bear without complaint the humiliation of unfair criticism from the sisters, as well as bring assistance to her neighbors, even to her own detriment. "We know that while Sr. Faustina's community did not notice any traces of egoism in her, overcoming herself was not always an easy task for her," writes Tarnawska. "Numerous entries in her *Diary* speak to this. She was helpful, kind, and obliging, but how many times did she complain bitterly to the Lord Jesus for ingratitude and thoughtless or selfish abuse of her person, and finally about her own lack of strength?" This certainly wasn't surprising. As a very sensitive person, she experienced all injustices deeply. Externally, she was composed, but interiorly she had to purify herself in order to begin to love difficult or unfriendly people with a pure love.

In the opinion of the scholar Fr. Stanislaus Urbański, Sr. Faustina began a period of so-called spiritual betrothal in her mystical life at the beginning of 1933. "While previous mystical graces were only transient, during the period of the spiritual betrothal, the mystical union with God becomes more lasting, although it is not yet permanent." God communes intensively with the soul by "acts of love and light" and the soul, in spite of the passivity of human faculties, experiences an interior peace flowing from the sense of God's presence and the certainty of reaching a yet higher stage of union with God. This is what Faustina experienced in 1937, in an act of spiritual marriage — that is, a divinizing union of her soul with God, which would be permanent from then on. Nonetheless, in 1933, during the period of Sr. Faustina's spiritual betrothal, "she comes into ever closer contact with God, having an ever stronger certainty of the presence of God in her interior life," claims Fr. Urbański.

During this time, Faustina still had some moments when, discouraged by those around her who doubted her mystical experiences, she wanted to stop trying to fulfill Jesus' instructions, as she judged they were beyond her capability. This was also true during her probation period, when she planned to completely drop the idea of painting an image of Jesus. But, as she noticed, her plans came to naught.

One day, she went to adore the Blessed Sacrament at the neighboring convent of the Franciscan Sisters of the Family of Mary. While praying, she saw

Jesus, who said, "**Know that if you neglect the matter of the painting of the image and the whole work of mercy, you will have to answer for a multitude of souls on the day of judgment.**" Faustina continued, "After these words of Our Lord, a certain fear filled my soul, and alarm took hold of me. Try as I would, I could not calm myself. These words kept resounding in my ears: So, I will not only have to answer for myself on the day of judgment, but also for the souls of others." Shaken to the core, she went to the chapel after returning to her own convent and said to the Lord, "I will do everything in my power, but I beg You to be always with me and to give me strength to do Your Holy will" (*Diary*, 154). She continued to pray fervently for a spiritual director who would understand and guide her.

During her stay at the Warsaw convent, Jesus dictated a prayer to Faustina that she was to offer up for sinners: "**O Blood and Water, which gushed forth from the Heart of Jesus as a fount of Mercy for us, I trust in You**" (*Diary*, 187). He also declared that when she recited this prayer "**with a contrite heart and with faith on behalf of some sinner,**" He would give the sinner the grace of conversion (*Diary*, 186).

As a "sacrifice" and as an individual graced with the gift of reading human hearts and sensing which temptations various individuals experience, Sr. Faustina prayed for others and also took on the burden of their suffering. For example, she felt the temptation to commit suicide that tormented one of the wards. For seven days, she suffered her torments and prayed fervently for her. The richness of her interior life was taking a toll on Faustina's ability to fulfill her daily duties in the convent.

Mother Michael Moraczewska commented, "Sister, absorbed with her interior life, assisted the vestiary sister whom she was assigned to help with a lesser degree of zeal than usual."

The vestiary was the name given to the convent's storeroom for clothing along with the sewing room. Once it was laundered, clothing found its way here, and was then mended and re-distributed to the sisters.

Sister Suzanne Tokarska noted, "By then her head was full and her thoughts overflowed with the Lord Jesus' revelations and instructions. She was not concerned at all about work, however much there was of it. She needed a lot of time to get everything done. Often, when someone asked her to help out or to substitute for someone else, she wouldn't refuse, so that when she came late to the vestry, I used to get angry at her because there was so much work, and she had come so late — she calmly listened to everything, even with a smile. It irritated me that she didn't seem to care. And a moment later, as if nothing had happened, she said, 'Please, Sister, I'm going to go to say some prayers now.' At that point, I was at my wit's end. I complained to the superiors, but my complaints came to nothing, because the mothers knew of her interior experiences, and so they did not side with me. ... I was in such turmoil that I stopped saying anything, but just waited for the probation to finish as soon as possible so that I would be free of her."

The work also brought Faustina many tribulations or, as she wrote, gave her many occasions to practice virtues. "Sometimes I had to take linen to some sisters three times and still one could not satisfy them. But I also came to recognize the great virtues of some sisters who always asked for the poorest things from the vestiary. I admired their spirit of humility and mortification," she recalled (*Diary*, 179).

The nun whose room Faustina cleaned gave her plenty of opportunity to practice humility. It was either Mother Superior (Raphael Buczyńska) or an older, sickly sister of the first choir. She kept complaining that the room was poorly cleaned, with "'a speck of dust here and a spot on the floor there.' At each of her remarks, I did each place over a dozen times," said Faustina. This didn't help; the nun complained about her to the Directress, Mother Margaret Gimbutt, saying, "Who is this careless sister who doesn't know how to work quickly?"

"The next day, I went again to do the same job, without trying to explain myself," said Faustina. "When she started driving me, I thought, 'Jesus, one can be a silent martyr — it is not the work that wears you out, but this kind of martyrdom'" (*Diary*, 181). She also made the general remark, "I learned that certain people have a special gift for vexing others. They try you as best they can. The poor soul that falls into their hands can do nothing right; her best efforts are maliciously criticized" (*Diary*, 182).

During her probation, Sr. Faustina had one more responsibility that she deemed an honor. She accompanied the priest who visited sick sisters with the Blessed Sacrament. She carried the candle. "As a knight of Jesus I always tried to gird myself with an iron belt, for it would not be proper to accompany the King in everyday dress," she noted (*Diary*, 183). The iron belt that the sisters wore under their clothing was made from a fine, prickly mesh. Any movement caused pain. Wearing the belt, like wearing an iron bracelet on an arm or leg, was a form of penance. Faustina offered this mortification for the sick.

In March 1933, Faustina's younger sister Wanda — then 13 years of age — visited her at the Warsaw convent. From the *Diary*, we can infer that Wanda spent two weeks in the convent house on Żytnia Street. "When she told me of her plans, I was horror-stricken. How is such a thing possible? Such a beautiful little soul before the Lord, and yet, great darkness had come over her, and she did not know how to help herself. She had a dark view of everything," noted Faustina. She "worked with her" for two weeks, praying for her sister. "For no other soul did I bring so many sacrifices and sufferings and prayers before the throne of God as I did for her soul." She felt that she had been heard, that she "forced God" to grant Wanda graces. "When I reflect on all this, I see that it was truly a miracle," she wrote (*Diary*, 202).

The change was so great that after several years Wanda decided to enter the convent. Sister Faustina wanted Wanda to choose her congregation, but, in the end, Wanda probably joined the Ursuline sisters just before the outbreak of the Second World War. She was not there for long. She was deported by the Germans to the Third Reich during the occupation, and at the end of the war, she married an Englishman and settled down in the West.

Sister Faustina visited the convent on Żytnia Street twice more. She spent one night there in February 1935, when she stopped off in Warsaw on her return journey to Vilnius from her native village, Głogowiec. She wanted to meet with Mother General. She arrived in the evening, and in the morning left for Grochów, on Hetmańska Street, where Mother Moraczewska was staying at the time. The convent had changed since Faustina's previous visit. At the turn of 1933 to 1934, the sisters put up a three-story brick building there, in which they opened "Our Lady's Care Institute." It was intended for girls between 12 and 18 years of age.

Faustina took part in the devotion to the Sacred Heart of Jesus in the chapel on Grochów Street. During adoration of the Blessed Sacrament, she had a vision of Jesus, who "came out from the Host and rested in my hands. This lasted for a moment; immense joy flooded my soul," she recorded (*Diary*, 406). Faustina then had a long talk with Mother General Michael, whom she described as being "full of goodness, peace, and the Spirit of God" (*Diary*, 405). She didn't reveal the details of the conversation in her *Diary*, however.

The chapel where Sr. Faustina prayed back then no longer exists. The convent house where the chapel had been located was rebuilt after the war. A brick pavilion stands in the place of the wooden barracks where Faustina lived in 1929. And in place of the large vegetable garden that the sisters and their wards tended before the war, there is currently a park for the enjoyment of the ladies at the nursing home that is run by the Congregation. After the war, in 1950, the sisters' care institution was taken over by the nationalized Caritas Catholic Union, and Caritas changed the mission of the center five years later. In place of the girls' institution, a center for chronically ill women was established. Though the ownership of the home changed, the sisters continued to work there. They regained ownership of the property in the 1990s. It was then that they set about building a new nursing home. Today, about 100 female senior citizens needing continual professional care live in St. Joseph's Nursing Home for Women. The portrait of St. Faustina, as painted by Helen Tchórzewska for the saint's canonization, hangs in the chapel of the nursing home. There is also another valuable painting in the convent — an image of the Merciful Jesus, painted by Ludomir Sleńdziński in 1954. At that time, the painting was accepted by the Polish Episcopal Conference as intended for public veneration, but it never came to be so well-known or so venerated as the work of Adolf Hyła of Łagiewniki.

Sister Faustina came to Warsaw one more time in 1936, in March, when she was recalled from the convent in Vilnius. She saw an angel accompany her for the entire journey to the capital — and not for the first time (see *Diary,* 471, 490, 630, 706) — and then the angel disappeared when she arrived at her destination at the convent gate at Żytnia Street. She stayed there for four days. She left for the convent in Walendów on March 25, the feast of the Annunciation of the Blessed Virgin Mary. That same morning, before her departure from the Warsaw convent, she had a vision of the Mother of God during meditation. Mary reminded Faustina that her task was to tell the world of the great merciful love of God. She was to prepare the world for the Second Coming of Jesus Christ, who would "come not as a merciful Savior, but as a just Judge." The Mother of God urged Faustina, "*Speak to souls about this great mercy while it is still the time for* [granting] *mercy. If you keep silent now, you will be answering for a great number of souls on that terrible day. Fear nothing. Be faithful to the end. I sympathize with you*" (*Diary*, 635).

Several weeks later, in May, Sr. Faustina left Walendów and its affiliated house in Derdy, and set off for Łagiewniki, once again by way of Warsaw. It is not known whether she visited the house on Żytnia Street once more or whether she went immediately to the train station. She never returned to Warsaw again.

Chapter Five

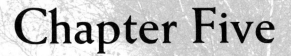

Ostrówek

1924-1925

'She Was No Stranger
to Us at Home'

THE FORMER HOME OF THE LIPSZYC FAMILY IN OSTRÓWEK, near Warsaw, still looks the same as in photographs from the 1920s: two stories high, built of larch wood, with four large porches and balconies. Only the color has changed. It used to be reddish-brown, and nobody remembers when the planks were painted white. Apart from this detail, the house still looks just as it did when Helen Kowalska lived and worked there — from July 1924 to August 1925 — in the last year before entering the convent.

Providence must have watched over this place. The house was not destroyed during the war, and after it ended, the owners took care to preserve the original layout of the rooms.

"Nothing has changed here," says Sr. Dominique Steć from the Congregation of Sisters of the Merciful Jesus while giving a tour of the house. "The floors, stoves, doors, and windows are all the same. The furniture was not preserved, but all you can see here now are period pieces."

Nowadays, this is the House of St. Faustina. In 2009, the building was purchased by the Catholic Diocese of Warszawa-Praga. Through the diocese's efforts, the interior has been restored, and the house now serves as a center of prayer for religious and priestly vocations.

"We called it the House of St. Faustina because Helen Kowalska was treated like a member of the family while working there," says Sr. Dominique, whose Congregation takes care of the house, the first of the many communities established in response to the wishes of Jesus, as revealed to Sr. Faustina. Adorning the walls of the ground-floor porch are pictures of Aldona and Samuel Joseph Lipszyc, as well as those of their seven children: the twins Maria and Thaddeus,

Sophia, Leopold, Nina, Visna, and Hedwig. Right next to them is a picture from 2009: six of the siblings are seated in front of the House of St. Faustina, without the late Leopold. When the picture was taken, the oldest — the twins Maria and Thaddeus — were 90 years old.

Helen Kowalska came to Ostrówek in the summer of 1924. The house, dubbed "the children's mansion" by friends of the Lipszyc family due to the fast-growing brood of offspring, stood almost completely apart. At the time, Ostrówek consisted of summer homes belonging to Tsarist officials, scattered about in the woods. The first cottages were built there after the opening of the St. Petersburg-Warsaw Railway line in 1862. One of its most important stops was located in the nearby town of Tłuszcz, almost four miles away. The same was true in 1924, though the train schedule for that year includes a stop — by request only — in the district seat Klembów (then called Kłębów), about one-and-a-quarter miles from Ostrówek. Because of the small sand dunes that had formed there, the Lipszyc family referred to the spot as "Górki," the Hills, though the name was not to be found on any map. They used a similar moniker for the place where their house was located in Ostrówek. Since that time, the village has grown in size and population. Many of today's Ostrowians commute to work in the nation's capital, compensating for a commute of more than 18 and a half miles with spruce trees in their yards and air clean enough to make a city dweller's head spin.

The inimitable atmosphere of the former Lipszyc home is not only due to the microclimate created by the neighboring forest reserve of Dębina, a remnant of unspoiled Mazovian forest with centuries-old oak trees. It is also, and perhaps above all, the feel of the place that God had chosen for Helen. Here, in Ostrówek, removed from the hustle and bustle of the city and surrounded by kind people, she prepared for entering the convent.

"I was touched by the goodness of God that entrusted Helen, Sr. Faustina, for this period of time in her life before the convent, to Aldona — who was pure, good, upright, fair, and had the law of God in her heart, even though she was not practicing," wrote Aldona's friend Sr. Catherine Steinberg of the Congregation of Franciscan Sisters of the Servants of the Cross in Laski after the war. When she met Helen in 1924, Sr. Catherine was not yet a nun. The then-Sophia Steinberg, or "Czarna Zośka [Black Sophie]" as her friends knew her, was 26 at the time and finishing her medical studies at the University of Warsaw. It was in her home in 1917 that Aldona met Samuel Joseph Lipszyc

("Mutek" to his family and friends), a handsome agricultural engineer who had spent several years in America.

The young newlyweds moved into the ground floor of the house in Ostrówek. It included a kitchen, three rooms, and two porches that also served as rooms in the summer. A well still stands in front of that house — forgotten and overgrown with moss. Until a few years ago, there also was a latrine, jokingly referred to by Samuel's sisters as a "Little Swiss House," which they adorned with a plaque bearing neat rhyming couplets: "Superphosphates brewed on site, much to growing plants' delight. Fertilizer's made right here, to ensure a bumper year."

The upper floor of the house belonged to Samuel's father Meyer Lipszyc, who, along with his wife, Chaya Sura, and his daughters, would come here from the capital for shorter or longer holidays. Meyer was a wealthy man. He began as an errand-boy and worked his way up until he became director and shareholder of the Meisel, Steinberg & Rittenberg Silk Ribbons factory, located at Mokotowska Street in Warsaw. He owned a vast apartment in the center of Warsaw, on Koszykowa Street, and also a villa in the district of Mokotów on Pilicka Street.

"The ground floor of our Hills home was rather simply arranged," recounts Maria Nowicka, the eldest of the Lipszyc daughters. "Most of the furniture was made of pine by the local carpenter, Mr. Wierzbicki: the wardrobe, table, chest, benches, and stools. We had iron-frame beds with straw mattresses. The straw would be replaced periodically. Our grandparents had better furniture: rugs, upholstered chairs, and wall hangings. They helped us financially, but our needs were ever-greater as children continued to be born."

It was not easy to make ends meet, even with the father's fairly high civil servant's salary. His children nicknamed Samuel "Salaam Alaykum" due to his custom of greeting others with the Muslim phrase for "Peace be with you."

Helen, called "Hela" by the Lipszyc family, worked and lived on the ground floor.

"She was a maid, and she worked hard in very primitive conditions without running water and electricity," remembers Maria Nowicka. "She worked together with my mother. The two of them ran the household. Although Helen was her maid, Mom never exploited her or any of our other housekeepers," Maria emphasizes.

Helen would get up early in the morning. She would light a fire in the kitchen stove and, in the winter months, in the tiled stoves in the rooms. She would bring water from the well. She did the laundry in a tub using a washboard, a rarity in the village; she ironed clothes with a charcoal flatiron; she scrubbed the wooden floors. Aldona Lipszyc wrote that "she was a hardworking girl. She performed any job willingly, without needing to be reminded, [working] independently."

Helen Kowalska and Aldona Lipszyc had hardly anything in common, sharing neither background nor education, neither social nor family status, nor piety. Perhaps age was the smallest of the differences between them. Helen was only nine years younger than Aldona. Yet, despite so many differences, the ties of understanding and goodwill that developed between them were something more than the usual relationship between an employer and a subordinate.

"Mom treated our Helen like an older daughter. She grew to love her very much," says Maria Nowicka, who repeatedly spoke with her mother about their former servant.

Aldona Lipszyc wrote about Helen in her memoirs: "She was no stranger to us at home: we all liked and respected her." Aldona Lipszyc was, as identified by Sr. Catherine Steinberg, a genius of motherhood. "The difficult material conditions, the increasing number of children, and her work around the house and in the garden did not diminish her willingness to come to the aid of others; she would find the time and energy to help," Sr. Catherine recalled. Thus, Aldona, though herself worn out after yet another childbirth, breastfed the child of an ill friend, or took on as a maid a single girl in the third trimester of pregnancy, only to help her in caring for her own infant later on.

"My mother was a fanatic of motherhood. She never had enough of children," says her daughter Maria.

This was also the kind of motherly love with which Aldona embraced the 19-year-old Helen at a difficult moment in her life — when Helen, having fled her family home, was growing in her decision to enter the convent. Besides, both Aldona and Helen liked children.

So Aldona Lipszyc could write of Helen's love of children, "She was cheerful, fond of children, and she played with them. I remember how she organized playing 'dress up' with them, and, putting on a costume herself, played along just like a child would. I remember her healthy, joyful laughter."

Maria Nowicka remembers Helen with her two golden braids pinned up around her head like a crown. She also recalls her warm relationship with the children.

"I don't think it's just that *we* loved *her*, but she loved us, too," Maria says. "She was a cheerful, very balanced, and nice girl."

Helen aided Aldona with the care of the four older children; she fed and dressed them. When she had time, she played with them, taking them on walks to the Dębina forest, telling them fairy tales, and taking them sledding in the winter. "We were always full of ideas, plans, and tasks. We regretted having to go to bed in the evening and having to put off until tomorrow excursions in the woods, hikes to the Struga River and, in winter, skating and sledding. We always had important tasks awaiting us: building forts, gathering and drying grass for bedding ... making furniture; picking blueberries, wild strawberries, bog bilberries, and mushrooms; cooking on our own small metal stove; carving out reed pipes and walking sticks; playing with clay; making 'Indian' headdresses or 'African' grass skirts. Oh, and making bonfires, which meant roasting potatoes and baking apples, and, above all, singing." Thus, Mary Nowicka remembers her childhood in her memoirs *Biało-zielono, biało-zielono* (*White and Green, White and Green*).

Not only the children, but also Aldona and Helen liked to sing. While they sang various songs together — from folk songs to patriotic songs, to tunes popular among the Polish gentry — Helen alone would sing religious songs. She began her days with the hymn "When the Morning Dawn Rises" (*Kiedy ranne wstają zorze*) and would sing in honor of Our Lady throughout the day. Aldona Lipszyc, who had a good singing voice and an ear for music, remembered that Helen sang a lot. Frequently, Helen sang a song that Aldona eventually learned from her, with the words: "Jesus hidden in the Eucharist; I am to adore, give up everything for Him, and live in His love." When Aldona learned about the life of Helen-Faustina years later, she realized that "this song summed up the entire content of her life."

Aldona did not remember Helen displaying her devotion other than through singing religious hymns while working. Helen did not impose her piety on the Lipszyc family; she respected their views. They were not religious. The head of the house, Samuel Joseph, was baptized but from a Jewish background. Aldona (née Jastrzębska), though she had been raised in a Catholic family in Tbilisi (at the time under Russian rule, now the capital city of Georgia), "while still in the Caucasus, due to some difficulties or disenchantment, [she] stopped receiving the Sacraments, and due to her extraordinary reliability and honesty, even in high school she was freed from the obligation of confession," as Sr. Catherine recalls.

"Mom did not practice, fast, or pray. She did not go to church, but I am sure she believed in God," claims Maria Nowicka. "She manifested Christianity with all of her life."

Helen must have seen this, too, since she later described Aldona as "pious" in her *Diary*, although she was not pious in the strict sense of the term. This was probably an expression of her affection and appreciation for Aldona's upright character. And this was despite the fact that she had also experienced spiritual suffering because of her. "The lady," she wrote of her, "pious as she was, did not understand the happiness of religious life and, in her kindheartedness began to make other plans for my future life. And yet, I sensed that I had a heart so big that nothing would be capable of filling it" (*Diary*, 15).

"My mother believed that having children, a family, is the greatest happiness and vocation for a woman. Therefore, she thought that it would be better for our Helen and for the world if she established a good, loving family and brought up children well," explains Maria Nowicka.

In this time, which was difficult for her, Helen experienced the presence of God quite strongly. This probably took place in the church in Klembów, which she attended most frequently with Frances Rybak, whose husband managed some of the Lipszyc fields, or with Apolonia Kurek, a resident of the neighboring village of Lipka. The church, built in the neoclassical style using funds donated by General Francis Żymirski, a hero of the Polish November Uprising against the Russians, still looks just as it did a hundred years ago. On the main altar is a remarkable 17th century painting of the Madonna and Child. The Virgin Mary, black-haired, with rather masculine facial features and an ear turned to the viewer, seems to be listening to what the people whisper to her.

Did Helen also speak to the "listening" Mary of the desires of her heart? It is likely that before this altar Helen made a private vow of chastity. This took place during the octave of Corpus Christi, between June 18 and 25, 1925.

"God filled my soul with the interior light of a deeper knowledge of Him as Supreme Goodness and Supreme Beauty. I came to know how very much God loves me. Eternal is His love for me," Sr. Faustina noted years afterwards. Some time later, she explained from a somewhat different perspective that this was the first time that she was granted the grace of being immersed in God for a moment, a "short little while." She recalled, "In simple words, which flowed from the heart, I made to God a vow of perpetual chastity. From that moment I felt a greater intimacy with God, my Spouse. From that moment I set up a little cell in my heart where I always kept company with Jesus" (*Diary*, 16). This brief moment of being "immersed in God," when God granted her the inner light of "deeper knowledge" — that is, an understanding of the things of God — was a flash of infused contemplation. It was her first step in the mystical life. Faustina would never call this state or similar experiences by this name, not being aware of these terms. She would, however, get to know their content well in the future.

Helen had made a firm decision to enter a convent. Nothing and no one could have talked her out of it anymore. Neither Aldona Lipszyc nor Helen's sister Jeannie — who came to Ostrówek to see Helen six months after she had left Łódź — could dissuade the aspirant. Helen had written to her family about her whereabouts and her plans. Helen's parents charged Jeannie with the task of dissuading Helen from entering the convent and bringing her home. In a conversation with Sr. Bernardine Wilczek in 1948, Jeannie recalled that she "honestly strove to convince Helen," but got nowhere. Instead, she spent just one night in Ostrówek and returned to Głogowiec in the morning.

Helen worked and saved money for her postulant's wardrobe. She would put away her entire wages. She never bought anything for herself. When she had appeared at Aldona's with a small bundle in hand, she was given a dress for work and underclothes. For her, this sufficed.

Aldona Lipszyc knew from the outset that Helen's stay was only temporary. Her departure, however, caused Aldona "great distress." When she went to visit Helen in the convent, she mistakenly ended up at the gate of the adjacent convent of the Franciscan Sisters of the Family of Mary, a congregation that only had one choir and did not accept servants.

Aldona Lipszyc recalled, "The sister with whom I spoke was outraged that the candidate they had accepted had misled them by not admitting that she had been a maid. ... Initially, I tried to explain that Helen was not a professional housekeeper, but a village girl who had worked for a short while in order to earn her postulant's wardrobe, but when I heard the accusation that she had deceived them, I was indignant and denied this charge vehemently: 'Our Helen could not lie. I have probably come to the wrong place, and she is not here.'" This incident and Aldona's response show the integrity of and intimacy between Helen and Aldona.

After entering the convent, Helen would confide the hardships and sufferings that she was experiencing as a postulant to Aldona. When, after the war, Sr. Catherine Steinberg learned about the events of Helen's life, it struck her that while Helen was preparing to join the convent in Ostrówek, she herself was experiencing a conversion. A year after Helen's departure, in 1926, Sr. Catherine was baptized. Although she could not recall any specific conversations she had

had with Helen, she remembered that at the Lipszycs' she had only heard "the very best" about her. Helen also impressed her greatly as someone who was "calm, serious, good-tempered." "She had something in her that aroused respect, something that could be called eminence."

Sister Bronislava Bojanowska, a neighbor of the Lipszyc family in Ostrówek and later a sister of the Congregation of the Ursulines of the Agonizing Heart of Jesus, remembered what Helen was like during this time: "I don't ever remember her being angry or upset. She was always balanced, peaceful. Sometimes she even struck me as somewhat phlegmatic due to her very mild reactions. It never occurred to me that her calmness and self-control were simply the fruit of her paying attention to what was concealed inside her."

Helen stayed in Ostrówek for a year. On August 1, 1925, she traveled to Warsaw to join the Congregation of the Sisters of Our Lady of Mercy in Żytnia street. Sister Catherine Steinberg is convinced that Helen-Faustina obtained for the whole Lipszyc family "great graces, and that she continues to watch over them." She recalled that Aldona, too, was convinced that she had experienced many instances of Divine Providence at work. Samuel Joseph Lipszyc died a week after St. Faustina's death, in October 1938, a year before the outbreak of the war. Thus, he avoided the Holocaust. Aldona and the children survived despite the fact that their Jewish surname alone was akin to a death sentence. Maria Nowicka, a liaison officer in the Home Army, the Polish underground resistance in World War II, evaded death at the hands of the Nazis several times, much to her own wonder.

Not only did the Lipszyc family survive, they also managed, at different times, to provide shelter for 13 Jews — in Ostrówek and in their home in Bielany in Warsaw. In 1996, Yad Vashem recognized Aldona Lipszyc by granting her the title of Righteous Among the Nations.

Maria Nowicka, who sometimes asks herself how she has managed to stay alive for so many years, explains, "I think I've lived this long so I can talk about our Helen."

Chapter Six

Skolimów

1925

'I Was in a Misty Place
Full of Fire'

TOWARD THE END OF AUGUST IN 1925, the town of Skolimów near Warsaw was slowly becoming deserted. Vacationers were packing their trunks, shuttering their summer residences, and bidding summer good-bye. They were returning to the capital. Those who could, however, stayed longer. This was also the case in the villa rented for the summer by the sisters from the Warsaw convent of the Congregation of the Sisters of Our Lady of Mercy. Though their living conditions were not ideal, their rental house was filled to the brim. Skolimów's clean air, pine forests, and access to the Jeziorka Brook enabled the sisters, as well as the girls in their care, to rest and grow in strength. As Mother Superior Michael Moraczewska remembers, in the autumn "only one of the sisters remained in the house, a convalescent, along with a companion," for whom the postulant Helen Kowalska served as a cook. Unfortunately, we do not know the exact date of Helen's arrival or departure. According to Mother Moraczewska, she was sent to Skolimów "soon" after entering the convent. In her *Diary*, Sr. Faustina mentions that this took place after certain dilemmas having to do with her choice of congregation, when, "shortly after this," she suffered some health problems and Mother Superior sent her "not far from Warsaw," to Skolimów, "for a rest" (*Diary*, 20).

Helen joined the Congregation on August 1, 1925. Three weeks later, she decided to announce to her superior that she was leaving. Jesus stopped her from taking this step. But Helen, most likely exhausted emotionally, began to feel worse physically. This happened no earlier than August 20. The phrase "shortly afterwards," used by Mother Moraczewska to specify when she sent Helen to Skolimów does not, therefore, refer to a time before the end of August. However, the wording "for a rest" used by Sr. Faustina may apply to both the time and nature of the trip.

Helen certainly traveled to Skolimów in the company of another sister. They traveled by carriage, a common means of transportation at the time, or by narrow-gauge railway train, which stopped in the neighboring town of Konstancin at the station next to the spa park. They could also have taken a coach bus operated by "Skowar," a bus line established in the 1920s by entrepreneur Herman Paulinek who had ties to Skolimów. At the wheel in six of the eleven James and Chevrolet buses sat Paulinek's sons, always punctual and reliable.

Unfortunately, we do not know the location of the summer residence rented by the sisters, or who it belonged to, or what it looked like. We do not even know whether it still exists. No mention of it is made in the annals of the parish in Skolimów, nor at the Congregation's general house, whose archives were destroyed during the Warsaw Uprising in 1944. Nowadays, Skolimów is a part of the Warsaw suburb Konstancin-Jeziorna, a small health resort town, known not only for its mineral-rich waters and graduation towers,[24] but also for the many mansions owned by wealthy businessmen and artists, which are clustered here. It has not changed much in the last hundred years.

In 1925, Skolimów was a designated resort village, which had been attracting people in search of peace, quiet, and fresh air since the late 19th century. On large forest plots allotted by the magistrate Wenceslaus Prekera, rich citizens of Warsaw would build homes, summer cottages, or establish inns visited by the trend-setters from Warsaw in the summer. The homes of the rich and of the bourgeoisie were designed by the best architects. Regrettably, many of the houses that were built of wood are no longer standing. In 1914, Skolimów counted 145 villas and inns, each built on large parcels of land 10,000 cubits — a little less than 65,000 square feet — in size.

Homes built in the typical Skolimów architectural style had several porches and were decorated with "lace-like" details in the Zakopane style. This, for example, is what the Mucha [The Fly] mansion — owned by Ladislaus Buchner, owner of a popular pre-war satirical magazine of the same name — was like. The Odpoczynek [The Rest] Inn, built in the beautiful Art Nouveau style, as well as the eclectic Zagłobin château belonging to Hugo Seydel, honorary consul of Serbia and owner of the natural health institute Hugonówka, have survived to this day.

In modern-day Skolimów, which is often associated with the nursing home for retired actors founded there in 1927, old villas stand side by side with new ones. The former, restored or awaiting better times, usually delight the onlooker with their architectural style. The latter often merely reflect the dubious taste of their owners.

There is a place in Skolimów that Helen Kowalska undoubtedly visited. Probably daily. It is the Church of Our Lady of the Angels. A new parish was established here in 1923, just two years before Helen visited. The church building was erected in 1906, based on the bold design by Bronislaus Brochwicz-Rogóyski and Ladislaus Kossowski, with an interesting façade and two soaring towers decorated with numerous pinnacles. The church was funded by the wealthy of Skolimów, not only Catholics, but also Protestants and Jews. After Helen's departure, the church was expanded — the main nave was lengthened, and two side-naves were added. But on the wooden altar hangs the same image of the Virgin Mary surrounded by angels, soaring much like the church's steeples and towers. The future saint — who as Helen Kowalska used to pray in this church — is commemorated by her portrait and the image of the Merciful Jesus, both enshrined in the sanctuary.

Helen mentioned Skolimów only once in her *Diary*, when she described the vision of purgatory that she experienced while she was staying in this resort town. It must have been very powerful, since she wrote about it in these terms many years later: "In a moment I was in a misty place full of fire in which there was a great crowd of suffering souls. They were praying fervently, but to no avail, for themselves; only we can come to their aid." She explained that her guardian angel had led her on this journey to purgatory, as recorded in her *Diary*. "I asked these souls what their greatest suffering was. They answered me in one voice that their greatest torment was longing for God."

Thus, Jesus showed Helen the suffering souls in purgatory for whom she should pray. He also told her: "**My mercy does not want this, but justice demands it**" (*Diary*, 20). From that point onwards, Helen was united more closely with the suffering souls. And thus Jesus was preparing her for her core mission — to proclaim the message of Divine Mercy.

Chapter Seven

Kraków-Łagiewniki I

1926-1928, 1933, 1935

'I Truly Would Not Be Able to Live without You, Even for a Moment, Jesus'

"THE GARDEN USED TO STRETCH FROM HERE TO THE CONVENT," explains Sr. Elizabeth Siepak — the author of a number of books about the saint — motioning broadly with her hand from the enormous Basilica of the Divine Mercy that was erected here in 2002 to the 19th-century convent complex. Before World War II, this area was covered with vegetable beds and rows of fruit trees. There were cabbages, carrots, and cucumbers, among other vegetables.

Sister Faustina Kowalska, a second choir sister, tended this very garden and now her portrait adorns the interior of the new basilica and the old chapel in the convent. Back in Sr. Faustina's time, there were greenhouses nearby where the sisters grew crops of vegetables, and there were also stables for the horses and barns for cows and pigs. This, along with a farm of a few dozen acres, was the basis of the food supply for the convent and the educational institution run by the Congregation of the Sisters of Our Lady of Mercy.

This was also the place where Sr. Faustina Kowalska — or rather, Helen Kowalska, who had joined the Congregation six months earlier in Warsaw — first arrived in Łagiewniki near Kraków on January 23, 1926. She would spend almost three years here in the "Josephinum," as the sisters dubbed the convent in Łagiewniki. She would also return here more than once — for the last time in May 1936, when she would remain until her death. In total, she would live in Kraków for more than five years, making it her longest period of residence in a convent during her 13 years of religious life.

In January 1926, Helen Kowalska came to Łagiewniki from Warsaw. She was supposed to finish her postulancy here, and then go through her novitiate.

She did not come alone. A professed nun came with her, and perhaps there were other postulants. The convent in Łagiewniki is a little over three miles from the Main Railway Station in Kraków. The sisters either changed trains for one heading to Zakopane or for Oświęcim (the town later known as Auschwitz) and got off a few minutes later at the Borek Fałęcki station (now called Łagiewniki), or they took a coach. Riding down St. Gertrude Street, Helen Kowalska would have been able to see the walls of the Royal Castle, whose cathedral has housed the tombs of Polish kings for centuries. Kraków — then a city with a population of about 200,000 inhabitants and the former capital of Poland — is endowed with a rich historical, academic, literary, artistic, and also political heritage. At the time, it was slowly giving way in importance to Warsaw, the current capital. Nevertheless, in the period between the two World Wars, it was still a prominent cultural center, with its Julius Słowacki Theater and its literary cafés that were meeting places for writers, actors, and painters. It was also an academic hub — home to the oldest Polish university, the Jagiellonian, and the well-known Polish Academy of Arts and Sciences. One fifth of the pre-war population of Kraków could be described as belonging to the intelligentsia class. As for industry and manufacturing, few Polish cities could match Kraków in status, especially given its food and clothing industries, construction companies, steelworks, and foundry.

Łagiewniki, currently situated where the southbound road from Kraków to the Zakopane resort in the Tatra mountains leaves the city, did not become a part of Kraków until 1941. In 1926, it was still a village with a population of just over one thousand. However, as a result of the discovery of shale and gypsum, the late 19th and early 20th centuries witnessed its dynamic development as an industrial town. It was then that the construction of brickworks, flour mills, paper mills, and bakeries began in these parts, as well as in nearby Borek Fałęcki where the Solvay soda factory was built — where Karol Wojtyła, the future Pope John Paul II, worked during World War II. The convent and an educational institution run by the Congregation of the Sisters of Our Lady of Mercy were built here at the end of the 19th century. The red brick neo-Gothic-style convent, designed by architect Karol Zaremba, is well-known by those with a special devotion to the Divine Mercy.

The chapel, the convent, and a large three-story house for the girls of the institution have not changed. From the outside, they look much as they did when Helen Kowalska saw them for the first time on January 23, 1926. However, the old outbuilding by the entrance gate has been replaced by a new structure that now houses the Faustinum Association, the Misericordia Publishing House, and some pilgrims' quarters. The inscription "Josephinum," which formerly spanned the gate, has disappeared. The sisters had named the estate in honor of St. Joseph, believing that they found this place through his intercession. The same statue of Our Lady of Mercy still stands in the main altar of the chapel. However, the side altar on the left, which once bore an image of the Sacred Heart, now displays the image of the Merciful Jesus, famous for the many miracles ascribed to it.

The same altar also houses the small casket with the remains of St. Faustina, and her portrait as painted by Valdemar Szajkowski. One thing that has completely changed is the landscape surrounding the convent. Towering above the old buildings is the Basilica of the Divine Mercy, designed by Witold Cęckiewicz, and consecrated by Pope John Paul II in 2002.

The establishment of the convent in Łagiewniki took place thanks to the generosity of Prince Alexander Ignatius Lubomirski, who made a fortune on shares of the Suez Company. The Congregation of the Sisters of Our Lady of Mercy had already established a religious house in Kraków in 1868. It was the second convent for the Congregation, with Warsaw being the first. Initially, the sisters lived in the rectory of the Church of the Divine Mercy on Smoleńsk Street in Kraków. Then, in 1871, they moved to a house at the intersection of Straszewskiego and Zwierzyniecka Streets.

They were forced to leave this property, however, and that was when Prince Lubomirski offered his assistance. Though he had lived in France for years, he had never forgotten Kraków. Among other things, he founded a home for street boys on Rakowicka Street, which is currently home to the Main Building of the University of Economics, and he also allocated one million francs for the new convent of the Sisters of Our Lady of Mercy. In 1889, the sisters purchased a few plots of land for the construction of the new religious house: 28 acres from Samuel and Bernard Wohlfeld and a few acres from local farmers — a total of about 37 acres. Some of the buildings were already completed two years later, including the chapel under the patronage of St. Joseph, which was dedicated by Cardinal Albin Dunajewski. The convent itself, the last to be completed, was finally finished in 1893.

In 1904, *Architekt* magazine described the convent complex thus: "The facility is located on the slope of the hills which surround Kraków, with a beautiful view of the city and the surrounding area. In the center stands the chapel, flanked on the left by the convent, and on the right by the house for the sisters' pupils.[25] The left wing on the second floor is made up of dormitories for the sisters and novices, as well as an infirmary with a kitchen and an isolation room; on the ground floor are the chaplain's apartment and a parlor for the sisters and the pupils, along with a refectory, kitchen, and recreation room. On the second floor of the right wing are the dormitories of the pupils, an infirmary, a pharmacy, a kitchen, and an isolation room, while the ground floor contains classrooms, work rooms, music rooms and, finally, spacious refectories; the laundry rooms are located in the basement."

The entire estate was surrounded by a fence, making it inaccessible to outsiders. The reason for this was the same for this and all other facilities run by the Congregation. The goal was to prevent the girls from having contact with people from their old way of life during the process of reforming their lives. The sisters only opened the chapel to local residents after World War II. The young Karol Wojtyła used to come here to pray on the way to his job at the Solvay factory. The wall that now separates the chapel and convent from the educational facility is newer — it was put up after the war, in 1962, when the Communist regime seized the institution from the sisters, along with part of their property. The sisters reclaimed their property in 1989. Since then, the sisters have run an organization in the building that provides spiritual and educational care to wayward girls and women in need of deep moral conversion. Thus, in addition to their work in the Shrine of the Divine Mercy, which is visited annually by approximately two million pilgrims, the sisters are still engaged in work similar to that which lay at the foundation of the Congregation.

From the time the convent in Kraków was established in the second half of the 19th century, the Sisters of Our Lady of Mercy never lacked candidates for the educational institution. Women and girls, either willingly or persuaded by their families, would come to the sisters, seeking an opportunity to turn their lives around. Most frequently, there were more candidates than available spots. In the period between the World Wars, the institution in Łagiewniki usually housed about 160 pupils. They learned bookbinding, embroidery, knitting, and also gardening and agriculture. The revenues derived from the sale of products and services (including laundry), along with minimal fees paid by the girls, were the main sources of the funds necessary to run the institution.

Many sisters were needed to keep such a large facility going. Before the war, Łagiewniki was home to between 30 to 40 sisters, and at times even more than that. According to the Vatican's 1926 statistical yearbook, when Helen Kowalska came to Łagiewniki, there were 53 sisters in residence — they were referred to as "members of the congregation," which includes professed nuns and most likely also novices. The Congregation of the Sisters of Our Lady of Mercy was the sixth largest among the 20 communities of women religious in Kraków at that time. The greatest number of convents belonged to the Daughters of Charity of St. Vincent de Paul, the Ursulines, the Felician Sisters, and the Albertine Sisters. According to the same document, in 1934 the number of sisters in Łagiewniki increased to 68 and, in 1939, to 75. In the interwar period, Kraków was an important religious center, not only because of the presence of many religious congregations for both men and women, and hundreds of historic churches and chapels, but also because of the radiance of holiness emanating from the saints that called Kraków home at the turn of the 20th century. Some of these include the following: St. Adam Chmielowski, St. Ursula Ledóchowska, St. Joseph Sebastian Pelczar, and the Blesseds Bernardine Maria Jabłońska, Angela Salawa, and Angela Truszkowska.

On January 23, 1926, the very day that Sr. Faustina arrived in Łagiewniki, a Sr. Henry Łosińska died. She was 29 years old. She worked as a shoemaker in the convent. Several days later, she visited Helen in the night with a request. Helen was to ask the Superior, Mother Margaret Gimbutt, to have Fr. Stanislaus Rospond — later Bishop Rospond — celebrate Holy Mass in her intention and to pray ardently for her soul. Because Helen was unsure whether this was a dream or not, she did not act on this request immediately. Only after two more visits from Sr. Henry did Sr. Faustina talk to the Superior. "Mother responded that she would take care of the matter," Sr. Faustina wrote, years later. "At once peace reigned in my soul, and on the third day this sister came to me and said, 'May God repay you'" (*Diary*, 21).

We know little else about what was happening in Sr. Faustina's life and heart as she was finishing her postulancy, her initial time of formation before her novitiate. It was probably a good time for her, since Sr. Joachim Głuc remembered that Faustina was incredibly cheerful and, at times, it seemed that "she could not control the joy and happiness resulting from her vocation.

"She was always smiling, beaming so much, that sometimes she even gave the impression of being absent-minded. The Novice Directress held her up as an example to us, saying that we should be as happy and fulfilled in service to God as Sr. Faustina was. Even when she was very weary and tired, her spirit was never low. She radiated joy," recalled Sr. Joachim.

The period of postulancy, that is, the first test, ended with the clothing ceremony. Helen, along with four other postulants, made an eight-day retreat beforehand. At last Friday, April 30, 1926, arrived. The archivist of the Kraków convent made the following entry: "Today we renewed our vows taken under the guidance of Fr. Kotowicz. Then, five postulants received their veils, five novices made their vows, and five sisters made their perpetual vows." Though the description was brief, the day itself was full of activity. Clothing day and the taking of vows took place twice a year in the Łagiewniki convent. Many guests came to attend the ceremony, and this time, on April 30, 1926, was no different. Mother General Leonard Cielecka came from Warsaw several days beforehand, and the main celebrant, Auxiliary Bishop Paul Kubicki, a friend of the Congregation, arrived from Sandomierz. The families of the sisters who were taking temporary or perpetual vows would also come, in addition to the families of those who, like Helen, were taking the habit.

The chapel in Łagiewniki, decorated with white flowers, was filled to overflowing. Father Joseph Andrasz wrote this about the ceremony: "Postulants approach the altar dressed like brides, in white robes, with tulle veils covering their long hair and wearing myrtle wreaths." Father Andrasz only became the permanent confessor of the sisters in Łagiewniki in 1933; however, from 1926 on, he came once a month to give a conference at the convent. Therefore, he probably witnessed that clothing day in 1926 in person. During the High Mass, the postulants asked Bishop Kubicki to accept them into the congregation. The bishop blessed each sister's habit, saying, "Put on the new self, which in the likeness of God has been created in the righteousness and holiness of the truth." The postulants left the chapel for a while in order to put on their habits. Helen was assisted in this by Sr. Clemens Buczek: "I said to her, 'Helen, let's hurry to put on your habit.' But dear Helen fainted. I dashed off to get the smelling salts to bring her round. … Later I would tease her about not having wanted to leave the world. I only found out after her death that the reason she fainted was not out of sadness at leaving the world, but because of something else."

This is how Helen-Faustina described this moment, years later: "The day I took the [religious] habit, God let me understand how much I was to suffer. I clearly saw to what I was committing myself. I experienced a moment of that suffering. But then God filled my soul again with great consolations" (*Diary*, 22).

When the sisters returned to the chapel wearing their habits, the bishop blessed their white veils. Placing the veil on the head of each novice, he spoke these words: "Receive this veil as a token of chastity, so that with a holy heart you may complete the race of your novitiate and Christ, the Bridegroom of virgins, may find you worthy of His purest image." Then came the time for the sisters to receive their new names. "From now on, you shall not be called by your worldly name, but you shall be called Maria Faustina," the celebrant told Helen Kowalska. The name Maria, in honor of the Mother of God, was given to each sister in the Congregation, but according to the Congregation's tradition, the sisters could choose an additional name. Sister Faustina chose the addition "of the Most Blessed Sacrament" to her name, and in time, she signed her *Diary* in that way: "Sister Maria Faustina of the Most Blessed Sacrament." However, she signed letters with a simple "Sr. Faustina."

No two sisters in the Congregation could bear the same name, which was why rare names, such as Faustina, had to be sought out. Faustina is a female form of the name Faustinus, which is derived from the Latin word *faustus* — blissful, blessed — and the verb *faveo, favi, fautum* — to favor, to be benevolent. The name Faustina. was given, for example, to women during the Roman Antonine dynasty as well as by early Christians to children, both male and female (for example, St. Faustinus). Today, the name is enjoying a revival. Saint Faustina is becoming the patroness of a growing number of girls baptized with her name.

The giving of a new name marked the end of the ceremony. Sister Faustina was now a novice. She was starting a new stage of her formation as a religious.

After the ceremony came the time for receiving congratulations and good wishes from guests and for meeting with family. Nobody from Faustina's family had come. Was it because, as one of her sisters explained years later, the invitation had reached them too late, or — which seems more likely — because Faustina's parents still could not come to terms with her decision, which she had made against their will? Several months earlier, when she had written to her parents asking them to send her a copy of her baptismal certificate copied from their parish baptismal register, her father had decided not to reply. Helen took care of things on her own, though. She wrote to the pastor, Fr. Wenceslaus Linowiecki, and was sent the necessary paperwork.

From the day of the clothing ceremony onwards, Faustina wore the habit and veil. For now, the veil was white. As a second choir sister, a coadjutor, her habit would differ in some respects from one worn by first choir sisters, that is, the directors in the Congregation.

"First choir sisters had longer veils, and the sleeves of their habits were wider. After their perpetual vows, they wore gold rings," recalls Sr. Amata

Strojewska from Walendów, who as a young nun belonged to the group of directors. "Coadjutors' veils were shorter and for practical reasons, their sleeves narrowed at the wrist, so as to be out of the way when working. They wore silver rings."

The division of members of religious communities into two choirs was abolished only after World War II, in the period both before and during the Second Vatican Council. In the case of Sr. Faustina's Congregation, this took place in 1962. This period also saw reforms concerning religious dress or habits. At this time, the sisters ceased wearing a belt from which they would suspend a long rosary. They had adopted this custom from the Jesuits who, from the time of the Congregation's inception, had had a significant influence on its spirituality. It was the Jesuit Fathers who had written the Constitutions for the sisters in Laval, France, and when the Congregation began its work in Poland, it, too, lived in accordance with the same Constitutions. Over time, Jesuits would become the Congregation's chaplains — and a close relationship between these two orders still exists.

Sister Faustina's novitiate in the Congregation of the Sisters of Our Lady of Mercy lasted for two years. The novices were given this time — provided by the 1927 Constitutions of the Congregation — to be initiated into "the understanding of the Constitutions, into pious meditations and frequent prayer, into understanding that which pertains to vows and virtues, and into the appropriate practice regarding the uprooting of the seeds of evil, the conquering of bad inclinations and the acquiring of virtues."

The Novice Directress at the beginning of Faustina's novitiate was Sr. Margaret Gimbutt. After seven weeks — in June 1926 — she was replaced by Sr. Mary Joseph Brzoza, a 37-year-old from Zakopane, who had just returned from observing the formation of the novices at the convent in Laval, France. She was "cheerful and full of love of neighbor" (*Diary*, 216), as Sr. Faustina described her, grateful as she was that Mother Brzoza was the first Superior who accurately recognized what was happening in her soul. Mother Brzoza gave Sr. Faustina support and understanding in times of difficulty. Sister Faustina's testimony about Mother Brzoza is important because certain methods used by the Novice Directress can only be understood while bearing in mind the importance of humility as a virtue for religious.

Sister Louise Gadzina recalls a time when the "Novice Directress, in order to encourage us to practice virtue, assigned each of us a flower to imitate. To Sr. Faustina. she said, 'You, sister, are a bouquet of flowers which has wilted in a vase and should be thrown into the garbage heap.' These words hurt me, because I saw her as the most beautiful flower in our Congregation. But she accepted this peacefully and without complaint."

It was a custom in the novitiate that a more experienced sister would become a guide, an "Angel," to a younger or less experienced religious referred to as a "soul." Faustina's Angel was Sr. Crescentia Bogdanik, who describes the experience thus: "My task was to introduce her to the religious life, and I admired the pace at which she was making progress. I never needed to tell her anything twice — as was usually the case with other novices. ... She carried out all her duties carefully, attentive that everything would be finished on time. There was always a kind of childlike joy on her face. Constancy in carrying out her duties was the virtue that was particularly apparent in her. I have sometimes thought about how best to describe Sr. Faustina, and the phrase 'joyful child of God' came to mind."

Life in the novitiate was divided into periods of prayer (common and individual), listening to lectures, and working. The novices' day started early, with prayer in the chapel. The Mass was preceded by Eucharistic Adoration and meditation. After breakfast, there were classes that took place in the spacious novices' hall on the second floor of the convent. The Congregation's historian, Fr. Joachim R. Bar, wrote, "Every day the novices read a book on asceticism for half an hour, and additionally *The Imitation of Christ* and the biography of a saint twice a day for 15 minutes. Moreover, the Novice Directress gave 30-minute lectures (three times a week on the Constitutions, once weekly on principal spiritual exercises for religious, and once weekly on the catechism)."

Novices were also trained in whatever tasks they would later be assigned for the needs of the convent and its educational institution. The rule was to spare the novice sisters from more strenuous and time-consuming work in the first year, as it was taken for granted that their spiritual development in the religious life took precedence. In the second year, they were ready to undertake the tasks that would be theirs later, provided that these didn't interfere with the "appropriate spiritual exercises for novices."

The superiors in charge of the novitiate assigned Sr. Faustina to work in the "children's kitchen." This was the name given to the kitchen where meals for the pupils were prepared, as opposed to the so-called "sisters' kitchen" where meals for the nuns were made. The former was located in the institution's building; the latter, in the convent. Faustina already began helping the sisters who did the cooking in the first year of her novitiate. Cooking for approximately 160 girls was a challenging task. Years later, Sr. Placida Putyra, who was also a novice at the time, remembered this period. She recalled that Faustina took great care that everything be clean. She would make sure that the dishes tasted good, and she would tell the sisters that they "should always do the cooking as if the Lord Jesus were coming to dinner." Sister Placida added that "she never complained that things were hard for her or that she didn't know how to do something. She always did everything she was told, and if she couldn't, then she said, 'The Lord Jesus will help, because it is He who wants me to do it.'"

Faustina would turn to Jesus in all matters, including ones like kitchen work. She spoke with Him as she would with her Lord and also her best friend. She trusted Him absolutely. Sister Placida remembered that one summer day the two of them were in the kitchen alone. The head cook was ill. Right then, half a cow's carcass was delivered to the kitchen. "I was worried: what would happen with the weather so hot, and so much meat? Sister Faustina answered, 'Don't worry, Sister, I will go to the chapel and ask the Lord Jesus what to do. He will surely give me good advice.' She left, and when she was back, she said that the more tender parts should be marinated, and the rest should be cooked so it does not spoil. Later, the head cook was surprised at how wisely this young woman had handled the situation."

At this time, Faustina's health was already poor, so when the Novice Directress sent her to work in the children's kitchen, Faustina was quite worried because — as she wrote in her *Diary* — she could not handle the cooking pots, which were huge. "The most difficult task for me was draining the potatoes, and sometimes, I spilt half of them with the water. When I told this to Mother Directress, she said that with time I would get used to it and gain the necessary skill. Yet the task was not getting any easier, as I was growing weaker every day. So I would move away when it was time to drain the potatoes. The sisters noticed that I avoided this task and were very much surprised. They did not know that I could not help in spite of all my willingness to do this and not spare myself. At noon, during the examination of conscience, I complained to God about my weakness. Then I heard the following words in my soul, **From today on you will do this easily; I shall strengthen you.**"

Faustina continued, "That evening, when the time came to drain off the water from the potatoes, I hurried to be the first to do it, trusting in the Lord's words. I took up the pot with ease and poured off the water perfectly. But when I took off the cover to let the potatoes steam off, I saw there in the pot, in the place of the potatoes, whole bunches of red roses, beautiful beyond description. I had never seen such roses before. Greatly astonished and unable to understand the meaning of this, I heard a voice within me saying, **I change such hard work of yours into bouquets of most beautiful flowers, and their perfume rises up to My throne**" (*Diary*, 65).

The moment in which Faustina saw the red roses in a pot full of potatoes was witnessed by Sr. Regina Jaworska. Having noticed earlier that the novice was having problems handling the pots, she wanted to help Faustina drain the water from the potatoes. But Faustina said that she would do it by herself. "Nevertheless, I stood beside her," Sr. Regina remembers, "ready to offer my help if needed. I could see how easily she did it. When she put the pot back and lifted the lid to let the steam out, I noticed a look of surprise on her face." Not until 20 years later, having read the *Diary*, did Sr. Regina realize what had happened. "She was seeing roses in the pot, when all I could see were potatoes," she concludes.

Father Andrasz points out that a similar miracle — regarded by many as mere legend — was performed by Jesus for St. Elizabeth of Hungary, the queen who, against her husband's orders, gave bread and money to the poor. One winter day, when her stern husband caught her taking bread to the poor, Jesus made him see roses instead of loaves in her apron.

The roses in the pot full of potatoes were to reward Faustina for her hard work, performed obediently out of her love for Jesus. "From then on I have tried to drain the potatoes myself, not only during my week when it was my turn to cook, but also in replacement of other sisters when it was their turn. And not only do I do this, but I try to be the first to help in any other burdensome task, because I have experienced how much this pleases God. O inexhaustible treasure of purity of intention which makes all our actions perfect and so pleasing to God!" she wrote (*Diary*, 65–66).

Faustina strove to fulfill all of her duties and to observe the rules of religious life as thoroughly as she could. She considered obedience to her superiors, which Jesus rigorously expected of her as well, to be one of the more important virtues. She saw the hand of God in her superiors' orders.

Sister Regina Jaworska recalls, "Once, while working in the cellar, a few of us were talking, telling one another stories from our lives. Sister Faustina came along and asked us whether we had permission to talk. We answered that we didn't. She ran off to the superiors and, a moment later, came back saying that we could talk freely, since we now had permission."

Sister Placida Putyra remembers, "She often had to endure bitter remarks about being too scrupulous, about pointing out the slightest violations of the religious rule. She did not mind, and she did what she saw as her duty, bearing any humiliation patiently."

Faustina's superiors at this convent in Kraków and in other convents, presented Faustina as an example of obedience for other sisters. This does not mean that the strict observance of all religious rules and superiors' orders came without effort. Even during her novitiate, Faustina would find the courage to point out their inappropriate behavior to more experienced professed sisters, which was not welcomed by them. Sister Placida remembers a conversation about priests and confessors between three sisters in the kitchen: "These were not edifying conversations. I was a little surprised that senior sisters could even talk in that way, and I wanted to leave the kitchen as fast as possible." She recalls, "Sister Faustina, who was working in the kitchen, on hearing this, said, 'Excuse me, but the Lord Jesus is not pleased by this, please stop this talk, Sisters.' I admired the novice's courage, which allowed her to stand up to the senior sisters."

When Faustina did not like something, she spoke up — both to superiors among the nuns and to priests. It is difficult to establish where the following incident took place, but it could have been in Vilnius, where she lived a few years later.

Sister Justine Gołofit recalls, "I can remember a certain priest who lived and worked among us, and that Sr. Faustina often and with great earnestness asked us to pray fervently for him, because his soul was in a deplorable state. She had enough courage to tell him this and to reprimand him. She was no respecter of persons where sin was involved, and she always reprimanded the person in private."

Faustina met Justine in Kraków, in the novitiate. She was her Angel. Sister Justine, a postulant at the time, was not very pleased with her Angel at first. Just the opposite. "Initially, I did not even like her. Outwardly, she was not very likable," she said about Sr. Faustina years later. Another time, she admitted, "This was because she was constantly scolding and admonishing me." However, a bond of friendship soon developed between the two women, and their friendship continued until Faustina's death.

Sister Justine Gołofit continues, "As a novice, she constantly prayed for me to earnestly love the Lord Jesus and to be a religious in accordance with the Sacred Heart. She repeated this to me often. Once, I was overwhelmed with temptations against my vocation, and I wanted to leave the Congregation as quickly as possible. I admitted this to her in private while we were working together. Sister Faustina was deeply concerned and, at the same time, reassured me that this was simply a demonic temptation. Should I succumb to it, I would be condemned. She presented this to me in such a terrible way that I was simply terrified. Her piercing eyes could read what was hiding at the bottom of my soul and would always see all my sins and failings."

Faustina was also the Angel to a younger novice, Louise Gadzina, who says, "She had such a good influence on people. Talking to her would make you take heart, because she could see the slightest sign of good in anything and lift you up. … I always admired how balanced and peaceful Sr. Faustina was, as well as admiring her religious spirit, dutifulness, and piety. She would suffer patiently, never complaining, but also never hiding the reality. I could hardly see any fault in her."

Sister Faustina spoke a great deal about Divine Mercy already when she was a novice. Sister Simone Nalewajk, who — unlike Faustina — always stressed Divine Justice, remembered this distinctly. "She always won me over with her arguments," Sr. Simone reveals. The sisters usually conversed during recreation time, which was devoted to resting, getting to know each other, and spending time together.

Sister Louise Gadzina recalls, "When she spoke about God, you could see that her soul was soaring, burning. She loved chatting during recreation, and at times like this, a circle of sisters formed around her, because she was open and eagerly advised us how to go about working. She was very kind to us, but never imposed herself on people who preferred to keep their own counsel."

Sister Regina Jaworska remembers, "We liked Sr. Faustina; she was dear to us. We would gather around her during recreation, and each of us wanted to be near her. We jokingly nicknamed her 'the lawyer' because she could speak beautifully, emphasizing what she was saying with hand gestures. She always directed the conversation to divine matters."

Sister Joachim Głuc recalls, "Even the older sisters liked talking with her, because the conversation was always edifying, pleasant, and concerned the things of God. One profited greatly from such conversation."

Once, during recreation time, as a joke, but also out of curiosity, Sr. Regina took a small notebook out of Faustina's pocket. "I wanted to see what she had written down. She chased me around the garden and did not let me have a look." This notebook was not yet the *Diary*, which Faustina did not begin until 1933, but this event does show that she was already taking notes concerning her spiritual life.

Mother Michael Moraczewska confirms this. She remembered years later that Faustina, as a newly professed nun, used to show her certain notes written down in pencil — "her inner enlightenment." Mother Michael merely flipped through the pages. She did not pay much attention to them. And she was not the only one to dismiss them.

Faustina talked about her spiritual experiences to her confessors, seeking advice and understanding. These, however, were elusive for a long time. Sister Faustina's spiritual experiences and her expectations were simply beyond the reach of those she talked to. This was also the case during her novitiate in Kraków, where the novice's confessor was Fr. Theodore Czaputa. This is brought to light by an event that was vividly remembered by Sr. Simone Nalewajk, Faustina's roommate.

One day, after confession, Sr. Simone went back to the room she shared with Faustina. A little later, Faustina came in as well. "She knelt down in front of her nightstand, on top of which stood a sacred image. She covered her head with her hands and started crying loudly," remembers Sr. Simone. "Her cries bordered on screaming. I felt sorry for her, and I ran immediately to fetch Mother [the Novice Mistress] and tell her what was happening. Mother ran to our cell right away and I went to the kitchen. I don't know what they spoke about. After some time, Sr. Faustina joined me in the kitchen, and although I could see she had been crying, she had fully regained her composure."

Sister Placida also remembered this incident, saying, "I asked her why she had been crying. And she replied, 'Oh, Jesus, even the confessor does not understand me, nobody understands me.'"

This was probably during Faustina's dark night of the senses, which she started experiencing near the end of the first year of her novitiate. This was a particularly important and, at the same time, extremely difficult period, the nature of which she learned and embraced only after it ended. That was the perspective from which she described it in the *Diary*. The dark night of the senses and the spirit is an experience known in its depths only to mystics. It is a time of a chosen soul's purification from earthly desires, passions, and affections. It is not the human being who purifies himself; it is God Himself who accomplishes this working inside the human being. Therefore, this spiritual process is often called a passive dark night of the senses and the spirit.

According to the greatest mystic of the Church, St. John of the Cross — as Fr. Stanislaus Urbański, Ph.D., tells us — the dark night "creates an organic unity of the senses and the soul, introduces an inner harmony, orders the passions, and gives birth to deep peace, to tranquility and humility. It also has an existential dimension, making the human being abandon everything and become completely focused on God." Thus prepared, the soul is ready for a greater and more perfect love. It is ready for union with God.

In some cases, purification takes many years. Faustina's was relatively quick, its first stage having taken about a year and a half. For comparison's sake, consider that Mother Teresa experienced something akin to the dark night, which lasted for almost half a century. However, in Sr. Faustina's life, there was one more period of the dark night: the purification of the senses was followed by a purification of the spirit. Both the night of the spirit and of the senses typically precede a period of mystical experiences, in which an individual who is chosen by God, as Faustina put it, "enters into intimacy" with Him. God reveals Himself "in flashes; that is to say, when God draws near," during so-called infused contemplation. Though these flashes are brief, the "light which has touched the soul is alive within it, and nothing can either quench or diminish it," Faustina explains. "This flash of the knowledge of God draws the soul and enkindles its love for Him" (*Diary*, 95). And suddenly, the soul is engulfed in darkness. It is immersed — as St. John of the Cross writes — in "emptiness, into that poverty and abandonment of all its faculties." It experiences spiritual aridity and darkness. It seems to the soul as though God has abandoned it. However, as Fr. Urbański explains, God continues to communicate with the soul through infused contemplation. But the light of God is so bright that the soul that has not yet passed through the purifications of the spirit and the senses is blinded. Instead of light, it sees darkness.

The mystical purification of Faustina's senses began near the end of the first year of her novitiate, probably in the spring of 1927. "My mind became dimmed in a strange way; no truth seemed clear to me. When people spoke to me about God, my heart was like a rock," she later said of her condition. "I could not draw from it a single sentiment of love for Him. When I tried, by an act of the will, to remain close to Him, I experienced great torments, and it seemed to me that I was only provoking God to an even greater anger. It was absolutely impossible for me to meditate as I had been accustomed to do in the past. I felt in my soul a great void, and there was nothing with which I could fill it. I began to suffer from a great hunger and yearning for God, but I saw my utter powerlessness. ... The abyss of my misery was constantly before my eyes. Every time I entered the chapel for some spiritual exercise, I experienced even worse torments and temptations. More than once, all through Holy Mass, I had to struggle against blasphemous thoughts which were forcing themselves to my lips. I felt an aversion for the Holy Sacraments, and it seemed to me that I was not profiting from them in any way. It was only out of obedience to my confessor that I frequented them, and this blind obedience was for me the only path I could follow and my very last hope of survival" (*Diary*, 77).

Faustina — who until recently had enjoyed "divine delights" and had been "immersed in God" — was now suffering terribly because of His apparent absence and because of her longing for Him and the closeness that she had experienced earlier. "My soul was in this state for almost six months." Faustina did not understand why "God was working very strangely" in her soul (*Diary*, 23). Unfortunately, she was unable to find anyone who could explain all of this to her. But even then, tempted as she was to doubt and reject revealed truths, to cease believing in the hope and love of God, she never stopped trusting in Him. "Even if You kill me, still will I trust in You!" she repeated in the words of Job (*Diary*, 77). She kept on begging God for help: "I ... reduced myself to dust under His feet and begged for mercy" (*Diary*, 23). As she wrote years later, her "very last hope of survival" in this "fiery trial" was obedience to her superiors and her confessor, who, in spite of her fears, ordered her to continue receiving the Eucharist (*Diary*, 77, 68).

Her spiritual torment was sometimes interrupted by a flash of God's presence. For instance, Jesus came to her on one occasion with the words **"I am always in your heart"** (*Diary*, 78). All joy, however, was short-lived. It was replaced by a period that she referred to as "the trial of trials." She felt absolutely abandoned by God: "It [the soul] sees within itself only sin. ... It sees itself completely abandoned by God. It feels itself to be the object of His hatred. It is but one step away from despair. ... The soul is drawn to God, but feels repulsed. All other sufferings and tortures in the world are as nothing compared with this sensation into which it has been plunged" (*Diary*, 98).

Faustina was tormented not only spiritually, interiorly, but also physically. The suffering affected her senses. She lost all her strength. Then, finally, the worst moment of her dark night arrived: the agony of the soul. This is how she described her unspeakable spiritual suffering later: "One day, just as I had awakened ... I was suddenly overwhelmed by despair. Complete darkness in the soul. I fought as best I could till noon. In the afternoon, truly deadly fears began to seize me; my physical strength began to leave me. I went quickly to my cell, fell on my knees before the Crucifix and began to cry out for mercy. But Jesus did not hear my cries. I felt my physical strength leave me completely. I fell to the ground, despair flooding my whole soul. I suffered terrible tortures in no way different from the torments of hell" (*Diary*, 24). Her soul was in agony.

"I wanted to die but could not" she wrote of the experience (*Diary*, 23). This lasted for 45 minutes. "I wanted to go and see the Directress, but was too weak. I wanted to shout, but I had no voice. Fortunately, one of the sisters came into my cell." It was Sr. Placida Putyra. She immediately summoned Mother Joseph Brzoza who, in the name of "holy obedience," told Faustina to get up off the floor. "Immediately some force raised me up from the ground and I stood up, close to the dear Mother Directress." Faustina felt "as if [she] had come out from the tomb" (*Diary*, 24).

Mother Brzoza recognized the nature of Faustina's experience. She knew that it was God Himself, trying and purifying her. She told the novice that God was calling her to great holiness: "The Lord wants to draw you very close to Himself since He has allowed these things to happen to you so soon. Be faithful to God, Sister, because this is a sign that He wants you to have a high place in heaven" (*Diary*, 102).

Faustina did not understand any of this yet. On that very same day, during evening devotions, her soul began to "agonize again in a terrible darkness." But even then, she did not lose her trust: "Jesus, I trust in You in the face of every interior sentiment which sets itself against hope. Do what You want with me," she told the Lord (*Diary*, 24).

For two more days, her face contained the traces of what she had experienced during the agony of her soul. She had a "deathly pale face and bloodshot eyes. Jesus alone knows what I suffered," she wrote (*Diary*, 104). And she felt as though she "had come back from the other world." Her physical condition, which "evoked pity," did not go unnoticed by the other sisters. They talked about it among themselves, not knowing the actual reason for it.

Faustina finished her novitiate and professed her first religious vows, the so-called temporary vows, during the period of her "passive nights." "A sister, just out of her novitiate, is so deeply united with the Lord Jesus that if she told me that she has spoken with Him — I would believe her at once," Mother Joseph said about Sr. Faustina while speaking to the younger novices. Felicia Żakowiecka's recollections suggest that the sisters guessed immediately to whom Mother Joseph was referring, and she herself did not deny it. This incident indicates that the Novice Directress recognized the depth of the young nun's spirituality. Other sisters also noticed a certain spiritual "distinctiveness" in Faustina.

The future saint made her first religious vows in Łagiewniki on April 30, 1928. The convent archivist noted, "Bishop Rospond, assisted by Fr. Kotowicz and Fr. Zieja from Radom, performed the ceremonies of perpetual vows, annual renewals, and investiture with the habit. Perpetual vows were professed by Sr. Callista and Sr. Norberta, dir.[ectors], renewals — by Sr. Renata, Sr. Bonaventure, dir., and Sr. Florentine, and Sr. Faustina, coadju.[tors]. Two postulants received the habit."

Sister Faustina was one of four religious (in 1926, five of them had started novitiate together) who made temporary vows of poverty, chastity, and obedience for one year. The ceremony was preceded by the so-called canonical examination. Faustina, like any other sister, had to answer fourteen questions. The questions concerned personal information: the place and date of birth, Baptism, and Confirmation, as well as whether she contributed a dowry to the Congregation or not. There were also questions as to whether she had been previously engaged or married; whether she had been in another religious congregation; her motivations for entering the Congregation of the Sisters of Our Lady of Mercy; whether she entered voluntarily; whether she knew the rules of the Congregation; whether she had any possible doubts before professing vows; and whether she was willing to voluntarily and earnestly serve God in the Congregation. The document containing Faustina's answers and bearing her signature is dated April 3, 1928.

The ceremony of the profession of vows took considerable time. It started in the convent. The novices, together with the Sister Directress, processed to the great hall where the professed sisters were waiting for them. Here, the novices knelt down and asked Mother General Leonard Cielecka (who was to be replaced in October by Michael Moraczewska) for permission to make the profession of vows. Next, holding lit candles, they processed to the chapel, where they asked the celebrant — the Auxiliary Bishop of the Kraków Archdiocese, Stanislaus

Rospond — to accept their first profession in the Congregation of the Sisters of Our Lady of Mercy. "By the grace of Jesus Christ, our Savior and God, these virgins here present are due to be blessed and dedicated to Jesus our Lord, and to be espoused to the Son of the Most High," proclaimed the celebrant. The sisters knelt down, bowing very low, until their faces almost touched the ground. Then the bishop blessed the sisters' black veils, placing one on each sister's head. He also blessed their crucifixes and the long rosaries which they hung from the belts of their habits. (The rosaries had medallions imprinted with the image of St. Ignatius of Loyola on one side, and of the Holy Family on the other.) Only then did each sister, with a lit candle in hand, recite the formula of the religious vows:

"Almighty Eternal God, I, [name of sister], though by all means unworthy to stand before You, but trusting in Your infinite mercy and prompted by the desire to serve You, in the presence of the Blessed Virgin Mary, the glorious patriarch St. Joseph, and the whole court of Heaven, vow to your Majesty, Poverty, Chastity, and Obedience, in the Congregation of Our Lady of Mercy. And I humbly ask Your infinite Goodness, by the Blood of our Lord Jesus Christ, to accept this sacrifice as a sweet fragrance, and as You have given me the means and the willingness to make this sacrifice, so give me abundant grace to fulfill it. Amen."

In this moment, the vows were completed. Faustina's parents witnessed the ceremony, this time having responded to her invitation. They were seeing their daughter for the first time in four years, since she left Łódź for Warsaw to look for a convent. As they were walking in the convent garden, her father asked, "My child, don't you feel bored here?" Faustina, according to family lore, responded with great surprise that she could not possibly be bored living "under the same roof as the Lord Jesus." Her parents finally came to terms with the choice their daughter had made. "We have to leave her here," Stanislaus Kowalski said. "This is the will of God."

Having made the vows — temporary ones for the time being — Sr. Faustina was now a professed nun. She would renew these vows four more times, year after year, and then make the permanent ones after five years in the Congregation. This event also took place in Łagiewniki.

Approximately six months after Faustina's first vows, the darkness in her soul ceased. This probably happened at the Łagiewniki convent, in the fall of 1928. "Once, when I was praying, Jesus pervaded all my soul, darkness melted away, and I heard these words within me: **You are My joy; you are My Heart's**

delight," she wrote (*Diary*, 27). From that moment on, she felt "as though my soul had been set free from everything" earthly and human (*Diary*, 102). She felt "inundated with Divine light. Since then, my soul has been in intimate communion with God, like a child with its beloved Father" (*Diary*, 27).

A few years later, Faustina was able to better understand what she had experienced during that period. Even so, this first dark night did not bring about the full purification of her senses and her spirit, which was why she was forced to endure one more period of "darkness," when her soul would once again endure torments. Yet, when that time of further purification arrived, she was already aware that everything that was happening was the work of God, who is closer to the chosen person in her spiritual suffering than she may think. When, "struck by divine light, [she] claims that there is no light," it is because this light "is so intense that it blinds her." Faustina would come to know that "after such sufferings the soul finds itself in a state of great purity of spirit and very close to God" (*Diary*, 109), but that during the period of suffering, she would not understand what was happening to her. "I would not have believed that one could suffer so, if I had not gone through it myself" she wrote (*Diary*, 104).

With the exception of Mother Brzoza, who recognized the source of Sr. Faustina's suffering, no one else was able to understand her, or help her, not even her confessor. Following her description of her dark night, Fausina twice made mention of a priest who, unable to comprehend what was happening in her soul, refused to hear her confession. This must have been a very disturbing experience for her.

Was this the reason for her tears, as remembered by Sr. Simone and Sr. Placida? That seems quite likely. Faustina described this experience several years later. Her writing is calm, without emotion, taking the form of a set of guidelines for those undergoing the same thing and of directions for confessors. Faustina stresses that it is important for a priest who does not understand what is happening in a person's soul to refer them to another "experienced and well-instructed confessor … Or else he himself should seek light in order to give the soul what it needs, instead of downrightly denying it confession." For in the latter case, such a priest "is exposing the soul to a great danger; and more than one soul may well leave the road along which God wanted it to journey. This is a matter of great importance, for I have experienced it myself. I myself began to waver; despite special gifts from God," she wrote (*Diary*, 112).

Sister Faustina stayed in Łagiewniki until the end of October 1928. She spent this time working in the kitchen — probably the one for the girls. She also supervised the novices who worked there. The head cook was Sr. Marcianna Oświęcimska.

Sister Joachim Głuc remembers, "Sister Marcianna would not treat all the sisters equally, and she was especially hard on the novices. Sister Faustina could not stand this injustice. Once, she even reported Sr. Marcianna to the Novice Directress for treating a novice harshly. Faustina herself was very kindly disposed towards the novices. She tried to make things easier for them and instructed them how to do the things they had problems with."

Sister Justine Gołofit recalls, "When the novices made a mistake or spoiled something, for example, when they put salt in the tea instead of on the potatoes, and then went out and served the salty tea, Sr. Faustina was the one who had to endure a lot of humiliation from the other sisters. Nevertheless, she never complained in front of anyone, and she always apologized calmly, with a smile, saying she had not been attentive and careful enough, and she always corrected the novice who had made the mistake gently and with great love. … She often said that each sister who cooked for the pupils should make an extra effort to prepare good, tasty meals for the glory of God."

Whenever working in the kitchen, here in Kraków or elsewhere, Faustina always wore her religious habit. Of this practice, Sr. Joachim Głuc remembers, "When other sisters tried to convince her to wear work clothes instead of her habit, she would reply, 'The Lord's bride should always wear the habit.'"

Not all the sisters understood her motives. Sister Beata Piekut remembered that some nuns felt bothered by her outfit. They said she was too prissy. "'She's always formally attired, never wearing the working habit,' they remarked enviously." In reality, the habit was heavier and much less comfortable for working in the kitchen, which was always hot. For Faustina, wearing it was not just a form of taking pride in being a religious, but also a kind of mortification. That was why she even avoided rolling up her sleeves while working.

Sister Faustina, as is apparent in the *Diary*, made use of various other forms of additional mortification. The Congregation's Constitutions did not counsel any particular penitential practices besides those generally required by the Church and also partial fasting on the eve of renewing one's vows and on certain feast days. The sisters' hard work, especially as carried out by the second choir sisters, was sufficiently difficult. What the Congregation's Constitutions encouraged was practicing regular mortification, "which above all it is necessary to base on continuously overcoming their inclinations, their tempers, and humor, and bearing the irritations inseparable from daily occupations, in patience in times of illness, disability, or suffering that befall them, and in self-denial."

The Constitutions also recommended that a few times a year, particularly on the vigils of the greater feasts, the sisters should ask their Superior for some sort of penance and "to perform them publically in the refectory for infringements of religious discipline." They could undertake other types of penance and mortification with the agreement of a confessor. (When these penances were of an external nature, they also needed the consent of the superiors.)

Sister Faustina had asked for such permission to wear a "hair shirt" for several hours or days, and she was granted it on certain occasions. The hair shirt was either a belt woven from very coarse animal hair, or an iron girdle with sharp ends. Such strips were worn around the waist, wrist, or leg. (Faustina was wearing the latter when she was visiting her family in February 1935 in Głogowiec; see *Diary*, 1248.)

Faustina left the Łagiewniki convent on October 31, 1928. "This morning, Sr. Zdislaus, Sr. Alexia, and Sr. Faustina left for Warsaw," noted the house chronicler. Unfortunately, nobody remembers whether during Sr. Faustina's three-year-long stay at the Łagiewniki convent — for example, during recreation or on a feast day — she ever left the premises of the Józefinum. Despite the fact that the Congregation was active and worked with the girls in the educational institution, it led a very cloistered life, limited to its walled-in campus.

Nonetheless, it is quite likely that during this period, Faustina did pray in the nearby Church of St. Joseph in the Podgórze, a district of Kraków. The village of Łagiewniki lay within the parish boundaries of this church, which counted 24,000 parishioners at this time. And because the Congregation also had a great devotion to St. Joseph, it is probable that the church, built towards the end of the 19th century like their convent, was near and dear to the sisters.

Sister Faustina came back to Łagiewniki five years later, on April 18, 1933. By then, she was an experienced sister, both in terms of the religious life and, most importantly, in the progress she was making in the mystical life. She had had many mystical experiences since her first dark night of the senses in Kraków. She had spent short periods of time in convents in Warsaw, Vilnius, Kiekrz,

Walendów, Biała, and more than two years in Płock. This is where Jesus appeared to her and asked that His image be painted and the Feast of Divine Mercy be established.

Sister Faustina came to Kraków to make a retreat preceding her perpetual religious vows. The sisters had made some changes in their activities since she had been at the convent last. Since 1932, they were running a soup kitchen for the unemployed living in Łagiewniki, organizing retreats for mothers, and leading Eucharistic Adoration for children.

Two days before the retreat started, Sr. Faustina took the so-called canonical examination, certifying the truthfulness of her answers with her signature. On April 21, the retreat began for the sisters. It was preached by the Jesuit Fr. Anthony Bronislaus Wojnar.

"It sometimes happens," Sr. Faustina wrote, "while I am listening to the meditation, that one word puts me in very close union with the Lord, and I no longer know what Father is saying. I know that I am close to the most merciful Heart of Jesus; my whole spirit is entirely plunged in Him, and in one moment I learn more than during long hours of intellectual inquiry and meditation. These are sudden lights which permit me to know things as God sees them, regarding matters of both the interior and the exterior world" (*Diary*, 733).

In the *Diary*, Sr. Faustina devoted much space to the description of the spiritual preparation for her perpetual espousal to Jesus. Because Jesus was her Master, she called herself a "little novice of Jesus," despite the fact that she had not been a novice for years now. She declared, "With the trust and simplicity of a small child, I give myself to You today, O Lord Jesus, my Master. I leave You complete freedom in directing my soul. Guide me along the paths You wish. I won't question them. I will follow You trustingly" (*Diary*, 228).

She also made many resolutions during this time of retreat. At least a few are worth mentioning here, as they will tell us much about Faustina. She made a pledge to improve in complying with the religious rule — she sometimes broke the silence, failed to react to the sound of the bell, or interfered with the duties of others. She also decided to "avoid sisters who grumble" and "take no heed of the opinion of others," but, in agreement with her own conscience, "in every action … be mindful of God" and "keep silence outside the time of recreation, and avoid jokes and witty words that make others laugh and break silence." Finally, she pledged to observe every detail of the religious rule. She wanted to avoid being "absorbed in the whirl of work," instead planning to take small breaks in order to direct her thoughts towards God. She obliged herself to "speak little with people, but a good deal with God" (*Diary*, 226), not to divulge her experiences to others, not to complain when suffering, but maintain calm and composure instead. She promised she would be at the service of the other sisters, not to speak about somebody in their absence, and would find delight in her neighbors' successes. "I will spend all my free moments at the feet of [Our Lord in] the Blessed Sacrament. At the feet of Jesus, I will seek light, comfort and strength," she wrote (*Diary*, 224).

The closer the day of her perpetual vows approached, the more Faustina's joy grew: "Meanwhile, each time I call to mind that in a few days I am to become one with the Lord through perpetual vows, a joy beyond all description floods my soul," she noted. She wrote down what she had learned through her mystical visions: "God makes known to me, even now, the immensity of the love He already had for me before time began; and as for me, I have just begun to love Him, in time. His love was [ever] great, pure and disinterested, and my love for Him comes from the fact that I am beginning to know Him. The more I come to know Him, the more ardently, the more fiercely I love Him, and the more perfect my acts become" (*Diary*, 231).

When she was thanking the Lord the night before for the grace of professing her perpetual vows, she heard, "**My daughter, your heart is My heaven**" (*Diary*, 238). Faustina was so excited that she could not fall asleep that night. She noted later, "Joy has driven sleep away."

Finally, on May 1, 1933, the long-awaited moment arrived. The celebration in the convent chapel was presided over by Bishop Stanislaus Rospond, who had also received Sr. Faustina's first temporary vows five years earlier. The ceremony was long, because it involved the investiture with the habit of nine postulants, the annual vows of five sisters, and perpetual vows, also made by five sisters: four first choir sisters — Sr. Bonaventure, Sr. Henry, Sr. Bernadette, Sr. Liguoria; and one second choir sister — Sr. Faustina. "Today I place my heart on the paten where Your Heart has been placed, O Jesus, and today I offer myself together with You to God, Your Father and mine, as a sacrifice of love and praise," she prayed during the Mass (*Diary*, 239).

The moment when — as prescribed by the ceremony of profession — Faustina lay prostrate on the floor, face down, was particularly touching. The choir was singing Psalm 130, *De Profundis*, in Latin: "From the depths, I have cried out to you, O Lord; Lord, hear my voice!" At this point, the sisters covered

Faustina with a pall, and the bells tolled as for a funeral. This sign and the psalm were symbols of her death to the world and the beginning of a life devoted solely to God.

Lying under the pall, Faustina prayed for many things, as she knew that on this day, God would not refuse her anything. Her first plea concerned a special cause: the triumph of the Church, especially in Russia and Spain. These two countries — Russia since the revolution in 1917, and Spain since the Republicans had come to power in 1931 — continued to witness the bloody persecution of Catholics. Faustina also asked for a blessing for Pope Pius XI, for the clergy, for light for priests who would be her confessors, for graces for the sisters, superiors, the Congregation's pupils, and the entire Congregation, for blessings for her family and for a few other individuals whom she does not name in the *Diary*, for the grace of conversion for unrepentant sinners and for those who need prayer most, as well as "to free all souls from purgatory." In this special moment, she also begged Jesus to "transform me completely into Yourself" (*Diary*, 240). She desired the power of the Spirit to obey His will in everything she did.

Next, Bishop Rospond blessed Faustina's ring, a token of her espousal to Jesus Christ: "Take this ring as a sign of the eternal covenant you are making with Christ, the Spouse of Virgins." As the bishop placed the ring on her finger, Faustina felt God suffuse all of her being. "Today my soul has lost itself in You, my only treasure," she wrote down of the words she had uttered in her soul. She also confessed, "I truly would not be able to live without You, even for a moment, Jesus."

As a response, she heard the following words of Jesus in her soul: "**My spouse, our hearts are joined forever**" (*Diary*, 239).

The ceremony was over. Now was the time to meet with family. No one from her family was there. So she took a walk by herself. Right at that moment, the sisters who had just professed their first temporary vows were preparing to pose for a group photograph near Our Lady's grotto. The two superiors, Mother General Michael Moraczewska and the Novice Directress, Mother Joseph Brzoza, sat down on chairs. Behind them stood the five temporarily professed sisters. Sister Faustina joined them. She stood to the side, on the right. Thanks to the fact that the sisters invited her to be in the picture with them, we can see what Sr. Faustina looked like on the day of her perpetual vows.

Sister Cajetan Bartkowiak, who received the habit that day, remembered years later that Faustina had a conversation with Cajetan's father who had come for her vows. "She engaged him in a very long discussion. I was none too pleased, because we had little time together and I loved my father very much and wanted to enjoy his company to the full." However, Cajetan soon forgot about this small moment of sadness and became closer to Faustina after that day.

Just before Faustina's perpetual vows — she was still in Warsaw at this time — she responded to the call of Jesus to become, like Him, a sacrifice offered to God for the faults of sinners. In Kraków, a few days after her perpetual vows, Faustina saw Jesus "covered with wounds" in the convent chapel, and He said to her: "**Look at whom you have espoused**" (*Diary*, 252).

Several months later, while making a Holy Hour, she had a similar vision. "Jesus was suddenly standing before me, stripped of His clothes, His body completely covered with wounds, His eyes flooded with tears and blood, His face disfigured and covered with spittle. The Lord then said to me, **The bride must resemble her Betrothed**." Faustina understood this image and these words well — to their very depths. She wrote, "There is no room for doubt here. My likeness to Jesus must be through suffering and humility" (*Diary*, 268).

Further, Sr. Faustina was to have a more prolonged conversation with Mother Brzoza during this stay in Kraków. "She clarified many things for me, and she set me at peace as regards my spiritual life, reassuring me that I was on the right path," she wrote (*Diary*, 222). This was important to Sr. Faustina, as — ever since Płock, where Jesus had appeared to her and asked for His image to be painted — she had been misunderstood by her confessors and the other sisters.

What turned out to be even more important during this stay was her confession with the Jesuit Fr. Joseph Andrasz. A few years later, he would become her spiritual director alongside Fr. Sopoćko, whom she would come to recognize in Vilnius later. In 1933, Fr. Andrasz was 42. He was a well-read theologian with an excellent and broad formation, the author of articles and books on asceticism, a valued confessor and priest, and — as Faustina described him — a man "filled with the Spirit of God." He worked for the Jesuit-owned publishing house Wydawnictwo Apostolstwa Modlitwy (Apostleship of Prayer) and was the editor-in-chief of the monthly magazine *Posłaniec Serca Jezusowego* (*The Sacred Heart Messenger*). He became the regular confessor to the sisters in Łagiewniki in 1933, not long before Faustina arrived there for the second time. Jesus had informed Sr. Faustina that He would provide Fr. Andrasz with the light necessary to know her soul, and that the priest's words would be His own.

Indeed, the Jesuit correctly recognized the nature of Faustina's spiritual life. The confessions that she made before her perpetual vows, as well as later, when she stayed in Kraków for another month, were very important to her. Father Andrasz assured Faustina that what she was experiencing was of a supernatural nature, a grace from God, and not an illusion — as many confessors up to that point (with the exception of Fr. Elter) and many sisters had told her. He reassured her in regard to all of her spiritual concerns and forbade her to refrain from her interior inspirations, but also directed her to tell everything to her confessors.

"Have confidence and walk ahead with courage," he said to Faustina the day before she left Kraków for Vilnius. He suggested that she should adhere closely to directions given by her future confessors. She recorded the effect of Fr. Andrasz's words thus: "An extraordinary, divine power came over me after that confession. Father stressed that I must be faithful to God's grace and said, 'No harm will come to you if, in the future, you continue to keep this same simplicity and obedience. Have confidence in God; you are on the right path and in good hands, in God's hands'" (*Diary*, 257).

Father Andrasz had given Faustina wings: "It seemed to me that I was running, not walking. My wings were spread for flight; I soared into the very heat of the sun, and I will not descend until I rest in Him, in whom my soul has lost itself forever," she wrote joyfully. "I am one with the Lord. It is as if the gulf between us, Creator and creature, disappears. For a few days, my soul was in a state of continuous ecstasy. God's presence did not leave me for a single moment. And my soul remained in a continuous loving union with the Lord. But this in no way interfered with the performance of my duties. I felt I was transformed into love; I was all afire, but without being burned up, I lost myself in God unceasingly. ... I had impeded and feared God's grace for so long, and now God Himself, through Father Andrasz, has removed all difficulties" (*Diary*, 142).

In a letter she sent to Fr. Andrasz on May 25, 1933, after she reached Vilnius, Faustina confided, "After these two confessions ... I feel strong and courageous. I fear neither suffering nor humiliations; not only am I not afraid, but I find joy and satisfaction in suffering."

After making her perpetual vows, Sr. Faustina felt overwhelmed with happiness. "My relationship with God, since perpetual vows, has been more intimate than it had ever been before. I sense that I love God and that He loves me" (*Diary*, 254). She also wrote, "I am continuously united with Him. It seems to me as though Jesus could not be happy without me, nor could I, without Him. Although I understand that, being God, He is happy in Himself and has absolutely no need of any creature, still, His goodness compels Him to give

Himself to the creature" (*Diary*, 244). And there is the sentence that speaks of her great unity with God: "I am in Him, and He in me" (*Diary*, 254).

By May 5, four days after the ceremony of taking perpetual vows, the sisters were starting to scatter to various other convents in Poland. Only Sr. Faustina stayed in Łagiewniki for almost a month. She helped out in the kitchen and the garden. She made an Ignatian retreat.

Mother Moraczewska recalls, "Knowing this soul, I understood well that she should have an experienced director, and therefore I desired that she stay in the Josephinum after her vows, in order to remain under the direction of Fr. Andrasz, whom she trusted immensely. But, strangely, this did not work out."

On May 6, a Sr. Borgia Tichy came to Łagiewniki from Vilnius. As the convent chronicler noted, she informed them about "the offering" to the sisters of Łagiewniki of a new religious. Sister Tichy left soon afterwards.[26] However, soon thereafter, a letter arrived from Vilnius, asking for a sister to be sent there to work in the gardens. Sister Faustina notes that "it was undecided whether I was to go to Rabka or to Vilnius" (*Diary*, 251). She did not reveal her preference to her Superior. She wanted Mother's decision to result purely from the will of God. Finally, Mother Michael asked her to come and see her: "Sister, you know how much I wanted you to remain here, but it cannot be."

Faustina was leaving with great regret. She wrote, "When I came out of the house, I looked at the garden and the house, and when I cast a glance at the novitiate, tears suddenly ran down my cheeks. I remembered all the blessings and graces bestowed on me by the Lord. Then, suddenly and unexpectedly, I saw the Lord by the flower bed and He said to me, **Do not weep; I am with you always"** (*Diary*, 259).

Sister Faustina left for Vilnius. She would stay there for almost three years and would return to Łagiewniki from Vilnius for the third time on October 19, 1935. At that point, she was once more able to talk with Fr. Andrasz. He was leading an eight-day retreat for which Sr. Faustina had come. Father Andrasz reassured her again that she was "in the good hands of a very good God" (*Diary*, 506) and that what she was experiencing was no illusion. He also said that she had a good spiritual director in Fr. Michael Sopoćko, and should follow his advice.

After All Saints' Day, on November 2, 1935, Faustina set off on a return journey to Vilnius.

Chapter Eight

Kiekrz

1929

The Time of 'Loving Repose'

"**O**NE AFTERNOON ... [I] stopped on the shore of the lake; I stood there for a long time, contemplating my surroundings. Suddenly, I saw the Lord Jesus near me, and He graciously said to me, **All this I created for you, My spouse; and know that all this beauty is nothing compared to what I have prepared for you in eternity**" (*Diary*, 158).

This is how Sr. Faustina described the encounter at the lake in Kiekrz, near Poznań, in 1929 in her *Diary*. Did she say anything in response to Jesus? Or was she so surprised and moved that she was at a loss for words? She writes nothing further about this. A few years later, however, she will be on such intimate terms with Jesus that she will talk to Him as to a Master and best friend at the same time.

The Little Kierskie Lake — one of the two in Kiekrz — is picturesque, and we know that Faustina was sensitive to the beauty of nature. The lake is rather small, not very wide and also shallow, with an irregular shoreline, surrounded by an abundance of trees, mainly alders and willows. Various birds nest in the dense clusters of reeds that stretch far into the water: wild ducks, grebes, coots, terns, laughing gulls, harriers, little bitterns, and many other species. From time immemorial, locals have referred to the lake as Święte (Holy Lake), or Półświęte (Half-holy Lake). Perhaps they sensed that one truly saintly encounter — between Jesus and a holy mystic — would be recorded in the eternal memory of the world right here.

Jesus stood next to Faustina — not opposite her. He stood beside her, and together they looked at the water's surface. How long did this last? Just a moment, or maybe longer? Did Jesus say anything else?

A view of Little Kierskie Lake close to the convent in Kiekrz.

Her encounter with Jesus and the words He spoke were, in Sr. Faustina's words, "a great consolation." Some months — perhaps a year or so — earlier, in the fall of 1928, she had come to the end of a very significant but difficult phase in her spiritual life: the dark night of the soul, when it seemed to her that God had abandoned her. After having undergone that experience, which is lived by every mystic at some point, she was enjoying a time of "loving repose," as she referred to it in her *Diary* (115). Meeting Jesus in Kiekrz was a part of this as well.

Faustina stayed at the lake until the evening. It happened to be her day off work. She was making a one-day retreat and had more time for individual prayer. The time at the lake passed so quickly that it seemed to her she had been standing there for only a short while.

Eighty-two years pass, and it is September 2011. It's the very same lake, the same willow tree lane along which Sr. Faustina walked. Only two of the trees are missing. On the shore stands a tall alder tree with a small shrine on it, decorated with numerous rosaries brought here by those who had come to seek echoes of that historic encounter before I did. A man sits on a bench. Once roused from a state of contemplation, he explains that since he moved here from Poznań two years ago, he cannot get enough of this view. A flock of swans drifts by without a sound. Silence. Nobody else is around.

The exact date of Faustina's encounter with Jesus is unknown. It took place between July 7, 1929, when Sr. Faustina arrived at the Kiekrz convent, and October 1929, when she returned to the Congregation's house at Żytnia Street in Warsaw. It must have been a sunny day, because she stayed at the lake until evening.

Faustina must have come here more often: the convent is just two or three hundred yards away. Once, all you needed to do was cross the convent's field, step over the railroad tracks which are part of the Poznań-Szczecin line, and run through the enormous orchard with 4,000 trees that once surrounded the convent. Sister Paula can still remember the taste of the pears that were grown here until the 1960s. Now, the walk from the convent to the lake takes somewhat longer since crossing the railroad tracks at the old spot is no longer allowed because it is unsafe. It is a prettier journey, however, since the lane was improved for Sr. Faustina's 100th birthday in 2005.

When Faustina came to Kiekrz in July 1929, the local community of Our Lady of Mercy had just been established. The sisters had settled here in March 1928, scarcely a year before. They came to the region of Wielkopolska (Greater Poland) in response to the invitation of Fr. Valentine Dymek, later the Archbishop of Poznań. They took over the care of a girls' home from the ladies of the Poznań society Przystań (The Haven). They took up residence in a house far from the center of a village that is itself nearly seven-and-a-half miles from Poznań. At first, they rented and then, in 1932, purchased a 40-acre farm from the Hübner family, who themselves were moving to Germany.

Kiekrz was located within Prussian-occupied territories until the end of World War I. In 1919, after the Polish victory in the Greater Poland Uprising of 1918-1919, the village was returned to the newly reconstituted Poland. At that time, many Germans decided to leave. In 1921, Kiekrz had a population of 459, of which 154 were Germans; six years later, in 1927, only 65 German inhabitants remained.

Having been moved to her community's different houses, Sr. Faustina now found herself in Polish territories for the first time, albeit territories that had been under Prussian rule for over a century. She must have noted differences between life in Kiekrz and in her home village of Głogowiec, where years of Russian rule had left their mark. In Kiekrz, the farmhouses were big and built of brick, while the farms were larger, with tens of acres of land each. In contrast, Głogowiec was inhabited by poor smallholders, who — like Faustina's father — cultivated tiny parcels of land, about seven to 10 acres in size. The houses were small, built of stone and clay, and had thatched roofs. In the Wielkopolska region, the soil was more fertile, and agricultural practices were more advanced.

Nonetheless, the living conditions in the spacious, two-story brick house where the sisters lived in Kiekrz were quite primitive. There was not even electricity. Initially, the house was occupied by four sisters and 20 girls placed in the Congregation's care by county authorities or Poznań's social services. The financial support for the girls' home came from the farm and orchard, and from 1934 on, when the sisters opened a bakery, from the more than 2,600 pounds (over a ton) of bread they baked weekly. The new source of income allowed them to increase the number of pupils to 40. This, however, did not take place until five years after Sr. Faustina's stay in Kiekrz.

Traveling by train, St. Faustina left Warsaw, changed trains in Poznań, and then arrived in Kiekrz. After that, she still had to travel the roughly two miles from the station to the convent. Her visit was short. She came in order to fill in for a cook, Sr. Modesta Rzeczkowska, who was ill. The Superior of the convent in Kiekrz was Sr. Xavier Olszamowska, the same sister who, a quarter of a century later, would be the person made responsible in the Congregation for gathering materials for the cause of Sr. Faustina's informative process for beatification.

The house, once hidden from the eyes of passersby by the orchard, is now clearly visible from the busy Kierska Street. Pale-colored plaster now covers the red brick of the convent walls, as well as those of a small utility shed that now holds a small exhibition of items from Sr. Faustina's time. These two buildings were already in existence in 1929. The bakery on the left, which was built in the 1930s, is now a story higher than it used to be. The largest building, to the right, with a children's playground in front of it, only dates back to the 1990s. It houses a shelter for single mothers and a daycare center for local children.

The interior of the convent has been rearranged slightly since Sr. Faustina stayed here. The kitchen where she worked was on the first floor to the left of the entrance. Now, only the old door remains. It leads to the chapel that has been expanded to include the space of the former kitchen.

The sisters called the convent in Kiekrz the House of the Sacred Heart after the chapel located there. According to Fr. Edward Nawrot — historian and author of a monograph about Kiekrz as well as the long-serving pastor of the local parish — the chapel on the site had been open to use by local villagers since its very establishment in July 1928, when it was consecrated by Bishop

Karol Radoński. In other religious houses, such openness to the public became the norm during World War II.

From 1929 onwards, the sisters in Kiekrz had a chaplain named Fr. Ladislaus Karasiewicz. Sources indicate that he was already here before July 1929 when Sr. Faustina arrived. At the time, he was a 39-year-old priest, well educated, a graduate of a German school where he studied classical languages. After several years of studies at the University in Freiburg and at the seminaries in Poznań and in Gniezno, he had to interrupt his studies and scholarly work due to a respiratory illness. He was leading the retreat on the day when Sr. Faustina encountered Jesus at the lake.

Did she tell Fr. Karasiewicz about this encounter during her next confession? We will never know.

It is highly probable that during her stay in Kiekrz, Sr. Faustina visited the local church under the patronage of St. Michael the Archangel and the Assumption of the Blessed Virgin Mary. A view of the Great Kierskie Lake can be enjoyed from the hill where this Baroque church with a Rococo-style interior is built. The church is located in the part of Kiekrz that was incorporated into the city of Poznań in 1987, while the convent remains outside the city limits. Perhaps the future saint visited the church with the other sisters and the girls from the home for the unveiling of the statue of Jesus in front of the church. The statue was funded by the people of Kiekrz in thanksgiving to God for their regained national independence.

Sister Faustina left Kiekrz, at the latest, in October 1929. The Superior of the convent, Mother Olszamowska, wrote as follows to Mother General Michael Moraczewska about Faustina: "My impression is that her interior life is very profound and that she has been granted special graces by God."

Chapter Nine

Płock

1930-1932

'These Words Do Not Come from Me'

THE BUILDING AT NO. 16 ON THE SOUTHERN SIDE OF THE SQUARE KNOWN AS THE OLD MARKET IN PŁOCK, Mazovia Province, is two stories high. Looking at it closely, one can observe a certain lack of harmony in the structure. On the right, a window — bigger than the others — has been walled up. There used to be a large glass door there in the 1930s. It led straight from the Old Market Square to the bakery belonging to the Congregation of the Sisters of Our Lady of Mercy where the residents of Płock could buy bread. Faustina Kowalska would stand behind the counter.

Nobody knows how long she worked there, but it is certain that this was her main occupation during her stay in the Płock convent. How many city residents — customers of the convent bakery — unwittingly met this holy mystic while shopping? How many of them spoke with her?

A plaque on the adjacent house informs passersby that it was in Płock that Sr. Faustina's mission began: "In this house, on February 22, 1931, St. Sr. Faustina had her first revelation of the Merciful Jesus." The phrase "in this house" refers to the premises, because the two-story building where the vision actually took place no longer exists.

Sister Faustina came to Płock in May or June 1930, and she remained there until November 1932. Her stay was occasionally interrupted by short periods when she would relocate to the house in Biała, which was affiliated with the Płock convent. The Guardian Angel Care Facility — as the Płock house was called — was home to over 30 sisters and approximately 100 wards, girls aged 14 to 18. The girls were given an elementary school education and received vocational training there. Laundering, embroidery, and the bakery were the primary means of sustenance for the house. The facility also had a special patron — Bishop Anthony Julian Nowowiejski, a man who did much for the development of the

city and the local church. As a young priest, he contributed to the foundation of the convent and its educational institution. In 1889, along with Mother
Columba Łabanowska, he founded the Congregation of Divine Love in Płock,
whose mission — much like that of the Congregation of the Sisters of Our Lady
of Mercy — was to provide care for women in need of deep moral conversion. In
1899, thanks to Fr. Nowowiejski's efforts, these two congregations were united
into a single entity.

In 1900, in the wake of this re-organization, a new convent complex
consisting of three one- and two-story buildings was established in the Old
Market Square in Płock. Located in the heart of present-day Płock, these
buildings occupy street Nos. 14, 16 — where the bakery used to be — and
18. Architecturally, they do not stand out from the other buildings surrounding
the Market Square. After renovations, they mirror their counterparts from pre-
World War II pictures. On the inside, however, none of the spaces can be said
to have remained unchanged since Sr. Faustina's time. The convent was heavily
vandalized after the Communist regime forcefully evicted the sisters and their
pupils in 1950 to make room for a vocational school for boys.

It is likely that a window replaced the door that used to lead to the bakery
while the boys' school was housed there. Eventually, the opening was walled
up completely. When the nuns returned to their house in 1990, they found it
almost entirely different, with the interior having been rebuilt and rearranged
repeatedly. The walls of the façade were supported by wooden posts. The only
parts of the building that have kept something resembling their original form
are the bakery and the laundry room, located in the battered outbuilding next
to house No. 16.

Photographs from 1928 show what the nuns' bakery looked like. Girls
from the school and the sisters, with rolled-up habit sleeves, are putting unbaked
loaves into the ovens using long-handled bread paddles. Perhaps Sr. Faustina
even helped the other sisters with the baking. It was done in two shifts — a
day and a night shift. In 2006, the sisters set up a multi-media, interactive St.
Faustina museum in the former bakery, which had so miraculously survived.
They recreated the bakery and a convent cell, complete with period pieces from
the saint's time.

The bakery in the Płock convent where Sr. Faustina would occasionally help out.

Sister Faustina's job in the bakery was to help Sr. Christine Korzeniowska. For a while, she was responsible for the cash register in the store. She had so many duties that — as Sr. Marceline Kobrzyniecka recalls — she would come to the store earlier than the other sisters and stay later. Perhaps it was during her stay in Płock that Sr. Faustina decided, "I will not allow myself to be so absorbed in the whirlwind of work as to forget about God. I will spend all my free moments at the feet of the Master hidden in the Blessed Sacrament" (*Diary,* 82).

Sister Faustina — who had a contemplative soul — learned to pray without interrupting her work. The religious rule of silence helped her. It was easier for her, however, to say short prayers while cooking (in Płock, she also spent some time working as a cook) than while serving customers behind the counter in the store. This kind of work, though, gave Faustina an opportunity to meet people and observe their various wants and hardships, all the ways in which they were in need of Divine Mercy.

Through the glass doors, she was able to take in the life of the city — with its population of more than 30,000 residents — which was just beginning to feel the painful effects of the Great Depression. Through the display window, she was able to catch glimpses of civil servants hurrying to city hall and of teenage boys running in the opposite direction to the Stanislaus Małachowski all-male high school — Poland's oldest school, the so-called "Małachowianka," which has been providing instruction uninterruptedly since the 12th century. She would see the residents of Płock walking in the park, which, before World War II, was located in the center of the Market Square. But what she could also observe were the dramatic events that took place here in the 1930s. Due to the growing economic crisis and the resulting unemployment, workers would picket in front of city hall demanding "work and bread."

On March 29, 1930 — shortly before Sr. Faustina arrived in Płock — riots broke out in front of city hall. A few people were wounded and over a dozen arrested. A year later, in July 1931 — during Faustina's stay at the Płock convent — "a crowd of the unemployed marched in the streets, shattering glass display windows as they passed. Stones were thrown at city hall, and the State Labor Agency building was entirely devastated," warned the city council in a special memo to the authorities in Warsaw. Two people were killed, and over a dozen wounded. In 1932, city councilors noted that "the squalor of the unemployed has become more dire, which means the city streets are teeming with them, especially women with babies who are demanding employment for their husbands and breadwinners. On more than one occasion, the police have had to drive crowds away from city hall." Petty crime and prostitution were on the rise. The Caritas organization, other charities, and municipal organizations were handing out meals and food stamps to the hungry. Beggars would come to the door of the convent of the Sisters of Our Lady of Mercy in the Old Market Square. They also came to the bakery where they would sometimes steal the bread.

Sister Bozenna Pniewska said of Sr. Faustina that "when a loaf of bread was stolen, she suffered not because of the material loss, but because of the offence to God, and she promised that she would pray for the person who stole the bread."

The pre-War location of the kitchen where Sr. Faustina worked is unknown. Sister Paulina Kosińska remembers that "the kitchen was a mere passage way — a hallway. It was so narrow that she had to have angelic virtue not to get annoyed with people who were constantly pushing past her [Sr. Faustina], and there was no other way to go around. The doorbell was always ringing, and she — always smiling, always composed — never showed any sign of impatience. The moaning and complaints only started when Sr. Faustina left and another sister took over her duties. … Only then did we realize how much she was able to put up with, never betraying any dissatisfaction in her words or gestures."

Sister Joachim Głuc recalls that "she was overjoyed when the sisters were happy with her cooking. She never refused anyone anything if the food stores in the cupboard allowed her to accommodate them."

Faustina did not describe these incidents in the *Diary*, which she only began to keep in Vilnius two years later. In the *Diary*, she scarcely wrote about her past — just a few notes about the most important events. One of these was her encounter with Jesus on February 22, 1931. This was when she heard His command that an image of Him should be painted in the form in which He showed Himself to her — with a hand raised in the gesture of blessing and two rays, red and pale, emanating "from beneath the garment, slightly drawn aside at the breast"— and with the signature "Jesus, I trust in You" (*Diary*, 47).

This was the moment when Sr. Faustina's mission to spread the message of Divine Mercy began. It was in Płock that Jesus first expressed His desire for the establishment of the Feast of Divine Mercy on the Second Sunday of Easter (the so-called Low Sunday) as Divine Mercy Sunday.

Jesus appeared to Faustina in her convent cell — a place that no longer exists. The building where Faustina lived on the second floor was located toward the back of the convent complex, to the left of the entrance. It was adjacent to No. 14 and the lot belonging to the Małachowianka high school. The building was still standing after World War II. In 1990, when the Congregation repossessed its property, the sisters placed a statue of the Merciful Jesus on the spot where the apparition took place. But recently, when the entire yard became a construction site, the statue had to be moved to the house in Biała. A new church, a retreat house, and a pilgrims' guesthouse are being built on the site. On the very spot where the Lord Jesus appeared to Faustina, the sisters are erecting a Blessed Sacrament chapel where there will be Perpetual Adoration. The surviving parts of the central building containing the bakery and the laundry room are to be incorporated into the new shrine, and the existing interactive multi-media St. Faustina museum is to be further developed. The sheer number of pilgrims — up to 200,000 a year — has made the expansion of the shrine a necessity.

Already during Jesus' first apparition to her in Płock, He communicated the promise to Sr. Faustina that whoever would revere the image painted according to His instructions would not perish but be saved. The renowned Polish theologian Fr. Ignatius Różycki — a professor of dogmatic theology who conducted a thorough analysis of the content of the revelations of Jesus to Sr. Faustina — wrote that the second promise, although not spelled out, stems from the role of the image itself in being "a channel *of grace*" of Divine Mercy. This means that anyone whose veneration of this image expresses their unyielding trust in Divine Mercy can receive "all salutary graces and all temporal blessings" sooner and to a greater extent.

Of course, "it is not the image that grants the graces, but Jesus, through the image," as the image itself does not have this power. A condition for receiving all the graces, as Jesus would tell Sr. Faustina in subsequent revelations, is that, in addition to one's trust in God, one should exercise mercy towards one's neighbors. Faustina once said to Sr. Damiana Ziółek, "I have heard the Lord Jesus say that, on the Day of Judgment, He will be judging the world only in terms of mercy, because God is all Mercy. And by acting out of mercy, or neglecting mercy, a person determines their own judgment."

In Płock, Jesus told Faustina of His demand for the establishment of the Feast of Divine Mercy. He would restate this demand several more times. Overall, Jesus spoke about it in 14 of His apparitions. During Mass on the first Sunday after Easter, a passage from the Gospel of St. John is read that describes the moment when Jesus, on the eighth day after His Resurrection, entered the Cenacle in spite of the locked door. He greeted the disciples gathered there with the words, "Peace be with you." It was Jesus as He was at that moment who appeared to Sr. Faustina, and this is how He wishes to be portrayed in the image. "This scene from the Cenacle," writes Sr. Elizabeth Siepak, "is all one with the events of Good Friday: the crucifixion, and the piercing of the Sacred Heart of Jesus with a lance. The Lord Jesus said: **'These two rays issued forth from the very depths of My tender mercy when My agonized Heart was opened by a lance on the Cross'** (*Diary*, 299). ... Saint Thomas, quoting here the Fathers of the Church, connects the symbolism of the water and the blood with the Sacraments of Baptism and the Eucharist, but the same symbolism can also be applied to the remaining Sacraments." In short, the image represents the merciful love of God towards man, which was most fully revealed in the life, Passion, death, and Resurrection of Jesus. This is why this portrayal of Jesus is called the image of Divine Mercy.

As Sr. Faustina noted in the *Diary*, just as Jesus made important promises to those who revere Him in His image, He made important promises in relation to the observance of Divine Mercy Sunday. Of all the promises relating to the various forms of Divine Mercy devotion, these are the greatest. Jesus told Faustina that anyone who goes to Confession and receives Holy Communion on Divine Mercy Sunday shall be granted **"complete remission of sins and punishment"** (*Diary*, 300). This implies not only the remission of temporal punishment due for one's sins, as granted by indulgences, but also remission of culpability itself. Father Różycki stresses that this promise is theologically permissible — that is, its lawfulness may be demonstrated from intrinsic reasons or extrinsic authority.[27] In order for the promise to have its effect, however, one must meet certain requirements, involving not only Confession and the reception of the Eucharist on Divine Mercy Sunday, but also having trust in God and being merciful towards one's neighbor — the foundation of the devotion of Divine Mercy. It is the ardent desire of Jesus — writes Fr. Różycki — "that the Feast of Mercy should be, for all people, and especially for sinners, an extremely effective recourse, incomparably more effective than all the other forms of the Divine Mercy devotion."

From the moment of her encounter with Jesus on February 22, 1931, Sr. Faustina prayed for a confessor who would help her understand what was happening in her spiritual life. At that time in Płock, and then throughout her entire religious life, she attracted the sisters' attention with the way she prayed.

Sister Paulina Kosińska remembers, "Sometimes, when she was kneeling in the chapel, it was as if she were asleep; she never sighed or moved. I thought, 'She is tired and has fallen asleep,' even though she was not kneeling in the pew, but directly on the floor in front of the Blessed Sacrament."

Many sisters remembered afterwards that Faustina would interrupt her work for a brief moment to go to the chapel and kneel before the Blessed Sacrament. Whenever she was able to — that is, after finishing all of her convent duties, and having received her Superior's permission — she would go to the chapel for Adoration. When she was alone, she lay prostrate in the form of the cross. She prayed the Stations of the Cross every day. This form of prayer was recommended but not obligatory for the sisters in the Congregation. Faustina, however, cherished it in a particular way.

She had a special reverence for the Blessed Sacrament, which was also expressed in her full religious name: Maria Faustina of the Most Blessed Sacrament. Receiving the Eucharist was the most important moment of her day. In it, she experienced the Real Presence of Christ. After receiving Holy Communion, she often experienced infused contemplation, accompanied by words heard interiorly and visions. This was quickly followed by the closest union of the soul with God — that is, a mystical union. In this state, writes Ludmilla Grygiel, Sr. Faustina experienced "a reiteration of the mystery of the Incarnation" of the Son of God and, mystically, she was able to repeatedly witness

His Passion. Ludmilla Grygiel adds that, in the history of mysticism, this is a rare case of experiencing "the close relationship between the Incarnation and the saving Passion, which brings out in strong relief the commonly known, but not always deeply comprehended, truth that Christ was born into this world in order to suffer and die for sinners." Sister Faustina would soon learn in the mystical union of her soul with God that the Incarnation of, and Redemption through, the Son of God, was the greatest expression of God's love towards mankind.

Faustina was already aware of the effectiveness of her intercessory prayer. For this reason, she asked Sr. Bozenna Pniewska — as one of the teachers who had direct contact with the girls — to point out an especially difficult pupil, promising to pray for her. Sister Pniewska recounts, "Indeed, the ward whom she included in her prayers converted, and as I have learned since, she died in a holy way. Once [Faustina] told me something that had to do with my own soul. I ignored it. Then she repeated, 'Please know this, Sister: these words do not come from me.' When I gave it some thought, I understood how great a significance this had for my spiritual growth."

In Płock, Sr. Faustina would pray before the Blessed Sacrament not only in the convent chapel, but probably in other nearby churches as well. Atop Tumskie Hill — only a few hundred yards from the house of the sisters — stands the massive 12th-century cathedral where Bishop Nowowiejski, a friend of the Congregation, celebrated Mass. While Faustina was living in Płock, an altar dedicated to St. Thérèse of the Child Jesus — a saint near and dear to her heart — was consecrated there. The cathedral is the oldest church in the Mazovia region and dates back to the greatest period in the history of Płock when it was the seat of the Mazovian dynasty. Its crypts are the final resting place of several Polish rulers. Not far from the convent, by the Old Market Square, there is one more church — St. Bartholomew's Parish Church — which is also the church of the Congregation. Masses for the pilgrims — now too numerous to fit in the small convent chapel of the Congregation of the Sisters of Our Lady of Mercy — are usually held here.

Chapter Ten

Biała

1930-1932

'I Follow the Truth, and It Frees Me from All Hardships'

THE PORCH WHERE FAUSTINA SAW JESUS NO LONGER EXISTS. The same goes for the house where she lived with the other sisters. Only its stone foundations remain, among which an orange cat warms itself in the September sun during my visit.

Jesus appeared to Faustina on this very spot while the roses were in bloom. It could have been 1930, 1931, or 1932, since it was during this time that Faustina lived at the Płock convent, from where she would come for shorter or longer stints to the Congregation's house in Biała, about six miles away. The Biała farm, with its 99 acres of land, supplied the food for the Płock convent and facility. It was also a place where the sisters came to rest, because in Płock's city center there was no room for recreation.

"Sister Faustina visited this place a few times to recuperate," says the Superior of the house, Sr. Tobias Wilkosz, interrupting her work in the garden.

Nobody knows whether the flower garden in the interwar period was located in the same place as it is today, but it is certain that it contained many rose bushes.

"One day, I had picked the prettiest roses to decorate the room of a certain person," Faustina wrote in the *Diary*. "When I was approaching the porch, I saw Jesus standing there. In a kindly way He asked me, **My daughter, to whom are you taking these flowers?**" Faustina was speechless. "My silence was my reply to the Lord, because I recognized immediately that I had a very subtle attachment to this person, which I had not noticed before. Suddenly Jesus disappeared. At the same moment I threw the flowers on the ground and went before the Blessed Sacrament, my heart filled with gratitude for the grace of knowing myself" (*Diary,* 71).

Who was this "certain person" for whom Faustina had picked the flowers? Was it, as some authors would have it, Mother General Michael Moraczewska, during a visit to the convent in Biała? This is difficult to verify, since we neither know the exact date of the incident nor the dates of the visits by the Mother General. Perhaps Sr. Faustina was carrying the flowers to the room of the chaplain, Fr. Peter Alexander Trojańczyk, who often visited Biała in 1930 through 1931, when he took up permanent residence there. Sister Romana Szulecka — who was not yet a nun at the time, although she did live in Biała where she met Sr. Faustina, under whose influence she joined the Congregation — believes that it was the Mother General. She knew, based on the sisters' stories, that the flowers were not intended for Fr. Trojańczyk's room. "The sisters used to say that it was impossible that she was taking the flowers to Fr. Trojańczyk, or that she had a special fondness for him. But Mother General, with whom she shared a mutual understanding, she loved much," remembers Sr. Romana.

The incident on the porch shows that Faustina's most important spiritual director was Jesus Himself. He was constantly watching over her and helping her to purify her soul from that which was not yet consumed by the fire of the dark night of the senses, which she had experienced as a novice and after making her first vows in Kraków. He was purifying her from all temporal attachments, even the one she felt for the Superior of her Congregation. He was aiding her in freeing herself from everything in her heart that was still of the world. He was doing this in order to help her soul enter into complete union with God.[28]

Nobody knows how many times Sr. Faustina visited Biała, or how long she stayed. On the basis of her notes in the *Diary* and two letters she wrote in Biała — in addition to what Sr. Zita Jastrzębska and other sisters related — it seems she visited Biała several times. Overall, she spent more than a year here. She came twice in the summer and once in the winter. The first time, and perhaps also later on, she was sent here by the Superior of the Płock convent, Mother Rose Kłobukowska, to benefit from a change of climate and to recuperate. This does not mean that Sr. Faustina was not working during these periods. Quite the contrary.

Sister Zita Jastrzębska — who met Faustina in Biała in 1930 or 1931 — recalled in 1966, "I do not remember exactly how long she stayed, perhaps a year, or less. From Biała she was transferred directly to Kraków."

Indeed, more than 30 years after certain events took place, Sr. Zita's memory failed her somewhat. It was in November 1932 that Faustina left Biała — or, more precisely, the main convent in Płock — and by that time, Sr. Zita was no longer there. Faustina did not go straight to Kraków, but to Warsaw. She did not go to Łagiewniki until six months after that. But Sr. Jastrzębska's memories reveal that — in the period when she was administering the Biała farm — Sr. Faustina stayed there for longer stretches; a few months at a time. Also, importantly, she stated that Faustina was sent from Płock to work in the kitchen.

It is likely that during her next stay in Biała, as can be deduced from a letter she wrote to Sr. Louise Gadzina, Sr. Faustina worked in the fields. Additionally, she helped Sr. Thecla arrange the flowers in the chapel, but this was not so much a duty as a pleasure. Possibly another reason why Mother Rose Kłobukowska sent Faustina to the small house in Biała was because of the interest she raised when the rumor spread among the sisters in Płock that she had seen Jesus.

Sister Faustina remembered well the summer when she saw Jesus on the porch in Biała. The house with a porch was still here in the 1980s. Then, after much effort, the sisters finally received permission from the Communist authorities to build a new home. The old house with a shingled roof, partly built of stone, did not retain heat very well. It was so cold that in winter you could scrape frost from the walls.

The Płock convent purchased the house together with a farm allocated from the Brwilno manor estate in August 1928. The building was not large. There were three windows to the right of the entrance and three to the left. On the ground floor, in addition to the chapel, there was a kitchen. The upper floor was occupied by the sisters and their wards, who would come in the summer to help with the farm work. The house was cramped and offered rather primitive living conditions. There was no electricity, running water, or sewage system. This is why the sisters were happy when they were finally able to build a large, two-story, L-shaped house in the 1980s. The expansion was all the more urgent as, by then, more sisters were staying there than before World War II. This is because some of the nuns settled in Biała after the Congregation was evicted by the Communists from its Płock convent in 1950. The house is a typical modernist "cube" similar to many others that have littered the Polish architectural landscape since the period of late Communism. The sisters built it very close to the old house for a simple reason: they had only 12 acres of land at this time. The rest of the farm had been seized by the Communists. Each scrap of land had to be used to the fullest.

Unfortunately, the old house stood too close to the new one to be left there. Eventually it was demolished. Today, the sisters would probably give anything to have been able to save it and have the chance to put together a memorial to St. Faustina.

Only old photographs can show us what the house where she lived looked like. One such picture has miraculously survived and shows three women in front of the house, Faustina on the left, another sister on the right, and a young woman wearing a dark dress and a white cap in the middle — probably one of the girls. The clothes suggest that it must have been a warm day — spring or early fall.

Sister Faustina was staying in Biała in the winter of 1930. This is quite certain, as on December 17, 1930, she sent a letter to Sr. Justine Gołofit from Biała. She gave Płock as her location at the top of the page, but went on to explain that she was in the affiliated house in Biała. "I am currently in Biała. Sister Aloysius and Sr. Zita are also here. It is very nice in Biała; the farmland is quite vast." Three sisters would usually reside in Biała. Perhaps it was during Faustina's stay — or perhaps the following winter — that an incident took place that was still talked about by the sisters many years afterwards. Sister Zita did not mention it, but she did contribute another piece of information that is not without significance for Faustina's story: "When we were in Biała, we could not receive Holy Communion every day. The chaplain only came once a week to celebrate Mass, and on other days two sisters would go to the parish church while the third stayed behind to keep an eye on the house."

One day, the frost was so bitter that one of the two sisters whose turn it was to go to church decided not to walk to the village. The other one was Faustina, who insisted on going alone, in spite of her Superior's protests. Sister Simone Nalewajk remembered, "She was allowed to go on condition that she put on the huge sheepskin coat, which was used by our coachman. Sister Faustina, without a second thought, put the coat on, even though it was larger than she was, and went to church." This story was retold in the convent for a long time afterwards.

From the sisters' house, you could see the tower of the church in Biała where Sr. Faustina attended Mass. The church, under the patronage of St. Hedwig of Silesia, stands on a tall hill. The shortcut to the church across the fields takes 10 minutes, but walking along the road takes much longer. The cruciform Gothic Revival church dates back to the late 19th century and was founded by Stanislaus Piwnicki, the owner of the nearby Srebrny estate. A portrait of St. Faustina and the image of the Merciful Jesus, which are displayed on the church's façade, remind passersby of the extraordinary inhabitant of the nearby convent house.

Sister Zita Jastrzębska remembers, "She [Sr. Faustina] was dutiful, kind, composed, and introverted. I remember having some issues with certain sisters in community life. But never with Sr. Faustina. She was always modest and humble."

Sister Zita was not the only one to characterize Faustina as composed and introverted. This must have been quite a change. Prior to joining the Congregation, her employers described her as having a lively character. The introversion must have come as a result of her spiritual experiences, her focus on them, and the growing union of her soul with God.

Humility is a difficult virtue, but it is particularly indispensable to the religious life. Sister Zita mentioned seeing Faustina cry after a strict reprimand from Sr. Aloysius. This was on the feast of Epiphany, on January 6. She does not say which year, but it could have been 1931. Sister Zita Jastrzębska remembers, "Sister Faustina went to church. She brought back blessed chalk and was writing [the names of the three kings] on the lintels of the doors with it.[29] Sister Aloysius scolded her, saying that this was not Faustina's responsibility, but hers, and demanding that she hand over the chalk to her."

Faustina definitely visited Biała in the summer of 1932; she wrote a letter to Sr. Louise Gadzina from Biała, dated August 2. Its contents indicate that she had been here for some time at that point, which is confirmed by Sr. Jastrzębska. "I have some spare time," Faustina wrote, "as I do not have to go to work in the fields because it is raining." She shared with Sr. Louise her reflections on the meaning of suffering, and she wrote that the sisters needed to pray for each other, for the girls, for all souls recommended to them, and for the entire world. "I live by faith and that is why I am happy and satisfied with what God gives me. It is true that in Warsaw I drew much profit for my soul from the help of the superiors, and I am grateful to God. But if God does not give me this help, then too I conform myself to His holy will just the same." She wrote this letter over a year after the apparition of Jesus in Płock on February 22, 1931. She did not mention this vision, only saying: "Dear Sister, I push onward, never minding if the sun shines, or if the rain is falling and the thunder rolling. I follow the truth, and it frees me from all hardships."

According to Fr. Joachim R. Bar, six sisters and about 20 girls lived permanently in Biała up until World War II. We do not know the source of Fr. Bar's information, as in fact the number of sisters and of their wards fluctuated. The nuns' recollections suggest that when Sr. Faustina was living here, there were fewer of them. In August 1932 — in the thick of harvest time — Faustina wrote:

"Three sisters are permanent residents: Sr. Thecla, Sr. Germana, and Sr. Isidora; and others come for the summer from Płock, so do the children [wards]. Currently, there are 13 persons to do the work." Thirteen sisters and wards — aided only by three men who would take care of the horses — worked 111 acres of fields, without any mechanical equipment. The work must have been incredibly hard. The farm in Biała supplied the sisters and pupils from the Congregation's house in Płock — about a hundred in all — with flour, milk, meat, and vegetables.

The food was transported to town by means of horse-drawn wagons. The sisters, however, would often walk all the way to Płock. They would take short-cuts through fields where there are now oil refineries, whose smokestacks can be seen from the Biała house windows. How many times did Sr. Faustina hurry along these paths?

What also remains from the Biała period are the memories of one of the wards, Ursula, who, having returned to the Płock convent, told Sr. Paulina Kosińska about "what intelligence Sr. Faustina has, and even more heart. After having worked so hard in the kitchen, instead of finally resting in the shade, she would entertain us to make our day more fun."

After 1990, the sisters recovered 82.7 acres — the majority of the land that had been seized from them. However, they no longer work the land, leasing it instead. They have different responsibilities now — running a preschool for local children and a home for single mothers, where 350 women have found refuge in the course of the last 20 years. But around the house, just like they used to, the sisters tend a fruit orchard and grow vegetables and potatoes. On hot summer days, they enjoy the shade of a great northern red oak that was there when Sr. Faustina first came to Biała.

Chapter Eleven

Walendów

1932, 1936

'My Love Deceives No One'

"IT IS NOT TRUE THAT SR. FAUSTINA LIVED IN WALENDÓW FOR ONLY A SHORT WHILE. She was here for 15 years." Sister Amata Stryjewska, with a smile on her lips, says nothing more. This almost 80-year-old nun, with a face that looks 20 years younger and an ailing heart, knows well what she is talking about because, after all, she "shared" a convent cell with St. Faustina. But this was many years after the future saint was sent to Walendów, located in the Warsaw suburbs, for the first time.

On the whole, the matter of Sr. Faustina's visits to the Walendów convent is confusing. Officially, she was here twice — in 1932 and 1936. The third time, right before her death, she really did come but by supernatural means — thanks to the gift of bilocation. She visited in order to meet with Sr. Placida Putyra. Finally and quite recently, she "spent" 15 years here.

Saint Faustina's last visit was completely different than the previous ones. Indeed, the word "visit" may seem like a bit of a stretch — but certainly not to those who venerate relics and who invoke the intercession of the saints.

"It all started in 1993," begins Sr. Amata. "After the beatification of Sr. Faustina, relics had to be prepared. Someone in the Congregation came up with the idea that I should occupy myself with this, seeing that I can no longer do strenuous work on account of my heart problems."

Thus, Sr. Amata Stryjewska — having taken the necessary oath — took on the preparation of the relics.

"I was given St. Faustina's precious bones by Sr. Beata Piekut, the vice-postulator of the beatification process. I would split them into tiny particles. Her precious ribs actually crumbled to powder when touched, because they were so riddled by tuberculosis, but the joints were very difficult to crumble. I toiled away at preparing those tiny splinters," recalls Sr. Amata. "I would place the bone on a white linen napkin, cover it with another napkin, and then hit it with a small hammer."

At first, Sr. Amata prepared 700 crosses for the Congregation. These were given to all the professed sisters. The crosses were opened up. Sr. Amata would place a drop of glue inside and then sprinkle in some powder from Sr. Faustina's bones. Next, it was time to prepare relics in capsules, which parishes and religious orders from around the world requested from the authorities of the Congregation. Sister Amata did not count how many of them she prepared. It was certainly in the thousands.

"I placed the relics in round brass capsules with a small glass viewing panel," she remembers. "I lined each capsule with red cloth. I then placed a little white textile 'flower' in it, and I glued a tiny bit of St. Faustina's bone to one of the petals. The capsule was signed and sealed in a box by the vice-postulator."

These brass capsules are now found in reliquaries displayed in churches worldwide.

"Sometimes, Mother General would call from Kraków requesting that 50 relic capsules be prepared for the following day," Sr. Amata continues. "So I sat down to work in the evening, and I got up from the table in the morning, not feeling tired at all. I would feel good during the entire following day, as if I had slept all night. It was the work and the power of God."

For Sr. Stryjewska, working with the relics of St. Faustina was something extraordinary, a gift from God and an opportunity for special prayers.

"I was happy that I could touch the holy bones. But I also realized that it put me under an obligation to be like her," says Sr. Amata. "I asked for and obtained many graces during this time. For myself, for others, and for the Congregation."

"Where did you keep the relics, Sister?" I asked.

"I can tell you that today. There was a special, well-secured place in my cell. Only two people knew about it: the vice-postulator and Mother General. I slept in one room with St. Faustina's precious bones. For 15 years in one cell!"

Turning to Sr. Faustina's stays there during her lifetime, she arrived in the Walendów suburb of Warsaw in November 1932. Above the gate leading to the property, the sisters placed an inscription with the name "Józefów-Ustronie (St. Joseph's Retreat)." The sign is gone now, but the same buildings are still there. On the right, there is a two-story administration building, to which a porch was added after World War II. On the left is the convent building, dating back to the early 19th century. The church right next to it was still under construction in

1932. Behind the church, on the left, is a large two-story house where the sisters' wards lived both before and after World War II. The outbuildings toward the back of the yard were built no more than 30 years ago. Before the war, there used to be a field where the gardens are currently located. Rows of potatoes and beets and patches of wheat used to grow just a few steps from the convent.

In 1932, Sr Faustina came to Walendów for an eight-day stay. Although it was only just over a week, it was very eventful. Here, she met the first confessor willing to assure her that her visions were supernatural and not a figment of her imagination. Here, too — as though to confirm the confessor's words — she saw Jesus exactly as she had seen Him in Płock, for a second time: with pale and red rays emanating from His Heart.

Sister Faustina came to Walendów for a retreat before beginning her third probation, that is, the five-month period of preparation before taking final vows. However, neither the admission to probation, nor her superiors' permission to go to Walendów for the retreat, proved easy to obtain. Quite the contrary. The admission to probation was decided by Mother General and the council of the Congregation, after consultation with the fully professed sisters of the convents where the candidate for the vows had spent any time. Some of the perpetually professed sisters in Płock opposed the admission of Sr. Faustina to these vows. After Jesus had appeared to Faustina in February 1931, asking that an image of Him should be painted, they judged her to be hysterical and endowed with an unhealthy imagination. Despite the unfavorable opinion of some of the sisters, Sr. Faustina arrived in Walendów on a November day in 1932, just as Jesus had foretold. She came with the Superior of the convent, Mother Valerie Wilczyńska. "Only Jesus can arrange things in such a way," she noted (*Diary*, 167).

The sisters probably traveled by horse-drawn carriage. The Walendów convent did own a Ford automobile in the 1930s, but nobody knows if they had it by 1932. It was easiest to travel from Warsaw by the Kraków route, nearly 12 and a half miles in the direction of Nadarzyn. A few years back, a few developments of exclusive single-family homes sprang up in Walendów and in neighboring Łazy. Their residents commute to the capital, and the majority of them would probably never guess that their fancy houses had been built on land that had once belonged to a religious congregation. In 1896, Count Gustav Przeździecki, who was active in bringing about both social and economic reforms, donated this property to the Congregation of the Sisters of Our Lady of Mercy. The Communist government confiscated it in 1950.

Sister Faustina must have heard about the convent in Walendów much earlier. It was an important place for the Congregation due to its enormous farm and an educational institution for approximately 100 girls. The farm was comprised of 505 "morgens" of farmland — about 741 acres — used mostly for fish ponds, but also with a mill, farm buildings, and an administrative building. Until 1913, only two or three sisters would live in Walendów to keep an eye on the farm and supervise the work of about a dozen families who occupied the former servants' quarters. The nuns did not move to Walendów from nearby Derdy until April 1913, when they had finished building the house for the girls, which had been started back in 1908. The construction of the convent was not completed until many years afterwards.

Farm work ensured the sisters and their wards a means of making a living. But the work itself was extremely hard. "There were only three of us there — Sr. Benigna, Sr. Sophia, and I — a postulant at the time," Sr. Zita Jastrzębska remembered, speaking of the time before 1913. "And the farm was enormous! Approximately 620 acres of land, about 138 acres of fish ponds, 50 cows, 24 horses. … You had to get up at one o'clock in the morning, wake the 10 milk-maids, oversee the milking and the cooling of the milk, and send the milk to a market in Warsaw before five in the morning. We produced about 560 liters of milk daily, for which we received up to 20 rubles.[30] Only after that did I wash up, put on my postulant's bonnet and walk to Derdy for Mass." In Derdy, there were 24 sisters. Later on, the work did not get any easier.

"The sisters were afraid of Walendów. They were worried when superiors sent them here," says Sr. Urbana Trybocka in the melodious accent of the Vilnius area. She has lived in Walendów since 1960 and can remember the older sisters telling her, as a very young nun, about the harsh living and working conditions in the convent before World War II. "They used to say with regret, 'We were given the farm as a present, but the work was so hard,'" adds Sr. Urbana.

Maria Olszewska, known as Camilla by the Congregation, remembers that time well. She is the only living ward of the Sisters of Our Lady of Mercy from that time in Walendów, where she has lived since 1931. She was sent there as a 13-year-old from another religious house, where she had been accepted as a young orphan. Even though she is over 90 years old, her health is amazingly good: she is active, cheerful, and has a phenomenal memory. While her hearing is getting worse, she is still a great singer.

Camilla was one of a hundred girls whom Sr. Faustina saw in Walendów in November 1932 when she came to make a retreat.

"We hardly had any contact with the sisters other than with those who were our caretakers," Camilla says. This is why, she explains, it is extremely unlikely that she ever spoke with the future saint.

The rehabilitation of the girls was carried out through work, as well as through general and religious education. Work and prayer, Mass, readings and spiritual reflection marked the rhythm of the day. The girls also belonged to the Sodality of the Blessed Virgin Mary, which required them to observe certain religious obligations and rules that, to a certain extent, resembled those followed by the nuns. However, due to their past or their dysfunctional family backgrounds, they could never join the Congregation. The girls were divided into two classes or groups.

"One group was assigned fieldwork and the other farm work, and the farm was huge, with horses, pigs, cows, sheep, chickens, ducks, and guinea fowl," says Camilla, who was in the field group. "Despite all that, the food was often scarce."

The wards' day began with a wake-up call at 5:30 a.m. Half an hour later, they attended Mass in the chapel. After breakfast, they went to work in the fields and on the farm. At noon, they had a break for lunch and a time of rest, during which the sisters read spiritual works to them. In the afternoon, they went back to work until supper at 6 p.m. Evening devotions at 7:30 p.m. marked the end of the day. Obligatory silence began at 9 p.m. In the fall and winter, the girls had more time for studying and for practical vocational training — courses in embroidery, cutting, and sewing. Discipline was strict.

"When one of us did something wrong, the punishment was kneeling for a long time or having a piece of paper stuck to our forehead. If you called someone 'stupid,' that is what the paper would say; for gossiping, it was a picture of a tongue," remembers Camilla.

All the girls wore the same uniforms: gray with stripes, for working; navy blue with white collars for festive occasions. They wore bonnets on their heads.

"Once, when we were at the market in Nadarzyn, people began to shout at us, 'Penitents, penitents!' and we did not know what that meant," Camilla says. She herself had been orphaned as a child, but most of the girls were sent here because of a shameful past, which had sometimes led them straight to a courtroom.

In November, the fields in Walendów are increasingly bare. It was like this in 1932 as well. Potatoes and beets had been harvested, and sheaves of wheat were stacked in granaries, waiting to be threshed. That year there was enough room and food to take in a group of nuns from the Congregation's other houses for a retreat. Sister Faustina was given a bed in a dorm, which was probably located on the second floor, possibly because it was easier for younger sisters to run up and down the wooden stairs than it was for the older ones, who therefore occupied the rooms on the ground floor. During the time of the retreat, there were no fewer than 12 or 13 sisters to a room. Up until 10 years ago, the sisters in the Walendów convent still lived in large rooms divided by curtains into several convent "cells." Today, each of the more than 20 sisters has a separate cell.

For many years, Sr. Amata Stryjewska slept in large dorm rooms shared with many others. It was not easy: "One sister is snoring; another wants the window open because she feels it's stuffy; another one wants it closed because she's cold; another is chatting away. But when you're young and enthusiastic, you can put up with anything. You also learn to accept these frustrations as a kind of mortification," she explains.

The 1932 retreat took place in the convent chapel upstairs in the wards' house. The statue of the Blessed Virgin Mary, the same that stands in the monastery gardens today, was on the main altar. The chapel was too small for the needs of more than 20 sisters and 100 wards (in 1931 there were 113 here), which is why the construction of a church began in 1930.

"We were building it with our own hands, the sisters and the wards," recalls Camilla Olszewska. "The construction was overseen by an engineer, Stanislaus Futasiewicz from Podkowa Leśna. He had two workers to help. We did the rest. The sisters would rinse the gravel, fire the bricks, and prepare mortar, and we, the wards, carried all that up the scaffolding."

The 1932 retreat was preached by Fr. Edmund Elter. This well-educated Jesuit, a graduate of the University of Warsaw, as well as universities in Rome and Paris, had been a professor of ethics at the Pontifical Gregorian University in Rome since 1926. He returned to Poland in 1932 and became a retreat director. Sister Faustina noted, "The father who preached the retreat came from America. He had come to Poland for only a short time, and it so happened that it con-ducted our retreat" (*Diary*, 172). The same sentence from the *Diary* quoted in the book by Maria Winowska differs somewhat: "The father who preached the retreat came from Rome."

Which version is true? Did Maria Winowska correct what the Sister had written to line it up with the facts? It cannot be ruled out that Fr. Elter had been in the States in 1932 and that he was planning to leave Poland, but things turned out differently. However, it is also possible that Sr. Faustina, writing the *Diary* from scratch in 1934, confused the facts slightly. Or perhaps someone else spread the rumor among the younger sisters that the retreat director was to leave for the States soon?

In any case, the future saint soon recognized the greatness of Fr. Elter's virtue. Faustina notes in the *Diary* that Jesus provided her with many guidelines for the time of the retreat. "**You shall strive to maintain a profound peace in respect to your communing with Me,**" was the first instruction. "**During this retreat, observe such strict silence that it will be as though nothing exists around you. You shall speak only to Me and to your confessor; you will ask your superiors only for penances**" (*Diary*, 169). The instructions for the retreat imposed a rule of silence on all the sisters. Their observance was not easy, because the nuns, who normally lived in different convents, often wanted to talk to friends they had not seen for a long time. It must have been a struggle for Sr. Faustina to remain faithful to the rule and the directions from Jesus. She describes how a sister from another house visited her in her cell and how they had not spoken for a long time. Faustina gave her a look intended to show that she would not break the silence. "She said to me, 'I didn't know you were such an eccentric, Sister,' and she went away" (*Diary*, 171).

Even before its beginning, Jesus promised Sr. Faustina that during the course of the retreat He would "remove all doubts" about her soul communing with Him. This was an important promise because ever since her experiences in the Płock convent and the incident with Mother Bartkiewicz in Warsaw, she felt an inner uneasiness. Confessors and superiors told her that her visions could be an illusion and that it was impossible for her to have revelations.

However, when she asked Jesus if she truly saw Him, or whether it was all an illusion, He replied: "**My love deceives no one**" (*Diary*, 29). Therefore, Jesus announced prior to the retreat that He would establish in Faustina's soul a certainty as to whom she was talking with so that even if she would want to have doubts, she would not be able to do so. "**And as a proof that it is I who am speaking to you, you will go to confession on the second day of the retreat to the priest who is preaching the retreat … [you] will present to him all your doubts concerning Me. I will answer you through his lips, and then your fears will end,**" Jesus said to her (*Diary*, 169).

It was, however, not easy for Faustina to fulfill this command. It meant that, once again, she was expected to unveil everything taking place in her soul to a new confessor — to tell him about all of the graces she experienced. "As for sins, it is always easy to do so, but in respect to graces I really have to make a great effort, and even then I do not tell everything" (*Diary*, 172). The second day of the retreat arrived. The time to go to confession and tell the priest about her conversations with Jesus was drawing near. The closer this moment came, the more terrible Faustina's torment grew.

"I felt a strange fear that the priest would not understand me, or that he would have no time to hear everything I would have to say. How am I going to tell him all this? ... My God, for a day and a half all has gone well, and now a life and death struggle is beginning. ... Satan tried to persuade me into believing that if my superiors have told me that my inner life is an illusion, why should I ask again and trouble the confessor?" She felt she would probably hear the same thing that Mother Jane Bartkiewicz had told her, that "the Lord Jesus does not commune with souls as miserable as yours" and that it was merely daydreaming, hysteria, and illusion. Faustina was thinking, "Look how many humiliations you have suffered because of them, and how many more are still awaiting you, and all the sisters know that you are a hysteric."

Yet, despite so many things racing through her mind, she did not give in to them. "'Jesus!' I called out with all the strength of my soul," remembered Sr. Faustina. "At that moment the priest came in and began the conference. He spoke for a short time, as if he were in a hurry. After the conference, he went over to the confessional. Seeing that none of the sisters were going there, I sprang from my kneeler, and in an instant was in the confessional. There was no time to deliberate" (*Diary*, 173-174). The confessor was a wise, spiritually mature priest. He quickly grasped the nature of the matter at hand. "Sister, you distrust the Lord Jesus because He treats you so kindly. Well, Sister, be completely at peace. Jesus is your Master, and your communing with Him is neither daydreaming nor hysteria nor illusion. Know that you are on the right path. Please try to be faithful to these graces; you are not free to shun them," she wrote in the *Diary*. The confessor stressed that she did not have to tell her superiors about what was happening in her soul. She was advised to do so only when the Lord Jesus explicitly told her to, and only after discussing the matter with a confessor. Should Jesus direct her to act externally, she should do so after having consulted with a confessor, "even if this costs you greatly," finished Fr. Elter. He instructed Faustina to pray for a permanent spiritual director, otherwise she would "waste the great gifts of God" (*Diary*, 174).

Father Elter was, therefore, the first priest to confirm that Faustina's experience was not an illusion, but a supernatural grace that came from God. It was God Himself, giving her a mission to carry out. On July 26, 1955, a month before he died, Fr. Elter testified under oath that he was deeply convinced that "the life of Sr. Faustina was entirely supernatural and that God was directing her in a visible way."

Sister Faustina left the confessional calm and happy. She immediately ran to the garden "to hide myself from the sisters to allow my heart to pour itself out to God" (*Diary*, 175). Perhaps she walked down the "spiritual alley," as the sisters called a tree-lined lane where the Walendów chaplains customarily walked while reciting the breviary. Sister Faustina decided to remain faithful to the inner inspirations given her in these words, "even if this costs you greatly. On the other hand, you must tell your confessor everything" (*Diary*, 174; see also 176). So much happened in Sr. Faustina's heart during the retreat. Outwardly, however, she did not show it.

Sister Seraphina Kukulska wrote, "I saw her making the retreat conducted by Fr. Elter, SJ, in Walendów. … She was no different from the rest of us, observing all the rules with the utmost precision; the preacher then remarked that he had met an extraordinary soul here."

During the final Mass of the retreat, Faustina renewed her temporary vows. Starting in the early morning, she felt that she was in a mystical union with God. She felt "completely immersed in Him," that her spirit was "submerged in God, in that ocean of love." On receiving Holy Communion in the chapel in Walendów, she suddenly saw Jesus, who told her: "**My daughter, look at My merciful Heart.** As I fixed my gaze on the Most Sacred Heart, the same rays of light, as are represented in the image as blood and water, came forth from it, and I understood how great is the Lord's mercy. And again Jesus said to me with kindness, **My daughter, speak to priests about this inconceivable mercy of Mine. The flames of mercy are burning Me — clamoring to be spent; I want to keep pouring them out upon souls; souls just don't want to believe in My goodness.**" After this vision, Faustina acknowledged, "throughout that whole day my spirit remained immersed in God's tangible presence, despite the buzz and chatter that usually follow a retreat. It did not disturb me in the least" (*Diary*, 177).

The chapel where Jesus appeared to Sr. Faustina for the second time, looking just as He does in the image of the Merciful Jesus, does not serve any religious function now. It is just one of many rooms in the former girls' home.

A few days later, when she was already back in Warsaw, God mystically allowed Faustina to learn His attributes: holiness ("The holiness of God is poured out upon the Church of God and upon every living soul in it, but not in the same degree"), justice ("His justice is so great and penetrating that it reaches deep into the heart of things, and all things stand before Him in naked truth, and nothing can withstand Him"), and the greatest one — love and mercy. "And I understood that the greatest attribute is love and mercy. It unites the creature with the Creator. This immense love and abyss of mercy are made known in the Incarnation of the Word and in the Redemption [of humanity], and it is here that I saw this as the greatest of all God's attributes" (*Diary*, 180).

Sister Faustina came to Walendów for a second time in March 1936. "I am going to Walendów for six weeks, and after six weeks there, I am to go to Kraków for good," she informed Fr. Sopoćko in a letter dated March 23, 1936. She wrote this from the convent on Żytnia street in Warsaw, where she had arrived on March 21. This was the first of her 19 letters to Fr. Sopoćko.

Faustina probably came to Walendów on March 25, 1936. She did not stay for the full six weeks, however. In a letter from nearby Derdy, dated May 10, 1936, she wrote that her superiors had moved her there from Walendów "soon after Easter." Easter Sunday fell on April 12 in 1936. The *Diary* suggests that Sr. Faustina was still in Walendów on April 25. However, a letter to Fr. Sopoćko dated May 10 indicates that the next day, May 11, she was to go to Kraków. This means that Sr. Faustina must have spent the six weeks (from March 25 to May 11) in the neighboring convents of Walendów and its affiliate in Derdy.

Things in Walendów had changed since her first stay there. Saint Joseph's Church — with a quadrangular tower that dominates the convent — was now completed. It was consecrated by Archbishop Stanislaus Gall in September 1934. At that point, however, the church was still unfurnished. The floor had no tiles, and there were no pews yet. Like other chapels belonging to the Congregation of the Sisters of Our Lady of Mercy in Poland, its characteristic shape is modeled on the chapel in Laval, France: a single nave, a simple, flat ceiling, the main altar located in the apse and two side altars. The main altar in Walendów features a triptych: Our Lady of the Scapular is depicted in the central panel, with images of St. Paul on the left and St. John on the right. Only the painting of Our Lady has survived.

The side altars had a statue of St. Joseph holding Jesus on the right (it is currently housed in the hall of the sisters' house) and one of Our Lady on the left. This statue was brought here from the chapel of the wards' house and is now to be found in the gardens. A painting of the Sacred Heart used to hang behind the statue of the Blessed Virgin Mary. It has since been replaced by a painting of the Merciful Jesus, with a portrait of St. Faustina below it. In it, the Sister looks like she does in her untouched photographs — simple, natural, smiling.

"When I arrived at Walendów, one of the sisters gave me this welcome: 'Sister, now that you have come to us here, everything is going to be all right.' I said to her, 'Why do you say that, Sister?' She answered that she felt this in her soul" (*Diary*, 636). The sister in question was probably Sr. Regina Jaworska, Faustina's peer, who was one of the witnesses during the process for her beatification. The future saint mentions the "dire straits" that the Walendów house was in at the time. One can guess that this refers to financial problems. The sisters had to tighten their belts in order to decorate the church, yet they did not succeed in finishing everything before the outbreak of World War II.

Three weeks before Sr. Faustina arrived, an important change took place at the Walendów institution. On March 6, 1936, a "Penitential Farming Colony" was established there. It operated until 1946. Following an agreement with the Ministry of Justice, about 100 female inmates were sent to Walendów. The purpose of the project was to protect the women from the harmful influence of hardened criminals and to ensure their full rehabilitation. Photographs from the period show the "colonists," as they were ironically called, dressed in uniform gray dresses and bonnets. The inmates were young women aged 18 to 30, who were serving their first sentence of no more than five to 10 years. This meant they were not imprisoned for especially serious crimes.

The Ministry provided a fixed amount of money for each inmate's basic keep, and she was expected to work to cover the rest. The women would work in the fields and gardens and would tend the farm. They also received instruction in reading and writing — as illiteracy was quite common among them — in addition to learning handicrafts and basic hygiene. Religious instruction and participation in religious practices played a significant role in their rehabilitation.

Sister Faustina mentioned neither the "colonists," nor the "penitents" in her *Diary*. In Walendów, the future saint helped in the refectory and worked in the so-called children's kitchen, which was located in the educational institution. This meant that she was cooking for both the inmates and the wards. The kitchen, outfitted with white-tiled stoves, was on the ground floor. One of the pre-war photographs shows sisters who were cooks in their full "outfit" — veils on their heads, habits with white aprons over them, and white over-sleeves. It is difficult to even imagine how uncomfortable and hot they must have been in this type of clothing. This is what Sr. Faustina was dressed like while working in the kitchen.

Her heart was occupied with other matters while she was at the Walendów convent. "I know that nothing now binds me to this earth but this work of mercy," she wrote of this time (*Diary*, 638). Sister Seraphina Kukulska remembered her as "focused, quiet, and therefore likely to be judged as not cordial towards others, but she behaved respectfully towards everyone."

In April 1936, Faustina wrote to Fr. Sopoćko that Jesus did not withhold "His light" from her, and that He was granting her "a deeper knowledge of myself."

In Walendów, in the spring of 1936, Faustina experienced — both in an actual and a mystical way — Palm Sunday, Holy Week, and Easter Sunday: "I experienced Palm Sunday in a wondrous way. Jesus allowed me to enter into the sentiments of His divine and merciful Heart; I saw many of the things that were happening at the time when the Lord Jesus entered Jerusalem," she wrote to Fr. Sopoćko. Faustina received the gift of participation in the spiritual Passion of Christ, beginning with His prayer in Gethsemane, when she took "part in the interior agony" that Jesus suffered in the Garden of Olives. "I also experienced in a special way Good Friday, Holy Saturday, and Easter Sunday, but each differently," she wrote. Faustina's share in the experience of Christ's Passion would be reiterated during Holy Week in the years that followed, and during her frequent meditation and contemplation of the Passion.

"Saint Faustina Kowalska is one of the few mystics who have experienced the sufferings of Christ, both physical and spiritual, in the present, by which I mean that they suffer with Him, and they attain the grace of participating in the salvific effect — in other words, they co-redeem," writes Ludmilla Grygiel. "The direct experience of the event in the Garden of Gethsemane is rare in the history of mysticism, and probably no one besides this Polish nun has experienced so fully and so thoroughly Christ's presentiment of the Passion and His spiritual anguish on Palm Sunday — the 'fear of the soul' — and then His sense of abandonment by the Father in Gethsemane."

At this time, Faustina's thoughts were focused on Jesus' command to create a new Congregation. She talked about it to her confessor, Fr. Aloysius Bukowski, a Jesuit. And she wrote to Fr. Sopoćko, "I feel an extraordinary interior force which drives me to action, and because of this, an indescribable torment afflicts my soul; yet I would not exchange this torment for all the treasures of the world, for it was caused by Divine love."

She was experiencing interior pain and perplexity because the Lord Jesus gave her instructions, but He did not give her the means to carry them out. On Palm Sunday 1936, Sr. Faustina had an important vision regarding this: she saw a new Congregation — the one the Lord Jesus was commanding her to establish. She saw "its external and internal growth in every detail" and that "not only will there be a female and a male congregation," but also "a huge association of lay persons, to which anyone can belong and by their deeds remind others of God's mercy, particularly by showing mercy to one another." She anticipated Fr. Sopoćko's response: "Please do not think these thoughts are [mere] madness, for they are the sincere truth, which will shortly be carried out in deed, and even if I were not to find anyone in favor of this work, still, I am not discouraged by anything, for it is enough for me to know that this is the Will of God."

Faustina already saw clearly that the new organization should consist of three branches: a contemplative one, an active one, and a lay association.

"This thought was evolving in Faustina's mind," says Sr. Elizabeth Siepak. "If we analyze all the fragments in the *Diary* and in her letters that concern the idea of a new Congregation, it turns out that it is about one single work within the Church. One work in three different aspects. The first two are formed by persons leading a consecrated life, that is, different religious congregations — contemplative and active ones, women's and men's organizations, and lay institutes — and the third one is made up of everyone who desires to live in this spirit and perform acts of mercy out of their love for Jesus."

In Walendów, Faustina met Sr. Beata Piekut who — many years later, in 1964 — was put in charge of the collection of materials about the life of Sr. Faustina in the Congregation and who later acted as vice-postulator in the process of her canonization. They first met a few years earlier, in 1932, in Kraków. Sister Beata, then a novice, remembered Faustina as "joyful, smiling," "as if she wanted to share her happiness with everyone." But they did not exchange a single word on that occasion. They only spoke to each other in Walendów, where they both arrived in March 1936 — each of them having been assured by the Mother

General that she was not going to stay long. Sister Beata was to return to Warsaw at Easter. Faustina, however, told her that she would not be leaving here soon. Sister Beata would stay until her final vows and beyond, but Faustina immediately added that God would reward her for it. How great must Sr. Piekut's amazement have been when she received a note from the Mother General the next day telling her that she was very sorry, but that she could not send her away from Walendów!

Sister Piekut was sure that Faustina had found out about the Superior's plans earlier. Not until many years later did she understand that she had been wrong about this. She remained in Walendów for the next 10 years running the Penitential Farming Colony's administrative office. Sister Beata remembered Faustina's words and the date of their conversation with great precision. It took place on March 25, 1936 — the day Sr. Faustina arrived in Walendów.

The sisters' conversation is retold in the Congregation to this very day. The older nuns passed it on to Sr. Urbana Trybocka in a slightly different version.

"Sister Faustina was only in Walendów for a short while, and she was to leave soon," says Sr. Urbana. "But Sr. Beata was staying. So she said to Sr. Faustina, 'You are so lucky, Sister. You stayed here only for a while, and you are leaving.' 'Because my soul requires this,' was the reply. 'Perhaps my soul would benefit from it, too?' Sr. Beata asked, and Sr. Faustina looked at her as if she was reading her soul, after which she said, 'Sister, you will stay here for a long time. You will not be lifted up on the altars, but you will be very useful in the Congregation.'"

One more extraordinary event links Faustina with Walendów. It was the result of a supernatural gift of hers that is seldom mentioned — bilocation. Such saints as Padre Pio, Anthony of Padua, and Catherine of Siena also had this gift. The event in question is an hourlong conversation between Sr. Faustina and Sr. Placida Putyra that took place in Walendów during a time when Faustina could not have been there. Sister Placida testified under oath in 1966 that the meeting took place "shortly before the death" of Sr. Faustina.

Nr. protok.	Nazwisko i imię	Data		
		przyjścia	wyjścia	śmierci
	Rok 1938			
165	Koszada Zygmunt	1/4	1/7	
167	Kowalczyk Tadeusz	2/4	15/6	
175	Kamysz Zofia	5/4	26/6	
179	Krasniewska Maria	6/4	3/5	
188	Knyzyński Stanisław	8/4		14/4
189	Kierczak Elżbieta	8/4	30/4	
199	Kostrewa Adam	12/4	19/5	
209	Kabacińska Maria	15/4	11/6	
222	Krzemiowska Henryka	19/4	29/4	
224	Kowalska S. Faustyna	20/4	17/9	
236	Kwinta Wacław	25/4	2/6	
249	Kostrzewski Andrzej	30/4	7/6	
254	Krzyżtoń Wincenty Walenty	2/5	30/6	
255	Król Wincenty	2/5	31/5	

Hospital chart. Item 224 contains the dates of St. Faustina's hospitalization.

It is well established that from May 1936 — from the time she left the Congregation's house in Derdy, which was affiliated with the convent in Walendów — until her death in October 1938, Faustina lived in the Łagiewniki convent. She only left Łagiewniki to go to the hospital in another district of Kraków, Prądnik, and to go to Rabka for a few days. She definitely did not go to central Poland. The visit in Walendów, therefore, could only have been possible by means of parallel presence in two places at the same time. Sister Faustina received this grace near the end of her life. She mentioned it in the *Diary*, although not in the context of her conversation with Sr. Placida, but in relation to prayer in the house of a dying man.

The sisters first met in Kraków as novices, in 1926, and then they both spent a month at the Walendów convent in 1936. They met once again "shortly before the death" of Faustina.

Sister Placida Putyra recalls, "Things were hard for me. I was considering leaving the convent. ... And then, Sr. Faustina arrives and tells me, 'I have come especially to see you.' She wanted to talk, but I did not, because it seemed to me that her life was a bed of roses, going smoothly, and that she would not understand me."

Sister Urbana Trybocka, to whom Sr. Placida told the story after the War, explains, "Sister Placida was suffering from nervous exhaustion. She kept saying, 'too little food, too much work, and too little time for prayer.' There were times that she needed to get up at three in the morning to supervise the milking of the cows. She had wanted to go to the Superior and tell her she was leaving. But somehow, this didn't happen. Suddenly, and as a complete surprise, Sr. Faustina turned up in Walendów. She was to stay only for breakfast. She said to Sr. Placida, 'Let's go for a walk and have a chat.' So they walked together down the 'spiritual path.'"

Sister Placida Putyra recounts, "Sister asked me how I was doing, and I replied, 'Bad, both in body and soul. I am stuck deep in the mud. Nobody understands me, and I have lost my trust in the superiors. There is nothing left for me but to leave.' Then, Sr. Faustina called to mind the conversations we used to have as novices, namely, how we should all respect our superiors and see the will of God in their commands. 'No one should be afraid of their superiors, but turn to them with confidence in the face of all hardships. ... Beware of avoiding the superiors, Sister.'"

"Placida was surprised that Faustina knew so much about her because she did not talk to anyone about her problems and intentions," continues Sr. Urbana. "When she started talking about some problem, Faustina was already finishing her thought. She advised Sr. Placida how to deal with the farmhands. One of them, when Sr. Placida criticized him, threw a pitchfork at her. She ducked and if not for that, she would have been injured. Sister Placida was very surprised that Faustina knew certain secrets of hers."

Sister Placida Putyra remembered, "She asked me to push unpleasant thoughts away, and she added, 'I pray for you, Sister, and I will continue praying, but you are the one who must change your life.' When I asked her why she had come, how she knew about my problems, she said nothing. ... After this conversation, I felt, in a strange way, spiritually restored. I regained confidence in my superiors and felt that I had been given new inner strength."

Faustina, who sensed the states of mind of other people, appeared in Walendów to help Placida, in order to dissuade her from leaving the Congregation and to strengthen her in her vocation. Sister Placida remained in the Congregation. She lived at the Walendów convent until her death in 1985.

Chapter Twelve

Częstochowa

1933, 1935

'The Mother of God Told Me Many Things'

"**S**O, SR. FAUSTINA CAME TO CZĘSTOCHOWA?" The vendors of the souvenir stands that densely crowd both sides of the sidewalk at the foot of the hill of Jasna Góra in Częstochowa respond to my question with surprise. "She walked down this road, down St. Barbara Street!"

Everyone is astonished. No, they didn't know. They also did not know that the future saint stayed in the convent that's located right behind them, at street No. 9/11. If they did, the souvenir stands that are impossible to miss would be selling St. Faustina holy cards and not just rosaries, angel figurines, small pictures of Our Lady and Pope John Paul II, and — more rarely — pictures of the Merciful Jesus, not to mention CDs, candy, and stuffed toys for every occasion.

The convent in Częstochowa is the only place that Sr. Faustina visited during the course of her religious life without actually living there for a longer period. She went there twice, each time for less than a day. She came to see Our Lady of Częstochowa at the Jasna Góra Shrine. The icon, famous for its many miracles, has been here at the monastery of the Pauline Fathers since 1382. Ever since then it has been continuously revered and constantly surrounded by the prayers of the people.

Faustina had already heard about the Black Madonna of Częstochowa as a child. She had seen a copy of the miraculous icon on the main altar of the church in Świnice Warckie. Her father had brought a small metal crucifix and glazed pottery figurines of Jesus and Mary from Częstochowa, and they were displayed in a place of honor in her family home. Stanislaus Kowalski made a pilgrimage to Jasna Góra, as have generations of Poles before and after him, in order to entrust various matters — of a personal nature or on the national scale, sorrowful and joyous — to the Blessed Virgin Mary. At present, the shrine is visited by about four million pilgrims each year. In 1933, when Sr. Faustina first came here, there already were over half a million of them yearly. Sister Faustina stopped in Częstochowa on her way from Łagiewniki to the convent in Vilnius.

She asked the Mother General for permission to go "at least for one day to Częstochowa so as to thank the Blessed Mother for many graces." This was an important period in Faustina's life. She had made her perpetual vows three weeks earlier, on May 1, 1933, in Kraków. She had a special reverence for and devotion to Our Lady, and not only because she belonged to a Congregation whose patroness is Our Lady of Mercy. Many years earlier, when she was still Helen Kowalska, she entrusted her difficult journey towards the religious life to the care of Our Lady. Much later, she wrote that the Virgin Mary "has taught me how to love God interiorly and also how to carry out His holy will in all things." It was also the Holy Mother who obtained the grace of untarnished purity for Faustina, which meant not only preserving her purity, but not being subject to any temptations against it. About the events that took place in 1929, she wrote, "Since that time I have experienced an increasing devotion to the Mother of God" (*Diary*, 40). Sister Faustina described her Marian apparitions and the conversations she had with the Virgin Mary in the *Diary* — especially in the entries after 1934, when she started writing regularly about her spiritual life.

The visitor's log kept at the Jasna Góra Shrine states that Sr. Faustina prayed here on May 28, 1933. Unfortunately, this date is incorrect. Her visit took place a few days earlier. Even now — more than 80 years later and with only the scant sources that are available — the actual date can be established. How so?

Sister Faustina mentioned leaving for Vilnius from Kraków in a *Diary* entry dated May 27, 1933. The distance from Kraków to Częstochowa is short, so she must have arrived there on the same day. It must have been quite late in the evening, though, since she could not go to the shrine until the next morning to pray there, as she recounts in the *Diary*. Therefore, one can make the claim that Sr. Faustina came to the chapel of Our Lady on May 28, 1933. This is also the date provided by the shrine's visitor log. The problem is that the dates provided by Sr. Faustina in the *Diary* and the one listed in the archives of the Vilnius convent do not match.

The convent archivist noted that Faustina arrived in Vilnius in the evening of Thursday, May 25, 1933. This date can be accepted as correct for two reasons — the first being that the archivist recorded events as they happened, while Sr. Faustina did not start writing the *Diary* until at least two months later, and what is more, she had to begin anew after it was burned in 1934. In a situation like this, mistakes are unavoidable. The second piece of evidence is even stronger — it is Faustina's letter to Fr. Joseph Andrasz, written in Vilnius just after her arrival from Kraków (via Częstochowa and Warsaw) and dated May 25, 1933. She therefore must have been in Częstochowa earlier than that. When? We will get to that.

The *Diary* tells us that Sr. Faustina went to Jasna Góra in the morning. She was present in the chapel of the Black Madonna at a moment that is familiar to generations of pilgrims — when the silver-and-gold shield that covers the miraculous image is lifted to the sounds of the hymn of Jasna Góra.

"I prayed without interruption until eleven, and it seemed to me that I had just come," she noted. "The Mother of God told me many things. I entrusted my perpetual vows to her, I felt that I was her child and that she was my Mother. She did not refuse any of my requests" (*Diary,* 260). Faustina does not provide any further details. Perhaps she asked for the same things that she had upon making her solemn profession — the triumph of the Church, especially in Russia and Spain; blessings for priests, her Congregation, her family; the repentance of sinners; the release of souls from purgatory; and, as for herself, the ability to fulfill the will of God in everything. She talked with the Holy Mother about the spiritual director for whom she had been praying for months. In a letter to Fr. Andrasz, written in Vilnius on the day of her arrival, she revealed that while she was praying in the chapel, she heard in her soul words of encouragement from Our Lady to speak courageously of God's mercy as being the greatest ornament of His throne. She also heard the following: "*Your spiritual director is the one who has completely set you at peace; be a frank child towards him.*" Faustina continued, "I understood at once that the Blessed Virgin was speaking about you, Father."

She was still under the deep impression that her confession with the Jesuit priest had made on her before leaving Łagiewniki. Her time in Płock had been difficult; after Jesus had appeared to her, the other sisters began to suspect her of being a hysteric. Following this, it was Fr. Andrasz who assured her that she was not experiencing any delusions, as believed by her other confessors and superiors, but a supernatural phenomenon. The first confessor to tell her this was Fr. Edmund Elter in Walendów, but she only confessed to him once, while she had several spiritually uplifting exchanges with Fr. Andrasz.

In her letter to Fr. Andrasz, then, she wrote, "Encouraged by the goodness of the Most Blessed Virgin Mary, I asked her: 'Blessed Mother, my Mother, please tell me whether this is the confessor whom Jesus promised me as a visible help?'" Our Lady confirmed that it was. Before that, in an interior vision, Faustina saw twice the spiritual director whom she was to meet in Vilnius, Fr. Michael Sopoćko. Father Andrasz, however, was also her spiritual director — that is, a few years later, when she returned to Łagiewniki in 1936 to live there once more.

Faustina prayed in the Jasna Góra chapel from 5 a.m. until 11 a.m., for six hours. She mentions going to Jasna Góra in her *Diary*, "to attend the unveiling of the image at five in the morning." At the same time, she suggests in the letter to Fr. Andrasz that she prayed there from 6 a.m. onwards. The apparent discrepancy can easily be explained. It is likely that in 1933, much like nowadays, the Pauline Fathers would open the gates to the monastery and the chapel at 5 a.m. and then uncover the icon of Our Lady at 6 a.m. The hours passed quickly for Faustina. However, the Superior of the house in Częstochowa, Sr. Seraphina Kukulska, began to worry. She "sent a sister for me, to tell me to come to breakfast and said she was worried that I would miss my train" (*Diary*, 260). The two nuns then ran down the street past the souvenir stands to the convent on St. Barbara Street.

The community of the Sisters of Our Lady of Mercy in Częstochowa was not among the largest ones in the Congregation. It had begun with difficulty in 1904, when three sisters from Warsaw started a daycare center for disadvantaged children and a sewing and embroidery workshop for girls in an apartment they were renting on St. Casimir Street. Four years later, the sisters moved into a house in the next street over — St. Barbara Street, which marks the beginning of the present-day convent. The house was purchased, in part, with a loan endorsed by Anthony Dobraczyński from Warsaw, the father of the well-known [Polish] writer Jan Dobraczyński and a friend of the Congregation.

In the 1930s, about 20 sisters lived in the convent, which by then had been expanded to include the neighboring building. They ran a large educational institution for morally neglected girls, officially named "The Most Blessed Virgin Mary Care Institute." In 1928, the sisters had 104 girls in their care; in 1936, 120. The girls, among other things, learned to embroider and sew. They also worked in the garden, traces of which remain behind the convent building. Today, instead of a girls' institution, the sisters run a therapeutic facility for children with physical and mental disabilities, and the spacious buildings now house an integrated school.

The sisters' house has been expanded and its façade has been renovated, which makes it more impressive than it was decades ago. In 1933, the convent was only half as wide as it is now. In 1936, three years after Faustina's first visit, the sisters built a large chapel, with an entrance from the courtyard. The adjacent two-story building with a garret, where a small pilgrims' hostel was established, was completed just before the outbreak of World War II.

In 1933, when Sr. Faustina was here, two rooms next to the gate served as the chapel. It was too small for the needs of the sisters and the wards, which is why they would walk to Jasna Góra or to the 17th-century church under the patronage of St. Barbara and St. Andrew located a distance down the street in order to attend Mass. The church was built on the very place where, according to tradition, a band of robbers abandoned the image of Our Lady in 1430 after having stolen it from Jasna Góra. Since then, pilgrims walk up and down St. Barbara Street — from the monastery of the Pauline Fathers to the spring, which is said to have bubbled up on the spot where the icon touched the ground. On their way, they pass the convent of the Sisters of Our Lady of Mercy and souvenir stands that sell small plastic bottles in the shape of the Blessed Virgin, with twist-off caps made to look like her crown.

After a rushed breakfast, Sr. Faustina made her way to the train station in the center of town. At that time, Częstochowa had a population of more than 130,000. Most of the city residents worked either in the textile industry, in the manufacturing of small items (mostly religious articles), or in providing services to the pilgrims. The convent is a little more than one-and-a-quarter miles away from the train station. We do not know if Faustina walked, or if one of the sisters gave her a lift in a horse-drawn buggy. In either case, she did not have much time. The 1933 train schedule shows that she had to change trains in order to get to Warsaw. At 12:10 p.m. she boarded a train for Piotrków Trybunalski. She was there at 2:15 p.m., and from there, she could catch a Warsaw train 10 minutes later. According to the schedule, she should have been at the main terminal in Warsaw by 5:40 p.m. There were also direct trains from Częstochowa to Warsaw. The first one in the afternoon left at 2:57 p.m. and was in Warsaw at 7:58 p.m.

But Sr. Faustina did not take this train. If she had, the Superior of the Częstochowa convent would not have had to send a nun after Faustina in order to prompt her to return. This means that Sr. Faustina arrived in Warsaw before 6 p.m. The train to Vilnius was scheduled to leave later in the evening, at 10:35 p.m., and was to reach its destination the next day at 7:20 a.m. The archivist of the Vilnius house recorded Faustina's arrival, adding that she came in the evening. We can deduce from this that Sr. Faustina, upon arriving in Warsaw, went to the Congregation's home on Żytnia Street, spent the night there, and continued her journey the next morning. The Vilnius train was leaving at 9:15 a.m. She got to Vilnius at 6:40 p.m. which means that she must have reached the convent in the evening of May 25, 1933.

Since she must have spent the previous night, from May 24 to 25, in Warsaw, it means that she prayed in the chapel of Jasna Góra in the morning of May 24. And she left the convent in Łagiewniki on May 23, not 27. This is what I believe to be the most likely sequence of events.

Sister Faustina's second visit to Częstochowa took place two years later, in the fall of 1935. Just as on her previous visit, she was only passing through. She was going back to Vilnius after an eight-day retreat in Kraków. She traveled through Częstochowa and Warsaw. She left Kraków for Vilnius on October 19. She probably made her way back home on Saturday, November 2. She was traveling with some of the other sisters. "On Saturday, we left Kraków and returned to Vilnius. On the way we visited Częstochowa," she wrote. "When I was praying before the miraculous picture, I felt that … are pleasing … " (*Diary*, 521). The sentence breaks off at this point. Something prevented Faustina from finishing her thought. This is all we know about her second visit to Częstochowa.

Chapter Thirteen

Vilnius

1929, 1933-1936

'Who Will Paint You as Beautiful as You Are?'

"**I**T'S A MIRACLE," SAY VISITORS TO THE VILNIUS CONVENT HOUSE AT 29A GRYBO STREET. "A miracle that this wooden house, only one of several belonging to the Congregation of the Sisters of Our Lady of Mercy, survived the inferno of the Second World War and after that, the Communist regime. And it happens to be the very house where Sr. Faustina lived."

After the war, it was saved from destruction by a professed atheist, who obtained permission from the Soviet authorities to spare the former convent from the wrecking ball and then used it as an orphanage. In 1961, the orphanage was enlarged by the addition of two wings constructed of concrete slabs. These buildings, like many other similar ones that still dot the post-Soviet cityscape, are now being renovated.

"City authorities had marked the wooden structure for demolition. But the orphanage director wrote to government offices, asking that they spare it for use as a warehouse. Thanks to her great efforts, she succeeded," says Petras Marcela, curator of the Prayer and Pilgrimage Center that has been operating in the miraculously saved house since March 2008.

The curator is sure that the orphanage director, who continued to live in the convent-orphanage building through to the mid-1980s, did not know anything about Sr. Faustina or her visions. But others certainly did know, like the people who would covertly place flowers in front of the house throughout the long post-war years, thereby running the risk of harassment by the Communist authorities. And it was here that those with a devotion to the Divine Mercy planted a large wooden cross after 1990, that is, after the collapse of the Soviet Union and the restoration of Lithuanian independence.

The words of the Chaplet of Divine Mercy drift from the open windows of St. Faustina's house. Petras Marcela says this prayer daily at 3 p.m. with the pilgrims who come to the house in the Antokol district after visiting the Shrine of The Divine Mercy in the center of Vilnius. The words of the prayer mingle with the noise made by the children from the orphanage and the decrepit Soviet-era four-story apartment buildings nearby. A playground stands on the spot of the former convent stables.

Saint Faustina's dark grey house, surrounded by the last of the trees from the sisters' once extensive garden, stands less than 110 yards from Grybo Street (formerly known as Senatorska Street). Saint Faustina's Congregation cannot repossess the property because it still belongs to the orphanage, which, in turn, falls under the authority of the Ministry of Education. And according to Lithuanian law, buildings like these may not be returned to churches or religious organizations. Consequently, the Ministry of Education has leased the Sister's former home to The Divine Mercy Assistance Fund for 20 years under the condition that the organization renovates it and opens up a house for pilgrims. The house was restored using funds from Ireland donated by those with a devotion to the Divine Mercy. The left wing of the house, which was consumed by two fires after the Second World War, needed more renovation than the right wing, where Sr. Faustina lived. Here, the original floors and some of the original windows and doors have been preserved. The room that Faustina shared with other sisters contains furniture from the period in which she lived: a narrow wooden bed, a little table, and a chair. In the next room over, in the presence of relics of St. Faustina and Blessed Michael Sopoćko, pilgrims pray the Chaplet of Divine Mercy.

Sister Faustina stayed at the Vilnius convent twice. She came to Vilnius for the first time on February 21, 1929, and stayed through June 11. The second time around she was there longer, nearly three years: from the end of May 1933 to March 21, 1936. This was a very important time for her personally as well as for developing the work of Divine Mercy. The image that Jesus had desired was painted in Vilnius, and it was here that it was publicly displayed for the first time. Further, the Lord Jesus dictated the Chaplet of Divine Mercy to Sr. Faustina in the Vilnius convent, and He also laid a new task before her while she was there: to establish a Congregation that, with its earnest supplications, will obtain Divine Mercy for the world.

Faustina probably got to know Vilnius better than Kraków or Warsaw, as she often walked its streets while carrying out Jesus' instructions regarding the painting of the image. Did she come to like this city, which the Nobel Prize-winning poet Czesław Miłosz reportedly described as "always adorned in red peonies and late lilacs, and baroque towers ascending to the sky?" Characteristically, Faustina never mentions a word in her *Diary* about the most important monuments that she would have seen in Vilnius, Kraków, or Warsaw. She delighted in nature rather than in the works of human hands — in the beauty of the world created by God. And since Vilnius enchants its visitors by means of a unique atmosphere coming from the combination of its architecture, its inhabitants, and its physical landscape, one can infer that, at the very least, she appreciated the city's geographical location. The city lies on hills covered with mixed forests, in the basin of the Neris River (Wilia in Polish) and its tributary, the Vilnia River (Wilejka in Polish).

Vilnius' medieval street plan was influenced primarily by the Baroque architecture of the Polish-Lithuanian Commonwealth — the palaces of grand magnate families and the churches they founded, where Polish and Lithuanian influences intermingled harmoniously. When Sr. Faustina was living here before the Second World War, the vast majority of the city residents were Poles who spoke in a characteristic singsong accent, but there were also Jews, who made up one-third of the population, and smaller ethnic groups: Russians, Lithuanians, Byelorussians, Germans, and Crimean Karaites.[31]

Vilnius, like Lithuania as a whole, was bound to Poland by a common history from the end of the 14th century onwards — starting in 1385 by means of a personal union through the marriage of the Grand Duke of Lithuania Ladislaus Jagiełło to the Polish Queen Hedwig (who was later canonized) and, starting in 1569, through a real union that was ratified in Lublin. After the First World War, which ended the Partitions of Poland, Vilnius was annexed to the Second Polish Republic, together with the region populated almost exclusively by Poles (called Central Lithuania). The rest of Lithuania became a separate state. In interwar Poland, Vilnius, with its population of 200,000 residents, had no economic significance, but it continued to be one of the largest cultural and academic centers. The Stefan Batory University, established in the 16th century, and the newer Academic-Research Institute of Eastern Europe were both located in Vilnius. The city also boasted a respected literary circle and several theaters where the greatest Polish actors of the day performed.

What did make an impression on St. Faustina was the Vilnius convent building complex, although it was no architectural masterpiece in and of itself.

On the contrary, she was struck by the fact that the convent was made up of "a few scattered tiny huts." "It seems a bit strange to me after the large buildings of Józefów," she wrote in her *Diary* in 1933, when she arrived here directly from Łagiewniki (261). But she must have had similar thoughts four years earlier, in February 1929, when she saw it for the first time.

The sisters' property was located on Antokol, one of several hills in the city, on the left bank of the Vilnia. This district of Vilnius was once famous for the magnificent gardens that surrounded the stately dachas and palaces of magnates. Today, it continues to be known for the Baroque Church of Sts. Peter and Paul, which is decorated with two thousand stucco figures rendered by the Italian artists Pietro Perti and Giovanni Maria Galli.

Sister Faustina travelled from Warsaw by train. The chronicler of the Vilnius house made the following entry for February 21, 1929: "Thursday, today, Sr. Faustina arrived from Warsaw for a few weeks to help the sisters in the kitchen. For Sr. Samuela is bedridden because of her continual ailment of a blood clot." However, in her *Diary*, Faustina gives 1928 as the year of her arrival in Vilnius. Taking into account that she recorded this information several years later, she could have been mistaken. But she also had a different explanation for her coming to Vilnius. She was supposed to replace a sister who worked in the kitchen, while this sister went to the Warsaw convent for her third probation in preparation for her profession of perpetual vows. From other convent sources, it is known that this sister was Petronela Basiura.

In that case, how was it that Sr. Samuela Wasilewska was listed in the chronicles of the Vilnius house as ill with a blood clot, and as the one whom Sr. Faustina was supposed to replace? Sister Samuela was probably the first to fill in for Sr. Petronela in the kitchen, but because she fell ill, a new replacement was needed. In the Congregation of the Sisters of Our Lady of Mercy, the third probation, which is a preparation for perpetual vows, lasts five months. The sisters usually professed their perpetual vows in late April or early May. After that, Sr. Petronela should have returned to work in the kitchen in Vilnius. That is why Sr. Faustina was supposed to fill in for her for just two months, but for unknown reasons she stayed longer, until June 11.

Sister Antonina Grejwul, who recalls Sr. Faustina's stay in Vilnius in 1929, claims that Sr. Faustina worked in the kitchen alone. "She cooked, washed the dishes, and also waited on the workers who were installing the electrical system. She never complained about having too much work." Faustina was a very good cook. Many nuns from various convent houses belonging to the Congregation echoed this sentiment. She probably liked to cook and, in particular, to bake cakes. She was praised for her skill in decorating cakes, for example.

In 1929, the Superior at the Vilnius convent was Mother Irene Krzyżanowska. The impression Faustina made on her was that of being a serious sister, "already schooled in the spiritual life." Renovations happened to be underway in the convent at 25 Senatorska Street (Grybo 29 is the postwar address). The sisters' cells were being renovated, so Sr. Faustina slept in the guest room. The renovations were probably one of the consequences of a fundraising appeal for material help for the Vilnius house — an appeal Mother General made to all convents in the Congregation two years earlier, in 1927. She was worried that "hunger was a real problem" for the sisters and their wards, and that if no help was given from the outside, they would have to close the convent.

Moreover, one of the wooden cottages went up in flames in 1928 and had to be rebuilt. According to the Vilnius city plan from 1929, five buildings stood on the plot of land that belonged to the sisters. This means that over the 20 years since the property was purchased in March 1908, the Congregation had added two cottages to the site and rebuilt one. The sisters bought the property for 24,000 rubles, back in the days of the Russian Partition, from the Tsarist General Vladimir Bykovsky. Princess Maria Radziwiłł donated money to the Congregation for this purpose. Archives reveal that in 1908, the property included a garden, a park, a tract of forest, and three wooden buildings. One of the buildings had fire damage and two were inhabited, of which "one tiny wooden house in the garden" had five rooms, a veranda, an annex, and two pavilions. This was the house where the sisters lived, which has been preserved to this day as St. Faustina's house. The kitchen, the laundry room (which had been newly-built in 1931), the sewing and embroidery workshop, the bakery, the wards' bedrooms, and the chapel were all located in other buildings.

In 1934, during Sr. Faustina's second stay in the Vilnius convent, the Congregation bought the neighboring plot of land from the descendants of a certain Mr. Puslovski. Thus, the property's size increased from 75,000 to nearly 420,000 square feet, that is, 10 acres of land. The sisters' home stood on the slope of a small rise. In heavy rain, the home stood in the way of the draining water, which meant that the walls of the house were damp with moisture; the house had no cellar. "The house was damp, and there weren't too many tile stoves[32] in the rooms, which must have had a negative impact on the state of Sr. Faustina's health," the custodian Petras Marcela explains.

Sister Faustina's second stay in Vilnius was significantly longer and began at the end of May 1933. "May 25, 1933, Thursday. Sister Faustina arrived in the evening by train. She professed her perpetual vows in Kraków," recorded the Vilnius convent chronicler. On the basis of her *Diary*, we are led to believe that Faustina arrived on May 28, but it is almost certain that she was mistaken. She wrote, "Today 27 [May 1933] I am leaving for Vilnius" (*Diary*, 259). Yet we know that Faustina stayed for one night in the Congregation's house in Częstochowa to visit the Shrine of Jasna Góra on the way from Kraków to Vilnius on May 25, 1933.

Sister Faustina was already familiar with the Vilnius house and knew Mother Superior Irene Krzyżanowska, who was kind to her, and some of the sisters — Felicia Żakowiecka and Fabiana Pietkun. But, above all, she was happy to see Sr. Justine Gołofit, with whom she was friends since her Kraków days, and who scrubbed the floor for her arrival. Other sisters — and there were 18 of them — also received Faustina "very warmly," which was "a great encouragement to endure the hardships" that lay ahead of her (*Diary*, 261).

"Days of work, of struggle, and of suffering have begun," she wrote in her *Diary*. "Everything continued according to the convent routine. One is always a novice, having to learn many things and to get to know about many things, because although the rule is the same, each house has its own customs; and thus, each change is a little novitiate" (*Diary*, 265). In Vilnius, this meant she had to get to know the customs of the convent house as well as the responsibilities entrusted to her. Sister Faustina was a good and experienced cook, but in the Vilnius house she was sent to work in the garden. In the spirit of obedience, she took up gardening, about which she had no clue. "The Lord Jesus will bless me, although I don't know how to garden," she said to Sr. Clementine Buczek before leaving Kraków.

Mother Irene Krzyżanowska remembered, "When she started working in the garden, she didn't know a thing. Gradually, she learned a lot and worked with a passion, particularly in the small greenhouse, eagerly gathering any information on the topic from more experienced gardeners." Mother Krzyżanowska recalls that Faustina visited "the Redemptorist Fathers, where she sought advice about running the garden, especially about taking care of the flowers." Nowadays no trace remains of the Redemptorist church or religious house on 7 Nemenczyńska Street. And the sisters' large garden has been divided up into smaller plots. The only remaining building, which was once part of the religious house, has become the children's ward in a tuberculosis hospital.

Sister Clementine Buczek, the head gardener of the Kraków convent, recalled years later that Faustina was taught gardening by a "missionary brother, a gardener" in Vilnius. Sister Clementine probably wouldn't have called a Redemptorist a missionary, although the Redemptorists' ministry was to lead popular retreats and missions among the people. In Vilnius, there was also a monastery of missionary priests (the Congregation of the Missionaries of the Precious Blood of Jesus). Their Baroque church — now a hospital — stands at the intersection of Subocz and Rasos Streets, that is, in the neighborhood of the convent of the Sisters of the Visitation, where Fr. Sopoćko lived in the chaplain's quarters. Was it here that Sr. Faustina came to learn gardening? Or perhaps she learned both from the Missionaries and the Redemptorists.

The sisters' garden in the Antokol district was large. It had to feed 19 sisters and 60 to 80 wards (in 1931, there were 37). It probably took up the majority of the nearly 10 acres of property. Vegetable beds, fruit trees, and bushes surrounded the wooden buildings and stretched out behind the sisters' house. Sister Faustina also placed great importance on growing flowers in the greenhouse, so that she could decorate the chapel altar with them all year long.

Sister Yolanda Woźniak remembered, "At that time, Sr. Faustina then had few workers in the garden, which resulted in various difficulties and unpleasantness, as she could not respond to everyone's needs. Watching how she bore those vexations without complaint and with a serene spirit inspired me."

Sister Justine Gołofit recalled, "More than once, they sent the worst girls to help her out, the girls the directress herself could not cope with. But Sr. Faustina succeeded; she had a good influence on them."

Sister Stella Kozłowska recalled a year that was particularly rainy. "The grass shot up and stifled the vegetable seedlings; I saw that Sr. Faustina was pained by this, and she would sometimes say, 'We must have more hands for work — I alone with the children cannot manage.' And, indeed, some of the vegetable beds were so overgrown with weeds that they had to be dug up, cleared with a sickle, and nothing grew there. Then, there was talk about her carelessness. I had to defend her as I knew that the accusations were false."

Faustina's difficulties in the garden were not so much due to the weather as to human weakness, to which consecrated persons are not immune. This was probably the main reason that too few wards worked in the vast garden with Faustina. Sister Fabiana Pietkun describes the reasons for the conflict. From her version of the story, we can conclude that when Sr. Petronela was the gardener (most likely the same sister whom Sr. Faustina replaced in the kitchen in 1929), Sr. Chrysostom Korczak, the girls' directress and later infirmary nurse, designated 14 wards to work in the garden. However, when Sr. Faustina became the gardener, they only gave her seven girls to help out.

Sister Fabiana Pietkun believed that "Sister Petronela was taking revenge on Sr. Faustina because Mother Irene gave Sr. Faustina the garden, while she was told to go to the farm instead. She often said, 'Why wasn't Sr. Faustina sent to the farm instead of me?' And she persuaded Sr. Chrysostom not to send her girls to the garden, so that Faustina wouldn't be able to manage. Sister Chrysostom didn't like Sr. Faustina, so she listened to Sr. Petronela and made Sr. Faustina's life miserable. ... Once, Sr. Petronela took a scythe and cut the cabbages right along with some weeds to show that Sr. Faustina was neglecting the garden terribly. Sister Faustina, very pained, came to me and asked if I could pray for Sr. Petronela so that the Lord Jesus would give her His grace, because the devil had so ensnared her that she in her fury did ... so much damage. Sister Faustina weeded and tended the remaining cabbages — little remained, really — and they grew so large that, as I live, never did I see such cabbages. ... Sister Faustina took me to see them and said, 'How good the Lord Jesus is! Have a look, Sister, at how He has blessed me.' ... Sister Petronela, seeing Faustina's goodness in spite of the fact that she vexed her so, had a change of heart and, later on, did not let anyone say anything bad about Sr. Faustina."

Despite various setbacks, Sr. Faustina must have coped well with her gardening duties, since the Superior General Michael Moraczewska recalled that "she received splendid results with the advice of other gardeners and thanks to her innate intelligence." Years later, she remembered making a visit to the Vilnius convent, during which she was showing around "guests from upper government circles who wished to visit the institution. One of the ladies said to me, 'The Sisters clearly must have a really expert gardener here.'"

After working in the garden, Faustina used to help the sisters in the kitchen.

Sister Vieslava Effenberg remembered, "Sister Faustina, having worked in the garden for the whole week, filled in for the sisters in the kitchen on Sundays and holidays."

Sister Antonina Grejwul recalled, "She was called in from the garden to make cakes, which were always a great success." Sister Joachim Głuc noted, "Other sisters would not have gone [to the kitchen], but Sr. Faustina went without a word, saying, 'Such is the will of God.'"

Sister Borgia Tichy remembered, "As an expert and gourmet cook, she always took over the management of the kitchen during house festivities, particularly when His Excellency Bishop Bandurski and other clerical or lay dignitaries came together to the house several times for the celebrations."

So Sr. Faustina had a lot of work and a variety of difficulties. But that was not what absorbed her soul and heart. What was most important during her stay in Vilnius was what took place in her spiritual life and the fulfillment of Jesus' instructions. In Vilnius, Faustina finally met the priest whom she had been praying for — a spiritual director and helper in fulfilling Jesus' will on earth. She had been praying fervently for someone like this since her stay in Płock. Although she ultimately met this priest in Vilnius, Jesus had given her an interior vision of him twice — but she didn't know his name yet. The first time was during her probation in Warsaw, and the second was in Kraków before she professed her perpetual vows. This promised confessor was Fr. Michael Sopoćko, today Blessed Michael Sopoćko.

Their first meeting most likely took place during the first week of Sr. Faustina's stay in Vilnius, that is, at the end of May or beginning of June in 1933. Once a week, the sisters made their confessions with Fr. Sopoćko, who came to the convent on Antokol for this very purpose. From the chronicles of the Vilnius house, it is clear that the first confession after May 25, that is, after Faustina's arrival, took place on Thursday, June 1, 1933. Sister Faustina also recorded her meeting with Fr. Sopoćko in the *Diary*. It immediately follows the information about her arrival in Vilnius and begins with the words, "The week for confession came" (*Diary*, 263).

But in Fr. Sopoćko's earliest memories about this, which were written down in his notebook on August 15, 1938, he wrote, "In 1933, I came to know Sr. Faustina, who told me right away that she had known me for a long time and that I was to be her spiritual director and proclaim God's mercy to the world. I didn't attach much significance to her words or treat them seriously." In memoirs written in January 1948, Fr. Sopoćko added that his meeting with Faustina took place in the summertime, in July or August. In his testimony from 1971, on the other hand, he spoke only of July. These discrepancies aren't surprising. After all, at the time, Fr. Sopoćko didn't know how important this meeting would be for him and for the future direction of his life.

As for Faustina, it was difficult for her to hide her joy, because Jesus' promise to her had been fulfilled. At the moment when she recognized that Fr. Sopoćko was the priest whom she had seen earlier with the eyes of her soul, she once again heard Jesus' words interiorly: "**This is My faithful servant; he will help you to fulfill My will here on earth**" (*Diary*, 263). Other sisters noticed Faustina's joy and were probably not just surprised, but also disgusted with her behavior immediately preceding confession.

Who was the priest that the Lord Jesus had chosen as a spiritual director and helper to Sr. Faustina in spreading the devotion to the Divine Mercy? Who was this person of whom the Lord Jesus said, "**His heart is, for Me, a heaven on earth**" (*Diary*, 574), and, at another time, "**Your director and I are one; his words are My words**" (*Diary*, 1308)?

Father Michael Sopoćko, born in the Vilnius region, was 45 years old in 1933 and had served as a priest for 19 years. He was familiar with parish work (from his work in Taboryszki), social work (he had organized Polish schools), as well as pastoral work in the military (he had served as a military chaplain for more than 10 years and had taken part in the Polish-Soviet war in 1920). He had experience in priestly formation (he was the Father Confessor in the Vilnius seminary) and had academic and teaching experience (he lectured in the theological department of the Stefan Batory University). In 1933, the year he met Sr. Faustina, he was finishing his habilitation thesis on the pastoral theology of the Jesuit Nicholas Łęczycki, a master of the spiritual life and a mystic. He defended his thesis one year later at Warsaw University.

He was a confessor at many men's and women's religious houses in Vilnius. In January 1933, six months before Sr. Faustina's arrival in Vilnius, upon the nomination by the Vilnius Metropolitan Archbishop Romuald Jałbrzykowski, he became the so-called ordinary or weekly confessor for the Congregation of the Sisters of Our Lady of Mercy. (The sisters also had an extraordinary confessor, who heard confessions four times a year.) Once a week, Fr. Sopoćko sat down in the confessional in the convent chapel on Grybo Street. Those who knew him emphasized his modesty, humility, simplicity, and ascetic lifestyle — as well as the good dose of common sense he administered in guiding souls. Father Sopoćko was rather reserved and didn't speak much about himself; rather, he listened to others. "Unusually zealous and filled with the Spirit of God, he was always a sober realist, far from exaltation, being guided above all by the demands of reason and discernment of current needs," wrote his student Fr. Stanislaus Strzelecki.

The meeting in Vilnius of these two individuals — a simple nun-mystic and a professor of theology — was a decisive moment in the development of the devotion to the Divine Mercy. It was an important meeting for Sr. Faustina, as up to this moment, Jesus had been her spiritual master exclusively. "Jesus often makes known to me what He does not like in my soul, and He has more than once rebuked me for what seemed to be trifles, but which were, in fact, things of great importance. He has warned me and tried me like a Master. For many years, He Himself educated me, until the moment when He gave me a spiritual director" (*Diary*, 145). While Jesus continued to be Faustina's master, she now found a tangible helper in Fr. Sopoćko, someone who would take her visions seriously. This was also a critical meeting for Michael Sopoćko, as it decided the further direction of his life. From the moment he became convinced that it was really Jesus who was conveying His message to the world through Sr. Faustina, he became intensely involved in spreading it. Despite many attacks, accusations, and much suffering, he was faithful to this work until the end of his life.

However, Sr. Faustina did not reveal her interior life to Fr. Sopoćko right away. According to Fr. Henry Ciereszko — the biographer and vice-postulator in the beatification process of Fr. Michael Sopoćko — this took place gradually. That is probably the reason why Fr. Sopoćko's memoirs give different dates for his first meeting with Sr. Faustina. During her first confession with him, she might have explained the reason for her happiness, but it was only later that she began to speak of her visions and revelations concerning Divine Mercy. It is possible that this only took place after several confessions, that is, after several weeks, although Jesus reassured her immediately that this was the priest whom He had promised her. Faustina herself admitted that she did not immediately reveal her soul to Fr. Sopoćko. What's more, she even planned to avoid him as a confessor. Why?

Where did this resistance of hers come from? After all, she had begged Jesus long and ardently for a spiritual director. Maria Tarnawska rightly notes that the answer can be found in Sr. Faustina's only surviving letter to Fr. Andrasz, which she wrote from Vilnius on the day of her arrival, May 25, 1933. In the forefront of her mind, Faustina still had the confession she had made in Kraków with Fr. Andrasz, who had confirmed her conviction that what she was experiencing came from God. Moreover, during her stay at Jasna Góra in Częstochowa, the

Blessed Mother confirmed that Fr. Andrasz was to be the guide of her soul. Faustina could not have known that this would come to pass three years later. She wrote to Fr. Andrasz, "Jesus promised me a visible help, because after all no one was able to put me at peace in such a way and before no one was I able to reveal my soul in such a way as before you, Father."

For all of these reasons, she had a hard time revealing her soul, despite the fact that in 1933, in Vilnius, she recognized Fr. Sopoćko as the priest whom Jesus had showed her in two visions. She already knew Fr. Andrasz; the Blessed Mother had told her that he would be a "visible help" to her; and Mother General had given her permission to write to him. This period of doubt probably lasted several weeks. It was only when Jesus warned Faustina that she opened up to Fr. Sopoćko. Jesus told her, **"As you will act towards your confessor, so I will act toward you. If you conceal something from him ... I too will hide Myself from you, and you will remain alone"** (*Diary*, 269).

This situation shows that although Faustina "recognized absolute obedience and tried to observe it strictly, in practice she had difficulty submitting her own wishes and judgments to the Lord's will. To no one does it come easy to lay oneself bare interiorly, even to reveal the most godly wishes and inclinations. This problem was to recur for Sr. Faustina more than once in her life. She had yet to suffer much within herself, to overcome and to work upon herself, before she could totally submit to the will of God without reservations," Maria Tarnawska points out.[33]

After Faustina finally revealed her soul to Fr. Sopoćko, she noted in her *Diary*, "Jesus poured an ocean of graces into it. Now I understand what it means to be faithful to a particular grace. That one grace draws down a whole series of others" (263).

As an experienced confessor and theologian, Fr. Sopoćko reacted with caution to the words of the nun: the claim that, according to Jesus, he was to help her spread the message of Divine Mercy. This is hardly surprising. Throughout his priestly life, he had probably met other individuals who had told him about their alleged visions. "I made light of her story and put her to a certain test, the effect of which was that Sr. Faustina began to seek another confessor with her Superior's permission. After some time she came back and declared that she would bear everything, but that she wouldn't leave me anymore," the priest recalled. Unfortunately, it is not known to which test he was referring. This was a time of trial for Fr. Sopoćko as well.

Sister Borgia Tichy remembered that several weeks after Faustina arrived at the Vilnius convent, the confessor declared that he would "probably be forced to give up this duty, as his health was not the best." However, during their conversation, Sr. Borgia sensed that he did not want to leave for health reasons, but for other reasons, about which "he couldn't speak, and which I could only guess at." Sister Borgia Tichy speculates, "He simply feared that if he wasn't careful he might get involved in some murky issues. These speculations about Fr. Sopoćko's reasons to leave were proven correct when Sr. Faustina was, at his urging, sent for a psychiatric evaluation at a private clinic. Once the results showed her to be psychologically healthy, her spiritual director evidently calmed down, and from that time on, there was no word about a change in confessors anymore."

Indeed, "fearing a delusion, hallucination, or fantasy" on the part of Sr. Faustina, Fr. Sopoćko first asked the Superior of the Vilnius convent, Mother Irene Krzyżanowska, for her opinion about Sr. Faustina and then requested this test of her psychological and physical health. The examination was carried out by psychiatrist Dr. Helen Maciejewska. She issued an assessment of the "excellent psychological health" of Sr. Faustina. After the Second World War, on January 6, 1952, she testified, "During the medical examinations, I never saw any neuropathic symptoms or any psychological abnormalities."

After Fr. Sopoćko received the "commendable report" on Faustina "on all counts," he continued to observe her. "Partly, I was not confident, I deliberated, I prayed, and I researched. I sought as well the advice of several enlightened priests on what I should do, without revealing what or whom it concerned," he wrote years later. He also presented the matter of Sr. Faustina's revelations to Archbishop Jałbrzykowski, the Vilnius metropolitan, who advised that he act with caution and not yield to delusions and ordered him not to talk about the visions to anyone. Archbishop Jałbrzykowski was also informed about Faustina's revelations by the Superior of the convent, as well as by Sr. Faustina herself, whose confession he heard twice in September 1935 in Fr. Sopoćko's absence. But the archbishop was skeptical about the authenticity of Faustina's revelations.

Sister Faustina had laid a difficult task before Fr. Sopoćko. He was to be her spiritual director, that is, someone who would lead her to sanctity, as well as someone who would help her to discern her revelations and visions and would support her in implementing Jesus' requests. "Characteristic of Fr. Sopoćko's spiritual direction of Sr. Faustina was that he kept at a prudent distance from what she told him about her interior experiences and visions, yet observed them attentively without making premature assumptions," writes Fr. Henry Ciereszko. "At the same time, Fr. Sopoćko focused his work on the spiritual growth of his penitent, for whom he felt responsible as her spiritual director."

As for Faustina, she saw the fruit of Fr. Sopoćko's guidance. "Oh, how great a grace it is to have a spiritual director! One makes more rapid progress in virtue, sees the will of God more clearly, fulfills it more faithfully, and follows a road that is sure and free of dangers. The director knows how to avoid the rocks against which the soul could be shattered. The Lord gave me this grace rather late, to be sure, but I rejoice in it greatly" (*Diary*, 331). At the same time, she occasionally wrote in her *Diary* what Jesus said to her, namely that, while He alone was the director of her soul, He also spoke to her through the mouth of her confessor and "earthly" director: **I Myself am your Director; I was, I am, and I will be. And since you asked for visible help, I chose and gave you a director even before you had asked, for My work required this. Know that the faults you commit against him wound My Heart. Be especially on your guard against self-willfulness; even the smallest thing should bear the seal of obedience"** (362).

In his contacts with Sr. Faustina, Fr. Sopoćko applied the advice of one of the Church's greatest mystics — St. John of the Cross. He treated her narratives of visions with detachment and did not ask for details. Father Stanislaus Strzelecki noticed that Fr. Sopoćko, "conscious of the unique nature of the paths of God's grace, did not accept anything *a priori*, nor did he reject anything *a priori*, which is positive proof of his prudence." Before making any judgment about the sister's revelations, he first assured himself of her personal holiness. He recalled in 1948, "She caught my attention with her unusual subtlety of conscience and close union with God: there usually was no material for absolution, and she never offended God with a mortal sin."

From the moment that Faustina, urged on by Jesus, decided to reveal to Fr. Sopoćko what was taking place in her soul and speak of her closeness with Jesus and her conversations with Him, her confessions became long. Sister Vieslava Effenberg remembered, "I was irritated by ... Sr. Faustina's long confessions and the sweet expression she had when she returned from making one."

Sister Vieslava was not the only one that was irritated by the future saint's long confessions. Faustina, wanting both to avoid the aggravation and the curiosity of the sisters, began to go to confession last. That didn't improve the situation. Father Sopoćko did not have the time to listen to her long "confidences in the confessional" either. He, therefore, recommended that Faustina write them down in a notebook and let him look at them every now and then. It seems that his lack of time was not the only reason for giving her these instructions. This meant that he could analyze the visions and revelations described by the sister when he was calm and collected, without the haste demanded by a waiting line of curious penitents.

Whatever the reason, thanks to Fr. Sopoćko's instructions, a unique document came into existence: the diary of the spiritual experiences of one of the greatest mystics of the Church. Had Fr. Sopoćko not given Sr. Faustina the directions in 1933 to write down "her soul's contacts with God," and had she not submitted to them obediently, we would never have found out so much about her visions. At the very least, we would not have gotten to know them from their direct source, but merely from what was related by her confessor and possibly, her superiors.

"I am to write down the encounters of my soul with You, O God, at the moments of Your special visitations. ... I have received this order through him who is for me Your representative here on earth, who interprets Your holy Will to me. Jesus, You see how difficult it is for me to write, how unable I am to put down clearly what I experience in my soul. Oh, God, can a pen write down that for which many a time there are no words? But You give the order to write, O God; that is enough for me," noted Faustina (*Diary*, 6).

The task of writing her *Diary* was not an easy one for Sr. Faustina. First of all, she was not well educated; she had only finished less than three grades of elementary school. Secondly, she didn't have circumstances conducive to writing. She was busy with work in the garden, and in her free moments, she had to conceal her writing from the other sisters. Faustina wrote on a nightstand, on her bed, and in some convents, like Vilnius, she wrote on a small table, separated from the other nuns by a screen. She was always on the watch, so that she could close and hide her notebook at any moment. In such moments, she stopped mid-sentence, and did not return to finish her thought.

Sister Borgia Tichy, Superior of the Vilnius house from December 1934 onwards, wrote, "She devoted her free time to writing her diary entries, which she hid scrupulously. This is what roused the sisters more than once to make many more or less spiteful comments, particularly because this was connected with more frequent contact with the confessor during the week. That is why she received the nickname among the sisters of 'kasztelanka' [her ladyship]."

Sister Vieslava Effenberg recalled, "Once, when Sr. Faustina was ill, I took her evening meal to her cell. Entering the dormitory, I heard the rustle of shuffled papers from behind the curtain of Sr. Faustina's cell, on account of which I remarked, jokingly, 'So, Sister, are you writing your life story that you hide it away so quickly?' to which she responded with a smile, 'Perhaps.'"

Another sister, Placida Putyra, also saw Faustina as she was writing, but that was later in Walendów in 1936. "During the day, she sometimes interrupted her work for a moment and went to her cell to write something down. Being curious, I peeked behind the curtain and saw that she was kneeling at her nightstand and was writing something quickly in her notebook," reported Sr. Placida.

But Sr. Faustina's greatest difficulty in writing had to do with something completely different — that is, in trying to convey what was really indescribable in words, because it related to the spiritual sphere, the contact of her soul with God. This is how Ludmila Grygiel described the task that Faustina was faced with: "She was supposed to convey what is beyond words (union with God) and describe what was inconceivable ('the immeasurable depth of Divine Mercy'), knowing that her description was 'only a faint shadow' of what she understood in her soul. ... The main 'plot' of her *Diary* did not concern external events, which are relatively easy to describe, but, rather, the essence of the merciful God, as learned through mystical experiences, the rules of His age-old action in the world, and also His direct participation in the history of salvation during Faustina's day."

Not only is the content of her *Diary* exceptional, but its form as well. While the author was uneducated and made spelling mistakes, her handwriting was elegant and regular. Most importantly, the text contains no erasures or changes. This leaves no doubt that what she conveyed — and particularly considering the unfavorable circumstances — flowed straight from her soul, from the inspiration of God Himself. "Many a theologian with many years of education could not even come close to solving these [theological] difficulties so accurately and easily as Sr. Faustina did," noted Fr. Sopoćko.

At first, Faustina wrote on loose sheets of paper and then in a notebook that her Superior bought for her at her confessor's request. She filled six such notebooks. She kept her *Diary* in her cell. Father Sopoćko would only take it occasionally for a few hours to look over, always on site at the convent. On December 15, 1971, he testified that he never changed anything in its content. Unfortunately, when he left for a few weeks for the Holy Land in 1934, Sr.

Faustina burned her *Diary* as per the advice of one she believed to be an angel, but who turned out to be Satan. She began the task of writing it anew on July 28, 1934.

Father Michel Sopoćko recalled, "I directed her to rewrite the destroyed contents as a penance. At the same time, she was having new experiences, which she also noted down, interweaving them with what she recalled from the burned notebook. That is why there is no chronological order in her notebooks."

The more Fr. Sopoćko became convinced of the authenticity of Sr. Faustina's spiritual experiences, the more earnestly he encouraged her to write them down. He continued to do so after she left Vilnius. Jesus also urged her to keep notes and instructed that she write more about His mercy and the goodness of God. Faustina saw Jesus as He was inspecting her *Diary*, checking what she was writing. He called her the secretary of Divine Mercy. "**You are the secretary of My mercy. I have chosen you for that office in this life and the next life**" (*Diary*, 1605). He also said, "**My daughter, you do not live for yourself but for souls; write for their benefit. You know that My will as to your writing has been confirmed many times by your confessors**" (*Diary*, 895).

Sister Faustina sometimes complained, "My Jesus, You see that I do not know how to write well and, on top of that, I don't even have a good pen. And often it scratches so badly that I must put sentences together, letter by letter. And that is not all. I also have the difficulty of keeping secret from the sisters the things I write down, and so often I have to shut my notebook every few minutes and listen patiently to someone's story, and then the time set aside for writing is gone. And when I shut the notebook suddenly, the ink smears" (*Diary*, 839).

The contents of Sr. Faustina's *Diary* and the way it was kept offer proof of the innate intelligence and abilities of this uneducated nun, but this is not the only evidence. For example, in 1936 in Vilnius, Sr. Faustina wrote a play to celebrate the feast of St. Borgia, the patron saint of the house Superior, Borgia Tichy. The skit, written in rhyming verse, was a conversation between four Jesuit saints: St. Francis Borgia, St. Stanislaus Kostka, St. John Berchmans, and St. Aloysius. Faustina and three other sisters acted it out.

With the exception of the superiors, most of the other sisters did not know of the *Diary's* existence, although they did see that Faustina was writing something. How surprised they were to find out about her *Diary* after her death!

Sister Beata Piekut, vice-postulator for Faustina's beatification process, recalled, "It seemed a bit strange to me that Sr. Faustina sometimes described very trivial, commonplace events. I don't view this as a lack of humility, but the impression of Sr. Faustina that I had formed from having direct contact with her was somehow different and more real; it doesn't match the picture one gets from her *Diary*. Sister Faustina's personality, as I used to know her, was somehow endearing, straightforward, and unsophisticated, and the text of the *Diary* seems to me to be trivial and unnecessary."

Sister Piekut emphasized that she always thought of Faustina as someone very prudent, tactful, and natural. "She knew how to get along with everyone, to understand anyone, to empathize with those who were sad and rejoice in the happiness of others." This is probably why Sr. Faustina's descriptions of daily life must have seemed "trivial and unnecessary" to Sr. Piekut.

At the same time, in the very form that it takes, Faustina's *Diary* testifies to her process of maturing in sanctity. In her *Diary*, Faustina not only describes "the contacts of [her] soul with God" and the message of Divine Mercy that Jesus entrusted to her to give to the Church and the world; she also describes the process of stripping herself of her own will and overcoming herself in her relations with others. Her *Diary* is a description of a life lived before God. Faustina was outwardly recollected, but interiorly, she experienced the joys and trials of everyday life. Sometimes, she complained in her *Diary* about unfair judgments, accusations, maliciousness, and affronts, which, as a sensitive person, she felt deeply.

She did not tell the other sisters about her suffering or complain to her superiors; instead, she confided in Jesus, her Bridegroom and best friend. He, in turn, told her, "**My child, you please Me most by suffering. In your physical as well as your mental sufferings, My daughter, do not seek sympathy from creatures. I want the fragrance of your suffering to be pure and unadulterated. I want you to detach yourself, not only from creatures, but also from yourself**" (*Diary*, 279).

Sister Faustina did not harbor resentments in her heart. With time, she learned to do what Jesus demanded of her — to bear humiliation in silence and humility and to show love and mercy to those who hurt her.

"Humiliation is my daily food," she wrote. "I understand that the bride must herself share in everything that is the groom's; and so His cloak of mockery must cover me, too. At those times when I suffer much, I try to remain silent, as I do not trust my tongue which, at such moments, is inclined to talk for itself, while its duty is to help me praise God" (*Diary*, 92).

Humiliation, unjust criticism, and gossip gave Faustina an opportunity to grow in virtue. And thus, those who caused her pain also had a role to play on her path toward sainthood. According to Sr. Fabiana Pietkun, of the 24 nuns who were then living in the Vilnius convent, four or five of them would sometimes refer to Faustina as a hysteric. There were three sisters in particular who gave her difficulty: Borgia, Chrysostom, and Benedicta.

Sister Fabiana Pietkun recalled, "She suffered much at the hands of Mother Superior (Sr. Borgia), who called her a hysteric. She wasn't liked because Sr. Chrysostom and others, including Mother Superior, said that she was self-taught and a know-it-all. ... Sister Borgia and Sr. Chrysostom sarcastically called her 'Superior' or 'spiritual director.' She suffered very much because of those sisters, but she did not complain; instead she ran to the chapel and sought comfort from the Lord Jesus. As for us, the younger sisters, she would always simply ask us to pray that one or another sister would improve, that the Lord Jesus would enlighten her so she would not offend Him anymore."

In light of this, Mother Borgia Tichy's opinion about Faustina becomes all the more valuable, as she notes, "She did not harbor unfriendly feelings to those who didn't like her, and she treated her 'enemies' just as she treated others, helping them with their various needs. Maybe these weren't great things, but she served others in an ordinary and constant manner."

Mother Borgia Tichy is portrayed in George Łukaszewicz's film *Faustina*, in which Dorothy Segda brilliantly plays the leading role. The history of the life of the saint is interwoven with Mother Borgia's own story, making it sound like a public examination of conscience with respect to Sr. Faustina.

Faustina once wrote in her *Diary* what she heard another one of the sisters say about her: "Sister Faustina must be either a fool or a saint, for truly, an ordinary person would not tolerate ... such things" (*Diary*, 632). She wrote this, as one might guess, about the spitefulness she experienced from Sr. Petronela Basiura when she worked in the garden of the Vilnius convent.

"The life of each person, wherever he or she lives, is marked by the cross. Sister Faustina also had a cross; one that was fitting for her. Without it, she would not have been credible; she would not have been a saint," says Sr. Elizabeth Siepak. "Her cross was a very heavy one: she bore the burden of her illness and, in connection with her prophetic mission, a great responsibility for the Church and people's salvation. Her struggle with many issues in community life was also a cross for her. Just like a family, a congregation is made up of people with various personalities and various weaknesses, because it is made up of ordinary people, not angels," she emphasizes. And she adds, "Sister Faustina saw the good in her suffering related to life in a community. She saw that suffering purified her of selfishness, of different weaknesses, and created space for love, and as a result transformed itself into a good for herself and others. Her purification made her capable of greater love, a more complete union with Jesus. She was becoming a free person, and as such, she was able to love everyone, even those who were not kind toward her, or who were not good to her. This cannot be achieved by means of the intellect, but only on the way of the cross."

Sister Justine Gołofit remembered that when she worked with Faustina in the greenhouse in Vilnius, Faustina always taught her to keep hurts hidden within herself and not to strike back because "that is not in keeping with Christian love."

Father Michael Sopoćko noted, "She was an extremely humble religious; she didn't put herself above the other sisters, she didn't hold any of them in contempt, but she felt humiliations intensely because she was sensitive."

Faustina put up with humiliations. When she noticed injustice or sin, however, she was capable of standing up and pointing it out. She did this face-to-face and not in the presence of others.

Sister Borgia Tichy described Faustina as "[s]eemingly quiet and calm, but not without a strong personality, which came to the fore quite often. She was uncompromising, sometimes too bold in criticising sisters who were her seniors either in rank, age, or office."

Sister Justine Gołofit recalled, "Sister Faustina never heeded any external circumstances; she was always brave enough to point out people's mistakes to them, face-to-face. She even told her superiors the truth. She did this with dignity and resolve, but also with respect, because she always saw God's authority in her superiors and would say, 'Even if a superior would be the worst among the sisters, she would still have complete authority from God and we should respect her.'"

Thanks to extraordinary grace, Faustina could read the secrets of hearts. She knew in a moment if a given person, or rather, his or her soul, was pleasing to God or not. She made use of this exceptional gift to render acts of mercy: she prayed for people who needed it, exhorted people to mend their ways and grow in virtue, and told others that they were pleasing to God.

Sister Justine Gołofit noted, "She often opened the eyes of our wards when they were living in mortal sin and then receiving Holy Communion without confession. This made a strong impression on them, because — how did she know? ... Her penetrating eyes read what was hidden in the depths of my soul; they always saw my sins and downfalls. I remember well how she would often let me know straight to my face when I succumbed to some fall. At those times, it hurt her greatly that I would be so bold as to insult the Lord Jesus and remain in this downfallen state for a longer period of time. She often repeated to me that nothing hurts the Lord Jesus as much as lack of trust. She would often repeat the phrase that though I had sins as scarlet, I was not allowed to doubt even for a moment that God can forgive me. It is just then that, with great trust, the perfect trust of a child, one [should] throw oneself at the feet of the Lord Jesus, cast down one's sins, and trust in Him."

Sister Justine continued, "She often told me that when a soul fears getting close to the Lord Jesus after a fall, then it wounds the Sacred Heart of Jesus horribly, for the lack of trust hurts Him more than the most terrible sins. She would often tell me when I had distanced myself from God for a longer period of time, 'It is a human thing to fall due to our weakness, but a thing of the devil to remain in sin and give in to distrust.' Her eyes read what was going on in the depth of my soul. I myself would avoid her glance, because at those moments she was saying to me, 'Sister, how could you allow such a horrible vacuum in your soul?'"

She spoke a lot about God to the wards who were helping her in the garden and in the kitchen. She encouraged them to make small sacrifices, to take small steps to change their lives. But she also offered up her own mortifications and penances that she had taken on for their needs. With her entreaties, she obtained God's mercy for them.

Sister Fabiana Pietkun remembered, "Sister Faustina often encouraged me to pray for one or another of the sisters who, in her opinion, particularly needed prayer for her improvement. ... In one case, I believe that, without Sr. Faustina's prayers, that sister would have either have lost her vocation or would have stepped onto a wayward path, but that religious mended her ways."

According to Sr. Justine Gołofit, the superiors would sometimes allow Faustina to stay in the chapel until midnight or longer. She spent these hours in prayer for the forgiveness of people's sins. "She prayed, and she loved to pray. She was always recollected when she was praying and immersed in her prayer. She prayed kneeling, but with her back straight. Her prayer was mental prayer. While praying, she rarely used devotional books or the Holy Scriptures," recalled Sr. Justine.

Many sisters remembered the fact that Faustina did not tend to use prayer books. With her eyes fixed on the Most Blessed Sacrament, experiencing higher mystical states, she was not able to pray by repeating learned formulas. "During prayer the soul experiences flashes of this light which make it impossible to pray as before," she wrote. "Try as it may to force itself to pray as it did before, all is in vain; it becomes completely impossible for it to continue to pray as it did before it received this light. This light which has touched the soul is alive within it, and nothing can either quench or diminish it. This flash of the knowledge of God draws the soul and enkindles its love for Him" (*Diary*, 95). She also wrote the following about this kind of prayer: "Such prayer, though short, benefits the soul greatly, and whole hours of ordinary prayer do not give the soul that light which is given by a brief moment of this higher form of prayer" (*Diary*, 815). At the same time, however, she also prayed in "ordinary" ways.

Sister Fabiana Pietkun remembered, "Sister Faustina always prayed while working. We would say the Rosary, the *Little Hours*, and other prayers, and none of this would hinder her in her work." Faustina did not promote among the sisters the forms of devotion to Divine Mercy that Jesus had communicated to her. In keeping with Jesus' instructions, she informed only her superiors and confessors about them. Nonetheless, she encouraged her friend Sr. Justine and the wards to frequently repeat the prayer "Jesus, I trust in You" and another short prayer that Jesus had taught her in Warsaw in 1933: "O Blood and Water, which gushed forth from the Heart of Jesus as a Fount of Mercy for us, I trust in You."

Sister Faustina only spoke about Jesus' revelations and her conversations with Him to her confessor and her superiors. Mother Borgia Tichy, who was skeptical of Faustina's spiritual experiences, admitted after the War that she had feared becoming the Superior of the Vilnius convent precisely because of Faustina's revelations. "On my part, my perspective, I didn't want to impede a thing of God — if that was what it was — with my skepticism. At the same time, I didn't want to get entangled in a murky situation."

Faustina did not confide her mystical experiences to others, even to her friends Damiana Ziółek and Justine Gołofit. When Sr. Justine asked her once if she had revelations, Faustina answered her "never to ask her about such things." But information about her supposed visions, as they were then called, reached some of the sisters. In spite of this, the majority of sisters, both in Vilnius and in other convents, were very shocked when they found out after Faustina's death (either during the War or after it had ended) that she had experienced such intimacy with Jesus.

Sister Louise Gadzina said, "Sister Faustina kept her interior life hidden, to the point that I did not know anything about her revelations despite the fact that I had such a close relationship with her."

Sister Odilia Kondraciuk noted, "I never suspected that Sr. Faustina had been given extraordinary graces. Nothing hinted at that."

The sisters at the Vilnius convent, however, did not fail to notice her aforementioned lengthy confessions or her fondness for conversations on spiritual themes.

Sister Vieslava Effenberg recalled, "For example, I didn't like it that Sr. Faustina sometimes walked away from the group during recreation, albeit with permission, so that she could chat, or as I saw it, 'confer with another sister.'"

Sister Fabiana Pietkun remembers, "We liked to gather around her at recreation, because she always had something to tell us. Often during recreations, she would ask a question which even the superiors did not know how to answer, and then the older sisters would say sarcastically, 'Oh, such an educated one, she read it out of books and is playing the wit.' They mocked her for 'sitting with her nose in books and not minding and not paying attention to her work,' though she always fulfilled her responsibilities very well and never neglected anything."

As can easily be imagined, the educated first choir sisters who were responsible for teaching the wards were reluctant listeners when Faustina began to explain things that they couldn't say much about. Faustina's knowledge did not come from books; it came primarily from her own inner knowledge.

Sister Borgia Tichy noted, "She liked to think of herself as mature when it came to matters of the spirit. When it came to this, she was somewhat stubborn in her opinions. She liked to guide the sisters on these topics, gathering them around herself, giving them her own direction. ... In a word, her weakness was that she thought of herself as a 'spiritual director.'"

Father Michael Sopoćko stated, "I don't know who taught Sr. Faustina the basics of faith or who taught her the basics of theology. ... Speaking with her, I discovered that though she was a simple nun, without any intellectual formation, yet she devoted her free time to reading ascetical books and enjoyed deepening her knowledge of theological truths concerning mysteries which are difficult to understand, such as the Most Holy Trinity or Divine Mercy, and she liked to talk about them, showing the proficiency of a true theologian. Listening to her speaking about these types of things, I came to the conclusion that Sr. Faustina had gained a proper understanding of these matters and that she had acquired it from her interior intimacy with God through continuous prayer and a life filled with a living faith."

The sisters did sense a certain uniqueness in Faustina. "There was something intangible that radiated from her person, which some sisters sensed at times and could irritate them. It was something positive, but it did not always meet with understanding, all the same," said Mother Borgia. That is why others would call her a "princess," to which Faustina responded, "Indeed, I am a princess, because the royal Blood of Christ flows in my veins." They would also call her "Royal Duchess" or "kasztelanka" (your ladyship). The latter nickname alluded to a person from some play performed by the wards of the institution, where one character was somewhat strange and stood out from the rest.

Yet, in spite of this, or perhaps because most of the sisters sensed Faustina's uniqueness and her strong bond with Jesus, they turned to her with requests for prayer for their intentions. They asked her to bring to Jesus their questions about certain matters — for example, whether they were making their confessions well, or whether Jesus had forgiven a particular sin. Sisters from both the first and second choirs also came to her with their difficulties with the wards and always received advice and comfort.

Father Sopoćko told Sr. Faustina the following, after the first period of his discerning what was happening in her soul: "If the things you are telling me really come from God, prepare your soul for great suffering. You will encounter disapproval and persecution. They will look upon you as a hysteric and an eccentric, but the Lord will lavish His graces upon you. True works of God always meet opposition and are marked by suffering. If God wants to accomplish something, sooner or later He will do so in spite of the difficulties" (*Diary*, 270).

From the moment Sr. Faustina revealed her spiritual life to Fr. Sopoćko, she insisted that he help her in fulfilling Jesus' instructions. Specifically, this meant painting an image of Jesus according to an apparition she had had in February 1931 in Płock. While Fr. Sopoćko was not yet fully convinced of the authenticity of her visions, he nonetheless made an effort to get the image painted, motivated by his "curiosity as to what the image would look like." After all, he realized that the painting of an image did not automatically mean that a devotion would follow. He also knew from the description in Sr. Faustina's visions that this representation of the person of Jesus would contain nothing contrary to any Church teaching.

Father Sopoćko's supportive stance and his involvement in starting the work on the painting were of decisive significance, but nothing could have taken place without the approval of Faustina's superiors Mother Irene Krzyżanowska and, certainly, Mother General Michael Moraczewska.

Conversations between Fr. Andrew Witko (the author of several books about Faustina and Divine Mercy) and Sr. Beata Piekut (the vice-postulator for St. Faustina's beatification process) reveal that the first person whom Fr. Sopoćko turned to with the proposal of painting the image of Jesus was the Bernardine nun Sr. Frances Wierzbicka. Among other works, she was the painter of two copies of the image of Our Lady of the Gate of Dawn (also referred to as "Our Lady of Ostra Brama"). Sister Wierzbicka, however, did not agree with certain suggestions made by Fr. Sopoćko and probably by Sr. Faustina regarding the image of Jesus. This information is confirmed in the *Diary*. Faustina recalled a conversation with "a certain person who was to paint the image but, for certain reasons, was not painting it" (354). Then, in a later fragment, we find out that person was a nun.

The second person whom Fr. Sopoćko asked to paint the image of the Merciful Jesus was his neighbor, the painter Eugene Kazimirowski. This artist, 61 years old at the time, was a graduate of the Kraków Academy of Arts and the Academy of St. Lazarus in Rome. He had also received scholarships at art schools in Lviv, Munich, and Paris. He painted mainly landscapes, portraits, and religious images. At the time, he had been a resident of Vilnius for 18 years. He taught at the teacher's college and was also a scene or set designer for the Great Theater and the Polish Theater in Vilnius. Nearly everything that he created was lost during the Second World War. His most valuable remaining work is the image of the Merciful Jesus, which he painted according to Sr. Faustina's instructions, perhaps out of considerations not so much artistic as religious.

Faustina first came to Kazimirowski's art studio on January 2, 1934. The studio was located at No. 2 Rasos Street (No. 6 today) near Rasos Cemetery, which is one of the most important and most beautiful Polish cemeteries. The building in which the studio was located was part of the Visitation Sisters' convent complex, at the center of which stood the huge late Baroque Church of the Sacred Heart of Jesus, boasting a cupola designed by distinguished architect

John Christopher Glaubitz, and an interior adorned with the frescos and the paintings of Simon Czechowicz. In comparison with the small wooden houses at the convent of the Sisters of Our Lady of Mercy, this massive convent complex, in which the Visitation Sisters ran a school for girls of noble birth, must have made quite an impression on Sr. Faustina.

Nowadays, on entering through the convent gates, one is greeted by a completely different view. The courtyard is divided in two by a shoddy white-brick wall, topped with coils of barbed wire. Behind it stands a guard tower covered with tarpaper. The view to the right is even more shocking — the former pearl of Baroque Vilnius now lies defaced. This scene is proof of the barbarity of the Soviet regime, which expelled the nuns from their convent and set up in the church a prison, which was running until 2008. To the left of the brick wall, a new and different world comes into view. The eye is drawn to a modest, neatly renovated two-story building, painted yellow-brown with red geraniums blooming in window boxes. This used to be the residence of the Visitation Sisters' chaplains, and until recently, it was the location of the prison administration. Eighty years ago, Sr. Faustina would come to this building on a regular basis. Over a period of about six months, from January to June 1934, she instructed the painter, Professor Kazimirowski, as to how Jesus was to appear in the image.

Kazimirowski lived on the first floor of the building, while Fr. Sopoćko lived on the second. The artist's studio was also located on the first floor, exactly on the spot where the chapel of the Congregation of the Sisters of the Merciful Jesus is today; that is, the first Congregation established according to Sr. Faustina's revelations, with the help of Fr. Sopoćko.

"Vilnius is important to us. It's here that the world was reminded of Divine Mercy, and from here the message spread to the entire world. This is where our Congregation was founded," says Sr. Anna Młynarczyk who lives in the Vilnius house of the Congregation of the Sisters of the Merciful Jesus, the residence of five sisters from Poland and Lithuania. They returned to Vilnius in 2001. They changed addresses several times until, in 2005, the Vilnius Metropolitan, Cardinal Audrys Juozas Bačkis, granted them the former home of the Visitation Sisters' chaplains, which had been reclaimed by the Church. The sisters say that it is a miracle that they find themselves in the very same place where their founder, Fr. Sopoćko, once lived and where the painting of the Merciful Jesus came into existence. "When we received this building in 2005, we were not aware of all this," asserts Sr. Anna.

The restoration of the chaplains' residence was made possible thanks to the financial help of Divine Mercy devotees. Inside the building, on the wall of the staircase in the entrance hallway, hangs a simple but immense wooden cross. It is a keepsake from Fr. Sopoćko. He made it himself while he was in hiding in Czarny Bór, close to Vilnius, during the Second World War.

The sisters have set up their chapel in what was once Kazimirowski's art studio. A one-to-one scale photocopy of the painting of the Merciful Jesus hangs on the wall — 8.5 feet by 4.5 feet in size. The painting takes up the entire height of the room. That was also the case when Kazimirowski painted it. He fitted the canvas to a large old frame that someone had given to him. Work on the painting lasted about six months. It is not known to what extent Fr. Sopoćko revealed to Kazimirowski the origins of the concept of the image. In his diary, Fr. Sopoćko wrote that he "partly" acquainted the artist with it, "requesting he keep the secret."

Sister Faustina would come to Rasos Street once or twice a week in the company of Mother Superior Irene Krzyżanowska, who was sometimes replaced by Sr. Borgia Tichy.

"In order not to draw the sisters' attention to Sr. Faustina's interior experiences," noted Mother Irene Krzyżanowska, "I would go with her to Holy Mass at the Gate of Dawn every Saturday morning, and after Mass, we would stop in at the painter's studio. Sister Faustina would give him exact information as to how he should paint the image of the Merciful Jesus."

The distance from the convent to the Gate of Dawn Shrine and then on to the Rasos district is a little more than 3.1 miles long. So every Saturday, the sisters had a long walk through Vilnius. Borgia Tichy's memories suggest that the visits took place on Sundays and that the sisters would get a ride to the Rasos district. It's possible that when Sr. Borgia accompanied Faustina, the routine changed.

The sisters first stopped by Fr. Sopoćko's apartment on the second floor. Sister Borgia Tichy remembered, "I stayed there on my own, and Sr. Faustina went down to the studio, accompanied by Fr. Sopoćko. She came back a short while later, and then we rode home."

Faustina gave Kazimirowski her instructions, but was troubled in spirit that Jesus was not as beautiful on canvas as she had seen Him. Father Sopoćko recalls that it was also very important to her that Jesus be portrayed in the same position as she had seen Him. He wrote, "According to Sr. Faustina, the image of the Lord

Jesus should appear in a standing and walking posture, as is often the case when we stop to greet someone. The eyes should be looking downward and the gaze merciful, as if He were looking down from the cross. His right hand should be raised to the height of His shoulder in order to bless, and His left hand should be drawing aside His robe in the area of His Heart, which remains hidden. From under the raised garment, there should be gushing forth two rays of light: to the right of the viewer, a pale one; and on the left, a red one. These rays are to be translucent, but they should appropriately shed light on the figure of the Savior as well as on the space in front of Him."

When Fr. Sopoćko asked Sr. Faustina what the two rays in the painting are supposed to represent, she told him several days later what she had heard from Jesus: "**The two rays denote Blood and Water. The pale ray stands for the Water which makes souls righteous. The red ray stands for the Blood which is the life of souls. … These rays shield souls from the wrath of My Father**" (*Diary*, 299).

In March 1934, while work on the painting was ongoing, Fr. Sopoćko went to the Holy Land for a few weeks. Two important events took place in the life of St. Faustina during this period of time. The first of these has been mentioned already: she burned her *Diary* because she was misled by the devil. The second event, of a spiritual nature, had more significance in Faustina's life and for her mission. It took place on Holy Thursday, March 29, 1934. That day, Faustina wrote down her act of oblation, which she had already offered at the time of the third probation in Warsaw. She gave herself to God as an atoning sacrifice for sinners. Jesus desired her to do this, "**especially for those souls who have lost hope in God's mercy**" (*Diary*, 308). In this way, step-by-step, Jesus was revealing the mission He had entrusted to her. Sister Faustina accepted it. The special act she recorded in the *Diary* explains what constitutes the sacrifice: "This offering consists in my accepting, with total subjection to God's will, all the suffering, fears, and terrors with which sinners are filled. In return, I give them all the consolations which my soul receives from my communion with God. In a word, I offer everything for them: Holy Masses, Holy Communions, penances, mortifications, prayers. I do not fear the blows, blows of divine justice, because I am united with Jesus. Oh, my God, in this way I want to make amends to You for the souls that do not trust in Your goodness. I hope against all hope in the ocean of Your mercy. My Lord and My God, my portion — my portion forever, I do not base this act of oblation on my own strength, but on the strength that flows from the merits of Jesus Christ" (*Diary*, 309).

Sister Faustina quickly began to experience the effects of the act she had performed, suffering spiritually and physically.

Meanwhile, work on the painting in the Rasos district was slowly drawing to a close. Sister Faustina must have expressed her dissatisfaction more than once during her visits to Kazimirowski's studio, because he changed the painting several times. In order to depict Jesus' stance as per Faustina's instructions, he even asked Fr. Sopoćko to pose for him, dressed in an alb. The artist also needed to capture the draping of the garments, the position of the arms, legs, and head, and the direction of the gaze. Father Witko, the author of many books on Faustina and Divine Mercy, points out that this caused criticism of the image years later: namely, that Jesus has the same stance that Fr. Sopoćko adopted while celebrating Mass.

The one thing that remained was the question of the inscription on the image. Faustina promised to tell the priest what it ought to be at her next confession. Upon leaving the confessional, however, she received an "inner understanding about the inscription." "Jesus reminded me of what He had told me the first time; namely, that these three words must be clearly in evidence: 'Jesus, I trust in You' ['Jezu, ufam Tobie']" (*Diary*, 327). She had heard these words during the revelation she had had in Płock in February 1931. Consequently, Fr. Sopoćko inscribed these words on a plaque and affixed it to the frame of the painting. The work was complete.

In his various memoirs, Fr. Sopoćko gives different dates for the completion of the painting. At one time, he wrote that the painting was completed in May; another time, he mentioned June; and yet another time, it was July 1934. Most likely, the painting looked ready in May, but the painter continued to make improvements till June or even July.

Mother Irene Krzyżanowska recalled, "When the painting was close to being finished, I went to the studio with Sr. Faustina; and we were to state our opinion on whether the image was good. Sister Faustina was not completely satisfied, which saddened Professor Kazimirowski. Despite certain reservations of ours, the image gave the impression of being something quite different from usual images."

It is probably this visit that Faustina described in her *Diary*, "When we had left the artist's house, Mother Superior [Irene] stayed in town to attend to some matters while I returned home alone. I went immediately to the chapel and wept a good deal. I said to the Lord, 'Who will paint You as beautiful as You are?' Then

I heard these words, **Not in the beauty of the color, nor of the brush lies the greatness of this image, but in My grace**" (*Diary*, 313).

Faustina calmed down after hearing these words of Jesus. She then told Sr. Borgia, "It is not what it should be, but that's how it must remain." Sister Borgia did not hide her critical opinion, however, when she saw the completed painting standing in a dark corridor in the convent of the Bernardine nuns several months later: "From an artistic point of view, the depiction of the Lord Jesus left much to be desired, beginning with the very disproportion of His person, the position of the feet, and the typically Byzantine face of Christ. I'm not surprised that Sr. Faustina wasn't satisfied with it, as she had at least a subconscious sense of beauty."

Father Sopoćko, who confessed in his memoirs that he did not like the painting very much from an artistic point of view, emphasized that Sr. Faustina "did not complain any more about the inaccuracy" of the image and "was satisfied on the whole." So he paid the painter and took the canvas upstairs to his apartment.

Kazimirowski also made smaller versions of the image. It is not known how many there were of them. In March 1936, Sr. Faustina took one of them from Vilnius to Warsaw and gave it to Mother Michael Moraczewska, asking her to hang it up in the chapel. Mother Superior refused, explaining that the image would puzzle the sisters. Instead, she placed it in the archives, which went up in flames during the Warsaw Uprising. Shortly after having the image of the Merciful Jesus painted, as early as August 1934, the Mother of God told Sr. Faustina that she would suffer because of the coming into existence of the image. The following day, August 12, Sr. Faustina fell seriously ill.

Sister Yolanda Woźniak remembered that there was "a great commotion in the house in the early evening. Sister Faustina supposedly went completely rigid; she said she was dying and asked for a confessor."

Faustina was transferred to the infirmary. Doctor Helen Maciejewska and Faustina's confessor, Fr. Sopoćko, were called.

Sister Leocadia Drzazga noted, "'People didn't really believe that she was ill, but the doctor who was summoned [Dr. Maciejewska] asserted Faustina's condition to be very serious and was doing her best to rescue her with injections. It was just then that Fr. Sopoćko administered Extreme Unction to Faustina."

Sister Faustina seemed to show the symptoms of a severe case of sunstroke and then those of an asthma-like attack. She was dying. She wrote in her *Diary*,

"Suddenly, I felt sick, I gasped for breath, there was darkness before my eyes, my limbs grew numb — and there was a terrible suffocation. Even a moment of such suffocation is extremely long. … There also comes a strange fear, in spite of trust" (*Diary*, 321). "After I received the last sacraments, there was a definite improvement. I remained alone. This lasted for half an hour and then came another attack; but this one was not so strong, as the doctor intervened. I united my sufferings with the sufferings of Jesus and offered them for myself and for the conversion of souls who do not trust in the goodness of God. Suddenly my cell was filled with black figures full of anger and hatred for me. One of them said, 'Be damned, you and He who is within you, for you are beginning to torment us even in hell.' As soon as I said, 'And the Word was made flesh and dwelt among us,' the figures vanished in a sudden whir" (*Diary*, 323).

Maria Tarnawska points out that this asthma-like attack, which bordered on death, caused changes in Faustina's spiritual life and mission. Jesus had said that He left her on earth because, first, His will had not yet been fulfilled in her, and second, she was not prepared to accept death as He had: **"When I was dying on the cross, I was not thinking about Myself, but about poor sinners, and I prayed for them to My Father. I want your last moments to be completely similar to Mine on the cross. … Pure love understands these words; carnal love will never understand them"** (*Diary*, 324).

Sister Faustina accepted this lesson. Because of her personal experience of the agony of death, she learned that, even in such a moment, she could still make an offering to God for sinners. Until this point, she had prayed primarily for the souls in purgatory. From this moment on, she began to pray more intensely for the dying, for whom this was the last moment in which they could turn to God with a plea for His mercy. The awareness that the dying "need prayers even more than the 'Holy Souls,' for the Holy Souls, although they are in purgatory, are souls that have been saved, while for those who are dying, this is their last chance of salvation," is not definitively expressed by Sr. Faustina until now. "This knowledge appeared only during her time in Vilnius," concludes Maria Tarnawska.[34]

Hedwig Owar, one of the sisters' wards, recalled, "Once every hour she would ask us to say short prayers [quickly shot out like a dart] for the dying. When we asked her why we were praying so often for the dying, she answered that all of this still wasn't enough, that it is necessary to pray continually, because each second somebody is dying on this earth and needs our help."

A short time after Sr. Faustina's attack of asthma-like suffocation, the tuberculosis, which had been consuming her body for years, was finally diagnosed. This only took place after Sr. Chrysostom Korczak was removed from her post as infirmarian. She hadn't fully believed that Faustina was suffering. The new infirmarian, Sr. Amata, took Faustina to get her lungs X-rayed. Doctor Oleński confirmed that she had advanced stage tuberculosis. Faustina later told Sr. Damiana Ziółek that before this happened, doctors had been treating her for three years for "nerves." It is not known when she contracted tuberculosis. She didn't have it at home or while working in the homes of different employers, who described her as a healthy person. It's true that when Faustina first showed up at the convent, Mother Moraczewska called her "a weak little girl," but that could have been because of Mother Michael noticing her generally unkempt appearance.

The image of the Merciful Jesus was complete and stood ready in Fr. Sopoćko's apartment. During this time, Sr. Faustina started having visions where she saw the living image of Jesus, of which the painting was just a copy.

The first of these visions took place in the fall of 1934. It was 10 minutes before 6 p.m. on Friday, October 26. Faustina and a few wards were coming in for dinner from the garden. The girls who were with her were Imelda, Edie, Ignacia, Margie, and Hedwig. Suddenly, Sr. Faustina saw Jesus just as she had seen Him in Płock, and as He had been painted. "The two rays which emanated from the Heart of Jesus covered our chapel and the infirmary, and then the whole city, and spread out over the whole world," she wrote (*Diary*, 87). This lasted for about four minutes.

One of the wards, Ignacia, also saw the unusual rays of light, but she didn't know where they were coming from because she did not see the figure of Jesus. She was so moved by this phenomenon that she told her friends about it. They laughed at her, saying that she was seeing things, that it must have been the lights of an airplane or searchlights. Ignacia would not allow herself to be convinced. She was certain that she had never seen that kind of light in her life. She also told Sr. Faustina about this. Sister Faustina could not tell her that she had seen Jesus, but she probably confirmed having seen unusual rays of light, too.

One month later, on November 28, 1934, a document describing this event was drawn up in the Vilnius convent house. It was signed by Sr. Faustina; Sr. Taida, who put together the document; the ward Ignacia; and Mother Krzyżanowska, who confirmed the credibility of the deposition.

During another vision, one that probably took place during Mass sometime in November 1934, Sr. Faustina saw "two rays coming out from the Blessed Host ... one of them red and the other pale. And they were reflected on each of the sisters and wards, but not on all in the same way. On some of them the rays were barely visible" (*Diary*, 336). Another time, she recalled, "One evening as I entered my cell, I saw the Lord Jesus exposed in the monstrance under the open sky, as it seemed. At the feet of Jesus I saw my confessor, and behind him a great number of the highest ranking ecclesiastics, clothed in vestments the like of which I had never seen except in this vision; and behind them, groups of religious from various orders; and further still I saw enormous crowds of people, which extended far beyond my vision. I saw the two rays coming out from the Host, as in the image, closely united but not intermingled; and they passed through the hands of my confessor, and then through the hands of the clergy, and from their hands to the people, and then they returned to the Host" (*Diary*, 344).

Faustina also had other visions of Jesus as He appeared in the painting and also visions of rays emanating from the Blessed Sacrament and spreading out to the entire world. In these visions, Jesus was clearly pointing to the links between His image as revealed to Faustina and the Holy Eucharist as the source of Divine Mercy.

Jesus also reminded Sr. Faustina of another of His wishes, which He had expressed for the first time during a revelation in Płock — the establishment of the Feast of Divine Mercy. "**I desire that the first Sunday after Easter be the Feast of Mercy**" were the words that Faustina heard in Vilnius in 1934 (*Diary*, 299). Jesus explained, "**Ask of My faithful servant** [Father Sopoćko] **that, on this day, he tell the whole world of My great mercy; that whoever approaches the Fount of Life on this day will be granted complete remission of sins and punishment. Mankind will not have peace until it turns with trust to My mercy. ... Proclaim that mercy is the greatest attribute of God. All the works of My hands are crowned with mercy**" (*Diary*, 300-301).

The request to proclaim and explain the essence of Divine Mercy was directed to Fr. Sopoćko. Faustina was just the intermediary. Now, with the image having been painted, it was he who had to take over carrying out the next tasks:

displaying Jesus' image in public and spreading the devotion to the Divine Mercy. Father Sopoćko still had misgivings and doubts regarding the instructions that Jesus was conveying to Faustina. He told her that there already was a Feast of Divine Mercy, celebrated on the second Sunday after Pentecost, as established by Pope Pius IX in 1855. For this reason, Faustina asked Jesus why she is supposed to speak about the Feast of Divine Mercy since such a feast already existed. "**And who knows anything about this feast?**" was the response she heard from Jesus. "**No one! Even those who should be proclaiming My mercy and teaching people about it often do not know about it themselves. That is why I want the image to be solemnly blessed on the first Sunday after Easter, and I want it to be venerated publicly so that every soul may know about it**" (*Diary*, 341).

Indeed, although Divine Mercy is present and praised throughout all of Holy Scripture, and people have invoked it in private prayer, the truth about this attribute of God had not become a part of common Catholic consciousness. It had not been emphasized enough. God was seen first and foremost as a stern and just judge, but not merciful. However, Divine Mercy is proclaimed by the Prophets and glorified in the Psalms — the most beautiful of these being Psalm 51, which speaks of sin and forgiveness. Father Henry Ciereszko points out that "from the books of the Old Testament comes the teaching that Divine Mercy is not above and beyond God's justice, but is revealed in His forgiveness of the faults and sins of the individual and nation that admits its sins and chooses to return once again to a life in accord with God's commandments."

God revealed the fullness of His mercy for humankind in Jesus Christ, especially in His Incarnation and Redemption. In numerous parables — of which the Prodigal Son is the most instructive — Jesus called to mind that God is a good Father who waits for contrite sinners who acknowledge their faults and sins. He wishes to forgive them and, raising them up from their fall, restores their dignity. In the Sermon on the Mount, Jesus said that only the merciful would receive mercy ("Blessed are the merciful, for they will be shown mercy" [Mt 5:7]), and He Himself showed mercy, healing the sick in body and soul. The confirmation of God's mercy for humankind found its culmination in the sacrifice that Jesus, God incarnate, made of Himself on the cross as an atonement for the sins of humankind.

It is in this context of the Incarnation and Redemption that Divine Mercy appears in the documents of the Council of Trent, different synods, and those written by various Popes. As a matter of fact, there were no particular prayers about the mercy of God in old devotional books, although there were references to it in many prayers. Bishop Ceslaus Domin counted 47 mentions of Divine Mercy in a post-Tridentine Missal, along with 27 references to a merciful God. In the current edition of the missal, these references are more frequent: the mercy of God is mentioned 81 times, and the merciful God, 57 times. According to Fr. Peter Kreis's findings, the liturgical texts of a Votive Mass in honor of the Lord's mercy were published in Cracovian missals from the 15ᵗʰ and 16ᵗʰ centuries, and the second Sunday after Easter was called the Sunday of the Lord's Mercy. In addition to this, at the intersection of Smoleńsk and Felicianek Streets in Kraków stands a 17ᵗʰ century church. The dedication above the main entrance reads, "IN HONOR OF THE DIVINE MERCY," and the short roadway encircling the church property bears the name Street of The Divine Mercy.

Along with love, Divine Mercy has also been the theme for reflections by the greatest theologians. Echoing the words of St. Thomas Aquinas, it was repeated for centuries that love desires to bring good to our neighbor, while mercy aims to rid him of the evil that afflicts him. "But of all the virtues which relate to our neighbor, mercy is the greatest, even as its act surpasses all others, since it belongs to one who is higher and better to supply the defect of another, in so far as the latter is deficient," wrote St. Thomas Aquinas. In his 1980 encyclical *Dives in Misericordia* — that is, about God who is rich in mercy — John Paul II presents this issue somewhat differently. The Pope did not view acts of mercy as the elimination of what is lacking, but as the drawing out of the good from under layers of evil; as the valuing of someone, lifting them up, and returning or restoring their dignity to them. Seen from this perspective, mercy does not contain an element of pity.

The message given to the world through Sr. Faustina provides a similar perspective on Divine Mercy, and theologians have deemed it in keeping with the Public Revelation of God in Jesus Christ. Jesus revealed His mystery to His "secretary of Divine Mercy" in stages. Faustina came to know this mystery in His Incarnation, Redemption, and in the very act of creation, consequently capturing it in a single sentence in her *Diary*: "Mercy is the flower of love." She also expressed this thought in another way, "God is love, and mercy is His deed. In love it is conceived; in mercy it is revealed" (*Diary*, 651).

It was in Vilnius that Jesus clearly defined the mission that He had entrusted to Faustina, telling her: **Your assignment and duty here on earth is to beg for mercy for the whole world. No soul will be justified until it turns with**

confidence to My mercy, and this is why the first Sunday after Easter is to be the Feast of Mercy. On that day, priests are to tell everyone about My great and unfathomable mercy" (*Diary*, 570).

Establishing the Feast of Divine Mercy was a much more difficult task than having the image of Jesus painted. It did not lie within Faustina's power. To fulfill the will of God, she could only speak to her superiors and confessor about this wish, and pray and offer up sacrifices for its intention. She herself celebrated this feast on the first Sunday after Easter in the way that Jesus had instructed her to, "through interior recollection and exterior mortification" (*Diary*, 280). And so she prayed for the conversion of sinners and for mercy for the world, and for several hours she wore a little belt of coarse cloth as a form of mortification.

Alongside demanding the establishment of the feast, Jesus also urged Faustina earnestly to ensure that the image be displayed in public. Consequently, she kept pressing Fr. Sopoćko to hang the image up in the church. But he was still in no rush to do so.

In November 1934, Fr. Sopoćko became the rector of St. Michael's Church located in Vilnius' Old Town. It belonged to the Bernardine Sisters. He took up residence in the convent, which had once been the ancestral palace of the Sapieha family and which had been donated to the Bernardine Sisters along with the church. Father Sopoćko took the image of the Merciful Jesus from Rasos and placed it in a convent corridor.

According to one version of the story, Fr. Sopoćko hung it on the wall, while according to another, he set it down on the floor facing the wall. In a letter in 1966 to Fr. Anthony Mruk — the postulator for Sr. Faustina's beatification process, who had accused him of displaying the image for public veneration without the permission of Church authorities — Fr. Sopoćko wrote that the painting had stood in one of the corridors in the convent. He could not place it in a church without the approval of the Metropolitan of Vilnius, Archbishop Jałbrzykowski, since it did present an old message in a new way. Yet Fr. Sopoćko was convinced that the image did not embody anything that was contrary to the Gospel. Nonetheless, he was embarrassed to ask the Archbishop for permission, "and all the more to speak about the origin of this painting." Years later, he admitted, "I was not eager to hang it in church because I was still in the process of examining the whole issue."

Jesus' desire for the public display of the image had not yet been fulfilled, just as a Feast of Divine Mercy had not yet been established. Despite this, in

February 1935, Jesus revealed to Sr. Faustina a new form of devotion to Divine Mercy — the call to glorify and proclaim His great mercy to others. He also linked promises to this call, for this life and the life to come: "**With souls that have recourse to My mercy and with those that glorify and proclaim My great mercy to others, I will deal according to My infinite mercy at the hour of their death**" (*Diary*, 379). In a later revelation, Jesus said these individuals already experience His care: "**Souls who spread the honor of My mercy I shield through their entire lives as a tender mother her infant, and at the hour of death I will not be a Judge for them but the Merciful Savior**" (*Diary*, 1075). He also promised to clergy who would preach sermons about Divine Mercy that they would be particularly effective in converting people: "**Tell My priests that hardened sinners will repent on hearing their words when they speak about My unfathomable mercy, about the compassion I have for them in My Heart**" (*Diary*, 1521).

Then, on Good Friday, April 19, 1935, Sr. Faustina heard these words of Jesus: "**I desire that the image be publicly honored**" (*Diary*, 414). Even before Easter, Faustina had told Fr. Sopoćko that the Lord Jesus was angry with him and was demanding that Fr. Sopoćko display His image in the Gate of Dawn for three days, during the celebrations marking the close of the Jubilee the Church was then celebrating, the 1900th anniversary of the Redemption. The closing of the celebration fell on the first Sunday after Easter. Just as Fr. Sopoćko was trying to figure out how to carry out this request, the phone rang. The pastor of the Shrine of the Gate of Dawn, Fr. Stanislaus Zawadzki, was calling to ask Fr. Sopoćko to preach sermons during the three-day celebrations for the close of the Jubilee at the shrine. Father Sopoćko agreed, but set one condition: the image of Jesus was to be hung as a decoration at the Gate of Dawn during the celebrations. Father Zawadzki consented to it.

Thus, Jesus' desire was to be fulfilled. One might guess that several factors influenced Fr. Sopoćko's decision. First of all, at that point, he had been Sr. Faustina's confessor for nearly two years and was increasingly capable of evaluating her spiritual life. He was reading her *Diary* in which Sr. Faustina wrote down Jesus' demands, and at the same time, he had been deeply exploring what the great theologians and the Gospels say on the theme of mercy as an attribute of God. Father Henry Ciereszko points out, "Father Sopoćko was aware of [Jesus'] demands. At the same time, he had researched revealed knowledge regarding the mystery of Divine Mercy and had analyzed the liturgy of the first Sunday after

Easter, so he must have noticed the convergence of the essential significance of the liturgy for that Sunday with the truth about Divine Mercy." Father Sopoćko was also aware that until then, the Divine Mercy had not been honored in a particular way on that day. Finally, there was the unusual coincidence connected with his having been asked to preach sermons at the Gate of Dawn Shrine precisely during the first week after Easter. So all this spurred him to action.

However, Archbishop Jałbrzykowski did not know about the displaying of the image; and he was away from Vilnius at that time. "In Fr. Sopoćko's opinion," writes Fr. Ciereszko, "this fact, among others, played a prominent part in the Archbishop's later — and not always favorable — stance toward Fr. Sopoćko's activities in spreading devotion to the Divine Mercy."

Sister Faustina must have been overjoyed to learn that the image of the Merciful Jesus was going to be displayed on the Sunday after Easter at the Gate of Dawn, which was the most important place for religious worship, not just in Vilnius, but in the entire Republic — of equal importance to the shrine in Częstochowa. The image, of course, was not hung in the windows of the Chapel of the Gate of Dawn. In no way did it impede the view of the miraculous image of the Mother of God. It was hung to the left of the chapel, in the front-facing upper window of the galleries on the side of the church dedicated to St. Teresa.

In this church, about two weeks after the image of Jesus was displayed at the Gate of Dawn, the heart of Marshal Joseph Piłsudski, who died on May 12, 1935, in Warsaw, was reposed. His body was buried in Kraków in Wawel Castle, but his heart was brought to Vilnius. One year later, on the anniversary of the Marshal's death, an urn with his heart, along with the remains of his mother that had been brought from Suginčiai in Lithuania, were all buried ceremoniously in a single tomb at the Rasos Cemetery.

Today, from St. Teresa's Church, there is still a passage to the galleries, and from there, stairs lead to the chapel of the Mother of God. The old 18th century wooden steps were recently removed. They had been worn away by pilgrims who used to ascend them on their knees, while whispering the prayers of the Rosary, in order to bow in homage before Our Lady of the Gate of Dawn. The new steps are made of faux marble, which has caused many individuals and institutions to rally in protest with good reason, but it is too late.

It is six in the morning. The veil in the window of the Gate of Dawn is being slowly drawn aside. And again, just as yesterday, the day before yesterday, and tens, even hundreds of years ago, the image of the Mother of God is unveiled to the eye, she who "shines in the Gate of Dawn," as Adam Mickiewicz wrote. From this place, from the gate above Ostrobramska Street winding up the hill, for over 400 years, she has observed the city, its inhabitants, and all that they have lived through from this place. This included the glorious period of the Polish-Lithuanian Republic. It included nearly 200 years of the regime of Tsarist Russia, with the repressions that followed the failed uprising of 1863 — the uprising that, instead of bringing independence, brought deportations of Poles to Siberia and increased the Russification of schools and government offices. It included the German occupation during World War I and the annexation of the city to the Second Polish Republic in 1920. It included years of sluggish post-war development, interrupted by the Second World War, which brought about the slaughter and ultimately the exodus of the Polish population from Vilnius. It included the years after the war until 1990, when Vilnius was the capital of the [Lithuanian] Republic, one of the United Soviet Socialist Republics (USSR), a time when religious faith was being destroyed as churches and monasteries were closed and turned into warehouses, prisons, and hospitals. Yet not even the Communists dared to touch Mary in the Gate of Dawn. The Mother of God of the Gate of Dawn remains ever clothed in her garment shining with gold. With a downward gaze, she crosses her hands on her bosom as if she were pressing to her heart all those who kept coming to her in those happy and tragic times, and those who keep coming to her today.

The Gate of Dawn, from which the road led to Medininkai, is the only gate preserved in the walls of Vilnius. Its Polish name — "Ostra" — derives from a district of the city that used to be called "the Sharp Point." Originally, beginning in the 16th century, the image of the Mother of God hung in a niche in the city wall. The first chapel, still constructed of wood, was built over the gate in the 17th century. The current neoclassical chapel dates from the first half of the 19th century. On July 2, 1927, a year and a half before Sr. Faustina's first stay in Vilnius and following an extensive restoration, the image of the Mother of God was crowned and given the title "Mother of Mercy." Among others, Marshal Joseph Piłsudski, President Ignatius Mościcki, and Cardinal Alexander Kakowski were participants in the celebration.

In 1932, changes in the chapel décor were completed. Approximately 14,000 ex-votos or votive offerings, which had been offered in gratitude for received graces, were hung on the walls. The ex-voto offered to the Mother of

God by Joseph Piłsudski hangs between the windows that face the altar; "Thank You, Mother, for Vilnius," reads the inscription on the silver plaque. Until World War II, three coats of arms used to hang on the outside of the chapel on the railings by the windows: the crest of Mary, the Mother of God was in the center (and is still there today); to the right was the crest of Poland; and to the left, of Lithuania.

In 1933, that is, when Sr. Faustina came to Vilnius for the second time, the inscriptions in Polish had once again been reinstated on the Gate of Dawn, "*Matko Miłosierdzia*" ("Mother of Mercy"), and "*Pod Twoją obronę uciekamy się*" ("To thy protection we flee"). They were changed into Latin during the Russian occupation.

The image of the Merciful Jesus was placed in the front window on the second floor of the galleries on the eve of the three-day-long ceremonies closing the Jubilee of 1900 years of Redemption. It was 7 p.m. on April 25, 1935. Sister Faustina witnessed this moment. She was among those who were decorating the image with wreaths of greenery. No one saw what Faustina saw, however. She saw "a sudden movement of the hand of Jesus, as He made a large sign of the cross." That evening, when she was in her cell, she also saw "the image going over the town, and the town was covered with what appeared to be a mesh and nets. As Jesus passed, He cut through all the nets and finally made a large sign of the cross and disappeared" (*Diary*, 416).

The image "looked impressive," recalled Fr. Sopoćko. In his opinion, it drew people's attention more than the painting of Mary, the Mother of God.

Mother Borgia Tichy recalled, "Some shook their heads or shrugged their shoulders, not understanding the subject of the painting; others marveled at the two rays, white and red, streaming not from His Heart but from underneath His raised garment in the area of the Heart. As far as I could tell, they considered the image to be a new rendition of the Sacred Heart of Jesus. Not attaching any more significance to it, they walked away."

The following day, Friday, April 26, was a typical spring day. The mercury in thermometers indicated that it was over 50 degrees Fahrenheit. Nearly 20,000 people gathered around the Gate of Dawn. Just a handful of people were able to fit into the small chapel and the galleries. The majority stood outside, on the narrow street bordered by St. Teresa's Church to the left and row houses to the right. Behind them stands to this day the ancient Eastern Rite church of the Basilians with "Conrad's prison cell," described by Adam Mickiewicz in the third volume of his epic poem *Forefathers' Eve*.[35] A Mass concluding the Jubilee of

Redemption was celebrated in the chapel. Father Sopoćko preached the sermon. He spoke of Divine Mercy. He later admitted that he spoke not "in connection with Sr. Faustina's experiences or the image, but in connection with the idea that Divine Mercy is redemption."

Faustina wrote, however, that when Fr. Sopoćko began to speak, "the image came alive and the rays pierced the hearts of the people gathered there, but not all to the same degree. Some received more, some less. ... Then I heard the words, **You are a witness of My mercy. You shall stand before My throne forever as a living witness to My mercy**" (*Diary*, 417). On the way back to the convent, "a great multitude of demons" surrounded Faustina. They threatened her with terrible tortures. "Voices could be heard, 'She has snatched away everything we have worked for over so many years!' When I asked them, 'Where have you come from in such great numbers?' the wicked forms answered, 'Out of human hearts; stop tormenting us!'" (*Diary*, 418).

This happened again on the days of the celebration that followed: she had visions of Jesus, appearing as He did in the image, with the rays of mercy spreading out to the whole world.

The image continued to hang in the gallery of the Gate of Dawn until Sunday, April 28. Sister Faustina wrote: "Toward the end of the service, when the priest took the Blessed Sacrament to bless the people, I saw the Lord Jesus as He is represented in the image. The Lord gave His blessing, and the rays extended over the whole world. Suddenly, I saw an impenetrable brightness in the form of a crystal dwelling place, woven together from waves of a brilliance unapproachable to both creatures and spirits. Three doors led to this resplendence. At that moment, Jesus, as He is represented in the image, entered this resplendence through the second door to the Unity within. It is a triple Unity, which is incomprehensible — which is infinity. I heard a voice, **This feast emerged from the very depths of My mercy, and it is confirmed in the vast depths of My tender mercies. Every soul believing and trusting in My mercy will obtain it**" (*Diary*, 420).

The *Vilnius Courier*, one of Vilnius' major newspapers, made no mention of the ceremony at the Gate of Dawn or about the display of the unusual painting. But the headlines left no doubt — the world was in ever-greater need of God's mercy. On the first page of the Sunday edition, the newspaper reported, "England concerned about German air defense build up," and "Germans building submarines." Inside the publication was an account of a meeting of the German neo-pagan movement: "God revealed Himself in the person of Hitler. The neo-pagan movement in the Third Reich."

After the completion of the Jubilee ceremonies at the Gate of Dawn, Fr. Sopoćko took the image of the Merciful Jesus back to the Bernardine convent. He once again placed it in the corridor. Sister Faustina urged him to hang it in the church. On June 20, 1935, on the feast of Corpus Christi, Fr. Sopoćko arranged for the image to be publicly displayed for several hours. It was hung up at one of the altars that was set up near the convent during the Eucharistic procession. But the image was returned to the corridor after the procession.

On December 15, 1935, Sr. Faustina wrote down these words of Jesus, "**Tell the confessor that the Image is to be on view in the church and not within the enclosure in that convent. By means of this Image I shall be granting many graces to souls; so, let every soul have access to it**" (*Diary*, 570). One of Fr. Sopoćko's excuses was that he did not have Archbishop Jałbrzykowski's permission. Meanwhile, he had not even asked for permission out of fear that he would not get it. Nevertheless, on April 19, 1936, nearly one year after the image had been displayed at the Gate of Dawn, he decided to hang it up temporarily in St. Michael's Church without the permission of the Archbishop. He hung it on the wall to the right of the entrance. This took place on the first Sunday after Easter, which was on April 19 that year. Sister Faustina did not witness this since she left Vilnius for Warsaw on March 21, 1936.

The image remained in the church until Corpus Christi, when it once again became an altar decoration during the Eucharistic procession. Then, it ended up in the church sacristy.

Father Sopoćko decided to display the painting in the church because he was increasingly convinced of the authenticity of Sr. Faustina's revelations. He was also influenced by the fact that her prediction of a serious misunderstanding with the Bernardine nuns where he was staying had come true. The reasons for the misunderstanding were financial.

When the misunderstanding reached its climax in January 1936, the priest asked Sr. Faustina for prayer. "To my great surprise, on the very same day, all my difficulties burst like soap bubbles," he noted.

As for Sr. Faustina, she wrote that on that day she took all of Fr. Sopoćko's sufferings on herself, and she experienced many of them, both external and internal. At once, she became the subject of many unpleasant and painful experiences, false accusations, and humiliations. It includes one where the

Superior, in punishment for something that Faustina did not feel was her fault, "told her to eat her dinner on the floor instead of at the table, which she humbly did," Fr. Witko writes of the incident. In the chapel, though, she began to cry and complain to Jesus. Then, she heard, "**My daughter, why are you weeping? After all, you yourself offered to undertake these sufferings. Know that what you have taken upon yourself for that soul is only a small portion. He is suffering much more**" (*Diary*, 596).

For his part, Fr. Sopoćko was astonished by the fact that Faustina described the reason for his difficulties "with complete accuracy. ... This precision was very striking, even more so because she had no way of knowing the details herself," he noted.

What Fr. Sopoćko read in her *Diary* about the agony of Marshal Piłsudski's death also made a strong impression on him. Sister Faustina did not give the name of the person, just the date of his death — May 12, 1935 — but from the description as well as from the recollections of Fr. Sopoćko, it is clear who it was about. Sister Faustina wrote, "Then I saw a soul which was being separated from its body amid great torment. O Jesus, as I am about to write this, I tremble at the sight of the horrible things that bear witness against him. ... I saw the souls of little children and those of older ones, about nine years of age, emerging from some kind of a muddy abyss. The souls were foul and disgusting, resembling the most terrible monsters and decaying corpses. But the corpses were living and gave loud testimony against the dying soul. And the soul I saw dying was a soul full of the world's applause and honors, the end of which are emptiness and sin. Finally a woman came out who was holding something like tears in her apron, and she witnessed very strongly against him. O terrible hour, at which one is obliged to see all one's deeds in their nakedness and misery; not one of them is lost, they will all accompany us to God's judgment. I can find no words or comparisons to express such terrible things. And although it seems to me that this soul is not damned, nevertheless its torments are in no way different from the torments of hell; there is only this difference: that they will someday come to an end" (*Diary*, 425-426).

Father Sopoćko recalled that when he asked Sr. Faustina what the final judgment on this person was, she responded, "It seems to me that Divine Mercy won out, through the intercession of the Mother of God." In his book *The Leaky Kayak and Divine Mercy*, John Grzegorczyk rightly noticed that it is possible Faustina was not able to help the dying man more effectively with her prayer because she did not yet know the Divine Mercy Chaplet, the words of which Jesus dictated to her later.

From her interior visions, Faustina saw that her confessor was very pleasing to God. She saw Mary, the Mother of God, shielding him with her mantle. Another time, when he was celebrating Mass before the image of the Mother of God in St. Michael's Church, she saw how Mary leaned out of the image and told him, "*Courage, my son; courage*" (*Diary*, 597). She also said something else that Sr. Faustina did not catch. When Sr. Faustina asked Fr. Sopoćko what the Blessed Mother had told him, he answered in surprise, "Nothing." But he quickly added that during Mass he had received an answer to some kind of question of his.

Sister Faustina knew that the cause of devotion to the Divine Mercy, in which Fr. Sopoćko was becoming increasingly involved, would become the source of his immense suffering. In 1935, she wrote, "Once ... I had an interior vision — quicker than lightning — of his soul in great suffering, in such agony that God touches very few souls with such fire. The suffering arises from this work. There will come a time when this work, which God is demanding so very much, will be as though utterly undone. And then God will act with great power, which will give evidence of its authenticity. It will be a new splendor for the Church, although it has been dormant in it from long ago. That God is infinitely merciful, no one can deny. He desires everyone to know this before He comes again as Judge. He wants souls to come to know Him first as King of Mercy. When this triumph comes, we shall already have entered the new life in which there is no suffering. But before this, your soul [of the spiritual director] will be surfeited with bitterness at the sight of the destruction of your efforts. However, this will only appear to be so, because what God has once decided upon, He does not change. But although this destruction will be such only in outward appearance, the suffering will be real. When will this happen? I do not know. How long will it last? I do not know." (*Diary*, 378).

After Sr. Faustina's departure from Vilnius in March 1936, Fr. Sopoćko began to seriously reflect on the concept of Divine Mercy. He searched the writings of the Church Fathers for confirmation that Divine Mercy was the greatest of God's attributes, as this would correspond with the content of Faustina's revelations. He had not found this notion among the writings of more recent theologians. "To my great joy, I found similar statements in the works of St. Fulgentius and St. Ildefonsus, and even more were found in St. Thomas and St. Augustine who

— commenting on the Psalms — discussed Divine Mercy at length, referring to it as the greatest attribute of God," he recalled. "From then on, I no longer had serious doubts as to the supernatural character of Sister Faustina's revelations."

He also admitted humbly, "There are truths that one knows and that one hears and speaks of often, but that one doesn't understand. That was the case with me as pertains to the truth about Divine Mercy. I had mentioned this truth so often in sermons, thought about it during retreats, repeated it in Church prayers — particularly in the Psalms. But I didn't understand the meaning of this truth, nor did I explore the full depth of its meaning — that it is the greatest attribute of God's activity outside the Most Holy Trinity. It took the simple nun Sr. Faustina ... who, led by her intuition, told me about it briefly and repeated it frequently, stimulating me to research, study, and reflect on this truth frequently. I cannot repeat here, or rather, put into words the details of our conversation, only indicate generally that at the beginning, I didn't really know what it was about. I listened, I was wary, I deliberated, researched, and asked others for advice. It was only after several years that I came to understand the importance of this work, the greatness of this idea, and became convinced myself of the effectiveness of this old, great, life-giving devotion that, in truth, had been neglected and was in need of revival in our times."

Father Sopoćko began to preach sermons, edit brochures, and write articles for theological newspapers and magazines on Divine Mercy, especially on "justifying intellectually and liturgically the need to establish the Feast of Divine Mercy on the first Sunday after Easter." The first brochure, entitled *The Mercy of God*, appeared in June 1936 with the image of Jesus from Kazimirowski's painting on the front. Sister Faustina was very happy about the publication of the brochure. Father Sopoćko sent some brochures to the bishops gathered at the plenary synod in Częstochowa, but he did not receive a response from any of them. In July 1937, at the Mariological Congress in Vilnius, he put forward a motion to petition the Holy See to establish the Feast of Divine Mercy on the first Sunday after Easter. The Mariologists of the conference supported his proposal, but Archbishop Jałbrzykowski opposed it. Father Sopoćko persisted in his efforts. He discussed this topic with, among others, the Apostolic Nuncio in Poland, Philip Cortesi, but without effect.

Ultimately, Fr. Sopoćko turned to Archbishop Jałbrzykowski, who was skeptical about Sr. Faustina's revelations, and asked for his permission to hang up the image of the Merciful Jesus in St. Michael's Church. This took place on

April 1, 1937. Archbishop Jałbrzykowski, who was the first to be in charge of the Metropolitan Archdiocese of Vilnius, which had been established in 1925, did not want to make the decision alone. He quickly called a commission and placed the Chancellor of the Curia, Fr. Adam Sawicki, at its head. On April 2, 1937, the commission viewed the image and issued a positive opinion on it. The Metropolitan, therefore, allowed Fr. Sopoćko to hang up the image of Jesus in St. Michael's Church, but he set one condition: it would not hang above the altar, and Fr. Sopoćko would not tell anyone of its origin. And that is what happened. On April 4, 1937, the first Sunday after Easter, the image was blessed and hung in the church, on the wall to the right side as one looks toward the main altar.

Thus, six years after the vision of the Merciful Jesus to Faustina, the Lord's desires regarding the image were fulfilled: it was painted, blessed, and displayed for public veneration on the day He requested.

Today, the image of the Merciful Jesus is no longer found in St. Michael's Church. In fact, there isn't even a copy of it there. The church, located on St. Michael's Lane near the churches of St. Anne and of the Bernardines, is no longer used for religious purposes. The building was restored after being destroyed during World War II, but instead of being used as a house of worship, it was converted into a museum of architecture. Much like the church, the city of Vilnius, and its inhabitants, the image has had a turbulent history. In December 1940, Archbishop Jałbrzykowski, who was not a supporter of devotion to the Divine Mercy, ordered the ex-votos or votive offerings, which had been hung in great numbers around the painting, to be removed and the image itself to be transferred to a side wall.

This did not stop the spread of the devotion, however. As Fr. Witko writes, the Archbishop was again forced to deal with the matter of Jesus' image. In 1941, he set up a commission to evaluate and conserve the canvas. In May, three experts (an art historian, a theologian, and an art conservator) declared that the "painting has been rendered artistically and is a valuable achievement of contemporary religious art." In 1942, the painting was returned to its prior location, at the side of the main altar. That is where it remained until 1948.

At the Yalta Conference three years earlier, in February 1945, three world superpowers — the United States of America, Great Britain, and the Union of Soviet Socialist Republics — divided up spheres of influence in Europe. They handed over Poland's eastern lands, along with Vilnius and Lviv, to the USSR. As in all of the territories handed over to the Communists, a battle with organized religion began in Vilnius. All convents and the majority of churches were shut down and turned into museums, warehouses, hospitals, and prisons. Of more than 20 Catholic churches in Vilnius, only six were open for worship after the War. In 1948, the Communists suppressed the Bernardine Sisters' convent as well. They deported the sisters and closed St. Michael's Church. Its furnishings were transferred to the Church of the Holy Spirit on Dominikańska Street, which was still being used for religious services.

According to what seems to be the most probable version of the story, the image of the Merciful Jesus was moved at that point as well. According to another account, found in the 1990 memoir of Vilnius resident Jane Rodziewicz-Stefanowska, the image of the Merciful Jesus was still hanging in the bare and deserted interior of St. Michael's Church in 1950, two years after it had been shut down, with the expectation that the painting would soon be disposed of. Then, Rodziewicz-Stefanowska, along with her Lithuanian friend Hedwig Starajte, bribed the worker charged with disposing of the rest of the church furnishings and took the image away, preserving it by simply rolling up the canvas.

The women hid it until 1955, when they handed it over to the pastor of the Church of the Holy Spirit, Fr. John Ellert, who placed the canvas in a storage room at the church. Information about where the image was being kept soon reached Fr. Sopoćko, who had been living in Poland in Białystok since 1947. According to the nuns of the Congregation of the Sisters of the Merciful Jesus, however, Fr. Sopoćko, their founder, found out about the painting a year later, in 1956. The information was relayed to him by his good friend Fr. Joseph Grasewicz, who had returned to Vilnius after being released from a Soviet prison. Father Grasewicz knew the Vilnius image of the Merciful Jesus well from before the war, when he had lived in the Bernardine convent and was a neighbor to Fr. Sopoćko.

Based on his research, Fr. Witko says that Fr. Sopoćko wanted to have the canvas brought to Poland and then transferred to the chapel of the convent in Łagiewniki. A plan was drawn up to smuggle the canvas across the Polish-Soviet border. One of the border guards had been bribed, and another individual had declared himself ready to bring the painting to Poland. Father Sopoćko waited on the Polish side of the border at a pre-determined time and location. But the transfer never took place. "The person we agreed would transport the painting of the Merciful Jesus didn't arrive. He later admitted, 'I could not bring it across the border, because it seemed to me that I would commit a sacrilege,'" writes Fr. Witko, who also describes the further history of the image in detail.

In the fall of 1956, the image made it to a wooden village church in Nowa Ruda, not far from Grodno in Belarus. It had been taken there by Fr. Joseph Grasewicz, who was promoting devotion to Divine Mercy in the parish. One year later, in 1957, he was transferred from Nowa Ruda. But he was not able to take the image away with him. The parish did not have a pastor, but people kept going to the church and praying before the image of the Merciful Jesus, to which they were very attached.

In 1970, the authorities closed the church in Nowa Ruda. The sanctuary's furnishings were taken to a church in nearby Porzecze, but not the image. It was hung high up close to the ceiling on the wall separating the nave from the sanctuary, and the workers did not have a ladder long enough to take it down. Consequently it remained in Nowa Ruda, where it was in danger of being destroyed at any moment. The Communists wanted to set up a warehouse in the church, but women from the neighboring villages prevented them from carrying out this plan, risking their lives through this very act. They would also come secretly to the deserted church to pray in front of the image of the Merciful Jesus. This lasted for over 10 years.

It wasn't until the fall of 1986 that Fr. Grasewicz managed to organize the transfer of the image to Vilnius. The scheme for this was well planned out. It had to take place covertly, as the local residents would not have given up the image voluntarily, and the authorities could have destroyed it if they found out about the attempt to take it away. Everything took place under the cover of darkness. Several people crept stealthily into the deserted church in Nowa Ruda. They climbed into the attic area and pulled the painting up there. They hung a copy in its place. Father Grasewicz then transported the original to Vilnius. He placed it in the Church of the Holy Spirit, traditionally called "the Polish church," since Masses were being celebrated there exclusively in the Polish language. The pastor of the church at the time was Alexander Kaszkiewicz, who later became the Bishop of the Diocese of Grodno. In this way, 30 years later, the image returned to the city in which it originated. It was hung above a side altar, to the right of the main altar, in the spot where a copy of it hangs today. The journey of the image, however, had not yet come to an end.

By the time the image returned to Vilnius in 1986, it was seriously damaged. It required restoration before being displayed on public view. Religious from the Congregation of the Sisters of the Merciful Jesus say that this was done incompetently, reporting: "Damaged areas were painted over with a new layer of paint. This treatment significantly changed the appearance of the face of the Lord Jesus. The inscription 'JESUS, I TRUST IN YOU' was added in red paint to the image. Moreover, in order for the painting to fit into the niche in the altar, its lower corner was folded under, and an oval-shaped piece was glued on at the top. These changes were not in keeping with the artistic composition of the image as painted by Professor Kazimirowski with Sr. Faustina's and Fr. Sopoćko's participation. This all was, in essence, a brutal tampering with the work that seriously reduced its original value."

In 2003, a second restoration was carried out, which, as the sisters indicate, returned the figure of the Merciful Jesus to its original appearance. "All added layers of paint were removed, damaged areas were repaired, and spots that had formed as a result of moisture or attempts to get rid of them with chemical substances were removed."

From the moment the image returned to Vilnius, the devotion to Divine Mercy began to spread with a renewed energy. In September 1993, several months after the beatification of Sr. Faustina, Pope John Paul II prayed before the image of the Merciful Jesus in Vilnius. This was as part of his papal pilgrimage to the Baltic States, which had regained their independence in 1990 after the fall of the USSR. The Pope met with several thousand Poles in the Church of the Holy Spirit. He appealed to Poles and Lithuanians to cooperate, to "listen to each other, so that the one faith, the same hope, and the love that unites everything would grow in them." These words were particularly fitting more than 10 years later, when tensions between Catholics — Poles and Lithuanians — arose because the image of Jesus was to be moved to another church.

The Vilnius Metropolitan, Cardinal Audrys Juozas Bačkis, made the decision to do this following John Paul II's pilgrimage to Poland in August 2002, when the Pope entrusted the world to Divine Mercy. At that point, Cardinal Bačkis decided to transfer the image from the Church of the Holy Spirit to the neighboring Church of the Holy Trinity, where he planned to set up a Shrine of The Divine Mercy. This decision was announced on March 14, 2004. One week later, on March 22, Fr. Miroslaus Grabowski, the pastor of the Church of the Holy Spirit, and Bishop Juozas Tunaitis signed an agreement to transfer the image to the Shrine of The Divine Mercy. But the transfer didn't take place.

Parishioners of the Church of the Holy Spirit declared that they would not give up the image. They kept watch over it night and day. They collected letters and signed petitions, which they sent to the bishops, and also sent a delegation to the Vatican. The parishioners argued that the Church of the Holy Trinity, which is 10 times smaller than the Church of the Holy Spirit, was too small to become a shrine. They also pointed out that devotion to the Divine Mercy up to that time had developed exclusively in the Church of the Holy Spirit, where pilgrims flocked as a result. No other churches in Vilnius hosted liturgical celebrations honoring the Divine Mercy, nor did any of them display copies of the image of the Merciful Jesus. Both parties in the conflict turned to John Paul II for help, but the Pope left the issue to be resolved by Cardinal Bačkis.

It is important to state clearly that the conflict had nationalistic overtones. The Poles treated the image as their own, as John Grzegorczyk aptly described — a national heirloom. They argued that since it was painted by a Polish artist according to the revelations of a Polish mystic, it should remain in a Polish church. Cardinal Bačkis, on the other hand, hoped that the change of the location and surroundings would help give devotion to the Divine Mercy a more international, universal character in Vilnius and in all of Lithuania. One sometimes hears the following question — not just in Lithuania, where there is a particular historical context for it — but also in the West: Why is it that the rays that emanate from the Heart of Jesus, who appeared to a Polish mystic, are in the Polish national colors? The response — that one ray is red like blood, and the other is not white, but pale like water — is not always convincing.

The Poles' protest vigil in the Church of the Holy Spirit lasted for 17 months. In the end, the image was transferred from there on the morning of September 28, 2005. "Mercy snatched by force" proclaimed the front page headlines of the *Vilnius Courier* the following day.

Several years have passed since then. One enters the narrow, single-nave Church of the Holy Trinity through a somewhat protruding apse, directly from the sidewalk on Dominikańska Street. Peering through the glass doors that separate the narthex from the nave, one can see the image of the Merciful Jesus as painted by Eugene Kazimirowski. It hangs above the front altar, framed by cream-colored marble. A contemporary, gold-filled image of Our Lady of the

Gate of Dawn is located on the wall to the right of the sanctuary, with her title as "the Mother of Mercy" etched in marble. On the wall to the left are found gold-filled, etched inscriptions of the invocation "Jesus, I trust in You:" in Polish, *Jezu, ufam Tobie*; in the corresponding Lithuanian, *Jėzau, pasitikiu Tavimi*; and in a variety of other languages.

The church has had a turbulent history since the 16th century when Ulryk Hozjusz, the father of the famous Cardinal Stanislaus, paid for its construction and King Sigismund the Old established a hospital next to it. It changed owners, was renovated, and was used as a warehouse during the Soviet era. Even in this place in a certain way, history has come full circle. After the War, for the one year before it was closed, from 1946 to 1947, Fr. Sopoćko celebrated Mass here.

Sister Faustina must have been happy that, after many hardships, the image of the Merciful Jesus was displayed in public, as Jesus had wished. But she quickly realized that this was not the last of the tasks that the Lord Jesus had set before her.

Not even a month had gone by after that event when, in May 1935, Sr. Faustina heard the following words interiorly: "**You will prepare the world for My final coming**" (*Diary*, 429). These words frightened her, and she did not write down exactly what this was supposed to mean — not then, nor during the days that followed. But we can see from her notes that she tried to stifle this voice within her, to avoid conversations with God, to feign being distracted, and, above all, to avoid carrying out this new task by giving the excuse that she was incapable of doing so. Father Sopoćko did not permit her to shy away from her interior conversation with God, but initially, she did not tell even him what Jesus' new request was.

Then, on June 9, 1935, Pentecost, she wrote down the following words of Jesus: "**By your entreaties, you and your companions shall obtain mercy for yourselves and for the world.**" She continued, "I understood that I would not remain in the Congregation in which I am at the present time" (*Diary*, 435). But she still did not reveal everything in her *Diary*. It wasn't until June 29, that is, more than a month after her first entries on this matter that, after a conversation with Fr. Sopoćko, she explained, "The secret is this: God demands that there be a Congregation which will proclaim the mercy of God to the world and, by its prayers, obtain it for the world" (*Diary*, 436). She also wrote down these words of Jesus: "**I desire that there be such a Congregation.**"

To leave her Congregation and establish another — this seemed like an unbearable task to Faustina. "I kept repeating to the Lord, 'I am unable to carry out Your plans, O Lord!' But, strangely enough, Jesus paid no attention to my appeals, but gave me to see and understand how pleasing this work was to Him. He took no account of my weakness, but gave me to know how many difficulties I must overcome" (*Diary*, 437).

Faustina knew that this new task was beyond her. She was aware of her own limitations: she was a religious from the second choir, uneducated, without financial resources, and to top it off, she was ill. It must have seemed incomprehensible to her that the Lord would now want her to leave the very Congregation that He had led her to and the one in which He demanded that she remain when she wanted to leave it at the beginning of her life as a religious. Her fear, then, is hardly surprising. On the contrary, it would have been surprising if she did not feel any fear. She sometimes complained to Jesus that He had burdened her with such a task. One time she heard the following in response, "**Will I not help you as I have done thus far? Repeat every one of My demands to those who represent Me on earth, but do only what they tell you to do**" (*Diary*, 489). So she behaved in keeping with Jesus' instructions.

Initially, Fr. Sopoćko kept what Faustina was telling him about the new Congregation at arm's length. He wanted to discern the issue better. He admitted that he even thought this was some kind of a temptation. At the same time, he told her to submit to the will of God and said that God could carry out His will with the help of the most incapable of individuals. Archbishop Jałbrzykowski, whom Faustina told of this desire of Jesus during confession in September 1935, advised her not only not to leave the Congregation but to avoid thinking such thoughts. Borgia Tichy, the Superior of the Vilnius convent at the time, was also set against these intentions of Faustina. Mother General Michael Moraczewska, whom Faustina told about the matter during her stay in Vilnius, expressed doubts as to "whether this idea comes completely from God, and whether you, Sister, have properly understood this inspiration." That is why her advice was "pray, consider, and wait." Similarly, Fr. Joseph Andrasz, whom she met during an eight-day retreat in Kraków in October 1935, told her, "Don't be in a hurry, Sister, until you have received more precise knowledge. The works of God proceed slowly, but if they are of Him, you will surely recognize them clearly. If they are not, they will disappear" (*Diary*, 506).

Meanwhile, Jesus urged Faustina to act. He said to her that He desired that **"such a Congregation be founded as soon as possible, and you shall live in it together with your companions. My Spirit shall be the rule of your life. ... Through your prayers, you shall mediate between heaven and earth"** (*Diary*, 438). Several months later, she also heard, **"Your purpose and that of your companions is to unite yourselves with Me as closely as possible; through love You will reconcile earth with heaven, you will soften the just anger of God, and you will plead for mercy for the world"** (*Diary*, 531).

The matter of founding a new Congregation would occupy the thoughts and heart of Faustina from then on until 1937, nearly until the end of her life. During this period, she would experience moments of doubt and then, once again, would feel a rush of courage and the will to act. Most importantly, what she experienced at this point was the purification of her own will and a complete reliance on the will of God, even to the point of agreeing to God disposing of her as He would. One matures to sainthood. Faustina was also maturing. After some time, she wrote, "I understood that all striving for perfection and all sanctity consist in doing God's will. Perfect fulfillment of God's will is maturity in sanctity; there is no room for doubt here. To receive God's light and recognize what God wants of us and yet not do it is a great offense against the majesty of God" (*Diary*, 666).

While Sr. Faustina was absorbed externally with the matter of having the image displayed publicly and the task of founding a new Congregation, interiorly she was in an ever more intimate communion with God. She was experiencing increasingly deeper states of mystical union in her soul with Him. According to Professor Stanislaus Urbański, this stage, known in mysticism as a spiritual betrothal, began for Faustina at the beginning of 1933 and lasted until 1937; that is, through the entire period of her stay in Vilnius. During the period of spiritual betrothal, the states of spiritual union with God last longer and are more permanent.

"Often during Mass, I see the Lord in my soul; I feel His presence which pervades my being. I sense His divine gaze, I have long talks with Him without saying a word; I know what His divine Heart desires, and I always do what will please Him the most. I love Him to distraction, and I feel that I am being loved by God," wrote Faustina on March 21, 1935. "At those times, when I meet with God deep within myself, I feel so happy that I do not know how to express it.

Such moments are short, for the soul could not bear it for long, as separation from the body would be inevitable. Though these moments are very short, their power, however, which is transmitted to the soul, remains with it for a very long time. Without the least effort, I experience the profound recollection which then envelops me — and it does not diminish even if I talk with people, nor does it interfere with the performance of my duties. I feel the constant presence of God without any effort of my soul. I know that I am united with Him as closely as a drop of water is united with the bottomless ocean" (*Diary*, 411).

In the summer of 1935, Sr. Faustina noticed, to her surprise, that she was experiencing in her soul and hearing Jesus tell her in the depths of her heart everything that Fr. Sopoćko had told her "about union with God and the obstacles to this union." "Perfection exists in this close union with God," she noted (*Diary*, 457).

In June 1935, Faustina experienced a mystical event in a physical way; her heart was pierced by a bright ray of light, which radiated from "that light," as she called God the Holy Trinity. This took place during Holy Mass. Jesus appeared to her at first; then she heard words regarding her mission; and when it came time for Holy Communion, the Christ, in His "unspeakable beauty," disappeared. A ray of light radiated from the great brightness and pierced her heart like an arrow. "An extraordinary fire was enkindled in my soul — I thought I would die of joy and happiness. I felt the separation of my spirit from my body. I felt totally immersed in God." Faustina, who was experiencing mystical rapture, wrote further, "Trembling with joy in the embrace of the Creator, I felt He Himself was supporting me so that I could bear this great happiness and gaze at His Majesty. I know now that, if He Himself had not first strengthened me by His grace, my soul would not have been able to bear the happiness, and I would have died in an instant" (*Diary*, 439).

Ludmilla Grygiel remarks that Bernini's statue representing the ecstasy of St. Teresa of Ávila would be a beautiful depiction of this experience "were it not for this tender gesture of God the Father" toward Sr. Faustina — one that is "unusual in the life of mystics" and which kept her alive.

Describing the aftereffects of her mystical experience, she wrote, "Holy Mass came to an end I know not when, for it was beyond my power to pay attention to what was going on in the chapel. But when I recovered my senses, I felt the strength and courage to do God's will; nothing seemed difficult to me; and whereas I had previously been making excuses to the Lord, I now felt the Lord's courage and strength within me" (*Diary*, 439).

Several months later, in September 1935, in an act of mystical union during Holy Mass, she came to know "more distinctly, than ever before, the Three Divine Persons, the Father, the Son, and the Holy Spirit. But their being, their equality, and their majesty are one ... Whoever is united to One of the Three Persons is thereby united to the whole Blessed Trinity, for this Oneness is indivisible." Faustina emphasized that, as in many other instances, she was unable to express this in words, but the "soul understands it well." She also underscored that she did not see this "with my eyes, as on previous occasions," referring to visions she had earlier, but "in a purely interior manner, in a purely spiritual way, independent of the senses" (*Diary*, 472).

On September 13, soon after the above event took place, Sr. Faustina described a vision that ended with Jesus dictating the words of a prayer to her that is now known the world over: the Divine Mercy Chaplet.

This took place in the evening of Friday, September 13. Faustina was in her cell when she saw an angel who, at God's command, was to punish the world for the sins committed by people. She prayed fervently and begged that time be given for repentance, but to no effect. Only when she began to pray "with words heard interiorly" did she see "the Angel's helplessness;" he could not "carry out the just punishment, which was rightly due for sins. Never before had I prayed with such inner power as I did then" (*Diary*, 474).

When she walked into the convent chapel on the morning of the next day, September 14, she heard the interior voice saying, "**Every time you enter the chapel, immediately recite the prayer which I taught you yesterday**." Having recited the prayer, she heard, "**This prayer will serve to appease My wrath**." The Lord Jesus told Faustina to recite this new prayer for nine days, instructing her exactly as to how she should say it using a rosary. First, one Our Father, one Hail Mary, the Apostles' Creed, and then on the large "Our Father" beads: "**Eternal Father, I offer You the Body and Blood, Soul and Divinity of Your dearly beloved Son, Our Lord Jesus Christ, in atonement for our sins and those of the whole world**." On the small "Hail Mary" beads: "**For the sake of His sorrowful Passion have mercy on us and on the whole world**," and at the end, three times: "**Holy God, Holy Mighty One, Holy Immortal One, have mercy on us and on the whole world**" (*Diary*, 476).

Father Ignatius Różycki counted 14 revelations of Jesus as recorded by Faustina in her *Diary* that are specifically related to the Divine Mercy Chaplet. Though she received the majority of them after having left Vilnius, the first one took place in that convent. To those who recite this prayer, Jesus made one general promise and several other promises regarding this life and the life of the world to come. Those who recite the chaplet and those for whom the chaplet is said will obtain great mercy at the hour of their death. "**Even if there were a sinner most hardened, if he were to recite this chaplet only once, he would receive grace from My infinite mercy**" (*Diary*, 687), Jesus told Sr. Faustina in September 1936, when she was already in Kraków.

On December 12 of that year, He once again reassured her that He would grant the grace of conversion at the moment of death to those for whom the prayer is said. "**When this chaplet is said by the bedside of a dying person, God's anger is placated, unfathomable mercy envelops the soul, and the very depths of My tender mercy are moved**" (*Diary*, 811).

Jesus also attached to the chaplet graces in the present life: "**The souls that say this chaplet will be embraced by My mercy during their lifetime and especially at the hour of their death**" (*Diary*, 754) He promised in October 1936, and in December He confirmed: "**Oh, what great graces I will grant to souls who say this chaplet**" (*Diary*, 848).

On January 28, 1938, He also gave the assurance: "**It pleases Me to grant everything they ask of Me by saying the chaplet**" (*Diary*, 1541). But in May 1938, He added that this would happen only if the requests were in keeping with God's will. The basic conditions for the fulfillment of these promises are trust in the Divine Mercy, steadfastness in prayer, and performing deeds of mercy.

In many revelations, Jesus told Sr. Faustina to keep speaking to the world about the Divine Mercy and to keep reciting the chaplet. "**It is a sign for the end times; after it will come the day of justice**," He told Faustina on December 25, 1936 (*Diary*, 848). Another time He instructed her to write, "**Before I come as the Just Judge, I am coming first as the King of Mercy. Before the day of justice arrives, there will be given to people a sign in the heavens of this sort: All light in the heavens will be extinguished, and there will be great darkness over the whole earth. Then the sign of the cross will be seen in the sky, and from the openings where the hands and feet of the Savior were nailed will come forth great lights which will light up the earth for a period of time. This will take place shortly before the last day**" (*Diary*, 83).

Sister Faustina was "conscious of [her] mission in the Church." She wrote of this in her *Diary* in September of 1935, a couple weeks after she received and recited the words of the chaplet for the first time. "It is my constant endeavor to plead for mercy for the world. I unite myself closely with Jesus and stand before Him as an atoning sacrifice on behalf of the world. ... My sacrifice is nothing in itself, but when I join it to the sacrifice of Jesus Christ, it becomes all-powerful and has the power to appease divine wrath" (*Diary*, 482).

Faustina had already agreed to be a sacrifice before God two years earlier during her probation period in Warsaw ("My name is to be: sacrifice" [*Diary*, 135]). Now she wrote, "My name is host — or sacrifice." She explained that in her call to become like Jesus on the cross, it was a sacrifice "not in words but in deeds — in the emptying of myself" (*Diary*, 485).

"Her sacrifice expresses the dynamic attitude of this apostle of mercy and determines the way she would fulfill her mission," writes Ludmiła Grygiel. "The symbol of the host denotes the most important aspects of her spiritual labors, which were based on the unceasing offering of her very self to God for other people." The symbol of the host indicates that hers was a hidden and passive intercession, and the host, which she wants to become, serves, as Jesus told her on the feast of Corpus Christi in 1935, as a means so that "**these rays of mercy ... will go out through all the world**" (*Diary*, 441). Faustina accepted this task "here and in eternity" (*Diary*, 483). Therefore, she pleaded with God for mercy for the world, for the Church, for Poland, for particular individuals, known and unknown, for the sisters, whose souls she was beginning to read, and for the wards, whose sins she began to feel physically through her internal stigmata, being able to discern how each of them had offended God by means of the type of pain she experienced.

The Chaplet of Divine Mercy was already known in the Church as a form of prayer. But neither was it as popular as it is today, nor did it look as it does now. Saint Gertrude of Helfta, a medieval mystic whose name is connected with devotion to the Sacred Heart of Jesus, used to recite some version of the chaplet in the 13th century (interestingly, Sr. Faustina chose her as the patron saint for a retreat she was making in the fall of 1936). Also, a prayer called the Chaplet of Divine Mercy had been known since the 19th century. The religious of the Congregation of the Sisters of Our Lady of Mercy used to recite it as well. This chaplet was even included in the prayer book that Faustina used and that had been published in 1931. The sisters used to say this chaplet during evening prayers. After an Our Father and a Hail Mary, they recited on the large beads: "Lord Jesus Christ, for whom nothing is impossible except this one thing, that You would not take pity on those begging Your mercy, have mercy on us!" Then, on the small beads, they would repeat, "Oh, my Jesus, [have] mercy!" They would end every decade with the Glory Be and then end the entire chaplet with the Our Father, the Hail Mary, and the Apostles' Creed.

The chaplet transmitted through Faustina has different wording. But that is not the only difference. The essence of devotion to the Divine Mercy — which Faustina wrote about unceasingly and which the professor and priest Fr. Różycki later described from a theological perspective — consists of two elements: complete trust in God as expressed in the words "Jesus, I trust in You," and exercising mercy toward one's neighbor. **"The graces of My mercy are drawn by means of one vessel only, and that is — trust. The more a soul trusts, the more it will receive,"** Jesus said to Faustina (*Diary*, 1578).

Mercy may be exercised toward one's neighbors in three ways: by deed, word, and prayer. **"In these three degrees is contained the fullness of mercy, and it is an unquestionable proof of love for Me. By this means a soul glorifies and pays reverence to My mercy,"** Jesus said (*Diary*, 742). Another time, Jesus said that one should perform at least one deed of mercy toward others throughout the course of a day, out of love for Him. Such a deed of mercy toward one's neighbor is accomplished by reciting the chaplet since one is begging for mercy "for us and the whole world." As for Faustina, He requested that she be the "first" to set herself apart by means of her trust in the Divine Mercy and that she perform acts of mercy toward her neighbor out of love for God.

Questions and doubts about the theological meaning of the wording of the chaplet arose in the wake of Fr. Sopoćko's promoting it, during and after the Second World War, and even after the Church had officially recognized the authenticity of Sr. Faustina's revelations. Specifically, the concerns had to do with the following part of the prayer: "Eternal Father, I offer You the Body and Blood, Soul and Divinity of Your dearly beloved Son, Our Lord Jesus Christ, in atonement for our sins and those of the whole world." One of the first theologians to raise questions was the professor Fr. Vincent Granat, rector of the Catholic University of Lublin, who died in 1979 and whose beatification process was initiated in 1995. He asserted, first of all, that the Divinity of the Son is one and the same as that of God the Father, and therefore it cannot be offered to the Eternal Father. Secondly, Divinity cannot be offered in sacrifice. Third and finally, Divinity cannot be an atonement for sins because that Divinity, that is, God, is the one who forgives sins.

To these objections, Fr. Sopoćko responded, "In the Person of the Son of God, there were united at the Incarnation two natures, the Divine and the human, and they were united in essence and eternally in such a way that the human nature does not [exist apart from the Divine nature] and it owes its being to the Eternal Word. This being so, during Holy Mass the Savior offers to His Father (and we also together offer) His whole self as a human being, and so both the humanity and the Divinity."

The objections of Fr. Granat and other theologians were only fully answered by the professor Fr. Ignatius Różycki. He explained that in the chaplet, the word "Divinity" does not refer to the Divine nature because "it is obvious that the Divine nature of Jesus Christ is identical to the nature of the Father and for that reason may not be offered to Him." The word "Divinity" in the chaplet does not mean the Divine nature common to the Three Persons of the Holy Trinity, but stands for the Divine Person of Jesus. It is precisely such a dogmatic definition about "the Eucharistic presence of the whole Jesus" that was accepted by the Council of Trent. The one reciting the chaplet, therefore, is offering to the Eternal Father the whole of Jesus — His Divinity, that is, His Divine Person, and His humanity composed of body, blood, and soul.

Father Różycki also makes reference to the Letter of St. Paul to the Ephesians, which, he writes, "speaks of the fact that Christ, in fulfilling His mission, was the first to offer Himself as a sacrificial offering for us. We can conclude from this Pauline text that the subject of the sacrifice offered by Christ to God the Father was His complete Self, that is, His complete humanity and His Divine Person. Thus, when we recite these words of the chaplet, we unite ourselves with the sacrifice of Jesus on the cross, made by Him for our salvation. In reciting the words 'Your dearly beloved Son,' we appeal to the love that God the Father bestows on His Son and, in Him, on all people. We have recourse to the strongest motivation in order for God to hear us."

Theologians, including Fr. Różycki, point to the fact that the wording of the chaplet is similar to the prayer dictated by an angel to the children in Fatima in 1916. One of the parts of that prayer goes as follows: "I offer You the most precious Body, Blood, Soul, and Divinity of Jesus Christ, present in all the tabernacles of the world, in reparation for the outrages, sacrileges, and indifference by which He is offended." The authenticity of the Marian apparitions in Fatima was officially recognized by the Church in 1930. Did Sr. Faustina know the Fatima prayer in September 1935 when she interiorly heard the words of the chaplet as dictated to her by Jesus? This is doubtful, as it was only after the Second World War that information about the apparitions in Fatima spread in Poland. Father Witko pointed out another interesting similarity, that is, that a similar question was raised regarding the chaplet as had been voiced about the angel's prayer in Fatima — that the Divinity of Jesus could not be offered to the Holy Trinity. Sister Lucia, one of the three children to whom the Blessed Mother appeared for several months, responded to this charge with a hint of irony, "Perhaps the angel had not studied theology."

The Divine Mercy Chaplet was the fourth form of the devotion that Jesus revealed to Sr. Faustina — after the image with the signature "Jesus, I trust in You," the Feast of Divine Mercy, and the spreading of devotion to the Divine Mercy. Somewhat later, in Kraków, Jesus would reveal one more: the Hour of Great Mercy. In her *Diary*, Faustina also wrote down other prayers given to her by Jesus — for example, the reflections for the novena preceding the Feast of Divine Mercy. Which of these were new forms of devotion still had to be determined.

Interestingly, Fr. Różycki, who was also one of the censors of Sr. Faustina's writings for her beatification process, accomplished this years later. The determining criteria were the promises that the Lord Jesus had made to all devotees of the Divine Mercy, not only to Faustina herself, as was the case with the prayer "O Blood and Water" or the Divine Mercy Novena. For this reason, in the adopted canon of the forms of devotion to the Divine Mercy, neither of these two prayers nor the Litanies to the Divine Mercy composed by Sr. Faustina or by Fr. Sopoćko are to be found.

Sometimes questions arise as to whether the content of Faustina's revelations did not flow out of her reading of religious literature. In the 1950s, Maria Winowska, author of the book *Prawo do Miłosierdzia. Posłannictwo Siostry Faustyny* (*The Right to Mercy. The Mission of Sister Faustina*), asked Mother Xavier Olszamowska, who was the sister in the Congregation handling the cause of the future saint, what Sr. Faustina used to read. Winowska most likely asked her about specific books by mystics of the Church. In July 1957, Mother Xavier wrote back that Faustina had not read the works of St. John of the Cross, those of St. Teresa of Ávila, or *The Story of a Soul* by St. Thérèse of the Child Jesus, to whom she had a special devotion. She didn't use a missal either, because, at that time, the sisters were not in the habit of using them. She only had a copy of the New Testament and a prayer book.

Ludmilla Grygiel, however, referring to a conversation with Sr. Beata Piekut, makes the claim that Faustina knew at least some fragments of *The Story of a Soul*. In the convent house in Kraków, and perhaps in others as well, the superiors often spoke about St. Thérèse; they would hold her up to the religious as a model to be imitated. Grygiel notes a "spiritual kinship" between St. Thérèse, the master of spiritual childhood, and St. Faustina, who was led along the "little way of spiritual childhood" by Jesus and her spiritual director, Fr. Michael Sopoćko. Her *Diary* reveals that, starting in 1934, Jesus often appeared to Faustina during Holy Mass, not as an adult "Teacher in the fullness of His strength and human adulthood," but as a small child (*Diary*, 333). When she once asked Jesus why He took on this form, pointing out that she sees Him nonetheless as "the infinite God, my Lord and Creator," Jesus responded that He would show Himself to her as a small child until she learned "simplicity and humility" (*Diary*, 335).

The Jesuit priest Fr. Joseph Majkowski suspects that Sr. Faustina also got to know some ascetical works from a series of books published by Fr. Joseph Andrasz. This is very likely, all the more so because Fr. Michael Sopoćko recalled Faustina reading ascetical works. As for Sr. Xavier, in her letter she informed Maria Winowska that Sr. Faustina's favorite reading was the life of the Servant of God Sr. Benigna Consolata Ferrero. This is interesting because Sr. Faustina had a lot in common with this Italian Visitation sister who died in 1916 at the age of 31. The similarities are not limited to their lives in the convent or their death at a young age. Sister Benigna also kept a diary in which she wrote down the revelations of Jesus. Father Henry Ciereszko writes that, in her Order, she, too, was known as the "secretary of mercy," because she proclaimed "that God is Love and Mercy, and that He awaits our faith and trust in His goodness, and desires to forgive sinners, if only they turn to Him with sorrow and contrition, without fear."

Another religious was also receiving similar revelations from Jesus during this same historical period. She is the Spanish religious Josefa Menéndez from the Congregation of the Sisters of the Sacred Heart of Jesus. She died in 1923 at a similarly young age — she was 33 years old. She also proclaimed, "God desires that people believe in His Divine Mercy, to expect everything from His goodness, and never to doubt God's forgiveness." Jesus cautioned that "the merciful Love of God is unappreciated, forgotten, and even scorned, and that humanity, valuing this Love, should aim to reciprocate it." With Sr. Josefa as His intermediary, Christ, "while assuring sinners of His merciful love, called for expiation for the sins of the world." This expiation should take the form of "atonement, love, and trust."

Can it be a coincidence that during more or less the same period of time three young religious from different parts of Europe received similar revelations about Divine Mercy, each several years after another? Isn't there some plan of God revealed through all of this? A last ditch attempt to save the world?[36] The revelations of the three nuns occurred during and just after the First World War, when atheistic Communism took hold in Russia, and shortly before the Nazis would stake a claim on world domination. It might have seemed that the evil existing in humankind and brought about by man's activity would prevail.

Neither the revelations of Sr. Benigna (probably on account of the events of the First World War) nor those of Sr. Josefa met with sufficient interest in the Church. It was one year after the death of Josefa Menéndez that Jesus reproachfully asked Helen Kowalska in Łódź's Venice Park, "**How long will you keep putting Me off?**" (*Diary*, 9). Several years later, when she was already Sr. Faustina, He began to reveal the great mysteries of the Divine Mercy to her and to urge her to act. He also gave her helpers: Fr. Michael Sopoćko, Fr. Joseph Andrasz, and, years later, Pope John Paul II.

The truth about the merciful love of God had always been a part of the faith of the Church, but through the centuries, it was as though dormant, seemingly forgotten.[37] It was characteristic of Jesus to remind three simple religious about this truth. He reminded Sr. Faustina through visions and revelations, but also in ways that reached beyond the senses during infused contemplation and the union of her soul with God. The history of private revelations shows that, as a general rule, they are either received by children (as was the case in Lourdes, Fatima, Gietrzwałd[38], and La Salette) or by simple, uneducated individuals (Guadalupe, Licheń[39]), which does not mean that they lack intelligence or spiritual sensitivity. The reasons for this seem understandable. The intellect and theological knowledge can be an obstacle to receiving revealed content that exceeds human intellectual capabilities.

Yet one also has to keep in mind that every apparition is burdened with the limitations of a given person. Cardinal Joseph Ratzinger, as prefect of the Congregation for the Doctrine of the Faith, included a reminder of this in his commentary on the third secret of Fatima. He observed that visions are "never simple 'photographs' of the other world, but are influenced by the potentialities and limitations of the perceiving subject."[40] They correspond to the measure and capabilities of the person receiving them.

Let us, however, return to Vilnius toward the end of 1935. Sister Faustina, urged on and sustained by Jesus, began to work on the constitutions for the new Congregation in November 1935. She modeled it on the Constitutions of the Congregation of the Sisters of Our Lady of Mercy from 1930. She prepared the rule for a cloistered order, because that is how she envisioned it at first, and that is what she had longed for at the beginning of her path as a religious.

The outline of the constitution for the new Congregation that Faustina left in her *Diary* says a lot about who she was and about how she viewed the Order of which she was a part; what she would have improved in its rule; and what she yearned for in community life. "There will be no distinction between the sisters, no mothers, no reverends, no venerables, but all will be equal, even though there might be great differences in their parentage," she wrote (*Diary*, 538). Candidates without a dowry were also to be accepted into the Congregation. The sisters should not only pray a lot, which is fundamental in a contemplative order, but they should also lead a very ascetic life ("We will have no meat. Our meals shall be such that not even the poor will have any reason to envy us" [*Diary*, 546]). They were to do all the chores in the convent on their own, on a rotating basis, so that each sister would get to know all the tasks: "Each sister, including even the superior, shall work in the kitchen for a month," she noted (*Diary*, 549). Further, Faustina placed great emphasis on the keeping of silence, which — in addition to the vows — she considered to be the most important rule of the religious life.

During this period of her stay in Vilnius, Sr. Faustina felt internally compelled to act. She told her superiors about this, wishing to receive their permission to leave the order and establish a new one. In a way, this meant passing her responsibilities on to others, and so it should come as no surprise that the matter was not easily resolved.

On January 8, 1936, Archbishop Jałbrzykowski received Faustina at his residence by the Vilnius Cathedral of St. Stanislaus and St. Ladislaus. At this point, Faustina had already been to this archcathedral basilica, which, in spite of the damage that has been inflicted upon it repeatedly, preserves the memory of the coronations, weddings, and funerals of the great Lithuanian dukes and Polish kings that had taken place there. The cathedral as it is today, and in which Faustina prayed, was built on the foundations of the first one from the 14th century and consecrated in 1801. Of the 11 chapels in the cathedral, the most beautiful is the early baroque St. Casimir's Chapel with his reliquary, modeled after Sigismund's Chapel on Wawel Hill.

On July 2, 1927, not long before Sr. Faustina arrived in Vilnius, a grand ceremony took place on the square in front of the cathedral — the aforementioned coronation of the image of Our Lady of the Gate of Dawn. Four years later, the square and cathedral crypts were flooded. Forgotten vaults containing the tombs of kings were discovered during the construction work that had been intended to strengthen the foundations. The coffins of King Alexander Jagiellon, of the wives of Sigismund Augustus — Elizabeth of Austria and Barbara Radziwiłł — as well as the urn containing the heart of King Ladislaus IV were uncovered. The re-burial of the rulers became a huge event.

Not far from all of this, on Zawalna Street (Pylimo today), stands the former church of St. George. Faustina would attend lectures there for religious sisters, encouraging other sisters to take part in them as well. We don't know the year, but Sr. Justine Gołofit recalled that they took place in the "summer time" on Sundays. At the time, the church was Catholic. It had been built in the 16ᵗʰ century by Calvinists, and nowadays it is a Calvinist church yet again.

During her meeting with Archbishop Jałbrzykowski, Sr. Faustina told him of Jesus' desire regarding the founding of a Congregation that would beg for Divine Mercy for the world. She had told the Metropolitan about this already, several months earlier, but this time she asked for his permission to do what Jesus was demanding of her. The Archbishop advised Sr. Faustina to give it more time, saying, that while "this thing is good in itself … there is no need to hurry" because "if it is God's will, it will be done, whether it be a little sooner or a little later" (*Diary*, 585).

Several times, Faustina put the same request to the Superior of her Congregation. Mother Michael Moraczewska recalled, "In the face of these renewed requests, I took a more decisive stance. … I told her, therefore, that as Superior General I am responsible for the sisters' vocations, and for this reason I cannot give approval for her project without deep reflection and without being assured that this is God's will and not a temptation of Satan. That perhaps it is the evil spirit who wants to pull her out into the world, so that there would no longer be Sr. Faustina, but once again, little Helen Kowalska. Then I told her, 'Right now, I don't have any special inspiration as you do, Sister. So please pray that the Lord God give me some kind of light on the matter, some sort of external or internal sign.'"

It was not only Sr. Faustina who encountered difficulties in the Congrega-tion as a result of her having received extraordinary graces from God. Faustina's case was also difficult for her superiors. Discerning whether they were dealing with a mystic or a hysteric — as some sisters nastily referred to her — required time, common sense, and a lack of prejudice. Fortunately, Mother General Michael Moraczewska was very prudent. Sister Faustina received even greater understanding and support from Mother Irene Krzyżanowska, who was her Superior in Vilnius for nearly two years and then for three years in Łagiewniki. Mother Borgia Tichy, on the other hand, did not understand the spirituality of Sr. Faustina, as was already mentioned earlier. On March 21, 1936, she sent her to Warsaw to speak with the Mother General about the matter of the new congregation.

Mother Borgia Tichy recalled, "After a short period of time, I received instructions from Mother General to send along Sr. Faustina's things, as she would not be returning to Vilnius."

Indeed, after consulting with her advisors, Mother Moraczewska decided to transfer Sr. Faustina from Vilnius to Kraków. Before she arrived in Łagiewniki, she was first sent to the convent houses in Walendów and Derdy for a few weeks. There happened to be a temporary need for a cook in those houses, and Faustina, as usual, did not resist being transferred from convent to convent, even for short periods of time.

Chapter Fourteen

Derdy

1936

'I Breathe a Whole Chestful of the Clean, Fresh Air'

"I AM CURRENTLY IN DERDY, ABOUT ONE MILE AWAY FROM WALENDÓW. ... Our small house in Derdy is truly like a house from a fairytale. It stands in the middle of the woods, and there are no buildings nearby. All is peace and quiet. Everything that surrounds me helps the concentration of my spirit. Little forest birds break the silence and praise their Creator with chirping. In everything around me, I see God!" Sr. Faustina wrote to Fr. Sopoćko on May 10, 1936. She was writing her letter in the silence of the convent house, which stood surrounded by a 32-acre park, awash in greenery. The sisters dubbed this house "St. Joseph's Retreat." Even today, though the park is smaller and a slew of mansions have sprung up in Łazy, a fashionable Warsaw suburb situated opposite the convent, it continues to be an enclave of silence, peace, and prayer.

Sister Faustina was at the convent in Derdy for only a short period of time. She spent a fortnight here, or perhaps several weeks, from April to May 1936. It is known that she left Derdy on May 11. She informs Fr. Sopoćko about this in her letter of May 10. After Easter, which fell on April 12 in 1936, she came from nearby Walendów. It could be that she began her stay in Derdy only after April 25, because she still wrote "Walendów" under that date in her *Diary*. This fact, however, is not conclusive since she also listed Walendów in the header of the letter that she wrote to Fr. Sopoćko on May 10. On the other hand, she wrote a few lines later in her letter that she was already at the house in Derdy. This was probably because at that time Derdy was a house affiliated with the Walendów convent. Therefore, Faustina could have been staying in Derdy both before and after April 25. This can no longer be clarified today.

In 1936, Sr. Faustina was already seriously ill. But in Derdy, it was as though she had gained renewed strength. The forest air suited her diseased lungs very well.

"I do some of the spiritual exercises in the woods, like the Rosary and some others, and in the meantime, I breathe a whole chestful of the clean, fresh air. I feel very healthy. I feel like I'm building up great stores of physical strength," she informed Fr. Sopoćko. Her superiors ordered her to nap for two hours every afternoon. She would therefore lie down in a lounge chair on the porch of the convent — at that time, a commonly used method for the treatment of tuberculosis.

The wooden building still looks just as it did in photographs from the time when Sr. Faustina lived there: a two-story house with a sloped roof and a porch that used to be thickly covered in grapevine. The interior boasts wood-paneled walls in warm beige and brown colors. It is modest, clean, and friendly. It is difficult to pinpoint precisely where Faustina's cell was located. It is certain that she slept on the first floor in the shared dormitory to the left of the entrance. In the late 1990s, this large space was divided up into smaller rooms. Every step of the narrow, wooden staircase leading to the chapel on the second floor creaks. This chapel was opened in 1934, two years before Sr. Faustina came to Derdy. She probably climbed the stairs several times each day. Kneelers for the sisters and the wards were arranged in a straight row that faced the altar. "At the feet of the Lord, I draw strength and courage to carry on the struggle," wrote Faustina. Mass, however, was rarely celebrated here. For the celebration of the Eucharist, the sisters would go to the church in Walendów. It was not until the late 1980s that a church was built next to the convent in Derdy.

In Derdy, Faustina worked in the kitchen. "My assigned task is so small that it seems to me more a rest than a duty: I look after the kitchen and pantry. I do not have the slightest difficulty with those tasks; I prepare meals for seven sisters and 36 schoolchildren," she wrote. Faustina was cooking for more than 40 people, but after having stayed in convents where she used to prepare meals for 100 people or more, the work was easy for her, frankly a respite. The large kitchen with a barrel-vaulted ceiling was located in the basement of the house for the wards, which stood next to the convent building.

The sisters began building a house for the wards in 1932. Four years later, when Sr. Faustina arrived, the second floor was ready. Faustina was the only cook in Derdy, but Sr. Seraphina Kukulska, the Superior of the Walendów house and the affiliated house in Derdy, used to delegate wards to help her. Sister Kukulska remembered one of them very well, as the girl was a recent convert and "had a very difficult personality, so no one wanted to work with her. While working with Sr. Faustina, this girl changed beyond recognition. That is the silent, godly influence that Faustina had on sinful souls."

It is not known whether Sr. Kukulska had in mind Hedwig Zalewska, who was there in Walendów and Derdy between the ages of 11 and 13. The fact is that during this period, because of her bad behavior at school, Hedwig had been sent to help in the kitchen as a punishment. "She told me later that Sr. Faustina comforted her and did some of the work for her," remembers Mrs. Camilla, that is, Maria Olszewska, a former ward of the sisters from Walendów.

In Derdy, the sisters ran an elementary school for their younger wards. The school was located in a wooden house, which to this day stands opposite the convent. It was founded by Fr. Justin Borzewski, a friend of the Congregation. He named it the House of St. Teresa the Great.

Sister Faustina saw Derdy for the first time long before 1936. She visited in November 1932, when, after an eight-day retreat in Walendów, she went with some other sisters to see the farm Count Przeździecki had donated to the Congregation one month earlier. It was the second time that the same property was being donated. The sisters received the Derdy farm for the first time in 1881, when the Countess Maria Alexandra Przeździecka, née Tyzenhauz, gave the Congregation 20 acres of sandy soil. Mother Teresa Potocka, the foundress of the Congregation, intended to use the land to set up a rest home there for the sisters. The sisters, however, quickly brought some of their wards to Derdy. This series of events was repeated several times in the history of the Congregation's houses. The religious would buy or would be given some property to create a place of rest, and then they would realize that there was a need to care for more girls and would, therefore, open a shelter for them instead.

The house in Derdy was in operation until 1913, when the religious moved to nearby Walendów. Moving to Walendów was the condition that Count Gustav Przeździecki, the son of Alexandra, set for giving the sisters a much larger farm there. Once this condition was fulfilled, the Count donated the farm to them. The house in Derdy was taken over by the Sisters of Charity of St. Vincent de Paul, who ran an orphanage there until 1930. For the following two years, the buildings stood abandoned. It was not until October 1932 that the daughter of Count Przeździecki, Princess Sophia Światopełk-Czetwertyńska, again donated Derdy to the Congregation of the Sisters of Our Lady of Mercy.

In 1936, while staying in Derdy, the thought of creating a new Congregation was first and foremost on Sr. Faustina's mind. "I am currently receiving much Divine light regarding this work. My soul has been more and more at peace, as I am convinced that God Himself is carrying out this work, and I am being used only as an inept instrument," she wrote to Fr. Sopoćko. "On the first Sunday after Easter, on the Feast of Divine Mercy, my soul was filled with such great strength and courage to act that really I cannot resist this enthusiasm. I feel that very soon everything will be resolved. I am ready for whatever awaits me! I long for the sufferings and adversities that await me. ... I feel that Jesus Himself speaks through my mouth and is giving me the answers to the various questions posed by the superiors. I am obedient to the voice of God, and nothing has changed in my soul — just as it was, it is in my heart — the Lord's gaze penetrates me through and through!"

In this letter, Sr. Faustina informed Fr. Sopoćko of a major decision. She decided that after arriving in Kraków, she would take "a decisive step in accord with the Divine desires." This would be taking leave of the Congregation of the Sisters of Our Lady of Mercy, in accord with the wishes of Jesus, to found a new order.

Mother General Moraczewska gave Faustina permission to send letters to Fr. Sopoćko by herself — that is, without first having them read by the Superior of the convent she was staying at, in this case, Derdy. These types of controls were outlined in the Constitutions of the Congregation. "I'm personally putting this letter in the mailbox, so you, Father, will surely receive it," Faustina informed him, from which one can infer that it was not always so. It is not known whether Faustina put the letter in the mailbox that stood by the village schoolhouse just over half a mile away from the convent, or in the mailbox in Nadarzyn that was located nearly two miles away. The special exception that Mother General made for Sr. Faustina shows her great trust in the future saint, but it also speaks the fact that the Superior wanted to avoid the spreading of information among the sisters about Faustina's plans to establish a new Congregation. Mother Moraczewska rightly foresaw that this could become the source of gossip and speculation, contributing to a generally negative atmosphere among the sisters.

On the last day of Faustina's stay in Derdy, as she said goodbye to her friend Sr. Justine Gołofit, she gave her a cross from the Holy Land, which she had received from Fr. Sopoćko. Sister Justine recounts, "Faustina told me in great confidence that 'in two years' time, in the fall, she was going to die, and that we would not see each other on this earth, [that is,] until in heaven.' Faustina warned me not to tell anyone as long as she was alive, and she did die two years later, just as she had predicted. This conversation took place in May 1936, and Sr. Faustina died in October 1938. She promised to remember me in a special way after her death and to pray for me a lot."

On May 11, 1936, accompanied by Sr. Edmunda Sękuł, Sr. Faustina left Derdy. They travelled to the convent in Łagiewniki by way of Warsaw.

Chapter Fifteen

Kraków-Łagiewniki II

1936-1938

'I Feel That I Have Been
Totally Imbued with God'

ON MARCH 23, 1937, THE TUESDAY OF HOLY WEEK, SR. FAUSTINA SAW HER CANONIZATION IN AN INTERIOR VISION. The ceremony was taking place simultaneously in Rome and in Łagiewniki. "Suddenly, God's presence took hold of me, and at once I saw myself in Rome, in the Holy Father's chapel and at the same time I was in our chapel. And the celebration of the Holy Father and the entire Church was closely connected with our chapel and, in a very special way, with our Congregation. And I took part in the solemn celebration simultaneously here and in Rome" (*Diary*, 1044). This is how she described what she saw, though she was unable to understand how it was possible.

But those who were present in St. Peter's Square and in Łagiewniki on Sunday, April 30, 2000 — *they* knew! A special simulcast made it possible. Two giant screens bringing the ceremony live from the Vatican stood in front of the convent in Łagiewniki. At the same time, the televised transmission from Łagiewniki was being shown on two giant screens in St. Peter's Square. In this way, what was happening in Łagiewniki became an integral part of the television coverage of Faustina's canonization in Rome, which was being broadcast to the whole world.

That day even the weather was similar in both cities. In Kraków, more than 70,000 pilgrims prayed in the scorching heat — rare at that time of year. There were more than 200,000 people in St. Peter's Square, including tens of thousands of Poles, and many pilgrims from the United States, Argentina, Mexico, and the Philippines. Polish Prime Minister George Buzek was there, along with various bishops and Fr. Ronald Pytel of Baltimore, Maryland, from the USA — whose healing through the intercession of then-Blessed Faustina Kowalska was recognized as the miracle for her canonization.

"The crowd was so enormous that the eye could not take it all in. Everyone was participating in the celebrations with great joy, and many of them obtained what they desired," wrote Faustina in 1937 (*Diary*, 1044) about what was going to happen in April 2000.[41] Indeed, such simultaneous participation in a canonization Mass would mark a first in the history of the Church. "And then suddenly I saw St. Peter, who stood between the altar and the Holy Father. I could not hear what St. Peter said, but I saw that the Holy Father understood his words," Faustina continued in her description of what she saw in the future.

Pope John Paul II, who presided at the canonization Mass, said, "By Divine Providence, the life of this humble daughter of Poland was completely intertwined with the history of the 20th century, the century we have just left behind. In fact, it was between the First and Second World Wars that Christ entrusted His message of mercy to her. Those who remember, who were witnesses and participants in the events of those years and the horrible suffering they caused for millions of people, know well how necessary the message of mercy was." He also called Sr. Faustina "a gift of God for our time."

Sister Faustina came from Derdy to the convent in Łagiewniki on May 12, 1936. Sister Felicia Żakowiecka, whom Faustina had known since the time of her novitiate, accompanied her on the way from Kraków's main train station. Faustina could see how much the city had changed since 1928, when she was last in Kraków for a longer time. The rebuilding of the city's main thoroughfare — the Aleje Trzech Wieszczów — was underway right then. The city's residents still harbored vivid memories of the royal funeral, which had been given to Marshal Joseph Piłsudski a year earlier, on May 18, 1935. He had been buried with the highest honors in the cathedral crypts on Wawel Hill. "I delight in Kraków," Faustina wrote in a letter to Sr. Justine Gołofit two weeks after her arrival.

In coming to Łagiewniki, Faustina returned to a convent that she knew well. It was here that she had her investiture ceremony and spent her two-year-long novitiate, which was completed with the profession of her first religious vows in April 1928. After that, she came to Łagiewniki twice more, though for brief stints: in 1933, when she made her perpetual vows, and in the fall of 1935 for an eight-day retreat. She also knew well the Mother Superior of the

Łagiewniki convent, Mother Irene Krzyżanowska. Mother Irene had previously been in charge of the house in Vilnius.

Faustina was assigned to work in the garden. She worked there with three other sisters under the supervision of Sr. Clementine Buczek, the head gardener at the convent. "I get on very well with Sr. Clementine, even though I did not expect to," Faustina informed Sr. Justine, adding, "I spend more time working in the greenhouse and the frames." As she told her friend, Sr. Faustina felt very happy at the time. Nevertheless, she did have a lot of work, which she mentioned in one of her letters to Fr. Michael Sopoćko. But, despite her declining physical strength, the results of her work were astonishing. Sister Clementine recalled that when Faustina worked in the garden, the nuns used to harvest huge amounts of cucumbers and tomatoes. Some tomato plants bore as many as 80 tomatoes, and a small strawberry patch yielded more than 330 pounds of fruit daily.

Sister Felicia Żakowiecka recounts that Faustina "was very prudent in coping with what went on between the garden and the kitchen, and she tried to satisfy all the sisters, providing what was needed. She did not refuse any sister her request because, as a former cook herself, she knew what the needs of a kitchen were. And this was no easy matter, because the sister in charge of the garden was rather parsimonious with supplying vegetables."

Once, when Sr. Felicia asked Faustina whether it was a good thing for her to work in the garden, Faustina replied that she was doing the will of God, and so it was very good for her. She added that, on the other hand, adversity could be found anywhere. "You just need to remember that it is God who gives adversities to us." Faustina did not mention her work in the garden or her everyday responsibilities in the *Diary*. Her heart — beginning with her time in Vilnius — was preoccupied with Jesus' request to establish a new Congregation that would plead for mercy for the world. Already during her short stay in Derdy, before she came to Łagiewniki, Faustina had resolved that it would be in Łagiewniki that she would take "a decisive step" and leave the Congregation in order to establish a new one. But she wanted to do this with the consent of her confessor and spiritual director who, in Łagiewniki, was Fr. Joseph Andrasz.

In fact, from this point until her death, Sr. Faustina had two spiritual directors because she continued to exchange letters with Fr. Sopoćko, consulting him on important matters. Father Andrasz, who held Fr. Sopoćko in high esteem, advised her to do the same. As for Fr. Sopoćko, he would visit Faustina in Łagiewniki or in the hospital in Prądnik whenever he was in Kraków or in southern Poland.

They would always talk for a long time. Many years later, Sr. Felicia Żakowiecka admitted that she would tease Faustina "sincerely and cordially" about having two spiritual directors. "I do not understand how one can have two directors of one's conscience," she would say to Faustina. And Faustina would respond "with a kind smile, but in all seriousness": "the Lord Jesus demands it."

Both priests were very careful when it came to the issue of the new Congregation. They did not give Faustina what she expected from them, that is, permission to leave her Congregation in order to establish a new one. Father Andrasz promised to give her direction in this matter on the feast of Corpus Christi, which fell on June 19 in 1936, and he told her to pray for this intention until that time.

Meanwhile, in his letters, Fr. Sopoćko continued to advise her as he had earlier: "[O]ne should maintain caution and not hurry in spite of the great pressure to act." At the same time, in a letter dated May 15, 1936, he told her of a certain Mrs. Hemplowa, who was looking for a suitable congregation, and who — not finding one — took an interest in Faustina's idea. She was willing to hand her wealth and possessions over to the new Congregation. On the one hand, Faustina saw in this the sign from God for which she had been praying, but on the other hand, she feared that it was still too soon. However, Mrs. Hemplowa, about whom nothing else is known, did not come to see Faustina in Kraków.

But the matter did not end there. Feeling impelled to act, and without waiting for Corpus Christi and for Fr. Andrasz's directions, Sr. Faustina made a decision on June 18 to leave her Congregation and establish a new one. But the next morning, before taking part in the Eucharistic procession at the Jesuit church on Kopernik Street, "the presence of God" left her and "a great darkness enveloped" her soul. So she changed her mind. She decided to "delay the matter a bit." However, later on in the same month, in June 1936, she wrote: "O my Jesus, how immensely I rejoice at the assurance You have given me that the Congregation will come into being. I no longer have the least shadow of a doubt about this, and I see how great is the glory which it will give to God. It will be the reflection of God's greatest attribute; that is, His divine mercy" (*Diary*, 664).

Faustina began to act once more. She wanted to go to Rome to ask the Pope for permission to leave the Congregation and to establish the Feast of Divine Mercy. Father Andrasz dampened her enthusiasm, explaining that it would be difficult for the Mother General to allow her to do this. On July 5, however, Faustina wrote to Fr. Sopoćko, "I feel that God's chosen hour for me to start acting has come."

In his response, which was written five days later, Fr. Sopoćko urged her to be calm: "Sister, the Feast of Divine Mercy, which the Lord Jesus is demanding through you, will be established without your going to the Holy Father; and besides, your going to Rome in person would not help the matter advance, and could even hinder it." Father Sopoćko advised her to prepare the ground first, that is, to make people, especially the bishops, aware of the need for such a feast. Once this was done, establishing a Feast of Divine Mercy would only be a matter of time. According to Fr. Sopoćko, Faustina should also not rush to leave her Congregation in order to establish a new one. "Sister, the way I see it at this point, such a Congregation would have to be established without you, as a diocesan congregation for the time being, and only afterwards would you be able to pass over to it as to an already existing one."

Faustina did not receive Fr. Sopoćko's suggestion with enthusiasm. She was still convinced that she was the one who would establish the new Congregation. She remained in this state of mind for at least another year. Before her death, though, she was already at peace about it. She knew then that the Congregation would be established, although she would not be the one to establish it. But back then, in 1936, she experienced times of doubt and fear, alternating with great enthusiasm and a willingness to act.

Mother Michael Moraczewska recalled, "Faustina suffered very much at that time. It was evident that the thought of leaving our Congregation, which she truly loved, was taking its toll on her ... on the other hand, it seemed to her that she ought to follow the will of God. So those few years were perhaps the most difficult period of her life. During those years, she was sad, depressed, but always in her proper place and doing her duty."

After one particular conversation with her Superior, walking away sadly, Faustina asked, "So what am I hearing in my soul; is it all an illusion?" Mother Michael is supposed to have answered her, "Sister, I sense that you have been given great enlightenment from God, but it is always possible to add something of one's own. It is possible that such a Congregation is to be established, but I very much doubt that it is you who is to be its foundress. So let us wait."

In a letter to Fr. Sopoćko dated August 9, 1936, Faustina promised to "proceed more slowly so as not to spoil anything," to arm herself with patience "despite these interior promptings" and to wait for "God's providence to take the first step." But this did not last long. In November, she made a retreat. "I received light in my soul that nonetheless, I ought to make the decisive step without paying attention to anything in the world. ... If I am to take an active part in this matter, then I must not only be allowed to leave the Congregation but must also be dispensed from my vows," she wrote to Fr. Sopoćko on November 19. At the same time, she bombarded him with questions as to whether he had already made any effort to establish the new Congregation. "Has anything been done about it or not yet, and are there any prospects for beginning this work or not? And, Father, do you anticipate that a person will be found who will carry out this intent of God as the Lord demands it? Have you, Father, already talked about this matter with the Archbishop or not?"

Father Sopoćko repeatedly spoke with Archbishop Jałbrzykowski about Faustina's case — about the new Congregation and about permission to publish a holy card with the Divine Mercy Chaplet. However, all of this was without success. Faustina had the same experience when an opportunity presented itself on September 14, 1936, during a visit by the Metropolitan of Vilnius in Łagiewniki. Archbishop Jałbrzykowski would invariably reply that it was too early to decide.

Mother Irene Krzyżanowska also opposed Faustina leaving the Congregation. Sister Faustina repeatedly asked Mother Moraczewska for her permission and on October 31, 1936, she told Faustina the following: "Sister, if the Lord Jesus wishes you to leave the Congregation, then let Him give me some sign that He is asking for this." She sensed, which she indicated to Faustina, that while Faustina herself might be in this matter the hidden spring through which God will be acting, she would not necessarily need to leave the Congregation.

Faustina prayed for God's light to discern well and do His will in this matter. She had already made an act of total submission to the will of God much earlier. But here, in the Łagiewniki convent, she wrote, "Perfect fulfillment of God's will is maturity in sanctity" (*Diary*, 666). And she added, "My sanctity and perfection consist in the close union of my will with the will of God. God never violates our free will" (*Diary*, 1107).

Sister Faustina was becoming more closely united with God and being given the graces to understand more deeply His Essence. She wrote Fr. Sopoćko in a letter from Kraków, "At present, my communion with God is the same as before, only with this difference: that right now such a great longing for God seizes me that I do not understand how one can go on living without Him. This love of God puts me into a kind of excruciating longing for Him! This strong desire for God must put an end to my imperfect life, and the fullness of life in Love, that is, in God, must follow!"

One Thursday in August 1936, while in the state known as mystical union, Sr. Faustina was making a Holy Hour (from 9 to 10 p.m.) when she was given to understand the mystery of the institution of the Eucharist. "During this hour of prayer, Jesus allowed me to enter the Cenacle," she wrote. She "was most deeply moved when, before the Consecration, Jesus raised His eyes to heaven and entered into a mysterious conversation with His Father." Faustina did not relate the content of the conversation, but she noted, "It is only in eternity that we shall really understand that moment." She focused on Jesus, whose eyes "were like two flames; His face was radiant, white as snow; His whole personage full of majesty, His soul full of longing." At this point, the inexpressible happened: the offering of the sacrifice. "At the moment of Consecration, love rested satiated — the sacrifice fully consummated." Faustina explained, "Now only the external ceremony of death will be carried out — external destruction; the essence [of it] is in the Cenacle" (*Diary*, 684).

Ludmilla Grygiel draws attention to the fact that Sr. Faustina, "with great precision and theological correctness, explains that the sacrifice of the Eucharist celebrated for centuries in the Church is the actualization here and now of Christ's offering of Himself in the Cenacle, an offering dictated by the 'longing' for the fulfillment of the will of the Father and obtained at the price of 'interior suffering.'" Her account, Grygiel emphasizes, of what happened at the Last Supper is "the only description of its kind in mysticism and, therefore, probably a unique experience."

Faustina was getting to know the mystery of mercy ever more fully. Jesus urged His "secretary" to write down each sentence in which He spoke about it, "**because this is meant for a great number of souls who will profit from it.**" Jesus told her not to be discouraged by the difficulties she was encountering in proclaiming His mercy, as they were needed "**for your sanctification and as evidence that this work is Mine**" (*Diary*, 1142). He directed Sr. Faustina to pray for God's mercy, to perform acts of mercy, and demanded from her exemplary trust in the mercy of God — that is, He asked of her everything that constitutes the basis for proclaiming and imploring mercy for people and the whole world.

In August 1936, Jesus dictated the text of a novena to Faustina, for her to pray privately. However, in December 1936, He made a further request: the praying of a novena that would consist of the Divine Mercy Chaplet being recited daily for the nine days leading up to the Feast of Divine Mercy. "**By this novena, I will grant every possible grace to souls,**" He proclaimed (*Diary*, 796).

Then, in October 1936, Sr. Faustina visited hell. In 1925, at the beginning of her path in the religious life, she was led by her guardian angel to purgatory, and from then on, she prayed more earnestly for the souls detained there. She was in contact with them.

Now, she was transported for a moment to hell. "I, Sister Faustina, by the order of God, have visited the abysses of hell so that I might tell souls about it and testify to its existence," she wrote formally. "It is a place of great torture. ... The kinds of tortures I saw: the first torture that constitutes hell is the loss of God; the second is perpetual remorse of conscience; the third is that one's condition will never change; the fourth is the fire that will penetrate the soul without destroying it — a terrible suffering, since it is a purely spiritual fire, lit by God's anger; the fifth torture is continual darkness and a terrible suffocating smell, and, despite the darkness, the devils and the souls of the damned see each other and all the evil, both of others and their own; the sixth torture is the constant company of Satan; the seventh torture is horrible despair, hatred of God, vile words, curses, and blasphemies. These are the tortures suffered by all the damned together, but that is not the end of the sufferings. There are special tortures destined for particular souls. These are the torments of the senses. Each soul undergoes terrible and indescribable sufferings, related to the manner in which it has sinned."

She wrote all this at the command of God "so that no soul may find an excuse by saying there is no hell, or that nobody has ever been there, and so no one can say what it is like." Then, she added something significant: "I noticed one thing: that most of the souls there are those who disbelieved that there is a hell." From that moment, she prayed even more fervently "for the conversion of sinners. I incessantly plead God's mercy upon them" (*Diary*, 741).

A little later, Faustina explained that the mercy of God sometimes reaches the sinner in the last moment, and "the merciful God gives the soul that interior vivid moment, so that if the soul is willing, it has the possibility of returning to God. But sometimes, the obduracy in souls is so great that consciously they choose hell" (*Diary*, 1698).

Sister Faustina experienced ever deeper mystical states, that is, the union of love with God. She wrote the following in November 1936: "My communion with the Lord is now purely spiritual. My soul is touched by God and wholly absorbs itself in Him, even to the complete forgetfulness of self. Permeated by God to its very depths, it drowns in His beauty; it completely dissolves in Him

— I am at a loss to describe this, because in writing I am making use of the senses; but there, in that union, the senses are not active; there is a merging of God and the soul; and the life of God to which the soul is admitted is so great that the human tongue cannot express it. When the soul returns to its habitual form of life, it then sees that this life is all darkness and mist and dreamlike confusion, an infant's swaddling clothes. In such moments the soul only receives from God, for of itself it does nothing; it does not make even the slightest effort; all in her is wrought by God. But when the soul returns to its ordinary state, it sees that it is not within its power to continue in this union. These moments are short, but their effects are lasting. The soul cannot remain long in this state; or else it would be forcibly freed of the bonds of the body forever. Even as it is, it is sustained by a miracle of God. God allows the soul to know in a clear way how much He loves it, as though it were the only object of His delight" (*Diary*, 767).

Explaining once again the source of her knowledge of God, Faustina writes that in such moments the soul receives the light of spiritual insight, thanks to which the soul is instructed "about things it has not read in any book and has not been taught by any person. These are times of great inner knowledge which God Himself imparts to the soul. These are great mysteries" (*Diary*, 1102).

Faustina experienced one such moment at the convent in Łagiewniki on Palm Sunday in 1938. She received "a deep inner light which gave me to understand, in spirit, all the workings of mercy. It was like a flash of lightning, but more distinct than if I had watched it for hours with the eyes of my body" (*Diary*, 1658).

Earlier, in May 1937, on the feast of the Ascension of Jesus, Sr. Faustina experienced such a profound union with God that she called it "an uninterrupted ecstasy of love." It started as usual: "Since early this morning, my soul has been touched by God. After Holy Communion, I communed for a while with the heavenly Father. My soul was drawn into the glowing center of love. I understood that no exterior works could stand comparison with pure love of God." And then she saw "the joy of the Incarnate Word" and was "immersed in the Divine Trinity." She continued, "When I came to myself, longing filled my soul, and I yearned to be united with God. Such tremendous love for the heavenly Father enveloped me that I call this day an uninterrupted ecstasy of love." She also noted, "This strong inner conviction, by which God assures me of His love for me and of how much my soul pleases Him, brings deep peace to my soul. Throughout this day, I was unable to take any food; I felt gratified to the full with love" (*Diary,* 1121).

During this period, Faustina was growing weaker physically. Tuberculosis was ravaging her body more and more. The disease had been diagnosed while she was still in Vilnius, but it hadn't started then. As she told Sr. Louise Gadzina, it was three years before going to Vilnius that she had begun to feel ill. At that time, tuberculosis was a veritable societal scourge — an authentic plague that reaped a plentiful harvest for death. It was primarily the young who contracted tuberculosis. The disease developed undetected for a long time. Although vaccinations were introduced in 1921, they were not effective in those who — like Faustina — had already been diagnosed with advanced-stage tuberculosis. And the first effective medication for tuberculosis — streptomycin — was not introduced until 1946, after the Second World War.

In September 1936, Sr. Faustina's health deteriorated severely. Doctor Adam Silberg, a specialist in the treatment of infectious diseases, examined her on September 19. He confirmed tuberculosis. He instructed her superiors to isolate Faustina from the other sisters so as not to infect them. Sister Faustina was therefore transferred from the common dormitory to the infirmary. She was very weak. A sudden deterioration took place on September 24. She noted in the *Diary* that the suffering that day was so great that it prevented her from "making even the slightest movement": "I could not even swallow my saliva. This lasted for about three hours. ... I resigned myself completely to the will of God and thought that the day of my death, so much desired, had come" (*Diary,* 696). It appears from this entry that the tuberculosis had attacked not only the lungs, but also the intestines, causing excruciating pain in that area a few hours after a meal.

From this point on, these attacks would recur. Exhausted by suffering, Faustina asked Fr. Sopoćko in a letter written the day after the attack to give her in writing "an absolution for the hour of my death." Father Sopoćko sent her the absolution. He also instructed Faustina to protect her *Diary* from destruction "just in case" and to supplement it. He asked her to carefully underline everything that, in her opinion, "was clearly of Divine origin" and especially the parts concerning the Feast of Divine Mercy and the establishment of a new Congregation. "If these things really are of Divine origin, then we have a strong duty to respect and faithfully fulfill everything," he wrote.

Not all the sisters believed in Faustina's illness. "Sister, you're not sick; they just wanted to give you some rest and that is why they have made up this illness," she once heard. Sister Felicia Żakowiecka recounts, "One sister in particular was very much averse to Faustina: she did not believe in her illness, and the type of piety practiced by Faustina annoyed the sister very much."

The illness kept on progressing, but Faustina had periods where her health improved suddenly, perhaps leading some sisters to believe she was feigning it. "Strangely, I got better, and that in a very short time. I now take part in all spiritual exercises and have even resumed my duties in the garden. I really do not understand this sudden improvement in my health," she wrote to Fr. Sopoćko on October 12, 1936.

Sister Brunona Sroczyńska, who worked in the infirmary until November 1936, remembered that Faustina "did not give in to the illness, and as soon as she was not confined to bed, she returned to her regular duties, doing her best to meet her obligations. Her serenity, peace, and steadfast spirit — considering the difficulties arising from her illness — were amazing. She never complained, even though it was sometimes noticeable that she was growing weaker. She did not let others sense what she was experiencing, and even her superiors were not aware of her condition."

In the *Diary*, Faustina noted her surprise that the Lord Jesus allowed Mother Irene Krzyżanowska, the Mother Superior of the convent, who generally showed great love of neighbor to sick sisters, to tell her that she should "get used to suffering."

In the fall of 1936, Sr. Chrysostom Korczak became the infirmarian in Łagiewniki. Faustina had met her in the same role in Vilnius and did not have good memories of her. Already in Vilnius, Faustina heard from Sr. Chrysostom that "she is guilty of coddling herself; that she does not have enough energy and that she gives in to her illness."

Mother Michael Moraczewska noted, "God allowed that the Sister Infirmarian — back from their shared time in Vilnius — did not really believe in Faustina's experiences, about which she already knew a little. At the same time, the sister in charge of assisting the sick was very much afraid of contracting tuberculosis. As a result, as I learned later, that poor, sick Faustina sometimes went without proper care."

Sister Chrysostom once called Faustina a hysteric who makes others take care of her. "Sister, you want to be a saint? Pigs will fly before that'll happen!"[42] she once snarled in anger. Sister Cajetan Bartkowiak witnessed this scene. She then heard Faustina replying, "Sister, I love you even more."

Sister Felicia Żakowiecka recalled, "Several sisters talked about her, saying that she spends too much time praying in the chapel, that she is spoiled; that she has arranged an aristocratic life for herself; and that they cannot comprehend that kind of perfection. These things reached her in a roundabout way, but she cared little for people's opinions. One could sense clearly that she cared only about pleasing the Lord Jesus."

Sometimes, however, Faustina complained to Jesus, hints of which she left on the pages of her *Diary*. "A certain sister is constantly persecuting me for the sole reason that God communes with me so intimately, and she thinks that this is all pretense on my part. When she thinks that I have done something amiss she says, 'Some people have revelations, but commit such faults!'" (*Diary*, 1527).

Another time she wrote that from the moment she entered the convent, one charge was repeatedly made against her, "namely, that I am a saint. But this word was always used scoffingly. At first, this hurt me very much, but when I had risen above it, I paid no attention to it" (*Diary*, 1571).

Some time later, in May 1937, more than a year before her death, Faustina wrote, "Oh, how sweet it is to live in a convent among sisters, but I must not forget that these angels are in human bodies" (*Diary*, 1126).

Sister Faustina strove for personal holiness, and she also knew that in this way, she would be useful to the Church: "I know very well that I do not live for myself alone, but for the entire Church," she wrote (*Diary*, 1505). She had wanted to become a saint from a very early age. Therefore, when she saw St. Thérèse of Lisieux — to whom she had a great devotion — in a dream during her novitiate in Łagiewniki, she did not hesitate to ask if she would become a saint. "To which she replied, 'Yes, you will be a saint.' 'But, little Thérèse, shall I be a saint as you are, raised to the altar?' And she answered, 'Yes, you will be a saint just as I am, but you must trust in the Lord Jesus'" (*Diary*, 150).

The *Diary* preserves a quite unusual witness of Faustina's striving for holiness and struggles with weaknesses. It is a "Chart of inner control" (*Diary*, 1352), that is an account of victories and failures. Other sisters also kept such records. They recorded to what extent they had kept the Commandments, vows and rules of religious life, and whether they had lived the Christian virtues. On Faustina's chart summarizing the year 1937 (*Diary*, 1355), there are dozens of victories and just a few failures to do with love of neighbor (three in one year) and humility (13 in one year). "When I hesitate on how to act in some situations, I always ask Love. It advises best," she noted (*Diary*, 1354). In the same year, she wrote, "I spend every free moment at the feet of the hidden God. He is my Master; I ask Him about everything; I speak to Him about everything. Here I obtain strength and light; here I learn everything; here I am given light on how to act toward my neighbor" (*Diary*, 704).

How was Faustina perceived by those who knew her best, by her confessors and superiors?

Father Joseph Andrasz gave this testimony: "Sister Faustina was well aware that holiness, for which she longed earnestly, and for which she came to the Congregation, does not consist primarily in visions and revelations, but in fundamental virtues. For this reason, while still in the world, but especially as a religious, she worked very hard on obtaining such virtues as purity of heart, humility, patience, conscientiousness, obedience, poverty, gentleness, diligence, active love of one's neighbor, interior recollection, deep piety, and above all love toward God. One should not think that she acquired these virtues — especially at their higher levels — without any difficulty. There is no doubt that she had her own petty sins that she fell into occasionally, whether in speech or in relationships with others, or in reacting with impatience, in minor vanities, or some small imperfections at work. ... She confessed them and sincerely asked God for forgiveness, but recovered from them with vigor. She mentions this in her *Diary*. And although she gave in to these imperfections from time to time (because holiness in this world, even heroic holiness, is not yet heavenly holiness), these shortcomings became less frequent and ever smaller, while the lovely flowers of the virtues grew in her more and more beautifully."

Father Michael Sopoćko wrote this description in 1948: "In terms of natural disposition, she was thoroughly level-headed, quite even-tempered, without a shadow of psychoneurosis or hysteria. Naturalness and simplicity characterized her relations both with the sisters in the convent, and also with persons outside the community. Externally, she did not differ from others in any way. ... Her emotionality was normal, kept in check by the will. She did not suffer from depression or irritation as a result of any failures, all of which she accepted with submission to the will of God. ... Mentally, she was prudent and could be characterized by her sound judgment on things. Morally, she was honest and truthful, without putting on airs, and moreover she stood out because of her humility, obedience, zeal, and angelic purity, making continuous progress in the love of God and neighbor. Sister Faustina's interior life was marked by an extraordinary subtlety and depth of spiritual beauty, which were the result of special illuminations of the mind and visions, and often the voice of the Lord Jesus, as well as her diligent cooperation with the graces and abundant gifts of the Holy Spirit, and above all, the gift of wisdom."

Mother Michael Moraczewska wrote the following about Faustina years later: "Regarding negative traits ... first of all, there was a certain exuberance of imagination, which sometimes discerned an extraordinary side to things where I did not see it. This inclined me to be even more reserved, although fundamentally I believed that she was an extraordinary soul, favored with exceptional graces from God. Secondly, I took exception to certain shortcomings in humility. It seemed to me that for her spiritual refinement, she would need to desire the last place, to seek out humiliations, whereas I noticed in her a great sensitivity to harsher treatment and a certain critical spirit. However, it should be noted that these defects were disappearing toward the end of her life, as was noticed both by me and her long-term Superior, Mother Irene. As for positive character traits, I would like to emphasize her sincerity, simplicity, obedience, a great transparency, gentleness, helpfulness, and discretion. Only a few sisters knew about her rich interior life, apart from which she did not stand out in any way."

Mother Borgia Tichy gives the following account of Faustina: "To all appearances, she was quiet and peaceful, but not without quite a temperament which would come to the fore somewhat frequently. ... She had love of neighbor that she tried to live by, but at the same time, she did not allow herself to be exploited in this respect, unless there was a definite need. The moment she thought her help was needed, she never hesitated to give it."

In 1966, Raymund Trillat, a French graphologist, claimed to determine the following about Faustina: "She is demanding, but she is guided by a sense of justice and grace. She is hard-working, with a smile on her face every day and with intimate spiritual aspirations. She is emotional, and this despite the rule that is conducive to reserved behavior; she is visibly marked by enthusiasm, zeal, a flame of love that is characteristic of those who are inspired or of great mystics. Her emotionality is significant, but it is kept in control by her spiritual balance. At first, she treats others with shyness, but later she is able to achieve, if necessary, the form of sacrifice. She is absolutely sincere, and there is no contrivance or changes of attitude in her. ... The conclusion is that both in the writings as in the reproductions of the face of Sr. Faustina, we see the radiance of a being marked by deep inspiration, which transcends human reason and understanding."

Professor George Strojnowski, a psychiatrist and retired researcher at the Catholic University of Lublin, tried to assess not so much Faustina's character but her mental health based on the *Diary*. In 1999, in the psychological monthly *Charaktery* (*Characters*), he published an article in which he made the claim that Sr. Faustina "was affected by mental disorders," and specifically by cyclophrenia (a bipolar disorder). The professor tried to back this up with quotes from the *Diary*, thereby proving only that he had no knowledge whatsoever regarding the topic of mysticism. His thesis about Sr. Faustina's mental illness was refuted by Henryka Machej, a clinical psychologist with 20 years of experience working with patients in a psychiatric hospital in Kraków, including those suffering from cyclophrenia. Comparing the behavior of her patients to what Sr. Faustina wrote about her interior life, and to the recollections of others about the future saint, she determined that "neither in her writings nor in the life of Sr. Faustina can I find any reason to assign any psychopathology to her, let alone this severe one." On the contrary, she emphasized that Faustina was a psychologically coherent personality.

This diagnosis is consistent with what the psychiatrist Helen Maciejewska stated when she examined Sr. Faustina in 1933 in Vilnius, issuing a statement about her "perfect mental health." In addition, Sr. Anna Tokarska of the Congregation of the Sisters of St. Joseph, who has dealt with the relationship between mystical experience and psychological norms, makes the claim that every mystic has a strong and extremely consistent and mature personality. This is one of the indispensable conditions of being a mystic. Professor Strojnowski was trying to find an erotic element in the mystical ecstasies of Sr. Faustina and in her relationship with Jesus. Saint John of the Cross wrote about this that "the love of God sometimes overflows also to the senses and then it is found to be sweet and tender." As Henryka Machej emphasized, "In contrast to patients with manic disorders, that which mystics experience has more in common with involuntary satisfaction (unprovoked by any actions or imaginings) than with sexual tension. The element of eroticism is sometimes evident in the early stages of the mystical life, prior to the purification from sensuality, which occurs at the second stage."

A discussion with Professor Strojnowski never took place — neither in the monthly, nor in any other forum — because the professor died two weeks after his publication in *Charaktery*.

But let us get back to Łagiewniki in 1936. Because Sr. Faustina continued to grow weaker, Mother Moraczewska decided to send her to a tuberculosis sanatorium in Prądnik, near Kraków. "When I was somewhat overcome by the fear that I was to be outside the community for so long a time alone, Jesus said to me, **You will not be alone, because I am with you always and everywhere**" (*Diary*, 797). Therefore, reassured, she went to the hospital on December 9, where, apart from a short break for Christmas, she stayed until March 27, 1937.

That day, the convent chronicler at the Łagiewniki House noted that Faustina, now in better health, had returned to stay permanently. The joy was premature.

Sister Yolanda Woźniak recounts, "She looked very gaunt, but she still worked in the garden depending on her physical abilities." And she was still thinking about establishing a new Congregation.

In May 1937, Mother Moraczewska arrived in Łagiewniki for the purpose of a visitation. On May 4, she told Faustina that she agreed to her leaving the Congregation. "So far, I have always held you back, Sister, but now I am leaving the choice up to you. If you want, you can leave the Congregation, or — if you want — you can stay," she informed her. Faustina was greatly surprised. After a brief moment, she asked Mother if she would take care of the necessary formalities. "To my response," Mother Moraczewska recalls, "that I would not know how to describe her motivations for wanting to leave the Congregation because of its origin in private revelation, she asked permission to go to see Fr. Andrasz, who, however — as it turned out — happened to be away for a while."

Sister Faustina was not only surprised but also terrified. She had been asking for consent, had waited for it for a long time, and, now that she had it, she felt that leaving the Congregation was beyond her capabilities. The Congregation gave her a sense of security, had taught her to agree with the will of superiors, who decided most matters for her, and now, she herself would have to take responsibility for creating a new religious structure and for the welfare of any girls who would want to share their lives with her. She felt alone and abandoned.

"When I had left Mother General, darkness once again descended upon my soul, as it had in the past," she noted in the *Diary*. "It is strange that, each time I ask permission to leave the Congregation, this darkness invades my soul, and I feel as though I have been left completely on my own." Mother Michael, to whom she immediately told this, responded, "That leaving of yours is a temptation" (*Diary*, 1115).

Two days later, on May 6, 1937, Faustina wrote the following to Fr. Sopoćko: "I discern that, with regard to this Congregation, God's time has not yet come, so I am leaving [it] to Divine Providence. Since the Archbishop has not given his permission, I too have less responsibility before God, and I will refrain from doing anything externally in regard to this matter until favorable external circumstances present themselves, which will be proof that God demands this." She did not mention anything about her conversation with Mother Michael, nor about Mother's decision. She did write, however, about the state of her soul: "For a few days my soul was plunged in darkness, but today the presence of the heavenly Father has dispelled the darkness, and I even experienced this great grace in a physical way. Rest assured, Father, that I shall not take any major steps without first consulting you."

A few days later, after Mother Moraczewska had finished visiting Łagiewniki's sister house in Rabka, she came back to her conversation with Faustina, who told her Superior "with sincerity and simplicity, that, the moment I gave her a free hand, she felt in her soul as though she was in a dark abyss, completely alone and abandoned, unable to take any step, and any thoughts of leaving the Congregation vanished." It was their last conversation on this subject.

Years later, Mother Moraczewska said that "the sudden darkness of soul" Faustina experienced at moments when she was close to making decisions was the sign from God that she — that is, Mother Moraczewska — had been waiting for. It was the sign that Faustina should stay in her Congregation, after all, because the new Congregation would be established by someone else, as Faustina would understand later. The result was that the matter of Sr. Faustina leaving the Congregation was closed in May 1937.

Faustina no longer spoke about this with the superiors, but in the *Diary*, she still returned to the subject several times. In June 1937, she wrote that during Mass she was given to understand that the new work was to have what one could call three aspects. The first will consist of "souls separated from the world" (*Diary*, 1155), that is, consecrated persons living in monasteries and convents, who will beg for mercy for the whole world. The second group will consist of those bound by vows, but living "in this egoistic world" (*Diary*, 1156), that is, lay members of religious congregations. By prayer and works, they will be obtaining mercy for the world. Finally, everyone can belong to the third "aspect" of the work. "A member of this group ought to perform at least one act of mercy a day; at least one, but there can be many more, for such deeds can easily be carried out by anyone" (*Diary*, 1157-1158).

Thus, Sr. Faustina described three ways of performing an act of mercy: firstly, "the merciful word, by forgiving and by comforting; secondly, if you can offer no word, then pray — that too is mercy; and thirdly, deeds of mercy" (*Diary*, 1158).

On September 3, 1937, referring to "that time" when she felt called to leave and start a new Congregation, she concluded, "This is the third year passing by since that time, and my soul has felt, in turns, enthusiasm and an urge to act — and then I have a lot of courage and strength — and then again, when the decisive moment to undertake the work draws near, I feel deserted by God, and because of this an extraordinary fear pervades my soul, and I see that it is not the hour intended by God to initiate the work. These are sufferings about which I don't even know how to write. God alone knows what I put up with, day and night" (*Diary*, 1263).

In August 1937, Fr. Sopoćko came to Łagiewniki for a few days. While reading the *Diary*, his attention was drawn to the text of the Divine Mercy Novena, which Jesus had dictated to Faustina for her personal use. Father Sopoćko liked this prayer so much that he copied it. He then took it, the Divine Mercy Chaplet, the image of the Merciful Jesus, and a Litany about Divine Mercy, which he had based on texts of Faustina's prayers, to 22 Szewska Street in Kraków, where Joseph Cebulski's prayer book publishing house and warehouse of devotional items had its headquarters. (In his memoirs, Fr. Sopoćko gives the name Piekarski; it could be that someone with that surname worked there.) The publishing house occupied part of the three-story building that is known to this day as the "Collegiate House," as it belonged to the Collegiate Church of St. Anne. Cebulski's company had received permission from the Kraków Archdiocesan Chancery for the publication of new prayers in honor of the Divine Mercy.

The publishing of the prayer book was supervised by Mother Irene Krzyżanowska, who, of all the superiors — as Sr. Faustina recorded twice — contributed most to the development of the work of the Divine Mercy. Mother Irene went to see the publisher on September 25, and two days later, on September 27, 1937, she went there accompanied by Sr. Faustina. They inspected larger and smaller images of the Merciful Jesus being prepared for printing, and Sr. Faustina made some comments.

A prayer book entitled *Chrystus, Król miłosierdzia* (*Christ, King of Mercy*), which had been put together by Fr. Michael Sopoćko, as well as holy cards with the image of the Merciful Jesus and with the text of the Divine Mercy Chaplet on the back appeared in print in October 1937. Mother Krzyżanowska sent copies of them to the Congregation's different convents. The prayer books were not used by the sisters in an official capacity, but were intended for private use. Things didn't turn out so well with the holy cards, however. People did not end up buying them, so Mother Irene started to give them away.

At that point, in September 1937, Sr. Faustina must have been very excited to see the text and images being prepared for publication. What Jesus had spoken about was happening before her very eyes. Slowly, though with difficulty, the message of God's mercy was spreading. It was making its way into the world.

The sisters walked from the publishing house on Szewska Street on to the Main Market Square. Faustina now had what was possibly her first opportunity to see this place, which has special significance for all Poles. The enormous Main Market Square is one of Europe's largest urban market squares. It is surrounded by houses that are hundreds of years old, and in the middle of it stands the impressive Cloth Hall. For centuries, the square was the heart of Poland. Here, kings received homage; here, the army of the Polish-Lithuanian Commonwealth took an oath of allegiance to the Constitution of May 3, 1791. Three years later, it is here that Tadeusz Kościuszko announced a general uprising in Poland (against the Russian Imperial forces, known as the Kościuszko Uprising[43]). The Main Market Square in Kraków remembers times of splendor and times of defeat, royal funeral processions and wedding processions.

For seven centuries, life here has been punctuated by a bugle call from the tower of St. Mary's Church — the church that the sisters entered in order to pray. It is not known whether Faustina was awed by the masterpiece created by Veit Stoss: an altarpiece carved in lime wood. In the center panel, the sculptor depicted the Dormition of the Most Holy Virgin Mary. On the side panels of the triptych altarpiece, which is adorned with dozens of more than life-sized figures, Veit Stoss carved the most important events in the life of the Mother of Jesus. Paintings by the greatest Cracovian artists — John Matejko, Joseph Mehoffer, and Stanisław Wyspiański[44] — surround Stoss's masterpiece.

In the midst of all this extraordinary beauty that was created for the glory of God, Sr. Faustina was thinking about spreading the message of His mercy. "Then I entered into an intimate conversation with the Lord, thanking Him for having condescended to grant me the grace of seeing how the veneration of His unfathomable mercy is spreading. I immersed myself in a profound prayer of thanksgiving," she noted (*Diary*, 1300).

This was the time when Faustina reached the fullness of mystical union with God, a fullness of which the great mystic St. John of the Cross wrote, "[It] comes to pass when the two wills — namely that of the soul and that of God — are united as one, and nothing separates them. And thus, when the soul rids itself totally of that which opposes the Divine will and does not conform with it, it is then that it will be transformed into God through love."

In this regard, Sr. Faustina's entry in the *Diary* on September 3, 1937, contains an extraordinary text, an "Act of Oblation" that is an act of total abandonment to the will of God: "From today onward, Your will, Lord, is my food. Take my whole being; dispose of me as You please. Whatever Your Fatherly hand gives me, I will accept with submission, peace, and joy. I fear nothing, no matter in what direction You lead me; helped by Your grace I will carry out everything You demand of me. I no longer fear any of Your inspirations nor do I probe anxiously to see where they will lead me. Lead me, O God, along whatever roads You please; I have placed all my trust in Your will which is, for me, love and mercy itself.

"Bid me to stay in this convent, I will stay; bid me to undertake the work, I will undertake it; leave me in uncertainty about the work until I die, be blessed; give me death when, humanly speaking, my life seems particularly necessary, be blessed. Should You take me in my youth, be blessed; should You let me live to a ripe old age, be blessed. Should You give me health and strength, be blessed; should You confine me to a bed of pain for my whole life, be blessed. Should you give only failures and disappointments in life, be blessed. Should You allow my purest intentions to be condemned, be blessed. Should You enlighten my mind, be blessed. Should You leave me in darkness and all kinds of torments, be blessed.

"From this moment on, I live in the deepest peace, because the Lord Himself is carrying me in the hollow of His hand. He, Lord of unfathomable mercy, knows that I desire Him alone in all things, always and everywhere" (*Diary*, 1264).

A month later, in October 1937, Faustina received a revelation about the Hour of Mercy, which became part of the devotion to the Divine Mercy. Jesus told Faustina that the hour of His death on the cross — three in the afternoon — is "**the hour of great mercy for the whole world." "At three o'clock, implore My mercy, especially for sinners; and, if only for a brief moment, immerse yourself in My Passion, particularly in My abandonment at the moment of agony. ... In this hour, I will refuse nothing to the soul that makes a request of Me in virtue of My Passion**" (*Diary*, 1320).

As Fr. Ignatius Różycki explained later, for the requests to be answered, one needs to meet three conditions: the prayer is to take place at 3 p.m., it should be addressed to Jesus, and one should appeal to the value and merits of the Passion of Jesus. In another revelation four months later, Jesus urged Sr. Faustina to reflect on His Passion at the Hour of Mercy and make the Way of the Cross, provided that her duties permitted it, and if this was not possible, to adore in the Most Blessed Sacrament for a moment His Heart, which is full of mercy, or to pray wherever she found herself at three o'clock. At this hour, she was to implore mercy for the world, especially for sinners (see *Diary*, 1572).

From this point onwards, Faustina tried to ensure that at this hour, she could get away from her responsibilities and pray — if not in the chapel, then in a secluded spot close to her workplace (for example, in the pantry). The wards would often see her in the pantry at three o'clock in the afternoon. She would be praying while lying prostrate, her arms outstretched in the form of the cross.

The Hour of Mercy was not included in the new forms of devotion to the Divine Mercy until much later — in fact, not until the 1980s. But there are places in the world where it is very popular. For example, watches that signal the Hour of Mercy at three o'clock have been in production for many years in the Philippines.

Sister Faustina was growing weaker. After returning from Rabka, she no longer worked in the garden. She did not have the strength for it. Starting in September 1937, she was the convent gatekeeper. Two weeks after taking on her new responsibilities, she was visited by her brother Stanislaus, who was then working in Kraków. He had plans to join a religious order of some kind, and Faustina encouraged him in this, but it never came to pass. Her brother saw that she looked different, but also that she was cheerful and smiling. He, therefore, did not suspect that she was so seriously ill.

Although her work was now easier, it still required effort and attention, because a lot of people came and went through the convent gates. Her new responsibilities put Faustina in contact with people burdened with a variety of miseries — material and moral. "When the same poor people come to the gate a second time, I treat them with greater gentleness, and I do not let them see that I know they have been here before; [I do this] in order not to embarrass them. And then they speak to me freely about their troubles and needs," she wrote (*Diary*, 1282).

During this period, there was high unemployment in Kraków, as through-out the rest of the country, which led to strikes and violent workers' riots. The unemployed were among those who knocked at the convent gate, looking for or even demanding work. The sisters, therefore, were sometimes afraid of these encounters. Beggars would also come to the gate asking for food.

Anna Burkata, one of the wards who was working in the kitchen at that time, recalled that "Sr. Faustina came several times from the gate to fetch food for the poor. Perhaps the fifth time around, Sr. Anna [the cook] angrily asked Faustina, 'Sister, how many more times are you going to come around and bother me?' To which Sr. Faustina answered calmly, 'Until I have fed the Lord Jesus.'"

On September 30, 1937, the bell rang at the convent gate. Faustina opened the door. She saw an emaciated young man. He was barefoot and his clothes were in tatters. "[He] was frozen because the day was cold and rainy. He asked for something hot to eat," Faustina related. "So I went to the kitchen, but found nothing there for the poor. But, after searching around for some time, I succeeded in finding some soup, which I reheated and into which I crumbled some bread, and I gave it to the poor young man, who ate it. As I was taking the bowl from him, he gave me to know that He was the Lord of heaven and earth. When I saw Him as He was, He vanished from my sight" (*Diary*, 1312). The gate at which Jesus rang the bell is no longer there. But the small bell itself has been preserved. It hangs in the reconstructed copy of St. Faustina's cell, which is located in the house that has replaced the old one-story building adjacent to the former convent gate.

Faustina continued her conversation with Jesus ceaselessly — an interior dialogue in her heart, or openly during her visions. She also felt her internal stigmata more frequently and intensely. These were not visible. They did not bleed like the stigmata of St. Padre Pio or St. Francis. They were spiritual stigmata like, for example, those of St. Catherine of Siena. Sister Faustina felt intense inner pain in the places where the five wounds of Jesus were and also pain on her head where the crown of thorns had been placed. She suffered more intensely on Fridays and when she met people who were not in the state of grace. Based on the kind of pain she felt, she was able to identify who offended God and in what way. Gently, she would encourage such people to go to confession and to change their lives.

Hedwig Owar, one of the wards, remembered, "[I]t seemed that she could read everything that was happening inside the soul. It was impossible to lie in her presence without her immediately recognizing it. She sometimes also pointed out to one or another of the girls that 'there's something not quite right inside of you; you could use a bath,' that is, go to confession. ... And sometimes her kind word would overcome the resistance of the girls who were not always willing to go to confession."

Sophia Matusik, another ward, recalled, "There was a great difference between Sr. Faustina's behavior and that of the other sisters. It often happened that I myself or some other girl from the institution did not behave as we should. This usually brought a reprimand from other sisters and insistence on an apology. Sister Faustina never demanded that we apologize to her and always treated others cordially and with love — everyone she came in contact with, whether she experienced hurts or kindnesses from them."

Hedwig Owar also recalls, "She never gave in to the mood of the moment; she always remained the same, but ... she did not tolerate any familiarities from the girls. She would tell us that she loved us very much, but she did not allow caresses and kept us at a distance."

In October 1937, Sr. Faustina made a retreat that would be the last one she participated in along with the other religious. It lasted for eight days. Jesus announced that the retreat would be for her "an uninterrupted contemplation," (*Diary*, 1327) and she wrote after it ended that she came out of it "thoroughly transformed by God's love. My soul is beginning a new life, earnestly and courageously; although outwardly my life will not change, and no one will notice it, nevertheless, pure love is [now] the guide of my life and, externally, it is mercy which is its fruit. I feel that I have been totally imbued with God and, with this God, I am going back to my everyday life, so drab, tiresome, and wearying, trusting that He whom I feel in my heart will change this drabness into my personal sanctity" (*Diary*, 1363).

Sister Faustina knew when she would die. In May 1936, more than two years before her death, Faustina told Sr. Justine Gołofit, when she was in Derdy, that she (Faustina) would die in two years. In the fall of 1937, she confided to Sr. Damiana Ziółek that she felt very sick and added, "I think that Jesus will not surprise me, because, after all, I am to die in the thirty-third year of my life." Meanwhile, toward the end of the year, her tuberculosis was so advanced that Faustina felt the decay of her own body. "It sometimes happens that I feel the complete decay of my own corpse. It is hard to express how great a suffering this is," she wrote (*Diary*, 1428). She also noted that one of the sisters, after talking with her for a while, "made a terribly wry face and said, 'Sister, I smell a corpse here, as though it were decaying. O how dreadful it is!'" Faustina, undeterred, told her to stay calm and not be afraid, because "'that smell of a corpse comes from me.' She was very surprised and said she could not stand it any longer. After she had gone, I understood that God had allowed her to sense this so that I would have no doubt, but that He was no less than miraculously keeping the knowledge of this suffering from the whole community" (*Diary*, 1430).

Faustina found it increasingly difficult to eat anything. "I also started at this time to suffer from pains in my intestines. All highly seasoned dishes caused me such immense pain that I spent many nights writhing in pain and in tears, for the sake of sinners," she wrote (*Diary*, 1428).

She also suffered from attacks of pain not caused by disease, but which were of a mystical nature. "At eight o'clock I was seized with such violent pains that I had to go to bed at once. I was convulsed with pain for three hours; that is, until eleven o'clock at night. No medicine had any effect on me, and whatever I swallowed I threw up. At times, the pains caused me to lose consciousness." This recurred several times, each time taking the same course, but doctors could not identify the root cause. The third time around, Jesus let her know that "He Himself allowed these sufferings in order to offer reparation to God for the souls murdered in the wombs of wicked mothers" (*Diary*, 1276).

Faustina began 1938 with suffering. "Welcome to you, New Year, in the course of which my perfection will be accomplished," she wrote (*Diary*, 1449). For two days, she had been unable to get out of bed. "I was feeling very bad, and a violent cough was weakening me. And together with this, a constant pain in my intestines and nausea had brought me to the point of exhaustion. Although I could not join in community prayer, I united myself spiritually with the whole community. When the sisters got up at eleven o'clock at night to keep vigil and welcome the New Year, I had been writing in agony since nightfall, and this lasted until midnight," she noted (*Diary*, 1451).

Faustina was coughing, spitting up blood, and had no strength. She felt so ill that she went neither to Mass nor to Confession, as she had intended, and barely made it to the next cell where she received Holy Communion. What caused her more pain than the physical suffering itself was the fact that the infirmarian still treated her illness with disbelief. "I had been in bed for two days, writhing in pain, and she hadn't visited me; and when she did come, on the third day, she did not even ask if I were able to get up, but asked irritably why I hadn't got up for Mass," she recounted. The infirmarian advised her not to give in to the illness, to which Faustina replied bitterly, "I knew that here one was regarded as seriously ill only when one was in one's last agony" (*Diary*, 1453).

It was probably as a result of such experiences that Sr. Faustina told Odilia Kondraciuk "never to pass by a sick sister's cell with indifference even before Mass; even at the time of silence, one should stop by and ask if she needed anything, water or tea."

Sister Felicia Żakowiecka said, "It seemed as if she felt forgotten and, though she did not complain about it, it probably did hurt her."

This situation must have lasted for a long time, since on January 21, 1938, Faustina wrote, "As long as one can move about and work, everything is fine and dandy; but when God sends illness, somehow or other, there are fewer friends about. ... [I]f God sends a longer illness, even those faithful friends slowly begin to desert us. They visit us less frequently, and often their visits cause suffering. Instead of comforting us, they reproach us about certain things, which is an occasion of a good deal of suffering." She continued, with sadness, "When God gives neither death nor health, and [when] this lasts for many years, people become accustomed to this and consider the person as not being ill. Then there begins a whole series of silent sufferings. Only God knows how many sacrifices the soul makes" (*Diary*, 1509).

Faustina wrote of another occasion that brought her suffering: "One evening, when I was feeling so bad that I wondered how I would get back to my cell, I came across the Sister Assistant [Sr. Seraphina], who was asking one of the sisters of the first choir to go to the gate with a certain message. But when she saw me, she said to her, 'No, Sister, you need not go, but Sr. Faustina will, because it is raining heavily.' I answered, 'All right,' and went and carried out the order, but only God knows the whole of it. ... Sometimes it would seem that a sister of the second choir is made of stone, but she also is human and has a heart and feelings" (*Diary*, 1510).

The morale among the sisters in the Łagiewniki convent was not the best at this time. This was due to the changes introduced by the Novice Mistress, Sr. Callista Piekarczyk. Sisters from the two choirs did their activities separately. Novices of the first and second choirs were not only separated for lectures, but even for recreation and the so-called "chapters of faults," the name given to the monthly meetings where sisters would publicly discuss their behavior.

Sister Damiana Ziółek remembers, "This instruction aroused considerable opposition from among the sisters of the second choir. The sisters felt humiliated. On first hearing about it, Sr. Faustina said, 'I don't know, but perhaps, if I were a novice, I would give up the habit.'"

Sister Fabiana Pietkun said, "Sister Faustina was afraid that all of this would lead to a division. She did not say this to reprove the superiors, but in order that prayers be offered for this intention [the healing of division]."

Faustina discussed the new regulation with her confessor, but after he assured her that it was just an experiment that could be done away with, she comforted other sisters of the second choir. Years later, Sr. Cajetan Bartkowiak recalled that Faustina had foretold a time would come when the division into two choirs would be abolished, and all the sisters would be treated equally. "I will not live to see that moment, but you will, Sister," Faustina would say. The tense atmosphere was eventually diffused, and after one year, the unfortunate regulation was withdrawn.

In February 1938, six months before her death, Sr. Faustina wrote, "I see that this earthly vessel is beginning to crumble. I rejoice in this, because soon I will be in my Father's house" (*Diary*, 1616). In a letter sent before Easter, on April 12, 1938, to her sister Jeannie, who lived with their mother in Głogowiec, Faustina wrote that she was already so ill that she could not work. She could only pray. "I'm already longing to be united with God. I am totally reliant on the will of God; as God wants, so let it be." Other sisters observed her condition. They felt that the moment of Faustina's death was approaching. Some begged her to remember them and intercede for them with God when she died. One of the sisters even told her to die as soon as possible, because she would be a saint, to which another sister retorted that this was not certain.

Faustina was receiving letters from other convents with similar requests. "Dear Sr. Faustina, we are very sorry that you are so gravely ill; but we are very happy that, when the Lord Jesus takes you away, you will pray for us, for you have a lot of influence with the Lord," she quoted in the *Diary* (1673). "When you die, Sister, please take me under your special care, for certainly you can do that for me," wrote one nun, and another declared, "How I am waiting for the time when the Lord Jesus will take you, because I know what will happen then; and I greatly desire death for you." Faustina noted, "I did want to ask her what she was thinking of, concerning my death, but I mortified myself and answered, 'The same thing will happen to me, a sinner, as happens to all sinners, if God's mercy does not shield me'" (*Diary*, 1673).

Faustina accepted the sisters' requests with a smile. Their letters witness, however, to the fact that they regarded Faustina as someone exceptional — someone who is close to God.

Chapter Sixteen

Rabka

1937

'That Will Remain a Secret Forever'

THE MOUNTAIN AIR IN RABKA DID NOT SERVE FAUSTINA WELL. The "mild, dry mountain climate" with very little wind and lots of sun — as it was glowingly described in pre-war brochures — was too harsh for her lungs that were already destroyed by illness. Sister Faustina came here in July 1937. Six months earlier, a guidebook for the "mountain spa," as Rabka was called, published a list of illnesses treated there, along with another list indicating which medical conditions would be aggravated by a stay in the town. In this second category, tuberculosis of the lungs was at the very top of the list. Not only were tuberculosis patients not treated in Rabka, they were even discouraged from staying there. Faustina's superiors must have been unaware of this, since they sent her to Rabka to improve her health.

Faustina was already seriously ill. She had stayed in the hospital in Kraków's Prądnik for many months. The Congregation had a house in Rabka, affiliated with the one in Łagiewniki. Sisters would go there to recuperate for a week or two — not just the ones who lived in the convent in Kraków, but also those from the Congregation's other houses. This was not surprising, as Rabka was recognized at that time as a prominent health resort not only in Poland, but also across Europe. It was renowned for its salt springs rich in iodine and bromine, and for a microclimate that boasted great health benefits for those with respiratory disorders, cardiovascular diseases, metabolic disorders, and rheumatism. Since the mid-19th century, when Julian Zubrzycki opened a center for balneotherapy in Rabka, offering "therapeutic baths and mineral waters," the number of visitors had been increasing yearly. In the 1930s, the spa resort was frequented by more than 20,000 visitors annually.

Sister Faustina was sent to Rabka for a longer period of time, not for several days, as was the case with other sisters. The Congregation's house in Rabka was to become the next place for her to live the consecrated life. It would also be a place of work for her, because Faustina, in spite of her illness, continued to work. She was sent to the Rabka convent as a cook. This valuable piece of information comes from the recollections of a former ward, Valerie Zielińska, nicknamed "Josie," who was still living there in 1990. She remembered an important detail concerning Sr. Faustina's stay. Although Josie "did not see her much" and only "in passing," words spoken by Mother Helen, stuck with Josie: "'The Kraków Superior sent Sr. Faustina here to cook. How can I put her in the kitchen,' [Mother Helen] said, 'if she has tuberculosis?'"

Before Faustina came to Rabka, she knew that she was not going to stay for long. She was also certain beforehand that she would leave Łagiewniki, even before the Superior of the Kraków house, Mother Irene Krzyżanowska, informed her about this. On July 15, 1937, she noted in her *Diary*: "Once, I learned that I was to be transferred to another house. My knowledge of this was purely interior. At the same time, I heard a voice in my soul: **Do not be afraid, My daughter; it is My will that you should remain here. Human plans will be thwarted, since they must conform to My will**" (*Diary*, 1180). Sister Faustina did not write that she was leaving in order to recuperate, but that she would be "transferred," although she must have been moved so that she could benefit from a change of climate.

Interestingly, when Mother Irene informed Faustina about her decision, she replied that she wanted to leave as soon as possible. She wrote on July 20: "I was not to leave until August 5, but I asked Mother Superior to let me go at once. … I asked her to let me leave as soon as possible. Mother Superior was a little surprised that I wanted to leave so soon, but I did not explain the reason for my wanting to do so. That will remain a secret forever" (*Diary*, 1198). We will, therefore, never know why she wanted to go to Rabka immediately. Nor will we know why she wanted to leave Łagiewniki quickly, or, rather, why she wanted to leave for Rabka with such haste. She had to shorten her stay, as everything happened according to what Jesus had said to her: "**Human plans will be thwarted, since they must conform to My will**." What was His will? He said, "**[I]t is My will that you should remain here**" (*Diary*, 1180).

Sister Faustina arrived in Rabka on July 29, 1937. She traveled from Kraków by train, taking in the views of "the beautiful countryside and the mountains" through the window. We do not know where the Luxtorpeda was that she took, a super-fast train with an internal combustion engine that was capable of traveling to Rabka from Kraków at what seems today to be an incredible speed of 80 mph.

Getting off at the station in the center of Rabka, Faustina must immediately have noticed the neo-Gothic spire of St. Mary Magdalene Church and perhaps that of the priceless historic church built of larch logs in 1606, which was right behind it. A year before Faustina came to Rabka, the Władysław Orkan Museum was established there, with an enormous collection of wooden folk figures of saints that had been collected from small roadside shrines. Indeed, in the front of the station, there is a statue of St. Nicholas, the saint particularly loved by children. It was erected in 2004 in this so-called "town of the children of the world," since it is the only spot in Poland where the majority of recuperating patients are children.

Before World War II, the center of Rabka was abuzz with activity. The resort town ensured that patients were not only given proper treatment, but also entertained. Those who preferred swimming in the river and sunbathing had "a modern beach along with a swimming pool" at their disposal; sports fans had access to soccer fields and tennis courts, and there was a children's playground as well. Visitors could also enjoy "restaurants; pastry shops; cafes; a modern and elegant Cafe-Club, which combined a social club and a reading room; two libraries; a movie theater; and more." In the summertime, there were concerts in Zdrojowy Park given by an "excellent orchestra" and guest artists who performed music and theatrical shows. It's hard to counter the impression that visitors to Rabka were offered much better entertainment than they are today. Only the views one can enjoy on the hiking trails from Rabka Valley to the Island Beskids are still the same. The trails' highest mountain peaks — Turbacz and Luboń Wielki — were familiar to Karol Wojtyła, who was then a 17-year-old high school student from the town of Wadowice, which is more than 31 miles from Rabka.

We do not know what impression Rabka made on Sr. Faustina when she got off the train. But the sisters welcomed her cordially, as she mentions in the *Diary*.

The convent, located 1.25 miles from the train station, sits on the slope of a small hill called Bania. Słowacki Street ends abruptly some 218 to 328 yards uphill, with house No. 12 at its very end, which is the convent. In 1937, when Faustina arrived here, the house was nicknamed "Loretto." It looked nothing like it does today. It consisted of two sections. The older and larger section was built of larch wood. It had a steep roof and two spacious verandas on the first and second floors. Next to it stood a smaller section built of stone with bedrooms upstairs, joined to the larger one by means of a passageway. It has since ceded its place to the main entrance of the current convent house. The convent was surrounded by a large garden with fruit trees, vegetable patches, and flower beds.

The sisters of Łagiewniki had purchased the one morgen-sized plot of land (probably around a couple of acres) in 1928 from the local pastor, Fr. John Surowik. It was located just up the hill from another house, a villa called "Olszówka." Initially, the nuns had plans to build a larger house and turn it, in part, into a hostel for laypeople. The income generated from renting rooms was to sustain the entire house. However, the Kraków metropolitan (and, later, Cardinal) Archbishop Adam Sapieha did not approve of this idea. The sisters, therefore, built a smaller wooden house, which cost them — according to the "Loretto's" convent chronicler — 15,000 Polish złoty to build. The house was consecrated by Bishop Stanislaus Rospond, a friend of the Congregation, on July 9, 1931. In time, the Congregation was compelled to enlarge the house since the sisters — two or three of whom lived there permanently — started taking in girls, most of whom were orphans and the daughters of poor highlanders, the original mountain folk of the region. The sisters gave the girls a rudimentary education by teaching them reading, writing, and arithmetic, as well as basic history and geography. In addition, they taught the girls practical skills such as sewing, embroidery, crocheting, and knitting.

It soon became clear that a workshop needed to be built. A stone building with three windows on the ground floor and an attic under its steep roof was finished in May 1936, one year before Faustina arrived. Old photographs show girls busy with their sewing. The nuns were open to technological novelties. For instance, they already had a perforating machine (an early version of a modern sewing machine) and a telephone, which made contact with customers easier. Handicrafts and a small farm were the main sources of income for supporting the house. In 1934, the sisters put up a small barn behind the house, where they kept two cows and two pigs, along with some rabbits.

When Faustina came to Rabka on July 29, 1937, the house had already been expanded and 20 girls were living there along with probably two or maybe three sisters. It is possible that there were also other nuns who had come here to rest in the summer. Unfortunately, Faustina's health deteriorated so much in Rabka that not only could she not work, but she had to stay in bed. "I feel strange sharp pains all through my chest; I cannot even move my hand. One night, I had to lie quite motionless, as it seemed to me that if I budged, everything in my lungs would tear. The night was endless. I united myself to Jesus Crucified, and I implored the heavenly Father on behalf of sinners. It is said that maladies of the lungs do not cause such sharp pains, but I suffer these sharp pains constantly. My health has deteriorated so much here that I must remain in bed, and Sister N. says I will not improve, because the climate of Rabka is not good for every sick person," she wrote (*Diary*, 1201).

"Here, in this room, stood Sr. Faustina's bed," says Sr. Vaclava Siemienik, the Superior of the convent in Rabka, as she opens the door to the room on the first floor. She invites me to the "Little Faustina" room, as the sisters call it — the first room on the left of the entrance to the building. The larch logs are now hidden under light-colored wood paneling. Valerie Zielińska, now deceased, remembered that there was a white wooden bed in this room. We do not know what the room was called then, as every room in "Loretto" had a name: "Sacred Heart," "Holy Family," "Mother of Mercy," "Our Lady of Częstochowa," "Saint Joseph," "Saint Michael," or "Saint Anthony."

In Rabka, Sr. Faustina got to spend time with Sr. Odilia Kondraciuk. They had met a few years earlier, during their third probation in Warsaw. Here in Rabka, Faustina told her how she imagined Jesus "in adulthood, walking through the world, full of compassion and mercy for people" — just as He appears in the image.

Sister Kondraciuk remembered, "She was full of love for her neighbor, easy-going, and natural toward others, free of exaggeration or eccentricity. She told me once, regarding certain circumstances, that it was not fit for a religious to curry favor with sisters."

We do not know if Faustina's poor health allowed her to leave the convent at all, apart from spending time in the garden and the pine forest adjacent to the property. (A few years later, during World War II, the German forces executed Jews from Rabka and from the whole county of Nowy Targ in this forest). Did she visit the enormous Zdrojowy Park, which covers almost 100 acres? Did she go to the "Łazienki" spa to try the healing mineral waters? Did she pray in the wooden chapel of St. Thérèse of the Child Jesus at the resort, or in the parish church of St. Mary Magdalene, which is decorated with beautiful, colorful art?

Under ordinary circumstances, Faustina would not have needed to go to the parish church or the chapel in the resort since "Loretto" already had a chapel of its own. Yet, since no priest was available until 1936, Mass was not celebrated there on a regular basis. Consequently, the sisters went to Mass at the resort chapel that had been erected in 1928. In "Loretto," the sisters and their wards would typically attend Mass celebrated by clergymen who came to Rabka for rest, Fr. Joseph Andrasz among them.

From 1936 on, Mass was celebrated daily by the Benedictine Fathers who arrived there from Belgium — three Poles and three Belgians. The Benedictines were running a dormitory, located in the nearby villa named "Jaworzyna," for boys attending the Dr. John Wieczorkowski All-Boys Junior High Sanatorium School. The sister chronicler for the Rabka house mentions two of the monks by name: Fr. Adalbert Matusewicz, who celebrated Mass every day in "Loretto,"and Fr. Hyacinth, who would come for evening devotions. This lasted until June 1939, when the monks left for their monastery in Tyniec, near Kraków. At that time, the Benedictines recovered the abbey that they had lost by the order of the Austrian emperor more than a century earlier in 1816.

In the summer of 1937, Faustina went to confession to one of the monks, either Fr. Adalbert or Fr. Hyacinth. It was a very difficult time for her. Physically, she was suffering so much that she was not always able to get up out of bed and walk to the chapel and, spiritually, she was experiencing the dark night once again. The confessor recognized what was happening to her. Faustina recorded his words: "[Y]ou are on the right path, but God may leave your soul in this darkness and obscurity until death. ... But in all things abandon yourself to the will of God" (*Diary*, 1205).

She experienced separation from God and the lack of His presence in her heart intensely, in spite of the cordiality with which the sisters embraced her. Despite the warmth that the sisters showed her, she desired solitude. "I demand nothing from creatures and communicate with them only in so far as is necessary. ... My communing is with the angels" she wrote (*Diary*, 1200). One day, she heard the singing of an angel, "who sang out my whole life history and everything it comprised. I was surprised, but also strengthened," she noted (*Diary*, 1202).

In the midst of this abandonment, Faustina made one-day retreats that she referred to as retreats of suffering. "O Jesus, in these days of suffering, I am not capable of any kind of prayer. The oppression of my body and soul has increased. O my Jesus, You do see that Your child is on the decline. I am not forcing myself further, but simply submitting my will to the will of Jesus" (*Diary*, 1204).

In Rabka, Sr. Faustina experienced a sense of being cared for by St. Joseph, who was especially venerated by the Congregation. He told Faustina to have a special devotion to him, promising to help her in the implementation of the work that God had entrusted to her. In the Rabka convent, Sr. Faustina began a novena leading up to the solemnity of the Assumption of the Blessed Virgin Mary on August 15. She prayed for three intentions: to be able to meet with Fr.

Sopoćko; that God would hasten the bringing about of the work that Jesus had entrusted to her; and for the intentions of the fatherland. Faustina prayed for Poland very much. Not a day passed — as she wrote in July of that year — that she did not pray for her country. She left Rabka on August 10, 1937, having spent hardly 11 days there.

Chapter Seventeen

Kraków-Prądnik Biały

1936-1937, 1938

'Saints Are Not Contagious'

ASIMPLE WOODEN BUILDING USED TO STAND A STONE'S THROW AWAY FROM THE CHAPEL OF THE JOHN PAUL II HOSPITAL IN KRAKÓW: this was the tuberculosis ward. Sister Faustina Kowalska received treatment there toward the end of 1936 and at the beginning of 1937. At that point, the hospital had a different specialization — it was an epidemiological and disinfection facility that primarily treated patients with tuberculosis and scarlet fever. It also went by a different name: the Municipal Institutes of Health and Tuberculosis Sanatorium. It included a tuberculosis sanatorium and was one of the most modern facilities of its kind in Europe.

The part of the hospital in which Sr. Faustina spent nearly four months was still standing long after World War II. It was not demolished until 1963. In 1938, Sr. Faustina also spent almost five months in the adjacent building, which was similarly constructed of wood. She did not leave until three weeks prior to her death.

Sister Faustina first saw Prądnik Biały — which at that point had already been a part of Kraków for a quarter of a century — on September 19, 1936. Accompanied by the sister infirmarian, she came in order to be examined by Dr. Adam Silberg, a 42-year-old specialist in treating contagious diseases. Next to the hospital chapel stands the present day administration building that used to house a recreation room for tuberculosis patients. The X-ray machine used to be located on the first floor of the same building. This must have been where Dr. Silberg took Faustina's X-rays. He confirmed with certainty that she had tuberculosis and recommended the superiors of the convent isolate her from her fellow sisters, so that she would not infect them.

Upon leaving the doctor's office, Faustina walked directly to the chapel, where she interiorly heard the following words: "**My child, just a few more drops in your chalice; it won't be long now.** ... My heart melted, and there was a moment when my soul was immersed in the whole sea of God's mercy. I felt that my mission was beginning in all its fullness. Death destroys nothing that is good," she wrote (*Diary*, 694).

That day Sr. Faustina returned to her cell in the "Josephinum" in Łagiewniki, but she soon found herself back in Prądnik, this time for longer. The superiors of the Congregation, seeing that Faustina's health was deteriorating, sent her there for treatment. On December 9, 1936, the infirmarian, Sr. Chrysostom Korczak, accompanied her to Prądnik from Łagiewniki, which was located around seven miles away. The hospital facility occupied several acres of land, planted thickly with pine trees. Nowadays, the old parts of the hospital stand adjacent to cutting-edge hospital wards. The former tuberculosis sanatorium, which consisted of the aforementioned wooden buildings, was separated from the rest of the facility by trees. It was considered to be a part of the hospital. During this period, tuberculosis was treated mainly by isolating infected patients and exposing them to fresh air. Each of the low wooden buildings contained 42 beds. In total, the unit had 126 beds (in addition to 120 beds for patients with scarlet fever). Two of the buildings were designated for pulmonary tuberculosis patients (one for men and the other for women), while the third was for those suffering from skeletal and articular tuberculosis.

The wooden, one-story buildings of the tuberculosis unit are clearly visible in photographs taken before World War II, which were carefully archived by hospital photographer Alfred Lipnicki. Inside each was a huge room with dozens of beds set up in two neat rows. Patients lay next to one another in an orderly fashion. Some photos show the nurses, dressed in the religious habits of the Sacred Heart Sisters — the nuns of the Sister Servants of the Most Sacred Heart of Jesus. In addition to the large patients' dormitory, each building also had separate sanitary facilities, rooms for doctors and nurses, a small kitchen, and isolation rooms. Sister Faustina was assigned to one of the latter on December 9.

"I have a private room to myself; I am very much like a Carmelite," she noted (*Diary*, 798). After 11 years in the convent, where she had always slept in large dormitory rooms and where individual cells were only separated by screens, this was quite a change for her. She felt like a nun in a contemplative order — alone in her room, dedicated to prayer and to uniting herself with God. But this was just a first impression.

It was not quiet in the isolation room. The walls were very thin. "My room is next to the men's ward. I didn't know that men were such chatterboxes. From morning till late at night, there is talk about various subjects. The women's ward is much quieter," she wrote. "It is very difficult for me to concentrate on my prayer in the midst of these jokes and this laughter. They do not disturb me when the grace of God takes complete possession of me, because then I do not know what is going on around me" (*Diary*, 803).

The tuberculosis sanatorium stood in the middle of a patch of pine forest. Patients would rest on two wooden, south-facing verandas that were surrounded by trees. On December 12, Faustina noted, "This afternoon, I had my first open-air rest" (*Diary*, 816). That same day, she was visited by Sr. Felicia Żakowiecka, who brought her some things she needed from the convent. This date is important, because on that day Faustina recorded that it was the first time she recited the Divine Mercy Chaplet near a dying person, and Jesus confirmed to her that this person experienced the mercy of God.

The agony of this anonymous patient started on December 11. Sister Faustina wrote, "During the night, I was suddenly awakened and knew that some soul was asking me for prayer, and that it was in much need of prayer. Briefly, but with all my soul, I asked the Lord for grace for her" (*Diary*, 809). "The following afternoon, when I entered the ward, I saw someone dying, and learned that the agony had started during the night" (*Diary*, 810).

This had happened at the same time she was interiorly asked to pray. "And just then, I heard a voice in my soul: **Say the chaplet which I taught you**. I ran to fetch my rosary and knelt down by the dying person and, with all the ardor of my soul, I began to say the chaplet. Suddenly the dying person opened her eyes and looked at me; I had not managed to finish the entire chaplet when she died, with extraordinary peace. I fervently asked the Lord to fulfill the promise He had given me for the recitation of the chaplet. The Lord gave me to know that the soul had been granted the grace." Faustina further added, "That was the first soul to receive the benefit of the Lord's promise. I could feel the power of mercy envelop that soul" (*Diary*, 810).

When she returned from the common dormitory to her isolation room, interiorly she heard, "**At the hour of their death, I defend as My own glory every soul that will say this chaplet; or when others say it for a dying person, the pardon is the same. When this chaplet is said by the bedside of a dying person, God's anger is placated, unfathomable mercy envelops the soul, and the very depths of My tender mercy are moved for the sake of the sorrowful Passion of My Son**" (*Diary*, 811).

From that moment on, Sr. Faustina would often experience a similar feeling — interiorly she was made aware that someone was dying and asking her for prayer. "I feel vividly and clearly that spirit who is asking me for prayer. I was not aware that souls are so closely united, and often it is my Guardian Angel who tells me" (*Diary,* 828). Elsewhere, she explains, "My vision is purely spiritual, by means of a sudden light that God grants me at that moment."

She would be awakened and pray for dying persons in the middle of the night, and then in the morning, she would find out that somebody's last agony began at that exact time. "I have a watch, and I look to see what time it is. On the following day, when they tell me about that person's death, I ask them about the time, and it exactly corresponds, as does the length of the person's last agony" (*Diary,* 835). She would keep praying the chaplet till the moment of death for the given person or for a shorter time when she sensed peace in her soul. She was obtaining trust in the mercy of God for the dying. She begged for the grace of salvation.

"God's mercy sometimes touches the sinner at the last moment in a wondrous and mysterious way," she noted. "Outwardly, it seems as if everything were lost, but it is not so. The soul, illumined by a ray of God's powerful final grace, turns to God in the last moment with such a power of love that, in an instant, it receives from God forgiveness of sin and punishment, while outwardly it shows no sign either of repentance or of contrition, because souls [at that stage] no longer react to external things. Oh, how beyond comprehension is God's mercy! But — horror! — there are also souls who voluntarily and consciously reject and scorn this grace! Although a person is at the point of death, the merciful God gives the soul that interior vivid moment, so that if the soul is willing, it has the possibility of returning to God. But sometimes, the obduracy in souls is so great that consciously they choose hell" (*Diary,* 1698).

Faustina recited the chaplet not only for the dying in her hospital unit, but also for those in other units. "The priest ... hastily leaves early for the city, so the sick are left without care, but it somehow happens that I usually stay with the dying, which makes me very happy," she once told Sr. Seraphina Kukulska. She also prayed for those who were dying far away from Prądnik — for sisters from the Congregation, family members. Her spirit, and later also her body, would be transferred to wherever they were.

Faustina prepared many patients for confession and Holy Communion. Patients who sensed she was close to God turned to her for spiritual help. They sought consolation and hope. They confided their complicated life stories to her. Faustina told them about God's mercy. Not everyone could understand how she — seriously ill herself — could possibly have the strength to listen to others, to hear their complaints and grievances. For this reason, some did not spare her their sarcasm.

She explained that there was room for everyone in her heart, just as there was room for her in the Heart of Jesus: "My heart is always open to the sufferings of others; and I will not close my heart to the sufferings of others, even though because of this I have been scornfully nicknamed 'dump'; that is, [because] everyone dumps his pain into my heart" (*Diary*, 871). This was a part of her mission, to speak about Divine Mercy to people who were sick in body and soul, to those who were in despair, with one foot in the grave. She would pray for them, offer up her own suffering, and make additional mortifications for them.

It is difficult not to speak of heroism when one reads what penitential practices she undertook during Lent in 1937. Since she was under the observation of nurses, she explained that she made minor resolutions: "Sleep without a pillow; keep myself a little hungry; every day, with my arms outstretched, say the chaplet ... occasionally, with arms outstretched, for an indefinite period of time pray informally. Intention: to beg divine mercy for poor sinners, and for priests, the power to bring sinful hearts to repentance" (*Diary*, 934).

Long vigils at the bedside of the dying and getting up frequently at night to be with them were certainly not recommended because of the condition of Faustina's health. Consequently, after some time, the superiors of the convent and her doctor forbade her to visit the other patients. From that moment on, Sr. Faustina kept on uniting herself with the dying spiritually — she prayed for them in her isolation room, while resting on the veranda, or in the chapel, the same chapel that serves patients from 1917 to this day. A few years ago, it was thoroughly renovated.

The wooden altar with a statue of Our Lady, the floor, and probably the confessional are what remains from the time when Sr. Faustina used to pray here. Her portrait now hangs in the sanctuary. Faustina tried to attend Mass every day at 6 a.m. There were times, however, when she did not have the strength to walk to the chapel, which was only 70 steps from her ward. Sometimes she could not get out of bed for several days in a row and would even be forbidden to do so by the doctor. But she was not deprived of the Sacraments.

When, on the fourth day after her arrival at the hospital, she reproached herself that due to various circumstances she had not gone to confession for three weeks, Fr. Andrasz appeared in her room. "Beforehand, we did not exchange a single word. I was delighted because I was extremely anxious to go to confession. As usual, I unveiled my whole soul. Father gave a reply to each little detail. I felt unusually happy to be able to say everything as I did. ... Suddenly his figure became diffused with a great light, and I saw that it was not Father A[ndrasz], but Jesus. His garments were bright as snow, and He disappeared immediately" (*Diary*, 817).

This was not the only time when Jesus, with whom Faustina's soul communed constantly, appeared to her in the hospital room. She had another vision of Jesus on January 14, 1937. He was "wearing a bright robe and girded with a golden belt, His whole figure resplendent with great majesty." Jesus assured her that He would not leave her alone in the fulfillment of the task that He had given her: "**Do whatever you can in this matter; I will accomplish everything that is lacking in you. You know what is within your power to do; do that**" (*Diary*, 881). Faustina explained that such visions had become increasingly rare at this time. She had walked a long way along the mystical path and was ascending to its very summit. Now, she wrote, "I more often commune with the Lord in a more profound manner. My senses sleep and, although not in a visible way, all things become more real and clearer to me than if I saw them with my eyes. My intellect learns more in one moment than during long years of thinking and meditation, both as regards the essence of God and as regards revealed truths, and also as regards the knowledge of my own misery" (*Diary*, 882). She was now enjoying a state of profound union with God, who was communicating Himself lovingly to this chosen soul who, in return, was growing in love and knowledge of Him.

Faustina was aware of her task "now and in eternity," which was to spread the message of the Divine Mercy and plead for mercy for the entire world. However, she knew that "this [work] is, as it were, secondary," because it resulted from the most important thing — close communion with God. First place is always reserved for "God and for the continual uniting of myself with Him through an ever purer and deeper love," she wrote in a letter to Fr. Sopoćko on December 20, 1936. The pure love into which she was being transformed would lead her to new mystical experiences, which are unimaginable for "ordinary" souls and which she described in her *Diary*.

During this stay in Prądnik, Faustina finished a second notebook and started a third; she left behind six in total. She was writing more now. Paradoxically, it was her illness that made this possible. She also had time to do what Fr. Sopoćko had asked her to, which was "to put both diaries in order" and to underline the words of Jesus. "If I was not ill, I would not have time to do this," she informed him in a letter dated March 24, 1937, shortly before she left the hospital.

Sister Faustina underlined the words of Jesus in pencil — delicately, with a broken line. She was certain which words came from God. She wrote, "These words were so filled with power and so clear that I would give my life in declaring they came from God. I can tell this by the profound peace that accompanied them at the time and that still remains with me. This peace gives me such great strength and power that all difficulties, adversities, sufferings, and death itself are as nothing" (*Diary*, 359.)

Faustina's writings from this period contain an increasing amount of rhyming verse. Faustina was not particularly talented as a poet and consequently, from a technical perspective, the poems are not very good. She wrote them down just like she made her notes: spontaneously, without deletions. However, it is not a question of their form, but their subject matter, which is suffering and death, but above all, the adoration of God — His love and mercy.

Faustina spent Christmas 1936 with the sisters at the Łagiewniki convent. She came from Prądnik for a short, three-day break. She was taken back to the sanatorium by her friend Sr. Damiana Ziółek and was once again settled in by December 27. On their way to Prądnik, the two sisters stopped at the church of St. Joseph in Podgórze, where they dropped off a woman with an infant. A few days earlier, someone had abandoned the child at the convent gate. The sisters found an adoptive mother who was now taking the child to be baptized. The parish baptismal register shows that the woman was Paulina Aksak, the wife of Stanislaus, who resided at No. 141 in Łagiewniki. The pastor, Fr. Thaddeus Siepak, christened the baby girl Barbara Maria.

The New Year began with suffering for Faustina, but also with getting to know new, deeper expanses of mysticism. After the passive purification of the soul and "recurring periods of purification from certain imperfections," as Professor Fr. Stanislaus Urbański notes, her divine visitations kept becoming more and more intense. They allowed Faustina to see the Lord as though "unveiled" and, due to the suspension of the activity of her human faculties, "to be immersed in God" for longer periods. "The Lord is leading me into a world unknown to me. He makes known to me His great grace, but I am afraid of it and will not submit to its influence in so far as it may be in my power, until I am assured by my spiritual director as to what this grace is," she wrote (*Diary*, 910) at the beginning of February 1937, aware of the dangers that exist on the spiritual path. What Jesus told her during this time could have frightened her.

It began, as it usually does in these states, from infused contemplation, which, in turn, progressed into union of the soul with God. When "God's presence pervaded" Faustina and her mind became "mysteriously enlightened in respect to His Essence," then, in one flash of Divine light, she came to an understanding of the mystery of the Holy Trinity, which has been the subject of theologians' careful consideration for centuries. "In spirit, I saw the Three Divine Persons, but Their Essence was One. He is One, and One only, but in Three Persons; none of Them is either greater or smaller; there is no difference in either beauty or sanctity, for They are One. ... When I was united to One, I was equally united to the Second and to the Third [Person] in such a way that when we are united with One, by that very fact, we are equally united to the two Persons in the same way as with the One. Their will is One, one God, though in Three Persons. ... In these moments, my soul experienced such great divine delights that I find this difficult to express" (*Diary*, 911).

At the end of this, Faustina heard words that greatly startled her. Jesus said, **"I want you to be My spouse."** The sister knew nothing about mysticism beyond what she had experienced herself. This is why she pondered over what this could mean. After all, for the last five years, since she had taken her perpetual vows, she had felt espoused to Jesus, her Bridegroom. She wrote, "And so I continued to reflect on what this could mean. I sensed, and came to realize, that this was some special kind of grace" (*Diary*, 912).

Sister Faustina's soul was already purified, stripped bare of anything human that could draw her away from God, to such a degree that she could be united with the Lord — her Bridegroom, from whom only the "veil of earthly life" was separating her. The process of union would be gradual.

To begin with, on March 18, 1937, Faustina experienced "the spiritual espousal of a soul with God," that is, a transforming union. This is an "extremely spiritual" grace, as Faustina wrote, that "brings me into great intimacy and communion with the Lord." And though she deplored that she was unable to describe its nature, she nonetheless made an attempt to do so: "This grace has drawn me into the very burning center of God's love. I have come to understand His Trinitarian Quality and the absolute Oneness of His Being" (*Diary*, 1019-1020). God, through the light of interior knowledge, "allows me to know His greatness and holiness and ... He gives me an exclusive knowledge of His love for me ... and also of how He gives Himself to a soul while suspending all laws of nature" (*Diary*, 1019).

Under that date, Faustina admitted further, "I would not know how to live without the Lord. Jesus often visits me in this seclusion, teaches me, reassures me, rebukes me, and admonishes me. He Himself forms my heart according to His divine wishes and likings, but always with much goodness and mercy." She ends the description with the words, "Our hearts are fused as one" (*Diary*, 1024). So what happened then?

The act of transforming union, writes Fr. Urbański, is characterized by "extreme love of the human being in union with the Holy Trinity." From that moment on, "the mystic yearns for God with a yearning that nothing can extinguish and from then on, every thought, every word, every deed is nothing more than a means by which one can give oneself even more fully to God and be ever closer to Him ... the soul enters ever more deeply into itself, reaching the depths where God dwells and where the soul reaches the deepest union with Him." As St. John of the Cross wrote, what essentially takes place are "substantial touches of Divine union between God and the soul." In this act in which the soul enters most deeply into its spirit, it unites with God in love.

The point of culmination finally arrived. It was 11 a.m. on Good Friday, March 26, 1937. Sister Faustina experienced the mystical espousal, an experience known only to a few among the mystics: "And He brought me into such close intimacy with Himself that my heart was espoused to His Heart in a loving union, and I could feel the faintest stir of His Heart and He, of mine. The fire of my created love was joined to the ardor of His eternal love. This one grace surpasses all others in its immensity. His Trinitarian Being enveloped me entirely, and I am totally immersed in Him. My littleness is, as it were, wrestling with this Immortal Mighty One. I am immersed in incomprehensible love and incomprehensible torture because of His Passion. All that concerns His Being is imparted to me also" (*Diary*, 1056).

Although Faustina disclosed the essence of her mystical espousal in this short description, it is hard to escape the impression that she often grieved over how difficult it was to express what she had truly experienced. "Words, which belong to the world of the senses, cannot fully express what she was experiencing in the realm of the spirit." The average reader can only have an inkling about her experiences. They can compare it to the love of two people who live in each other, permeate one another, and give themselves to one another through mutual love. This "spousal unity of hearts" which came to be in that moment between Jesus and Sr. Faustina, the spiritual merging of "two loves," as Ludmila Grygiel describes it, is a sign of the greatest intimacy and the closest union. Maria Tarnawska wrote simply that, from that moment on, "Jesus permeates her to the extent that any tangible boundary between what is Faustina, and what is God, disappears, as He is in her."[45]

Father Urbański makes clear that in this union, it is not a matter of substantial transformation, that is, a conversion of human nature into the divine. Rather, it is the matter of "a profound spiritual transformation and the complete change of a human being's interior through the act of love." However, following St. John of the Cross, one must add that this union in love takes place between a transformed soul and the entire Most Holy Trinity, its Three Persons, and this comes about by means of the "same spiration of love that the Father breathes into the Son and the Son into the Father — the spiration of love who is the Person of the Holy Spirit."

From the moment of her mystical espousal to Jesus, Faustina would remain in a loving union with God, as though in an unceasing ecstasy, which no external events would be able to disturb. Her soul would no longer experience any further torment, unrest, dryness, or suffering caused by love. Nothing would, any longer, mar her inner peace, which stemmed from "possessing" God.

On the day following the mystical espousal, Faustina left the hospital. This marked the end of the first of her two treatments in Prądnik. This particular stay had lasted almost four months. Initially, Faustina was to remain at the hospital until March 3, but, as she informed Fr. Sopoćko in a letter, her stay had been extended.

She returned to Łagiewniki on Holy Saturday, March 27, 1937. The house chronicler noted that Faustina had returned "for good, and in better health." And indeed, the prognosis was better, though she did not return "for good," even if she stayed for a longer time.

A year later, Sr. Faustina arrived at Prądnik for a second time. It was the Thursday after Easter, April 21, 1938. She was supposed to stay at the sanatorium for two months, perhaps longer. She stayed for almost five months.

On April 20, the day before going to the sanatorium, she wrote, "I was very worried that I would be put in bed in a ward and be exposed to all sorts of things." She complained to Jesus, who asked her to remain calm. She heard interiorly, "**All is ready; I have ordered, in My own special way, a private room to be prepared for you**" (*Diary*, 1674).

Sister Felicia Żakowiecka remembered, "When we arrived, a private room for Sr. Faustina had already been prepared, and the Sacred Heart Sisters even placed two bouquets there. We were caught by surprise: what is this? We then found out that a man who had suffered from tuberculosis had died unexpectedly three hours earlier. Sister Faustina said to me with great peace and joy in her quiet voice, 'How good the Lord Jesus is! He heard my prayer.' There was joyous surprise in her eyes."

Three nurses from the Sacred Heart Congregation (Sr. David Cedro, who was a nurse in her ward, and two nurses from other wards — Sr. Alana Wilusz and Sr. Medarda Podrazik) hurried to welcome Faustina. Doctor Silberg confirmed the seriousness of the condition of Faustina's health. She, in turn, wrote, "I felt a peace so great that, if death had come at that moment, I would not have said to it, 'Wait, for I still have some matters to attend to.' No, I would have welcomed it with joy, because I am ready for the meeting with the Lord, not only today, but ever since the moment when I placed my complete trust in the Divine Mercy, resigning myself totally to His most holy will, full of mercy and compassion" (*Diary*, 1679).

The following day, something happened that surprised even Faustina. The previous evening, Sr. David had told Faustina that she was not to go to the chapel in the morning because she was "too tired" to do so. In the morning, Faustina made her meditation nonetheless and waited trustingly for Holy Communion, believing that she would receive it. "When my love and desire had reached a high degree, I saw at my bedside a Seraph, who gave me Holy Communion, saying these words: 'Behold the Lord of Angels.' When I received the Lord, my spirit was drowned in the love of God and in amazement. This was repeated for thirteen days" (*Diary*, 1676). The Seraph "was surrounded by a great light, the divinity and love of God being reflected in him."

The angel also brought Faustina Holy Communion on the first Sunday after Easter, the Sunday that Jesus demanded be established as the Feast of Divine Mercy. That day, Faustina renewed the oblation she had made of herself "as a holocaust for sinners" (*Diary*, 1680) and also for the intention of spreading the mission of mercy to the whole world. Not long afterwards, she wrote in the *Diary*, "In spite of Satan's anger, the Divine Mercy will triumph over the whole world and will be worshipped by all souls" (*Diary*, 1789).

During this stay in the Prądnik hospital, Faustina was visited by the sisters from the "Josephinum" more frequently than the first time around.

Sister Felicia Żakowiecka recounts, "We had heartfelt conversations, mostly on spiritual matters."

Sister Seraphina Kukulska remembered, "I always found [her] in a serene — or even cheerful — mood, sometimes almost as though she were beaming, but she never unveiled the secret of her happiness. She felt very happy in Prądnik and never complained about her suffering. ... Whenever I visited her, I could feel an interior attraction, something I could not comprehend, but I could not bring myself to have a spiritual conversation with her, because I had been unfavorably disposed toward her due to the influence of other sisters. Now I can see how one can misjudge a soul with whom the Lord Jesus Himself unites so lovingly."

Mother Irene Krzyżanowska recalled, "These visits brought me spiritual joy. Our conversations were always filled with a Divine atmosphere. Staying with her for longer periods, I felt the presence of God."

It was during visits like this that Faustina foretold the outbreak of a war to some of the sisters. She told them that it would be a great, long, and terrible one. She had visions of enormous devastation, exterminations, and persecution of the clergy. She told Fr. Sopoćko that Poland would see "very hard times. She saw her fellow citizens being deported to the east and west." Faustina prayed for Poland daily and kept on offering sufferings for her. She wrote, "My beloved native land, Poland, if you only knew how many sacrifices and prayers I offer to God for you!" (*Diary*, 1038). In the last year of her life, she interiorly heard these words of Jesus: "**I bear a special love for Poland, and if she will be obedient to My will, I will exalt her in might and holiness. From her will come forth the spark that will prepare the world for My final coming**" (*Diary*, 1732).

These words have been interpreted in different ways. Today, it is hardly questioned that this "spark" is the message of the Divine Mercy.

Sister Faustina, transformed by Love — divinized[46] — was slowly approaching the moment of her immersion in God for all eternity. "I have already felt for half a year as though I were in eternity," she told Sr. Damiana Ziółek in the spring of 1938. Faustina's condition was very serious, but Dr. Silberg no longer forbade her to go to the chapel if she had the strength to do so. He used to see her walking there, leaning against the wall. "Anyone else would not be capable of doing that, but I cannot forbid her to do it," Dr. Silberg would say. He, too, would come to Faustina for conversation about spiritual matters. "Sometimes they talked in such a serious manner that I did not dare interrupt them when I came to see her," recalled Sr. Alfreda Pokora. (On June 8, 1938, Sr. Alfreda replaced the infirmarian Sr. Chrysostom Korczak, who had not been well disposed toward Faustina.)

Little is known about Dr. Adam Silberg, who became the director of the hospital in 1937. This is because the hospital archives went up in flames during World War II. We do know that he was a convert and that he had a young son named Casimir. There is no reliable information about what happened to him or his family after the outbreak of the war, in the course of which he died.

Sister Alfreda Pokora remembered, "When I was visiting her in Prądnik, I usually found Sr. Faustina writing in one of her notebooks. I once jokingly told her that she was to be promoted to become a saint. In response to which she asked, 'Why?' 'Because you are writing your hagiography,' I answered. She smiled and said, 'How do you know?'"

The most important guest Faustina received in her hospital room was Jesus Himself. She already lived in such intimacy with Him that she treated Him, as she already had for a long time, like her dearest friend. This is well illustrated by the exchange that took place between Jesus and Faustina in May 1938, in the hospital gardens. Faustina went out to the garden immediately following the 6 a.m. Mass. There were no patients around at this early hour, so nobody could interrupt her contemplation about "the blessings of God." "My heart was burning with a love so strong that it seemed my breast would burst. Suddenly Jesus stood before me and said, **'What are you doing here so early?'**" Faustina replied: "I am thinking of You, of Your mercy and Your goodness toward us." She then asked, in a natural and free manner, "And You, Jesus, what are You doing here?" Jesus responded that He was there to meet her in order to "**lavish new graces**" on her (*Diary*, 1705). This was an exchange between two loving hearts.

In early June 1938, before Pentecost, Faustina made the final retreat of her life. It lasted for three days and was directed by Jesus Himself. Jesus dictated which fragments of the Gospel Faustina should read and what topics she should meditate on, and He gave talks — about spiritual warfare, about prayer and sacrifice, and on mercy, the contents of which she wrote down. On the first day, Jesus instructed her, or rather reminded her, how to overcome the difficulties in daily life: "**Never trust in yourself, but abandon yourself totally to My will**" (*Diary*, 1760). On the second day, His lesson was on how to rescue the souls of sinners: "**I want to see you as a sacrifice of living love, which only then carries weight before Me. ... All its power rests in the will**" (*Diary*, 1767). On the third day, He reminded her what the nature of her mission was: "**I desire that your heart be an abiding place of My mercy. I desire that this mercy flow out upon the whole world through your heart**" (*Diary*, 1777).

On June 17, 1938, the first Friday after the feast of Corpus Christi, Sr. Faustina's health deteriorated rapidly, probably as a result of internal bleeding. "I felt so unwell that I thought the longed-for moment was approaching. I had a high fever and spat up much blood during the night. ... In the afternoon, my temperature dropped suddenly to 35.8°C [96.4°F]. I felt so weak that it was as if everything inside me were dying. But when I steeped myself in profound prayer, I understood that it was not yet the moment of deliverance, but only a closer call from my Bridegroom" (*Diary*, 1786). Faustina complained to Jesus that He was misleading her because He was showing her "the open gate of heaven" and yet leaving her on earth. But Jesus promised that "**it will not be long now**" (*Diary*, 1787).

The last months of Sr. Faustina's life were filled with happiness, which flowed from her union in love with God. In some of the last entries in her *Diary*, she wrote, "My soul is one hymn in adoration of Your mercy. I love You, God, for Yourself alone" (1794). "The moments which are most pleasant to me are those when I converse with the Lord within the center of my being. I try my very best not to leave Him alone. He likes to be always with us" (1793).

Soon, after the bout of illness she experienced on June 17, Sr. Faustina finished writing the *Diary*. She was too weak to continue. Or was it, perhaps, that she had written down everything she had to pass on to the world about the Divine Mercy? She anticipated that her notes would be published after her death, to be "given for the comfort of souls." For this reason, in early June, she managed to leave an instruction on a loose sheet of paper: "No one is permitted to read these notebooks and the notes contained in them — Fr. Andrasz must first review them, or Fr. Sopoćko — considering that they contain the secrets of a conscience. It is God's will that all of this be given to souls for comfort. The notebooks themselves are not to be given to the sisters to read, the superiors excepted, until they are printed."

One of the last entries in the *Diary* was about the gift of bilocation. Jesus informed Faustina that she was going to go see a sinner in agony, who was dying in despair. She was to recite the chaplet, by the power of which the man was to receive trust. "Suddenly, I found myself in a strange cottage where an elderly man was dying amidst great torments. All about the bed was a multitude of demons and the family, who were crying. When I began to pray, the spirits of darkness fled, with hissing and threats directed at me. The soul became calm and, filled with trust, rested in the Lord. At the same moment, I found myself again in my own room. How this happens … I do not know," she wrote (*Diary*, 1798).

It is most probable that Faustina finished writing the *Diary* before June 24. Why this date? First, notes made after June 17 are very rare, taking up only two and a half pages in print. Second, Faustina does not provide information, as she did on June 17, about the further deterioration of her health, which took place on June 24. That day, an alarmed Mother Irene Krzyżanowska came from Łagiewniki to see Faustina. The following day, a confessor arrived and administered the last rites to Faustina.

Sister Alfreda Pokora remembered, "Seeing the grave condition of the sick sister, I asked her whether she wished to be taken home, so that she could die in the company of the Congregation. A joyful smile was her response … then, after a moment of reflection, I finally heard these words from her: 'I am not going to die yet, so please leave me here for now, Sister, because my presence in the convent would be too much of a bother since one of the sisters would always have to be near me.' A moment later she added, 'But please do whatever you see fit and what the superiors wish.'"

In July, Faustina had a visit from Mother Michael Moraczewska, who was making an official visit to the convent in Łagiewniki. Faustina happened to be feeling a little better that day and was even going outdoors to rest on the veranda in order to get some fresh air and walk to the chapel. Mother Michael noted that the sister was looking ill, but "she did not give the impression of one who was seriously ill."

Mother Moraczewska recalled, "This last meeting of ours left me with the most pleasant impression and memory. Sister was immensely delighted. She was telling me with animation about various episodes from her hospital stay and the single hour that I had at my disposal between my arrival and my departure by bus passed like a moment. We did not specially touch upon any interior matters. Only a short while before we parted company, she joyfully said, 'Oh, dear Mother, what beautiful things the Lord Jesus tells me,' and pointing to where her notes lay, she added, 'Dear Mother, you will read all of this.'"

Toward the end of August, Faustina wrote a farewell letter to Mother General. "I completely abandon myself to God and His holy will. *An ever-greater longing for God pervades me; death does not frighten me; my soul abounds in profound peace.*" She was thankful for all the goodness she had received and apologized for all her shortcomings and mistakes. She ended her letter with the words, "Good-bye, dearest Mother, we will see each other in heaven at the foot of God's throne. And now, may God's mercy be praised in us and through us."

That same month, Mother Michael found out that Faustina's health had deteriorated. On August 24, Sr. Camilla Sosnowska, who was also a patient at the hospital, phoned the convent to pass on the message that Faustina was feeling significantly worse. Mother Krzyżanowska arrived immediately and spent the night at the bedside of the sick sister. The following day, the chaplain, Fr. Theodore Czaputa, arrived from the "Josephinum." He heard the sick sister's confession and administered the last rites. Faustina received the Sacrament piously, but, she told one of the sisters, "I knew that, anyway, I was not going to die."

Father Sopoćko visited Faustina a number of times in late August and early September, having arrived in Kraków to attend a theological convention. He later wrote, "This is a soul closely united with God, who alone directs her and perfects her through suffering. She has a deep understanding of the truths of God and a profound intuitive sense of Catholic teaching." They talked for an hour and a half about various matters, including the new Congregation that had been on Faustina's mind so frequently in the last few years. Father Sopoćko concluded that everything that she had said about the new order was probably an illusion. Faustina promised to talk about it with Jesus and give him an answer during their next meeting. Meanwhile, the next day, as Fr. Sopoćko celebrated Mass for Faustina's intention, the following thought came to him suddenly: "Just as she had been unable to paint that image, but only gave instructions, she would be unable to establish the new Congregation, but would only give general directives."

During his next visit on September 2, when Fr. Sopoćko asked Faustina what she had to say about the new Congregation, she replied that she did not have to say anything because Jesus had already enlightened him with an answer during the celebration of the Holy Eucharist. Father Michael Sopoćko recalled,

"This answer shook my spirit, because Sr. Faustina did not know the thoughts I had during the Mass I celebrated."

Faustina did, however, tell him some important things that he should observe in the future. First of all, he should never cease spreading devotion to the Divine Mercy, but work toward establishing the Feast of Divine Mercy on the first Sunday after Easter. She told him in detail of the difficulties — and even persecution — he would encounter in connection with this matter, but that he was not permitted to stop spreading the message of Divine Mercy. She told Fr. Sopoćko, "The world will not last for much longer, and God still wants to grant graces to people before its end, so that no one will be able to excuse themselves at the judgment, that one did not know about the goodness of God and did not hear about His mercy."

As for the matter of the new Congregation, he was to be "rather indifferent," not become too involved, and he would know from certain signs who should act in this matter and how. She warned him that the Congregation should not accept individuals "from other congregations, where they had already gotten used to behaving in a certain way, and certainly not to persuade individuals to change congregations, because that would draw down upon itself the displeasure of the superiors of these established congregations." She foretold, "God Himself will bring a person from the world, one who will display the signs that will signal that they are the one chosen for the task."

It happened just as she predicted. A few years later, in Vilnius, a group of six women came together, who — on April 11, 1942, in the chapel of a convent belonging to the Discalced Carmelites — made private vows in the hands of Fr. Sopoćko. They were the ones to start the Congregation of the Sisters of the Merciful Jesus, which was officially founded on August 25, 1947.

Father Sopoćko remembered, "She also told me that she could see the first home of the Congregation, a spacious home but poor. But there reigns in it a great spirit — next to it there is a church. ... When I visited the house of the new Congregation in Myślibórz near Gorzów in 1947, I found that everything corresponded perfectly."

Near the end of her life, Sr. Faustina, who had initially experienced an interior struggle connected with the task of establishing a new Congregation and later even became actively involved in working toward this goal, understood what her role in all of this was to be. As Maria Tarnawska aptly pointed out, Jesus, who had demanded such a great sacrifice from Faustina — the sacrifice of leaving her

Congregation in order to establish a new one — Himself prevented this from taking place. "He did not want her to act, but to be *willing* to act." Faustina once noted in the *Diary*, "It is not the greatness of the works, but the greatness of the effort that will be rewarded. What is done out of love is not small" (1310).

Sister Faustina sensed that this was her last conversation with her spiritual director. Father Sopoćko noted, "She bid me farewell, promising to pray for me here and after death." He left her hospital room, but immediately returned because he noticed that he had not given her the copies of the booklets with published prayers to the Divine Mercy. When he half-opened the door, he saw Faustina in ecstasy: "I saw her immersed in prayer, sitting up, but almost floating above the bed. Her eyes were fixed on some invisible object, her pupils greatly dilated." Faustina did not notice that the priest, who wanted to withdraw, had come in. "She soon came to, noticed me. and apologized that she did not hear me knock or walk in." She bade Fr. Sopoćko farewell with the words, "See you in heaven."

Father Michael Sopoćko recalled, "I felt great pain and bitterness in my soul that I had to bid farewell to this extraordinary being and that I was now so abandoned by everyone. But I realized that it is I who, above all, had to trust in the Divine Mercy."

Sister Faustina was dying. The Superior of the convent decided to bring her to Łagiewniki, so that she could die at home. Faustina left Prądnik on Saturday, September 17. As a parting gift, Dr. Silberg asked his patient for the holy card of St. Thérèse of the Child Jesus that she kept by her bed — as a witness of "all her suffering."

Sister Alfreda Pokora added, "A few days after Sr. Faustina's death, I went to the director's [Dr. Silberg's] house, and noticed that this holy card was hanging above the bed of his 6-year-old son. I anxiously asked whether the holy card had been disinfected, and I received this answer: 'I am not afraid about the spread of the illness, because … Sr. Faustina is a saint, and saints are not contagious.'"

Chapter Eighteen

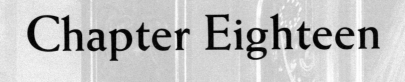

Kraków-Łagiewniki III

October 5, 1938

Death

ON SATURDAY, SEPTEMBER 17, 1938, 18 DAYS BEFORE FAUSTINA DIED, the infirmarian, Sr. Alfreda Pokora, brought her to the convent in Łagiewniki. They traveled a little more than six miles between the convent and the hospital in Prądnik in an open carriage.

"Our journey was very difficult," Sr. Alfreda recalled years later. "I thought that I would not manage to get her home alive. She fainted several times, much to my distress. Noticing my anxiety, Sr. Faustina — in spite of her own severe suffering — reassured me, saying, 'Sister, please don't worry, because I will not die on the way.'"

The sisters in the "Josephinum," which Faustina had left five months earlier, were aghast at her condition and appearance. Sister Stella Kozłowska described Faustina thus: "Her face was gaunt, and its shape had changed. Her skin was yellow, and her eyes were huge and sunken with dark bags underneath. Her gaze was intense, searching and penetrating." The former infirmarian, Sr. Chrysostom Korczak, who earlier had not really believed that Faustina was sick and had been mean to her at times, now burst into tears at the sight of her, saying, "Sister, look at you! You're like a skeleton." Father Andrasz later recorded these words, which were passed on by word of mouth.

Faustina was placed in an isolation cell for gravely ill sisters in the main building of the convent. "She is very frail. She can't get up at all anymore and hardly eats anything. She is completely resigned [to the will of God], and she awaits — in a way that is uplifting for all of us — the moment when she will be united with the Lord Jesus. And she is not at all afraid," noted the convent chronicler.

Two sisters took care of Faustina: the infirmarian, Sr. Alfreda Pokora, and Sr. Amelia Socha, who had tuberculosis of the wrist. Other sisters visited Faustina, though the superiors advised caution due to the danger of infection. The warning was aimed particularly at the young religious. Faustina herself did not let them get too close, saying, "Dear little Sister, take better care of yourself."

During such visits, Faustina told Sr. Anna and Sr. Clementine that a great and terrible war was going to break out and would last for a long time. She also revealed to Sr. Clementine that the sisters would remain in the convent in Łagiewniki, but that they needed to pray a lot. Both sisters acknowledged that they didn't take Faustina's words seriously and didn't remember them until one year later when the War began and the Germans wanted to expel the sisters from the convent in the "Josephinum" in 1940 (the first of their three attempts to do this).

Sister Stella Kozłowska recounts, "Not one of the sisters who visited Faustina heard a word of complaint or mention of herself. The sole subject of conversation was always the Lord Jesus. Speaking tired her enormously, so she would usually only respond to questions and would often repeat, 'Not much longer now, not much longer.'"

Sister Alfreda Pokora remembers, "Sister Faustina's final weeks were very edifying. She always showed great kindness and patience, requesting nothing for herself. When asked if she was suffering greatly, she would answer, 'Yes, very much, but I'm fine with it.'"

Faustina spoke about her illness in similar terms to Mother Irene Krzyżanowska, adding that the Congregation would have "much good" on her account. The Superior of the Łagiewniki convent noticed at this point that Faustina's fretfulness about spreading the devotion to the Divine Mercy had left her. She was already at peace about this, confident that it would take place. "There *will* be a Feast of Divine Mercy, I can see it. I only want the will of God," she would say.

Sister Clementine Buczek asked her once whether she was afraid of death. "Why should I be afraid?" she replied, suddenly full of vigor. "All my sins and imperfections will burn away like a piece of straw in the flames of Divine Mercy."

Mother Irene Krzyżanowska writes, "Shortly before her death, when I came to see Sr. Faustina, she sat up in bed, asking me to come closer, and she told me the following: 'The Lord Jesus wants to exalt me and make me a saint.' I sensed a great dignity in her without a shadow of pride, and had the odd feeling that Sr. Faustina accepted this assurance as a gift of God's mercy. I left her room moved by all of this without fully realizing the significance of those words."

On Thursday, September 22, following the Congregation's custom, Sr. Faustina apologized to the whole Congregation for any involuntary misconduct or negligence on her part. Three days later, on September 25, she saw Fr. Michael Sopoćko for the final time (this is the date Fr. Sopoćko gives in *My Memories of the Late Sr. Faustina*, while in the *Diary* it is September 26). Father Sopoćko came to Łagiewniki on his way from Częstochowa, where he had been taking part in a convention of the Catholic Youth Association. A Plenary Meeting of the [Polish] Episcopate was being held there at the same time. Father Sopoćko took that opportunity to hand the bishops letters requesting the establishment of the Feast of Divine Mercy. This news made Sr. Faustina very happy. They did not speak for long. "She did not want to continue to speak with me, or perhaps she could not, saying, 'I'm busy communing with the Heavenly Father,'" recalled Fr. Sopoćko, to whom Faustina had seemed like an "unearthly being." He remembered that she told him then that she would die in nine days.

Their last meeting confirmed him even more in the conviction of the truth of the message proclaimed by Sr. Faustina. He also had no doubts at all that what she had written in the *Diary* about a Seraph bringing her Holy Communion in the hospital in Prądnik "really happened."

Sister Amelia Socha spent many hours at Faustina's bedside. "Both sisters liked, understood, and loved each other very much," recalled Sr. Alfreda Pokora. A week before Faustina's death, Amelia said to her, "Sister, how good the Lord Jesus is to let you die so young and so consciously. How much I, too, would like to contract pulmonary tuberculosis and die one year after you." Sister Amelia, who suffered from tuberculosis of the bones, feared becoming an invalid and a burden to the Congregation. Faustina understood her motives, so she promised her, "Sister, if I shall have any graces with the Lord Jesus, I will ask that one year after me, He will take you." Just over a year after the death of Sr. Faustina, on November 4, 1939, Sr. Amelia died. The cause was pulmonary tuberculosis.

Faustina's cell was on the second floor of the convent. Its window overlooked the courtyard and chapel. Nowadays, you have only to look up to the right while walking in the direction of the Shrine chapel in order to see it. You can't miss it. The place where the saint was dying is marked with a plaque. The room is located within the convent enclosure, so pilgrims cannot visit it.

Faustina's cell was very small. One entered it from the main corridor by way of an anteroom that contained a fold-out bed for the sister whose duty it was to watch over the sick. During her last night, from October 4 to 5, Faustina was watched over by Sr. J. (we do not know her name), who, at that point, had only seen Faustina for the second time.

Sister Stella Kozłowska recalls, "Sister Faustina pleaded earnestly not to have anyone keep vigil near her, so when she saw a sister coming into the room to be with her, she said in a whisper, 'My God, I hope the sisters will not be burdened with me much longer, as they have got so much work to do.'"

The dying Faustina asked the sister watching over her to go to sleep and promised to ring when she needed any help. That night, the bell rang several times. Faustina asked for water in a weak voice. However, she did not drink a single drop, She would just rinse out her mouth. Thirst was burning her inner organs. "I could drink a whole little bucketful," she had told Mother Superior earlier. However, her esophagus and her intestines, consumed as they were by tuberculosis, did not allow her to swallow a single drop of water. She also asked to be turned over onto her other side. The sister taking care of her recounted later that she "did not feel any flesh when she touched her, only bones," and that the sick sister groaned when she touched them.

The morning of Wednesday, October 5, promised to be a fine one in Kraków. Sister Amelia had morning duty at Faustina's bedside. Faustina asked her to sing some pious hymn, and when she excused herself because of her bad singing voice, Faustina herself quietly sang, "Neither the eye has seen, nor the ear heard, nor has it entered the thought of man, what awaits a virgin in heaven."

At 4 p.m., Fr. Andrasz came. He granted Sr. Faustina the last rites. Faustina was conscious. She was suffering immensely. A few hours before her death, she asked for an anesthetic injection, but a moment later, she decided against it, after all. She offered up this pain to God as well.

Her final agony began in the evening. "Today Jesus is going to take me with Him," she announced.

"The bell rang during dinner. Everyone knew that Sr. Faustina was dying. We left everything and whoever was there went to see her," remembers Sr. Euphemia Traczyńska, a young and newly-professed sister at the time. "The chaplain [Fr. Theodore Czaputa] and several sisters were already in the infirmary," while others prayed in the corridor. They were reciting the prayers for the dying. "At some point, Sr. Faustina beckoned Mother Superior to come near and told her she was not going to die just yet, and that when she was about to die, she would let them know. So the sisters left; they went straight to the chapel. ... Nothing was announced after prayer, so all the sisters went back to their duties."

Sister Liguria Poznańska was the one keeping vigil over Faustina that evening. When her agony started, Sr. Liguria ran to wake up Sr. Amelia and also woke up Sr. Euphemia by mistake, who wanted to be present at Faustina's death, having heard Sr. Amelia say that Faustina would be a saint. And only those two sisters — Euphemia and Amelia — were present at the moment of Sr. Faustina's death. Sister Liguria had run to wake up someone else, but not Mother Superior Krzyżanowska, who, during Sr. Faustina's beatification process, testified that she did not learn of Faustina's death until morning.

Sister Euphemia Traczyńska recounts, "It was somewhere around eleven at night. When we arrived, Sr. Faustina appeared to open her eyes slightly and give a little smile. Then she bowed her head and already ... Sr. Amelia was saying that perhaps she is no longer alive, she died. ... We kept on praying. The Gromnica [a candle blessed on Candlemas Day and lighted at the bedside of a dying person] was burning the entire time."

Sister Maria Faustina Kowalska died on October 5, 1938, at 10:45 p.m. The following day, October 6, the nuns moved her body to the crypt. The casket was open up to the time of the funeral.

Father Joseph Andrasz remembers, "In the casket, Faustina regained her freshness and loveliness; she was far more beautiful than during her life."

Mother Irene Krzyżanowska recalls, "None of the sisters feared the deceased, as usually happens in such cases. Sister Faustina's face radiated peace."

A lot of people came to the crypt: sisters, wards, girls, and farm workers. The funeral was held two days later on the feast of Our Lady of the Rosary, October 7. Jesuit Fathers Theodore Czaputa, Ladislaus Wojtoń, and Thaddeus Chabrowski all came to the "Josephinum." The Requiem Mass began following Morning Prayer at 8:30 am. The priests did not wear black vestments, but white. Father Wojtoń celebrated Mass at the high altar in front of the image of Our Lady of Mercy, and Fr. Chabrowski at the altar of the Sacred Heart of Jesus, where today there hangs the image of the Merciful Jesus, beneath which the relics of St. Faustina are to be found.

After the Mass, the funeral procession led by Fr. Czaputa made its way toward the convent cemetery, located at the back of the garden. The nuns carried the casket with Faustina's body on their shoulders. They laid her in the sisters' common tomb.

None of Helen-Faustina Kowalska's family members attended the funeral. Faustina did not want her relatives to be notified of the funeral, due to the high cost of travel. But Natalia Grzelak, her sister who lived in Łódź, knew that Helen-Faustina had died even before news of her death arrived from Łagiewniki.

It was night when Natalia saw her sister in her room. "She was as white as a communion wafer, so thin, with folded hands. And she said to me, 'I have come to say goodbye to you, because I'm leaving. Remain with God. Do not cry, you mustn't cry!' She kissed me on the cheek, and I couldn't say a word. I just pressed my face into the pillow. When she left, I started to cry. ... Then, the door opened again, and my sister stood there, so white, and said: 'I have asked you not to cry, and you are crying. There's no need to cry, and I beg you: do not cry!'"

In the morning, Natalia travelled with her husband to Głogowiec. "I'm arriving at the village, and there is weeping there. The news had already arrived that Faustina died."

In the "Register of the Deceased" of the convent in Łagiewniki, there is recorded: "Sister Faustina, of blessed memory, arrived at a complete union with God in her relationship with Him — through loving and seeking the will of God in every event and in every order given by her superiors."

She was 33 years old. She lived for 13 of those years in the Congregation.

PART TWO

St. Faustina's Mission —
Proclaiming Divine Mercy
to the World

1938-2002

"THANK YOU, MY DEAR SR. FAUSTINA." "Dearest St. Faustina, thank you so much for everything." "Dearly beloved St. Sr. Faustina — Protectress of all sinners and those in need of your aid, pray for us." The date is August 15, 2011, and the guest book at the Łagiewniki convent is full of these and similar entries.

On this day, when all the basilicas of Kraków are exhibiting their most valuable treasures to the public, the Sisters of the Congregation of Our Lady of Mercy have put the *Diary of St. Maria Faustina Kowalska* on display. It is the first time that the original hand-written spiritual writings of one of the greatest mystics in the history of the world are being shown publicly. People flock to see St. Faustina's original writings, and the line shows no sign of getting shorter for the seven hours that the manuscript is on view.

The sisters from Łagiewniki have placed the six notebooks of various thicknesses — some with squared and others with lined pages — in a glass display case. The first notebook is opened to the page where Faustina describes her vision of Jesus on February 22, 1931, in Płock. The sixth lays open to the last page. As visitors near the display, their conversations die down. Heads bow in silence, in contemplation, sometimes with emotion and almost always with amazement. The neat, even handwriting in no way betrays that the author barely finished three grades in elementary school. Only in the last notebook, which was written a few months before Faustina's death, does the handwriting change. Written with a trembling hand, the letters are larger. Yet there are still no erasures or corrections — as is true of all 477 pages.

"The manuscript is in very good condition. It's not damaged in any way. It is only missing one page, which was ripped out by an unknown person, as was noted in the published edition," explains Sr. Elizabeth Siepak, who is chief editor and press secretary for the sisters.

The majority of those who are coming to see the original *Diary* know its contents well. For them, the display provides an opportunity to express their love and gratitude to St. Faustina. In other display cases, the sisters have placed dozens of the most interesting examples of foreign-language translations of the *Diary*, written both in the most widely spoken, as well as the more exotic, languages. No one, not even Sr. Elizabeth Siepak — who seems to know everything about the devotion to the Divine Mercy — can tell into how many languages the *Diary* has already been translated. One thing is certain: It is the most frequently translated Polish book.

A few years before her death, Sr. Faustina wrote: "I feel certain that my mission will not come to an end upon my death, but will begin" (*Diary*, 281). She was calm. She knew that despite immense obstacles, the devotion to the Divine Mercy would endure and grow. "There will come a time," she noted, "when this work, which God is demanding so very much, will be as though utterly undone. And then God will act with great power, which will give evidence of its authenticity" (*Diary*, 378).

Almost a year after Sr. Faustina passed away, World War II broke out — something she had predicted to several people. It was during the war, when it seemed that evil had prevailed, that people began to seek help from the Divine Mercy. The forms of devotion that were based on Sr. Faustina's revelations started to spread quickly and spontaneously. The center of the Divine Mercy devotion was then Vilnius. From there, it began to spread to other countries as refugees migrated to escape the violence of a world at war. Increasing numbers of people gathered to pray in front of the image of the Merciful Jesus, which from April 1937 onwards was displayed in St. Michael's Church in Vilnius. Tangible signs of their devotion began to accumulate around the image, as many of the devotees would leave behind ex-votos[47] or votive offerings in thanksgiving for graces they had received from the Merciful Jesus. Meanwhile, the devotion was being promoted tirelessly by Fr. Michael Sopoćko, who preached on God's mercy in the churches of Vilnius and distributed booklets with prayers to the Divine Mercy.

Since Vilnius was first occupied by the Soviets and then by the Germans during World War II, the message of God's mercy was able to spread quickly with the help of those being deported by the Soviets in cattle trains heading eastward, as well as by soldiers traveling through Vilnius who fought on the different fronts of World War II. By means of these refugees and soldiers, prayercards with the Divine Mercy Chaplet reached as far as Siberia and Kazakhstan. From there, they were taken by the soldiers of General Ladislaus Anders to the Middle East and later to Italy. In France, this mission was taken up by the Pallottine Fathers.

Further, the message of Divine Mercy was being spread overseas during World War II by the Marian Fathers of the Immaculate Conception. Its principal promoter early on was the Marian Fr. Joseph Jarzębowski, who considered it a grace of Divine Mercy that he successfully escaped the Nazis by journeying from Warsaw through Vilnius (where he met Fr. Sopoćko), and then through Siberia and Japan to reach his fellow Marians in the United States in 1941. Inspired by Fr. Jarzębowski, Marian Fr. Walter Pelczynski quickly got to work spreading the message in the United States of America. By 1944, he had formed the first Divine Mercy Apostolate in Stockbridge, Massachusetts, which exists to this day. The Marian Fathers — mainly through the efforts of Fr. Julian Chrósciechowski — were also promoters of the Divine Mercy devotion in Great Britain.

During these early years of spreading the Divine Mercy devotion, Fr. Michael Sopoćko was the first one to speak publicly about the important role that Sr. Faustina had played in bringing these new forms of devotion into the life of the Church. He announced that she was the one to whom Jesus gave the order to paint the image being venerated by the faithful in Vilnius. News of this spread quickly among Divine Mercy devotees and in the convents of the Congregation of the Sisters of Our Lady of Mercy. The majority of the sisters were surprised, since they had not been aware of the intimacy between Sr. Faustina and Jesus. Her revelations were known only to a few superiors — primarily Mother General Michael Moraczewska and Mother Irene Krzyżanowska. Mother Borgia Tichy and Mother Rose Kłobukowska were privy to them as well. Certain sisters had sensed something extraordinary about Faustina's spiritual life. Now, they could better understand her words and behavior. During her visits to some of the Congregation's houses in 1940 and 1941, Mother Moraczewska confirmed the information the sisters were learning about Faustina from other sources.

Sister Beata Piekut remembers, "Mother General called all the sisters together and officially informed us that supposedly — I emphasize, supposedly — all of this took place. In conclusion she said, 'Be informed, Sisters, but don't go telling anybody about it.'"

The news of Sr. Faustina's revelations caused more and more people, mostly from Kraków and the surrounding areas, to come to Łagiewniki, where the tomb of the mystic lay in the convent cemetery. The sisters also prayed near the tomb of Faustina, asking for God's mercy for their convent and its inhabitants.

Mother Irene Krzyżanowska remembered, "Three times, there was imminent danger of being expelled from the convent by the Nazis. At this threat, all the sisters went to the tomb of Sr. Faustina to ask her intercession to the Divine Mercy so that we would be left in peace."

The first small image of the Merciful Jesus, based on the image displayed in Vilnius, appeared in the Łagiewniki chapel while Sr. Faustina was still alive. Mother Irene Krzyżanowska placed it on the side altar where an image of St. Joseph was enshrined. It was late 1937 or early 1938. The image was one of the ones being printed by Cebulski's publishing house in October 1937. On February 6, 1941, the convent chronicler of the house in Łagiewniki noted that Fr. Joseph Andrasz, the chaplain of the house, blessed two images of the Merciful Jesus, which were hung in the wards' classrooms. Fr. Andrasz also took this opportunity to speak about Sr. Faustina's revelations. Unfortunately, the convent chronicler does not indicate who painted the two images, which were not of the best quality. It appears that the painter was an amateur, modeling them after the image of Jesus found on the holy cards printed up in 1937 and based on the description found in the *Diary* of Sr. Faustina. It is unlikely, due to the turmoil of World War II, that the painter visited Vilnius to see Kazimirowski's image. Although quite poor in artistic merit, these two images were kept in the convent.

The image painted by Adolf Hyła, which was hung up in the convent chapel in March 1943, came about somewhat differently. From the beginning of the war, the chapel was open to the public. The sisters opened it both because of the extraordinary circumstances brought about by the Nazi occupation and due to the great interest of those devoted to the Divine Mercy in the place where Sr. Faustina had lived and died.

Adolf Hyła, a 42-year-old art teacher, also would come to the chapel in Łagiewniki. He taught at the Augustus Witkowski VIII National High School of Mathematics and Natural Sciences in Kraków. He had spent five years as a Jesuit novice and had started to study for a degree in philosophy and law, which he did not complete. He had also spent a short time studying drawing and painting in the studio of the renowned Kraków artist Hyacinth Malczewski and had received national certification as an art teacher at the secondary school level.

After the Nazis occupied Kraków, Hyła lost his job and his apartment in the city center. Along with his wife and her family, he moved to Łagiewniki, where they lived in a cramped apartment at 36 Urocza Street, not far from the convent of the Sisters of Our Lady of Mercy. At this point in time, he started devoting more time to painting, which he had treated as a mere hobby before the war. He painted primarily religious images, landscapes, and portraits. In November 1942, he offered to paint an image for the convent chapel as an ex-voto in thanksgiving for graces received and for the survival of himself and his family: On November 9, 1939, the Gestapo had arrested seven teachers from the school where he was teaching.

Mother Irene Krzyżanowska, the Superior of the Kraków house at the time, and Fr. Joseph Andrasz asked Hyła to paint an image of the Merciful Jesus. They provided him with the excerpt from the *Diary* that describes the apparition of Jesus to Sr. Faustina in 1931 in Płock and a print of a copy of Kazimirowski's image. The copy had been done by the painter Lucy Bałzukiewicz, who lived in Vilnius until 1946 and was a student of the well-known painter Olga Boznańska.

Father Andrew Witko accurately describes the origin of the image of the Merciful Jesus painted by the brush of Adolf Hyła. The image was ready by late 1942, but the sisters Mother Krzyżanowska and Sr. Callista Piekarczyk rejected the work, having decided that the image was "not suitable for public veneration."

However, soon after this, Sr. Felicia Żakowiecka, Sr. Clementine Buczek, Fr. Joseph Andrasz, and the chaplain Fr. Theodore Czaputa also gave their feedback, and the painter made alterations to the work. The image was then blessed by Fr. Andrasz on March 7, 1943. The next day, the image of the Merciful Jesus was hung on the side wall toward the rear of the chapel to the right of the entrance in place of a confessional, which was moved nearer to the side entrance.

Seven months later, on October 6, another image of the Merciful Jesus was brought to Kraków, painted by an artist from Lviv, Stanislaus Kaczor-Batowski. The work had been commissioned by Mother General Michael Moraczewska. The Warsaw convent on Żytnia Street already had a painting by Batowski, and the sisters liked it so much that they ordered another one — as a gift for the chapel in Łagiewniki. The sisters in Kraków had to choose, then, which painting to hang in the chapel: Hyła's or Batowski's. The problem was solved by the Archbishop of Kraków, Cardinal Adam Sapieha, who, after examining both, said, "If Mr. Hyła's image is an ex-voto, let it be the one in the chapel."

It turned out, however, that due to its size and shape, Hyła's work would not fit on the side altar where the sisters usually placed an image of Jesus when celebrations devoted to the Divine Mercy were taking place. Therefore, Hyła had to paint another image. The sisters asked him, since he was already at it, to change the following in his depiction of Jesus: "the Semitic look, the black hair, the transparent robe, and the sternness of the gaze." Hyła accepted the suggestions. The face of Jesus in his second painting looks different. Hyła's first painting eventually made it to the sisters' Wrocław convent, where it has remained ever since. Fields and meadows make up the background of the Wrocław image.

In his second painting, Hyła painted the landscape of Łagiewniki with a meadow in bloom as the backdrop. On April 16, 1944, the first Sunday after Easter (also known as Low Sunday), this painting was blessed by Fr. Andrasz and displayed in the chapel of the Łagiewniki convent for public veneration. It was enshrined in the side altar on the left side of the sanctuary. Initially, the painting was placed above that altar only on the first Sunday after Easter, and on the third Sunday of each month, when devotions to the Divine Mercy were celebrated in front of it. Otherwise, the painting hung on the rear wall.

The young Karol Wojtyła saw this image and possibly even prayed before it, as he would stop by the Łagiewniki chapel to pray there during World War II. At the time, he was working in the nearby Solvay chemical factory.

"Even now I recall the street that goes from Borek Fałęcki to Debniki that I took every day going to work … with the wooden clogs on my feet. They're the shoes that we used to wear then," he reminisced dozens of years later, in 2002, on a visit to the International Shrine of Divine Mercy as Pope John Paul II. He continued, with great emotion, "How was it possible to imagine that one day the man with the wooden shoes would consecrate the Basilica of Divine Mercy at Łagiewniki of Kraków?" Truly, this could only have been orchestrated by God Himself.

While Karol Wojtyła worked at Solvay and used to stop by the Łagiewniki chapel to pray, he was also a student at the clandestine theological seminary in occupied Kraków. He knew little about Sr. Faustina at this time. However, because of how his life turned out, he encountered the devotion to the Divine Mercy right at the outset of his path to the priesthood. Later, he became the greatest proponent of this very devotion.

Already during the war and even more so after it ended, it was Łagiewniki that became the center of the Divine Mercy devotion. This came about because of the territorial changes that meant Vilnius, the original center, became a part of the USSR. But an even more important factor was that Sr. Faustina's tomb was in Łagiewniki and the image that had been painted according to her revelations hung in the convent chapel. Every third Sunday of the month, the homily during the Mass was dedicated to the topic of Divine Mercy, and a service to the Divine Mercy was celebrated on the first Sunday after Easter. In 1951, the Metropolitan of Kraków, Cardinal Adam Sapieha, even attached to that Sunday a plenary indulgence.

The Divine Mercy devotion spread spontaneously among believers. In Poland and abroad, images with the inscription "Jesus, I trust in You" appeared in churches, and people began reciting the Divine Mercy Chaplet, the Divine Mercy Novena, and the Litany of the Divine Mercy. Fragments of Sr. Faustina's *Diary* were copied by hand and distributed.

As it turned out later, this spontaneity caused the message and devotion to the Divine Mercy, as conveyed by Sr. Faustina, to be interpreted as each devotee thought fit. Consequently, it was distorted at times. This was true for all the different forms of devotion as well. Unfortunately, in the early postwar years, there was a shortage of theological works that could explain the essence of the devotion transmitted by Sr. Faustina. Both of the spiritual directors of Sr. Faustina promoted the Divine Mercy devotion in their writings. Father Joseph Andrasz published a short book entitled *Miłosierdzie Boże ... ufamy Tobie!* (*Divine Mercy, We Trust in You!*), which has been translated into 12 languages. Father Michael Sopoćko also published a few booklets and a weighty treatise in Latin on Divine Mercy. The two priests differed, however, in their approach to the topic. While Fr. Andrasz popularized the devotion to the Divine Mercy as described by Sr. Faustina, Fr. Sopoćko believed that it would be better for the growth of the devotion if the focus was not on Sr. Faustina's revelations, but on Divine Mercy as extolled in the Bible.

The devotion was growing at the grassroots level, but it was still not authorized by the Church. In September 1946, the Polish Episcopal Conference, headed by the Primate August Hlond, who was well disposed toward the devotion, began proceedings to recognize it officially. The Episcopate approached the Vatican Congregation for Divine Worship and the Discipline of the Sacraments with a request to establish a Feast of Divine Mercy on the first Sunday after Easter. It waited half a century for a positive reply.

In April 1948, two years after the Episcopate's motion, members of the Theological Society — whose conference Fr. Sopoćko also attended — decided to submit a similar request to the Holy See. Primate Hlond warned the theologians that, based on information he obtained from the Vatican, it appeared that the Congregation "is not accustomed to establish feasts to celebrate individual attributes of God, as only a Divine Person can be the subject of worship." Consequently, the theologians did not send the request.

Unfazed by all of this, Fr. Sopoćko, along with the Superior of the Congregation of the Sisters of Our Lady of Mercy, Mother Rose Kłobukowska, appealed to the Metropolitan of Kraków, Cardinal Sapieha, to prepare the beatification process for Sr. Faustina and to appoint a postulator. The Cardinal, however, took no such action. The one who did was the Superior General of the Pallottine Fathers. At the request of Mother Kłobukowska, he appointed a postulator and vice-postulator for the process. The sisters began to collect information about Faustina, recording the reminiscences of the sisters and of her family and friends. It was at that point, in 1948, that Sr. Bernardine Wilczek visited Helen Kowalska's family in Głogowiec for the first time in order to record the memories of those close to her.

While the Episcopate continued to wait for a response from the Vatican, the devotion to the Divine Mercy continued to grow spontaneously. It was under these circumstances in 1951 that the principal committee of the Episcopate asked Archbishop Romuald Jałbrzykowski — the Vilnius metropolitan who had been forced to leave Vilnius and move to Białystok after the War — his opinion of the new forms of devotion to the Divine Mercy as transmitted by Sr. Faustina.

Skeptical as always with regard to Faustina's revelations, Archbishop Jałbrzykowski responded, "The mercy of God I worship, and I always beg it of God, but my opinion on the devotion to the Divine Mercy, proposed on the grounds of the revelations and visions of Sr. Faustina, is very negative," he wrote in the introduction to his opinion. He invoked the Code of Canon Law then in effect that dictated great caution in matters concerning the approval of new prayers, religious practices, or images, as well as the decree of the Congregation of the Holy Office (whose name was changed to the Congregation for the Doctrine of the Faith [CDF] in 1965) that prohibited the introduction of new forms of worship or devotion. Further, he described "the method of promoting this devotion as not compliant with the spirit of Holy Church." Archbishop Jałbrzykowski forbade this form of devotion in his archdiocese. Many authors believe that his opinion and decision were, to a certain extent, influenced by his personal antipathy toward Fr. Sopoćko.

Two years later, the Episcopate began to examine the question of whether or not images of the Merciful Jesus should be displayed in churches. This was in September 1953, before the arrest of Cardinal Wyszyński by the Communist authorities. Earlier, on May 14, 1953, the Holy Office announced that a feast of the Divine Mercy was not to be introduced.

The Holy Office's relator, Fr. D. Hudal (the Vatican official overseeing the investigation), declared that there were some objections regarding Sr. Faustina's revelations. Even though he admitted that he did not find anything contradictory to the Catholic faith in them, he stressed that, above all, there were certain reservations he had concerning the image of the Merciful Jesus. As he admitted several years later, these reservations about the image were probably rooted in the fact that devotion to the image risked being associated with an excessive, even disproportionate faith in the image's power, so that trust in the Divine Mercy was no longer central. He advised against displaying the image in churches and against supporting an increase in devotion to it.

Four months later, in September 1953, Francis Barda, the Bishop of Przemyśl and a member of the Episcopate Commission, expressed his negative opinion about the image of the Merciful Jesus during one of the meetings of the Episcopate. He criticized the work of Adolf Hyła in terms of its liturgical and artistic value. These opinions of Archbishop Jałbrzykowski, an expert from the Holy Office, and now another by Bishop Barda caused the Polish Episcopate to recommend that priests remove images of the Merciful Jesus from their churches.

One should mention that by this time, Adolf Hyła had already made multiple copies of the image in question. According to Fr. Peter Szweda, Hyła painted a total of 230 copies of the image of the Merciful Jesus before his death in 1965. He would only change the landscape in the background, tailoring it to match the local landscape of the church that had commissioned the work.

What were Bishop Barda's objections to Hyła's painting? The available literature does not make it clear, but it can be assumed that his reservations were similar to those of Fr. Michael Sopoćko. The objections likely concerned the non-liturgical nature of the painting. They had to do with the incongruence between the representation of Jesus in Hyła's painting and the description of the risen Lord as He is presented in the Gospel of St. John, which is read on the first Sunday after Easter. The Evangelist describes the moment when Jesus appears to the Apostles in the Upper Room eight days after His Resurrection. He entered the room despite the barred doors; greeted the disciples, showing them the wounds on His feet and hands; and bestowed on them the power to forgive and retain sins.

In a letter from August 1968, Fr. Sopoćko wrote to Fr. Julian Chróściechowski that Hyła's picture was non-liturgical for several reasons: first, the background shows a landscape typical of the Beskid Mountains, which contradicts the universality of the message. Second, Jesus' gaze should be as though He were looking down from the cross, as Sr. Faustina wrote, and not as Hyła painted Him, looking "straight into the eyes of the beholder." Father Sopoćko's third basic objection concerned the position of Jesus' hand — it should be raised to the height of the shoulder as if granting absolution and not up at the height of the forehead.

Jesus asked of Sr. Faustina that the Church establish the Feast of Divine Mercy on Low Sunday, but He did not mention that the image He wanted painted should depict Him as He is described by St. John. Jesus had said to Sr. Faustina, **"My gaze from this image is like My gaze from the cross"** (*Diary*, 326). This, too, can be reconciled with Jesus' gaze at the disciples when He entered the Upper Room, as it was customary at this time to feast while reclining on couches. And what about the hand?

Father Sopoćko said that Jesus' hand should be raised to shoulder height. As in the letter just cited, he would sometimes explain that the hand ought to look as though it were raised in a gesture of absolution. In his memoirs, however, he wrote that it should be a gesture of blessing, because that was how Sr. Faustina described her vision of Jesus. One can deduce from this that both gestures were similar — they were both very precisely defined by the liturgical rules of the Tridentine rite. The priest was first to put his hands together at chest height, and then he was to bless the faithful by making the sign of the cross. In this position, the hand does not rise much higher than the shoulder. It can be assumed that Fr. Sopoćko instructed Kazimirowski to paint his version of the image with the hand of Jesus in this precise position. Is that how Sr. Faustina saw it? Or maybe it was just as Adolf Hyła depicted it? Today, liturgical regulations do not outline these issues as minutely as they did before Vatican II, and priests raise their hands higher in the gesture of blessing.

Father Sopoćko feared that the lack of approval of Sr. Faustina's revelations by the Church might hinder the spreading of the devotion to the Divine Mercy. For this reason, he would differentiate between the revelations and the devotion. He kept on asserting the image's consistency with the account in the Gospel of St.

John, whereas Fr. Andrasz promoted the revelations of Sr. Faustina as described in the *Diary*.

Father Sopoćko also disagreed with the interpretation of the image presented by Fr. Joseph Andrasz in his brochure *Divine Mercy, We Trust in You!*, published in 1947. Father Andrasz wrote that Jesus is wearing a white robe in the image "like a doctor in a hospital; He is walking the earth, healing sick mankind." For this reason, Hyła kept painting Jesus "against the backdrop of the sea, the mountains, flowers, factories, etc., which is not in accord with the vision of Sr. Faustina." The opinion of Fr. Sopoćko opposing this interpretation is cited by Fr. Anthony Mruk, SJ, the postulator of the beatification and canonization cause of Sr. Faustina.

Under the influence of criticism and pressure, Adolf Hyła changed the background of the image of the Merciful Jesus in the Łagiewniki chapel. He covered up the meadow and flowers with dark paint and painted a floor beneath Jesus' feet. According to some sources, this took place in 1952, while others suggest 1954. The second date seems more likely. If he had done it earlier, the accusations from Bishop Barda and the artistic committee of the Archdiocese of Kraków regarding the non-liturgical nature of the painting — although unavoidable — might not have been as pointed.

In fact, while evaluating images that Fr. Sopoćko submitted for a competition in June 1954 in which the Archdiocese of Kraków participated, this same artistic committee would declare that one of them — painted by Thaddeus Okoń — bears a resemblance to the images by Hyła, "from which, in accordance with the aim of the committee, it should differ." The aim of the committee was to weaken the link between the revelations of Sr. Faustina and the image of Jesus in the Hyła painting.

In his negative assessment of Hyła's image, Fr. Sopoćko also said that it should be "rejected, due to [the] effeminate appearance [of Jesus that is] inadmissible in images ordered to the liturgy[48] and the lack of harmonization with the liturgy of the first Sunday after Easter, with which this image should be associated."

A different opinion about Hyła's image was given in later years by the professor Fr. Ignatius Różycki. He considered the image by Adolf Hyła as only "not in keeping with one particular detail of the Płock vision of the Merciful Jesus: namely, the second ray is distinctly white. It is extremely difficult, however, to depict a watery liquid or a pale luminous ray using paint, although for the good of the devotion, this should be striven for. Yet one should expect that the

Lord Jesus will put up with the fact that the execution of the painting will not correspond to our intentions or the painter's in this regard."

Although critical of the image by Hyła, Fr. Sopoćko was wholeheartedly for spreading the Divine Mercy devotion. This is why the recommendation to remove the Hyła images from churches made him uneasy. So he began trying to convince the bishops that the image of the Merciful Jesus did not need to be associated with the revelations of Sr. Faustina, which had still not been officially recognized by the Church. Instead, it could be interpreted independently from them. One could also, he argued, paint a new image depicting the meeting of Jesus with His disciples in the Upper Room, according to the Gospel of St. John. He succeeded in convincing Bishop Barda, who was not opposed to the devotion to the Divine Mercy itself, to organize the competition in June 1954 (cited above) for a new image.

Three artists participated in the competition: Thaddeus Okoń, Anthony Michalak, and Ludomir Sleńdziński. Hyła declined to participate, because of the compromise it would involve in trying to reconcile the Gospel scene of the appearance of the risen Jesus in the Upper Room with the revelations of Sr. Faustina. The committee recognized the work by Ludomir Sleńdziński as best in conveying the scene from the Gospel of St. John. Father Henry Ciereszko relates that the committee concluded that "because of the rays denoting Blood and Water, which symbolize the Church emerging from the side of Christ with sacraments that cleanse the soul (Baptism and Penance) and give life (the Eucharist and others), [Sleńdziński's work] can be considered as an excellent exposition on the liturgy of the first Sunday after Easter."

Adolf Hyła, however, wrote the following to Fr. Sopoćko in a letter dated July 31, 1954: "The result of this compromise is an image that does not represent the scene from the Gospel, but constricts the understanding of God's mercy. After all, according to the Gospel (John 20:19-24), the Lord Jesus, after entering the Cenacle through a barred door, greeted the disciples with the words, 'Peace be with you,' showed them the wounds of His hands and side, breathed the Holy Spirit on them, and spoke the words that instituted the Sacrament of Penance. Out of all this, the image shows only the floor and door of the Cenacle, but Christ Himself is doing something different: He is pointing to the rays of Blood and Water gushing from His side as well as giving a blessing. At the same time, the image limits the concept of Divine Mercy expressed in the vision of Sr. Faustina, because it limits it only to mercy manifesting itself in the Sacrament of Penance."

Nonetheless, the favorable assessment of Sleńdziński's painting expressed by the artistic committee of the Archdiocese of Kraków was shared by the major Commission of the Polish Episcopate. It authorized the displaying of images painted according to Sleńdziński in churches, albeit with one caveat: they could not be placed above the altars, that is, as part of the altar itself. In the years that followed, Fr. Sopoćko made every effort to have the image of Jesus in the version painted by Sleńdziński copied and hung in churches in Poland and abroad.

However, neither this image, nor the later image of Jesus painted at the request of the Marian Fathers in 1957 by Adam Styka, met with the popularity of the work of Adolf Hyła. This is all the more surprising when one considers that, in terms of artistic merit, both of the later paintings seem to convey the elusive element of spirituality in a more effective way. They are less literal. And yet, the image of Jesus as painted by Hyła most likely resonates better with popular piety. Perhaps the popularity of his vision is also proof of what Jesus said to Sr. Faustina: "**Not in the beauty of the color, nor of the brush lies the greatness of this image, but in My grace**" (*Diary*, 313). So, in spite of the recommendations of the Polish Episcopate, the faithful were not "turning away" from the Hyła image, which by this time had already become popular, but were hanging it in their homes and churches. They were venerating it and receiving graces by means of it. Thus were fulfilled the words of Jesus, spoken to Sr. Faustina when He was instructing her to have the image painted: "**I desire that this image be venerated, first in your chapel, and [then] throughout the world**" (*Diary*, 47).

Before the image of the Merciful Jesus painted by Adolf Hyła became known the world over, it had been venerated in the Łagiewniki chapel since 1943. However, the first image of the Merciful Jesus was hung in the chapel of the Sisters of Our Lady of Mercy in Płock as early as 1939. A little later, in 1940, a copy of the image by Kazimirowski, as painted by Lucy Bałzukiewicz, hung in the convent chapel of the Congregation in Vilnius after it had been given to the sisters by Fr. Sopoćko. It is the image by Hyła, however, found where the mortal remains of St. Faustina rest, that has become the most widely recognized.

Other forms of devotion to the Divine Mercy developed spontaneously alongside the veneration of the Merciful Jesus in the image. Those with a devotion to the Divine Mercy passed along transcribed excerpts from the *Diary* of Sr. Faustina, some of which were even printed up in Paris. Yet Fr. Michael Sopoćko knew — as is emphasized by Fr. Henry Ciereszko, the postulator for his beatification process — that without official recognition by the Church of the supernatural character of Sr. Faustina's revelations, one could not use these excerpts in order to popularize the Divine Mercy devotion. Indeed, doing this could even prove detrimental to the cause.

He wrote about this concern in a letter to Mother Irene Krzyżanowska some two weeks after Faustina's death: "The case of the devotion to the Divine Mercy is similar to the devotion of the Sacred Heart, from which it cannot, of course, be separated. If the latter form of devotion waited for over 200 years to be recognized, and was not recognized because St. Margaret had said so, but because the Church had considered it appropriate, in accord with revealed teaching and beneficial in its consequences, then the same could happen with the devotion to the Divine Mercy. All public revelation came to an end after the time of the Apostles. All later revelations have been private and oblige no one to believe them even after the Church, of her own initiative, declares their authenticity on the basis of Scripture and Tradition. Therefore, we should be careful in our efforts in this direction and not link the devotion with the sanctity of a given person, unless God were to expressly request this by some sort of a sign. Otherwise, it is possible to harm the cause, or at least to put it off, as happened with the devotion to the Sacred Heart of Jesus."

Consequently, Fr. Sopoćko does not refer to the revelations of Sr. Faustina in his published works. He also does not make references to her holy life, but points to the biblical, theological, and pastoral grounds for the Divine Mercy devotion. He insisted, as he also wrote in his letter to Mother Krzyżanowska, on "the timeliness, aptness, beneficial effect, if not indeed the necessity of this devotion." He once confessed to Mother Krzyżanowska that only once, during a conversation with Archbishop Jałbrzykowski, did he make reference to the revelations of Sr. Faustina: "I regret having done so even that one time, as I think this is what stopped him from supporting this cause." He believed that when "God wishes to show particular graces through the intercession of the late Sr. Faustina, for which the Congregation can and should pray, only then will it be possible to include even this factor which, however, will not be the decisive one." Father Sopoćko, who died in 1975, devoted the majority of some 200 of his publications, brochures, and books to the biblical foundation of being devoted to Divine Mercy.

Yet, regardless of what Fr. Sopoćko was saying and writing, another trend was developing as the devotion spread where the emphasis was placed on the revelations of Sr. Faustina and, what was worse, sometimes on incorrect inter-pretations of them. Years after, Bishop Paul Socha, who served as an auxiliary bishop in a couple of dioceses in Poland, wrote that these errors were caused by a tendency in popular devotion that "often seeks the extraordinary and tries to interpret certain promises of private revelations too mechanistically, or applies more importance to them than to the same contents of the public revelation in the Church." In this particular case, there was an erroneous "interpretation of the message and promises, especially those associated with celebrating the Feast of Divine Mercy." There was also a misinterpretation of the image — an understanding of it that was "effusively sentimental and effeminate." In certain Polish circles, there was even a tendency with the image to interpret it as bluntly "nationalistic; namely, that the red and white color of the rays emanating from the bosom of Jesus were to symbolize the national flag of Poland." Of course, in the *Diary*, Sr. Faustina described the color as not white but "pale," symbolizing the water that flowed along with the blood from the pierced Heart of Jesus on the cross.

The Vatican became involved in the issue of the spontaneous spreading of the devotion to the Divine Mercy. In January 1957, three months after Primate Stefan Wyszyński's release from internment by the Communists, the Holy Office asked Cardinal Wyszyński to collect the bishops' opinions on this matter. Seventeen bishops responded to the Primate's survey.

"The devotion in question is quite widespread among believers in Poland. However, it has not yet been officially approved by the bishops," the Primate wrote to the Vatican in May 1957. He also informed the Vatican that, in the last few weeks, he had been receiving numerous letters in which thousands of believers were calling for the establishment of the Feast of Divine Mercy. From the information he sent to the Vatican, it is evident that, at the time, the Divine Mercy devotion was most widespread in the Tarnów Diocese: individual devotion was recorded in 143 out of 320 churches, and public devotion was in 18. Images of the Merciful Jesus were hanging in 161 churches. In the Dioceses of Gdańsk, Łódź, Łomża, and Siedlce, the Divine Mercy devotion was weakly propagated; in the Poznań Diocese, not at all. The Primate also included the opinion of the then-deceased Archbishop Jałbrzykowski, which had been prepared in 1951. All the bishops agreed that while the devotion to the Divine Mercy as such was good, the form it took was problematic, especially given the questions that were being raised regarding Faustina's revelations. Therefore, the bishops took varied stands on the devotion's development: ranging from outright rejection (Białystok), to reservation and waiting for the opinion of the Holy See (for example, Płock), to benevolent tolerance and temporary permission to exhibit the image in churches (Tarnów).

Primate Stefan Wyszyński's assessment was sent to the Vatican in May 1957, the same month that he announced the beginning of the "Great Novena" to Our Lady, Queen of Poland, in Jasna Góra (that is, at Częstochowa). This was a nine-year-long pastoral program intended to prepare Poles to mark a millennium of Christianity in Poland. It was no secret that for this time of preparation, the Primate was not overly interested in spreading any other devotion than the Marian one that constituted the very core of the Novena. Along with the bishops' opinions, Primate Wyszyński sent a copy of Sr. Faustina's *Diary* to the Vatican. It was not the Polish original, but a copy that had been typed up a few years earlier and translated into Italian. Between 1950 and 1952, this copy was officially certified three times by the Chancery of Kraków as being in accord with the source. Unfortunately, the text still contained many errors. The *Diary* was poorly copied and had been badly translated.

Mother Moraczewska had charged Sr. Xavier Olszamowska with typing it out. Along with Fr. Andrasz, this sister had also numbered the pages. Father Andrew Witko writes, "Sister Xavier considered it appropriate to change certain terms, add or leave out certain words, and even inadvertently omitted more extensive passages. Certain phrases became almost close to heresy."

In his introduction to the first critical edition of the *Diary*, Fr. George Mrówczyński wrote, "The number of demonstrated errors amounts to a dozen or so single spaced, typewritten pages." The errors include the omission of whole sentences and pages of the text, as well as the alteration, replacement, or addition of many words. One very serious error was that the copied text gave no indication which words were Faustina's and which were those of Jesus. Sister Faustina would often make the transition from using her own words to quoting the words of Jesus all in the same sentence. The lack of differentiation led to misinterpretations. One example reads as follows: "On page 161 of her manuscript, we read: 'But God has promised a great grace especially to you and to all those [here Faustina proceeds to quote the Lord Jesus; later, she would underline the words of Jesus with a pencil, as instructed by Fr. Sopoćko, to identify words she was sure came from the Lord] who will proclaim My great mercy' (*Diary*, 378). This sentence, when lacking quotation marks around the words of Jesus, is unclear to say the least, but it also could be taken to say that God has promised a great grace to those who proclaim the great mercy of the author, which is, of course, heresy," explain the sisters from the Congregation of Our Lady of Mercy.

The main objection raised by the relators or experts of the Holy Office supervising the case in the 1950s was that, according to the revelations of Sr. Faustina, veneration of the image of the Merciful Jesus, celebrating the Feast of Divine Mercy, and reciting the Divine Mercy Chaplet could be interpreted as each possessing unlimited power that could operate by itself, as if veneration of the image itself or promotion of the devotion to Divine Mercy were sufficient in themselves to achieve eternal life.

"Deciphering the *Diary* is, despite appearances, not an easy task," says Sr. Elizabeth Siepak, who has frequently referenced the manuscript. "Although her handwriting is nice and even, Sr. Faustina nonetheless rarely used punctuation, made use of various abbreviations, and sometimes, writing in a hurry, would omit some letters — or would simply make mistakes. She underlined the words of Jesus with pencil with lines that are, at times, almost imperceptible, which is why one could inadvertently overlook them."

According to Sr. Siepak, the first copies of the *Diary* were meant only to transmit its basic content, not to serve as critical editions — hence, the "omissions" or "improvements" of Faustina's notations that had occurred.

Certainly, the sharp protest that Archbishop Anthony Baraniak, the metropolitan of Poznań, made public in March 1958 harmed the cause. The Archbishop, formerly the secretary of Cardinal Hlond, objected to attributing a prayer for the beatification of Sr. Faustina to the then-deceased primate. The prayer in question was published in 1949 in London in Fr. Sopoćko's book *Miłosierdzie Boże — jedyna nadzieja ludzkości* (*Divine Mercy — the Only Hope for Mankind*). Archbishop Baraniak did not respond to the book until nine years after it had been published. The Archbishop also protested against "all the insinuations and assertions" in the Italian translations of Fr. Sopoćko's books that supposedly indicate Cardinal Hlond had supported the new forms of devotion to the Divine Mercy proclaimed through Sr. Faustina.

Father Sopoćko found himself in a difficult situation. He explained that the prayer for the beatification of Sr. Faustina was given to him by Sr. Xavier Olszamowska, who testified under oath that she had received it from Primate Hlond. There was no reason not to believe her. Cardinal Hlond's sympathy for spreading the devotion of the Divine Mercy is documented. For example, in 1946, the Conference of Bishops of Poland turned to the Vatican to request the establishment of the Feast of Divine Mercy; in 1947, Cardinal Hlond himself financed the publication of Fr. Sopoćko's Latin treatise about instituting the proposed Feast of the Divine Mercy.

Finally, on November 19, 1958, the Holy Office passed a decree on the matter of the visions and revelations of Sr. Faustina. However, it was not released until nearly four months later — on March 6, 1959. The wording of the two statements differs significantly. The document from November 1958 contains five points: the Holy Office declared in it that "the supernatural character of Sr. Faustina's revelations is not to be insisted upon," that is, it implied *de facto* that they are not supernatural. The other points are a consequence of the first: a feast of Divine Mercy should not be introduced and spreading images and writings that propagate forms of devotion transmitted through Sr. Faustina is forbidden. However, the Holy Office left to the "prudence of bishops" the gradual removal of the images painted according to the sister's visions and placed above the altars of churches, as well as their eventual replacement with other images that "approach the concept of Divine Mercy in a proper manner." In the last and fifth section of the document, the Holy Office issued a very serious warning (*gravissimum monitum*) to Fr. Sopoćko, ordering him to "cease the defense and propagation of these revelations and this devotion." The decree was received by the Primate Stefan Wyszyński, who brought it to the attention of the ordinaries of the dioceses, the Mother General of Sr. Faustina's Congregation, and Fr. Sopoćko.

However, according to canon law, this type of document must be made public in order to be valid. Its contents were published in *L'Osservatore Romano* on March 6, 1959, in the form of a Notification. This published version was much milder than the decree from November 19, 1958. As Fr. Sopoćko concluded, "The Notification almost canceled out the decree." It can be summed up in the following two points: the Holy Office forbade the spreading of images and writings promoting the devotion to the Divine Mercy in the forms presented by Sr. Faustina, and it left "to the prudence of the bishops" the matter of removing images exposed for public devotion. That was all.

The upshot of all this was that the Holy Office withdrew its judgment on the authenticity of Sr. Faustina's revelations and no longer expressed a formal position regarding the Feast of Divine Mercy. As for the recommendation to remove images, it was given to the bishops in such a mild form that they could choose to remove them or leave them if they wished to.

What happened in the four months between the adoption of the decree and the publishing of the Notification? What led the Holy Office to relax its stance? The answers to these questions are probably hidden in the Vatican archives.

Father Sopoćko accepted the Vatican's position calmly. He noted in his journal, "This decree was no surprise to me, as the devotion to the Divine Mercy did not follow the proper course. The Sisters of Our Lady of Mercy, and along with them, the Marian Fathers and the Pallottines put more emphasis on the revelations of Sr. Faustina and her canonization than on the dogmatic, liturgical, and psychological justifications for the devotion. Above all, the image of the Most Merciful Savior itself became distorted. … In the wake of all that, the Notification of the Holy Office had to put a stop to this, and in doing so, [led to] serious and thorough examination and treatment of this devotion." Many years later, Bishop Socha (cited earlier) drew similar conclusions. "The ban from the Holy See dealt not so much with the devotion to the Divine Mercy, but with distortions based on spreading it in forms that lack any true theological content, and, sometimes, are laden with a superficial and simply erroneous interpretation of the revelations."

Nonetheless, the Notification caused much confusion. Images of the Merciful Jesus were removed from many churches, both in Poland and worldwide. Priests ceased to celebrate devotions to the Divine Mercy and to distribute holy cards with the image of the Merciful Jesus. The growth of the devotion was restrained, but not destroyed. Those devoted to the Divine Mercy continued to pray privately in their own homes, using the words of the Divine Mercy Chaplet and other prayers transmitted by Sr. Faustina.

Images of the Merciful Jesus did not disappear from all churches, however. A copy continued to hang in the chapel of the Pallottines in Częstochowa. In Łagiewniki, the painting by Adolf Hyła not only hung in the convent chapel, but it was enshrined in a side altar. How could this be? News about the Notification of the Holy Office reached the sisters on the Saturday before the third Sunday of the month, when the image was customarily transferred from a side wall to the side altar. On the following day, a service dedicated to the Divine Mercy was to be celebrated in front of it.

On Monday, Sr. Imelda Wróbel and Sr. Beata Piekut went to see Archbishop Eugene Baziak, then the apostolic administrator of the Archdiocese of Kraków, with the question: what to do with the image? The archbishop told them to leave it where it was, which was as part of the altar. When Sr. Imelda was surprised and pointed out that in this way another image — that of the Sacred Heart — would be covered up, Archbishop Baziak responded, "And does the Merciful Lord not have a heart?" The image remained above the altar, and it continues to hang there to this day.

Although this was a difficult time for those devoted to the Divine Mercy, Fr. Sopoćko was optimistic. "As for the future, I am completely at peace, because Sr. Faustina foretold it all," he wrote in one letter. He knew that this was just a "moment" or a "time," after which "God will act with great power, which will give evidence of its [the devotion's] authenticity" (*Diary*, 378).

When Sr. Faustina saw her own canonization in an interior vision in March 1937, she also saw how many obstacles lay ahead on the path: "Then some clergy whom I did not know began to examine me and to humiliate me, or rather, what I had written; but I saw how Jesus Himself was defending me and giving them to understand what they did not know" (*Diary*, 1045).

As for Fr. Sopoćko, he must have had in mind what Faustina told him before she died: he was to be prepared "for the greatest difficulties and abandonments; disappointments, ingratitude, and persecution" — for a series of failures, bitterness, sadness, and abandonment by all. "When I turn to God in prayer, I will find no consolation there either, only emptiness in the soul and silence. And so [it will be] until death," he recorded.

Following publication of the Notification, those theologians who were convinced of the supernatural character of Sr. Faustina's revelations were faced with two tasks. Father Anthony Mruk, who was among their number, describes these tasks as follows: First, they had to present a theological justification for devotion to the Divine Mercy without any reference to Faustina's revelations. Second, they needed to provide a theological interpretation of the new forms of devotion transmitted by her. The Pallottine Fathers and the professor Fr. Ignatius Różycki played an important role in this work.

The Pallottines established in Częstochowa the Studium Miłosierdzia Bożego (Center for the Study of Divine Mercy), which took up the task of preparing an academic analysis of Divine Mercy. The Center organized theological symposia: the first one took place in 1966 in Częstochowa; the next one, two years later, in Ołtarzewo near Warsaw; and another in the 1970s. At the same time that such academic efforts were underway to provide theological justification for the new forms of the Divine Mercy devotion, Sr. Faustina's cause for beatification was also gaining momentum.

One person who never doubted the supernatural character of Sr. Faustina's revelations — or her sanctity — was Karol Wojtyła, that Solvay factory worker who would walk in his wooden clogs during World War II to the sisters' chapel in Łagiewniki. Some years later, in 1958, he became an auxiliary bishop of Kraków, and then in January 1964, the Metropolitan Archbishop of Kraków. Archbishop Wojtyła gave a good deal of thought to what could be done to revoke the Notification issued by the Holy Office.

Whether he decided on this approach himself or whether someone advised him, he came to the conclusion that it would be best not to seek the retraction of the Notification directly, but first to demonstrate the sanctity of Sr. Faustina. Approval for Sr. Faustina's beatification would result in recognizing the supernatural character of her revelations, and, consequently, would underscore the authenticity of the forms of devotion she had received through those revelations. Years later, it turned out that this foresight proved to be accurate.[49]

In fact, on September 14, 1965, Archbishop Wojtyła and his friend Fr. Andrew Maria Deskur[50] met with Cardinal Alfredo Ottaviani, then secretary of the Holy Office, in the vestibule of St. Peter's. The meeting came towards the end of the procession after Mass for opening the fourth session of the Second Vatican Council. Father Deskur, who had introduced Wojtyła to the revelations of Sr. Faustina when they were both seminarians during World War II, insisted that the Archbishop take advantage of the occasion by asking Cardinal Ottaviani whether it would be possible to begin the process for Sr. Faustina's beatification while the Notification regarding her revelations was still in force.

Surprised, the Cardinal responded, "What, you haven't begun it yet? Start as soon as possible, while witnesses are still living." This was hardly seven years after the Notification had been published.

Archbishop Wojtyła immediately instructed his Auxiliary Bishop Julian Groblicki by phone to begin the preparations for the diocesan process. So when Archbishop Wojtyła returned from Rome, and Sr. Beata Piekut showed up at his office, she heard that the secretary of the Holy Office "not only did not forbid, but in fact ordered" the initiation of the process for the beatification. Sister Piekut — who had been entrusted by the Congregation with Sr. Faustina's cause in place of Sr. Olszamowska — also recalled other words of Archbishop Wojtyła regarding the process: "If you had begun it right away, Faustina would have been raised to the honors of the altar by now. Everyone would have known where the image and the new forms of the Divine Mercy devotion came from. But you started from the wrong end."

This is not exactly what had actually taken place. Father Sopoćko and Mother General Rose Kłobukowska did approach the Metropolitan of Kraków, Cardinal Sapieha, in 1948 about initiating preparations for the beatification process, but without success.

Archbishop Wojtyła advised Sr. Piekut to act quickly: she should search for witnesses, collect evidence, and organize the beatification tribunal. Even earlier, when Fr. Sopoćko inquired about the initiation of Sr. Faustina's process on August 21, 1965, the Archbishop replied, "This cause is my priority; perhaps it will yet begin this year." Indeed, the informative process, conducted by Bishop Julian Groblicki, Archbishop Karol Wojtyła's delegate, began on October 21, 1965. It lasted only two years.

The postulator on the diocesan level was Fr. Isidore Borkiewicz, a Franciscan. The beatification tribunal, chaired by Fr. Joseph Szczotkowski, held 75 sessions, officially questioned 45 witnesses, collected the writings of the Servant of God, confirmed the absence of public devotion to her — which is an indispensable condition for the beatification process — but also confirmed the existence of the necessary private devotion to her. This was the initial stage, during which information on the life and virtues of the candidate for sainthood was being collected. Archbishop Wojtyła knew that great care had to be taken in dealing with the matter of the revelations of Sr. Faustina and the devotion to the Divine Mercy. "We are presently treading lightly," he was supposed to have told the sisters in Łagiewniki, asking them to discontinue celebrating Mass at the altar of the Divine Mercy. The idea was "not to create even the semblance of spreading the devotion in the forms transmitted by Sr. Faustina, because this could be detrimental to the cause," wrote Bishop Paul Socha.

The process in the Archdiocese of Kraków ended on September 20, 1967. On that day, Karol Wojtyła, who had been raised to the dignity of a Cardinal in June of that year, went to the chapel in Łagiewniki to pray before the tomb of Sr. Faustina. While the process was still underway, on November 25, 1966, the remains of the Servant of God had been exhumed and transferred from the convent cemetery to the chapel.

On January 31, 1968, the Congregation for the Causes of Saints in Rome, which had received the documents regarding Sr. Faustina, initiated the next stage of the beatification procedure. This stage lasted significantly longer. Father Anthony Mruk was appointed postulator in the process, and Fr. Isidore Borkiewicz was appointed the vice postulator. "From the very beginning, the Congregation proceeded cautiously," recalled Fr. Mruk, "often seeking the opinion both of the Congregation for the Doctrine of the Faith and of the Polish bishops."

One of the Consultors of the CDF concluded in 1969 that the process, if it was to be conducted at all, should be separated from the matter of Sr. Faustina's visions and revelations. The Conference of the Episcopate of Poland issued its *nihil obstat* ("nothing stands in the way") to the continuation of the process on April 30, 1970.

The most important task before the CDF was the examination of Faustina Kowalska's *Diary*. Since one of the reasons for issuing the Notification was the erroneous transcription and poor translation of the *Diary* into Italian, Fr. Anthony Mruk demanded "a critical edition of this document." A second copy of the original *Diary* had already been prepared in 1967. It had been put together by Sr. Beata Piekut and Fr. Isidore Borkiewicz and had been translated into French. Father Mruk also made a request that the Congregation for the Causes of Saints include at least one Pole as a theologian-censor of Sr. Faustina's writings, due to "the specificity of Polish spirituality, sometimes incomprehensible to Western theologians." This task was given to the professor and priest Ignatius Różycki; the second censor was an Italian.

Father Różycki shrank from being involved in Sr. Faustina's beatification process for a long time. Years later, he confessed, "For more than a quarter of a century, I harbored a deep mistrust both in relation to the heroic sanctity of Faustina, and above all the revelations with which — as she herself assured — she was favored." He considered himself warranted to think this by what he learned from "those in the know" regarding Faustina's case. He believed her to be "a victim of hallucinations on the grounds of hysteria, so that not only were the alleged revelations devoid of any religious value, but at the same time, the heroism of her life was a lost cause."

For this reason, as he wrote, he categorically and decisively refused to participate in the process of beatification of Sr. Faustina begun in 1965. One day, however, out of curiosity, "just that — to kill time," he began to flip through the pages of the *Diary*. He read all of it. And then something changed. He decided that the case was "well worth the effort of a thorough scientific investigation."

As a result, he completely changed his mind. He became convinced that the "sanctity of Faustina is truly heroic, and her revelations bear all the hallmarks of being of supernatural origin."

We know that Fr. Różycki was already involved in the process in 1967, as he appears in an anecdote related by Sr. Beata Piekut about Cardinal Karol Wojtyła. It goes like this: Fr. Różycki asked Sr. Piekut to let him see the manuscript of the *Diary*. But "Cardinal Wojtyła did not permit us to give even a trancript of the *Diary* to anyone. So I went to ask him what I should do," recalls Sr. Piekut, calling to mind a conversation she had with the Cardinal on November 20, 1967. "He told me this: 'Let the Reverend Professor take the trouble to go to Łagiewniki and there acquaint himself by examining everything on site. You, Sister, are not going to keep transporting the original *Diary* around with you.' With a smile, he added: 'You, Sister, are travelling with the *Diary* to Fr. Różycki; and the tram derails. You, Sister, die; no harm done; you will go to heaven. The *Diary* is beyond recovery. That's the worst.'"

The manuscript of the *Diary*, which was — and still is — diligently guarded by the Congregation, was not sent to the Vatican's Congregation for the Causes of Saints either. Instead of the original, the sisters sent exact photographs of all the pages to Rome. "A photograph was made of each page, and since at that time such delicate photographic paper did not exist as is presently available, the shipment was of a significance size," Sr. Piekut recalled. "So we were sending the *Diary* in parts by mail, just as we had done with other extensive documents, but only until a lady miraculously found one of the parcels in a waste paper basket used by town hall."

In Poland under the Communist regime, international mail was subject to inspection by the secret police. Certainly, this was the case with anything sent by Church institutions. After the discarded package was found, any documents necessary for the beatification process were taken to Rome by priests who happened to be traveling there. Most often, Cardinal Wojtyła himself carried them.

Carrying out a thorough theological analysis of the *Diary* took Fr. Różycki a long time. He didn't finish working on it until 1979. The resulting work, however, was enormous and very extensive — about 500 pages long. As Fr. Anthony Mruk put it, "This work earned him special recognition in the Congregation." By comparison, the analysis of the other expert evaluating the writings from a different perspective than the theological one, completed in 1970, was less than 60 pages long. Both censors expressed favorable opinions about the nature of

Sr. Faustina's revelations. They confirmed their authenticity and supernatural character.

To this day, the analysis carried out by Fr. Różycki constitutes the theological foundation of the forms of devotion to the Divine Mercy transmitted by Sr. Faustina. Professor Różycki thoroughly analyzed 82 revelations of Jesus recorded by Faustina. He defined the essence of the new forms of devotion to the Divine Mercy and demonstrated their compliance with the centuries-old tradition of Catholic teaching about the mercy of God. He refuted the argument — often raised by theologians critical of Sr. Faustina's revelations — that they promote the worship of God in only one of His attributes: mercy.

One of the most prominent theologians of this group was the professor Fr. Vincent Granat, who at that time was rector of the Catholic University of Lublin. Father Granat wrote of his opinion, "It is not advisable, and the Catholic Church does not desire or follow the practice of revering only a single attribute of God," which would be the case if a feast of Divine Mercy were established. "The mercy of God is one of the Divine attributes, and if we were to honor it by means of a separate feast, then it would also be proper to institute other feasts in order to render worship to individual Divine attributes. Such a stance would result in the blurring of the unity of God and would lead to the danger of polytheism," claimed Fr. Granat.

Professor Fr. Różycki countered that worship of the Divine Mercy is not honoring one particular attribute of God, but the rendering of worship to the Triune God. The revealed teaching about the nature of God is that He is "utterly simple, uncomplicated, there are in Him no parts whatever: in other words, everything that is in God, that is, in His substance, is God. And so God is not only wise but He is Wisdom; He is not only omnipotent but He is Omnipotence; in relation to the world, He not only reveals His providence, but He is Providence; not only does He love us, but He is Love; He is not only merciful but He is Mercy. Therefore, Wisdom, Providence, Omnipotence, Love, and Mercy, which are the same as God, have the right to our religious worship," he explained.

He also explained how to understand the fact that in the *Diary* of Sr. Faustina, mercy is called an attribute of God — and even the greatest attribute of God. This cannot be understood, he wrote, in a strictly philosophical and theological sense, but must be understood in the biblical sense, just as it is depicted in the Old and New Testaments. In the first sense, mercy is identical with the nature of God. "In this sense, all the attributes of God are God, one and the same. Therefore, they are all without exception absolutely equal to each other: Divine Mercy is as infinitely perfect as His Wisdom or Power, because it is similarly God Himself, and thus the same God as Divine Wisdom and Divine Power." In biblical terms, he explained, mercy — though sometimes called an attribute — implies the "active manifestation of God's love towards man."

In the Old Testament, the expression of this love was God's calling and guiding of the Chosen People. In the New Testament, it was the sending of the Son of God and the work of Redemption. According to Fr. Różycki, the true meaning of the statement that "mercy is the greatest attribute of God" in the biblical understanding is as follows: "The results of the activity of Mercy-Love make the greatest impact on the world and, in this respect, Mercy surpasses all the other attributes of God." Sister Faustina summed up this biblical relationship between love and mercy in these simple words: "God's Love is the flower — Mercy the fruit" (*Diary*, 949).

The word "mercy" in the revelations of Sr. Faustina is synonymous with love, compassion, goodness — and it also denotes Jesus Himself. This kind of mercy is like all attributes that God has. It is the unfathomable, incomprehensible, inexpressible, inexhaustible, and never-ending Mercy of the Triune God, of God the Father, but most frequently of Jesus Christ. The Mercy of the Triune God is the object of the devotion, and Jesus as the incarnate Mercy of God occupies the main place in it because — as Fr. Różycki reasoned — the devotion can be directed toward the Divine Mercy, as well as to the Merciful Jesus. Even the chaplet, which is addressed to the Mercy of God the Father as the Giver of all the graces associated with this prayer, represents Jesus, because He is "the Way, the Truth, and the Life," according to the Gospel.

The valuable input from Fr. Różycki also included the definition of the essence of our devotion to the Divine Mercy: trust and mercy toward one's neighbor. "Trust to the degree that without trust the devotion that Jesus desired does not exist; and without trust, it is impossible to obtain the promises attached to this devotion by any other concrete acts. Trust is the fundamental and intrinsic act of the devotion to such a degree that it alone, without the other specific acts of the devotion, already guarantees the attaining of all the general promises that the Lord Jesus attached to this devotion." Jesus spoke as many as 34 times about trust to Sr. Faustina and nine times about trust as a condition for obtaining the benefits flowing from the devotion. "**The graces of My mercy are drawn by means of one vessel only, and that is — trust**" (*Diary*, 1578).

The result, Fr. Różycki kept emphasizing, is that no external act of the devotion brings about the results promised by Jesus if it does not express trust and is not performed with trust. "For Jesus, to worship the Divine Mercy is the same as to turn to Him in an act of trust." Trust alone, without performing any specific forms of devotion, "shall ensure that all the ordinary effects of the devotion are achieved." However, a person who wishes to obtain some of the extraordinary effects that Jesus linked with certain acts of the devotion must not only trust, but also carry out those acts. "For example, the one who desires to obtain the complete forgiveness of all sins and punishments must receive Holy Communion on the Feast of Divine Mercy, that is, on the first Sunday after Easter."

What is this trust of which Jesus speaks? It is not a feeling, but an attitude. Father Różycki mentions that it includes faith, hope, humility, and repentance. In addition to trust, the essence of the devotion is mercy extended to others. Jesus said to Sr. Faustina, **If a soul does not exercise mercy somehow or other, it will not obtain My mercy on the day of judgment** (*Diary*, 1317). Mercy can be extended by way of deed, word, or prayer. Jesus demanded that devotees of the Divine Mercy perform at least one act of mercy each day. Thus, devotion to the Divine Mercy teaches the true Christian attitude.

On the basis of the *Diary*, Fr. Ignatius Różycki identified five forms of devotion to the Divine Mercy. They are the Feast of Divine Mercy, the image with the signature "Jesus, I trust in You," the Divine Mercy Chaplet, the Hour of Mercy, and spreading the worship of Jesus, who is the Divine Mercy. The criteria for distinguishing these forms of devotion are the promises that Jesus attached to them that hold good for everyone and not only to Sr. Faustina herself, as in the case of the prayer "O Blood and Water ..." or the Novena to the Divine Mercy.

After the censors of the Holy See's Congregation for the Causes of Saints successfully examined the writings of Sr. Faustina and reached a positive conclusion, its prefect, Cardinal Pietro Palazzini, signed a decree authorizing the continuation of the beatification proceedings. This took place on June 19, 1981. Work then began on preparing the so-called *Summarium* (summary) of the informative process, which was then completed in 1984, as well as the investigation into the heroic nature of the virtues displayed by Sr. Faustina. After all, she was to be raised to the honors of the altar not because she was a mystic, or because she transmitted the message of the Divine Mercy to the world, but because she lived the Christian virtues in a perfect way.

This part of the process, however, progressed slowly. In 1984, a new relator was assigned to the cause — that is, the person who would prepare the treatise on the heroic virtues of Sr. Faustina. Father Michael Machejek succeeded Fr. Ambrose Eszer in this capacity.

While all of this was taking place, the Notification was still holding back the spread of the devotion to Divine Mercy. More than once, when visiting the Roman Curia, Cardinal Karol Wojtyła would inquire about the possibility of the Notification's reassessment. In November 1977, he officially asked the CDF whether it was possible to revise the Notification issued in 1959. This was after one favorable opinion had already been issued by a censor involved in the beatification process of Sr. Faustina and Professor Różycki was nearing the end of his work.

In response, the Congregation once again examined the matter of the spread of the devotion, and on April 15, 1978, it issued a decree (published June 30) revoking its decision from 20 years ago. The ban regarding spreading the devotion to the Divine Mercy in the forms transmitted by Sr. Faustina was rescinded by the same decree. The Congregation justified its decision on the basis of the following reasons: the receipt of some original documents that had been unavailable in 1959, a general change in circumstances, and a favorable opinion expressed by the Polish bishops.

Divine Mercy devotees the world over must have felt joy and relief. Even though the forms of devotion transmitted by Sr. Faustina continued to be used both in Poland and throughout the world, the Vatican's prohibition constituted a major obstacle to the devotion's growth. Moreover, the lack of a clear official interpretation of the revelations of Sr. Faustina could lead to a distortion of the forms and essence of the devotion. This situation lasted for almost 20 years. "A time," Sr. Faustina had foretold (*Diary*, 378). Unfortunately, Fr. Sopoćko did not live to see the repeal of the Notification. He died on February 15, 1975. However, even though he was dying, he could be at peace about the growth of the devotion to the Divine Mercy. He had a worthy successor — Cardinal Karol Wojtyła, who further guided the cause.

The revoking of the Notification took place during the pontificate of Pope Paul VI, six months before the second conclave of 1978, at which Cardinal Wojtyła was elected Pope upon the unexpected death of John Paul I. This, too, must have been orchestrated by God Himself. Had the CDF announced this decision after October 16, 1978, Pope John Paul II would immediately have been accused of playing favorites in matters that were presented by the Church in Poland. Questions as to whether all the procedures were properly followed would inevitably have come up.

The election of Pope John Paul II was an important moment in the history of the progress of the Divine Mercy devotion. One could assume that this was the moment Sr. Faustina was describing when she predicted, "God will act with great power, which will give evidence of its [this work of Divine Mercy] authenticity" (*Diary*, 378).

Already in 1981, three years into his pontificate, John Paul II acknowledged that from the moment of his election, he believed that proclaiming the message of Divine Mercy was his specific mission. He brought Sr. Faustina's beatification process — which he himself had initiated in Kraków — to a close. Later on, he canonized Faustina, established the Feast of Divine Mercy in the Church, and, finally, entrusted the entire world to Divine Mercy.

A year earlier, on November 30, 1980, the Pope promulgated the encyclical *Dives in Misericordia*, which is about God being "rich in mercy." It was John Paul II's second encyclical and the first ever devoted to Divine Mercy in the history of the Church. Interestingly, the Pope wrote it without making any references to Sr. Faustina's revelations in the text. Later, it turned out that he was not familiar with the entire text of the *Diary* while he was writing the encyclical. It was read to him only after the assassination attempt on May 13, 1981. This shows that his conviction about the importance of the role of Divine Mercy had been growing in him independently of Sr. Faustina's revelations.

In the encyclical, the Pope provided a theological explanation of what mercy is. He presented it as active love that "makes itself particularly noticed in contact with suffering, injustice, and poverty, in contact with the whole historical 'human condition,' which in various ways manifests man's limitations and frailty, both physical and moral" (*Dives in Misericordia*, 3). Mercy, he wrote, is like another name for love, yet it is "the specific manner in which love is revealed and effected vis-á-vis the reality of the evil that is, in the world, affecting and besieging man, insinuating itself even into his heart and capable of causing him to 'perish in Gehenna'" (*Dives in Misericordia*, 7).

Such love does not imply indulgence toward evil, harm, offense, or insult that demand amendment. It does not cancel out justice, but exceeds it. The Pope wrote, "Mercy is manifested in its true and proper aspect when it restores to value, promotes, and *draws good from all the forms of evil* existing in the world and in man" (*Dives in Misericordia*, 6, emphasis in original). Such love — and this is its significant characteristic — does not wound the dignity of man. On the contrary, it allows a person to see himself as he is while keeping his dignity. At this point, the person finds himself only one step from conversion, from turning back from the path of evil.

Pope John Paul II emphasizes that Christ, revealing God's mercy toward man, also demands that people make showing mercy towards the other a guide for their lives. In the Sermon on the Mount, Jesus says, "Blessed are the merciful, for they shall receive mercy" (Mt 5:7). The Pope stressed, "Man attains to the merciful love of God, His mercy, to the extent that he himself is interiorly transformed in the spirit of that love toward his neighbor" (*Dives in Misericordia*, 14).

A year later, in 1981, the first official edition of the *Diary of Sr. Faustina Kowalska* appeared in print. This edition was prepared on the basis of the second copy of the original *Diary*, which was prepared in 1967 for the beatification process. Footnotes and indices had also been added. The *Diary* was prepared for publication by Fr. George Mrówczyński, an official involved in Sr. Faustina's information-gathering process, and by Sr. Beata Piekut, whom Faustina had told decades earlier that she would be very useful to the Congregation.

A note made by Sr. Beata attests that four copies of this transcript were sent to Rome and given to Jesuit Fr. Anthony Mruk, the general postulator of Sr. Faustina's cause. It was only in June of 1979, at the time of Pope John Paul II's first visit to his native land, that Sr. Beata approached Marian Fr. Seraphim Michalenko, the vice postulator of Sr. Faustina's cause for North America, with the request that the Marian Fathers publish the *Diary* in 1981 — in time for the 50th Anniversary of Sr. Faustina's mission, the beginning of which was the revelation of the Merciful Jesus in Płock. For several reasons, particularly because of restrictions placed on religious publications by the Communist government, the *Diary* could not be printed in Poland.

In order to publish the *Diary*, Sr. Beata supplied Fr. Seraphim with the transcript of the *Diary* text on film. The *Diary* was then prepared for publication by the Marian Fathers at their Marian Helpers Center in Stockbridge, Massachusetts, near the Shrine of The Divine Mercy, which was later granted a national designation as a shrine by the U.S. Bishops. The actual printing of the *Diary* then took place in Rome. Pope John Paul II received the first copy.[51] This first edition of the *Diary* bears the publisher's locations and date — Kraków, Stockbridge, Rome, 1981 — on the title page. It is the basis for making all translations into other languages.

Does the published *Diary* correspond to the original? Is anything removed or suppressed from it? These questions are still posed today by those who have heard about the first inaccurate copies of Sr. Faustina's texts. Then others still speculate that Sr. Faustina described an image of the Sacred Heart of Jesus with a Polish flag, but this fragment was expurgated. "Those are absurd insinuations," Sr. Elizabeth Siepak said tersely about the alleged description of the flag. "There is not, and there never has been, such a text in the *Diary*."

The official declaration of Fr. Ignatius Różycki, the Polish censor of Sr. Faustina's writings, reads as follows: "I declare that the text of the '*Diary*' of Sr. Faustina Kowalska, found on pages 31-691 of this typescript that I have compared with the manuscript of Sr. Faustina, is in complete concordance with the original. Kraków-April 16, 1979."

Faustina's beatification process was finally completed in 1992 — 27 years after her cause started. For almost a quarter of a century, her case had been ongoing in Rome. On March 7, 1992, Pope John Paul II signed the decree on the heroic virtues of Sr. Faustina Kowalska; and on December 21 of that year, he signed a decree concerning a miracle brought about through her intercession. A miracle is a sign for the church, a "heavenly seal" that confirms the sanctity of the candidate for sainthood. One could suppose that the prefect of the Congregation for the Causes of Saints — Cardinal Pietro Palazzini — received such a sign well before the end of the process. Sister Piekut claims it was through the intercession of Sr. Faustina Kowalska that his mother was restored to health. But proper procedure had to be followed.

To the beatification documents, the Congregation attached 100 narratives of a variety of cases of healings and graces obtained through the intercession of Sr. Faustina up to 1966. These included only a sampling of graces received out of the hundreds about which the sisters were notified up to the start of the process at the diocesan level. None of these, however, were selected to be investigated more closely by the Congregation. Instead, they investigated the miracle of the healing of Maureen Digan from the United States.

For many years, Mrs. Digan had suffered from lymphedema, also known as lymphatic obstruction. She underwent more than 50 surgical procedures before the age of 25. One of her legs had been amputated to the hip, and the other one was to be removed as well. Maureen had lost her faith, but the faith of her husband, Bob, remained strong. For many years, he had sought the intercession of many candidates for sainthood for his wife's healing, but his prayers seemed to have gone unanswered. In spite of all this, Bob continued to believe strongly in the possibility of a miracle.

Then, after watching an amateurish film about Sr. Faustina and the message of the Divine Mercy, Bob became convinced that his wife would be healed through the intercession of Sr. Faustina. So he brought her and their 8-year-old son to Poland, Their son Bobby was afflicted with a neurological disorder involving progressive myoclonic seizures that was known as "Baltic myoclonic." The family arrived in Poland on March 23, 1981, which was Bobby's birthday.

It was near Sr. Faustina's tomb in the chapel in Łagiewniki that Maureen Digan first underwent a spiritual transformation on March 28, 1981. Then, on that same day, she sensed that she had been physically healed immediately after concluding a novena to the Servant of God, Sr. Faustina. The incessant pain in her leg, which was one of the symptoms of the illness and about which she complained, immediately ceased. In fact, her illness disappeared suddenly, completely, and, from a medical point of view, inexplicably. It would later become evident that the healing was also permanent.

Bobby, the Digans' son, also received a healing, and he lived for the next 10 years without any externally observable evidence of seizures. Even though several encephalographic tests during that time revealed strong spikes in his brain's activity, indicating seizures, Bobby did not even exhibit any twitches, which is a common symptom of the onset of seizures. Further, Bobby's death in 1991 was not related in any way to the illness from which he was healed.

On the return journey home from Kraków, the Digans were already able to take Bobby off his seizure medication, something doctors warn people not to do without medical advice and supervision.

In 1989, Bobby underwent what was expected to be a routine operation to correct scoliosis. Unfortunately, the operation did not go well. Due to surgical complications, Bobby became paralyzed and his alimentary canal was destroyed by acid so that, for over a year, he was unable to receive food or drink on his own.

In May 1991, Bobby, who was confined to his bed, called his mother into his room. "Mommy," he said, "I have something to tell you. God is going to send His Son, Jesus, to take me to heaven soon. Don't be sad, and don't cry." He then asked her to bring his daddy in. Bobby died on May 23, 1991, at the age of 18. To this day, neither Maureen nor Bob Digan can talk about Bobby without it bringing them to tears. They still miss him terribly.

On April 18, 1993, on the Octave of Easter, which is the Feast of Divine Mercy, Sr. Faustina Kowalska was declared blessed. This event took place in St.

Peter's Square in Rome, and the Digans were there. Pope John Paul II marked the occasion by recalling Faustina's words: "I feel certain that my mission will not come to an end upon my death, but will begin" (*Diary*, 281). He then continued: "And it truly did! Her mission continues and is yielding astonishing fruit. It is truly marvelous how her devotion to the merciful Jesus is spreading in our contemporary world and gaining so many human hearts! This is doubtlessly *a sign of the times — a sign of our 20th century*. The balance of this century which is now ending, in addition to the advances which have often surpassed those of preceding eras, presents a deep restlessness and fear of the future. Where, if not in Divine Mercy, can the world find refuge and the light of hope? Believers understand that perfectly."[52]

The beatification of Sr. Faustina meant that she could now be venerated publicly. Locally in the Church in Poland, the liturgical memorial of Blessed Faustina Kowalska could now be observed on October 5, the day of her passage to life in God. The beatification was a special day for those devoted to the Divine Mercy, though they were aware that only her canonization would permit her liturgical memorial to be celebrated in the Church worldwide. Just before the beatification, the Bishops of Poland petitioned the Pope for the establishment of the Feast of Divine Mercy on the first Sunday after Easter for the Church in Poland.

The feast had already been celebrated since 1985 in the Archdiocese of Kraków, thanks to the efforts of Cardinal Francis Macharski, who was greatly devoted to the Divine Mercy. In 1995, the Vatican's Congregation for Divine Worship and the Discipline of the Sacraments gave its consent for the celebration of this feast in all the dioceses in Poland. Thus, the request that the Polish Episcopate had made in 1946 was finally granted. Now, it was only a matter of time before the Feast of Divine Mercy would be observed in the whole Church.

Before this took place, Pope John Paul II visited the chapel in Łagiewniki in 1997, during his sixth pilgrimage to Poland. In front of the image of the Merciful Jesus where he had prayed during World War II and before the little casket with the remains of then-Blessed Faustina Kowalska reposing beneath it, he said that the message of Divine Mercy had always been dear to his heart. "It is as if history had inscribed [this message] in the tragic experience of the Second World War. In those difficult years, it was a particular support and an inexhaustible source of hope, not only for the people of Kraków, but for the entire nation. This was also my personal experience, which I took with me to the See of Peter and which, in a sense, forms the image of this pontificate."

The mercy of God was needed by the people during the war. It was the source of hope after the war, and it continues as such to this day. As John Paul II pointed out in Łagiewniki, "There is nothing that man needs more than Divine Mercy — that love which is kind, which is compassionate, which raises man above his weakness to the infinite heights of the holiness of God." That is why, he continued, "the Church rereads the message of mercy in order to bring with greater effectiveness to this generation at the end of the millennium and to future generations *the light of hope.*"

Three years later, during the Great Jubilee Year of the Incarnation, Pope John Paul II repeated this message in St. Peter's Square when he declared Sr. Faustina a saint. It was on April 30, 2000 — on the first Sunday after Easter.

According to canon law, no new process to establish the recognition of heroic virtue had been necessary for the canonization — all that was needed was the recognition of a miracle through the intercession of then-Blessed Faustina. The Congregation recognized as medically inexplicable the healing of a priest, Fr. Ronald Pytel of Baltimore, Maryland, in the United States. He had been diagnosed with a serious heart dysfunction, had an artificial valve inserted, and was given the prognosis of, at most, a few years to live — and this was provided that he avoided any physical exertion. The healing occurred suddenly in 1995, and it remained permanent.

In his homily, the Pope said that by the act of the canonization of Sr. Faustina Kowalska, he wished to convey the message of Divine Mercy to the new millennium. "I pass it on to all people, so that they will learn to know ever better the true face of God and the true face of their brethren. ... It is this love which must inspire humanity today, if it is to face the crisis of the meaning of life, the challenges of the most diverse needs and, especially, the duty to defend the dignity of every human person."[53]

Thanks to a two-way live video feed, both those in St. Peter's Square and those in Łagiewniki could participate in the canonization ceremony. In the presence of more than 250,000 people gathered in the two locations, in addition to the millions watching on television, John Paul II established in the universal Church the Feast of Divine Mercy for the first Sunday after Easter. At this point, the desire that Jesus had expressed to Sr. Faustina in February 1931 in Płock was fulfilled — 69 years later.

The role of John Paul II in propagating the message of the Divine Mercy and fostering the growth of its corresponding devotion cannot be overestimated. Without Fr. Michael Sopoćko, Sr. Faustina would not have been able to have the image of the Merciful Jesus painted. Without Fr. Andrasz, it would not have been possible to spread devotion to the Divine Mercy so widely throughout the world. And without the personal involvement of John Paul II, whose entire pontificate was permeated with teachings about Divine Mercy, it would not have been known to the faithful throughout the world.

Well aware of the condition of the world and mankind today, Pope John Paul II knew that what people needed most was to have recourse to Divine Mercy. He preached this message in hundreds of his homilies, speeches, and letters. He kept on exhorting humankind to accept mercy, to bring it to other people — to the whole world. He considered this as one of the main tasks of the Church in today's world "in which there is so much evil, both physical and moral," full of threats to human freedom, conscience, and religion. All of this, he emphasized, causes great anxiety both in individuals and society about the future of humankind and the world, and about the meaning of human existence. The answer to this — he declared — is Divine Mercy because "in the mercy of God the world will find peace and mankind will find happiness."

Therefore, John Paul II decided to entrust the whole world to Divine Mercy. This took place in August 2002 when the Pope came to Łagiewniki once again, although he was already very ill. Many advised him against making this trip, but he personally wished to consecrate the new basilica as the world center of the Divine Mercy devotion. "I am convinced that this is the special place chosen by God to sow the grace of His mercy," he said on August 17, 2002.[54] John Paul II continued, "I do so with the burning desire that the message of God's merciful love, proclaimed here through St. Faustina, may be made known to all the peoples of the earth and fill their hearts with hope. May this message radiate from this place ... throughout the world. May the binding promise of the Lord Jesus be fulfilled: from here there must go forth 'the spark which will prepare the world for His final coming.'"[55]

On May 8, 1938, Sr. Faustina had a vision that she describes as follows in the *Diary*: "Today, I saw two enormous pillars implanted in the ground; I had implanted one of them, and a certain person, S.M., the other. We had done so with unheard-of effort, much fatigue and difficulty. And when I had implanted the pillar, I myself wondered where such extraordinary strength had come from. And I recognized that I had not done this by my own strength, but with the power which came from above. These two pillars were close to each other, in the area of the image. And I saw the image, raised up very high and hanging from these two pillars. In an instant, there stood a large temple, supported both from within and from without, upon these two pillars. I saw a hand finishing the temple, but I did not see the person. There was a great multitude of people, inside and outside the temple, and the torrents issuing from the Compassionate Heart of Jesus were flowing down upon everyone" (*Diary*, 1689).

Was the image from which the temple rose in this vision the image of the Merciful Jesus? Was this great temple the Basilica in Łagiewniki? Did the "hand finishing the temple" belong to John Paul II? Let us leave these questions unanswered, even though we are aware that the greatest fruit of John Paul's II's pontificate shall remain the discovery of the Divine Mercy by millions of believers. The reintegration of the Divine Mercy devotion into the mainstream expression of faith and the life of believers, the growth of the devotion, and the deepening of the teaching about it all became possible thanks to the Polish Pope.[56]

Could the pontificate of John Paul II, marked by the proclamation of Divine Mercy, have come to an end on anything other than the vigil of the Feast of Divine Mercy, April 2, 2005? Not by Divine intervention, but by human decree, the beatification of the Pope then took place on May 1, 2011 — on the Feast of Divine Mercy. Thus, John Paul II once again directed people's gaze beyond himself, toward God, who is Mercy.[57]

The Shrine in Łagiewniki — where the image of the Merciful Jesus and the tomb of St. Faustina are found — is visited each year by about two million people from nearly 90 countries. The mission of St. Faustina has not come to an end. It goes on.

ENDNOTES

Part One

[1] Interestingly, the First Sunday of Lent is celebrated by Eastern Rite Catholics as the Feast of Orthodoxy, commemorating the defeat of iconoclasm and the restoration of sacred images to the Churches of the East.

[2] Polish last names with the –ski suffix are inflected, i.e. for a woman they end with –ska (e.g., Helen Kowalska) and for a man they end with –ski (e.g., Joseph Kowalski).

[3] "At that time the Congregation was divided into two choirs, the so-called director sisters and the coadjutor sisters. The membership to one or the other was decided by the Congregation's governing body on the basis of the candidate's intellectual level, age, and abilities. The director sisters' task was to manage the Congregation and the penitents' homes. The coadjutor sisters did the manual work and served as helpers to the director sisters, especially in the area of physical labor (Const. Congr.)." *Diary*, endnote 61.

[4] Any icon or image to be used in a liturgical context must be approved by the Church for such uses.

[5] Indeed, acceptance of Faustina's visions was complicated by an earlier false visionary at Płock, a Polish nun named Felicia Kozłowska who, in 1893, claimed to have received revelations about Divine Mercy. After the revelations, she took on a mission of reforming the Polish clergy. As a result of her claimed revelations, the Mariavite community appeared in Poland at the end of 19th and beginning of the 20th century. The group initially remained within the Church, seeking recognition from Rome of both Kozłowska's purported revelations and canonical erection of the Mariavite movement. However, the claimed revelations were condemned as hallucinations, the foundress and Mariavite Minister General Fr. Jan Kowalski were excommunicated by Pope Pius X, and the Mariavites became a breakaway sect.

[6] Merriam-Webster defines marl as "a loose or crumbling earthy deposit (as of sand, silt, or clay) that contains a substantial amount of calcium carbonate."

[7] Prior to their entry into the novitiate, sisters in the Congregation of the Sisters of Our Lady of Mercy had to answer fourteen questions. The questions concerned personal information: the place and date of birth, Baptism, and Confirmation; whether she had any debts. There were also questions as to whether she had been previously engaged or married; whether she had been in another religious congregation; her motivations for entering the Congregation of the Sisters of Our Lady of Mercy; whether she entered voluntarily; whether she knew the rules of the Congregation; whether she had any possible doubts before professing vows, and whether she was willing to voluntarily and earnestly serve God in the Congregation.

[8] "A man's lightweight silk or woolen robe worn as a housecoat, especially on the Sabbath and holidays." Sol Steinmetz, *Dictionary of Jewish Usage: A Guide to the Use of Jewish Terms* (Rowman & Littlefield, 2005), pg. 30.

[9] "A high fur hat trimmed with plush, worn usually on weekdays. From Yiddish, borrowed from Polish, 'saucer.'" Ibid.

[10] "Shtrayml. A hat trimmed with fur pieces, usually sable, worn by Hasidim on the Sabbath and holidays. Anglicized as *shtreimel*. From Yiddish, derived from Polish *strój*, 'fancy dress.'" Ibid.

[11] In the "Positio" of the beatification cause of the Servant of God Sr. Faustina, presented by the canonical lawyer Rev. Luigi Giuliani, it is stated that Helen Kowalska was confirmed in February of 1922 in Aleksandrów. However, in the biography of Sr. Faustina, elaborated for the same "Positio" by Sr. Sangwina Kostecka of the Congregation of the Sisters of Our Lady of Mercy, November 6, 1921, appears as the date of the Confirmation of Helen Kowalska. In the documents kept in the Chancery of the Diocese of Łódź, Sr. Kostecka found the information that the Bishop of Łódź, Vincent Tymieniecki, conducted his first pastoral visit in Aleksandrów on October 29-30, 1921. Further, "on Saturday after the solemn ingress, the Bishop presided over the celebration of vespers. The next day, he conferred the Sacrament of

Confirmation, celebrated the solemn Holy Mass, preached a sermon …" That happened on November 6, 1921. The next mention in the chronicles of the Diocese of Łódź about conferring the Sacrament of Confirmation is found in July 1924. Father Seraphim Michalenko, MIC, the vice-postulator of the beatification process of Helen-Faustina Kowalska in the United States, gave October 30, 1921, as the date of Confirmation of the Servant of God, which was included in the book of his sister, Sr. Sophia Michalenko. This incoherence of dates most likely resulted from this: that Fr. Michalenko failed to detect the further information of the chronicler connecting the October visit of Bishop Tymieniecki with the conferring of Confirmation.

[12] One *złoty* (the Polish unit of currency) is equivalent to 100 *groszy*. Though currency reforms have taken place several times in Poland since St. Faustina's time, the name of the currency has remained the same to this day.

[13] Merriam-Webster defines cretonne as "a strong cotton or linen cloth used especially for curtains and upholstery." Once familiar in America, the term is rarely used today.

[14] Giedroyc (July 27, 1906 – September 14, 2000) was a Polish journalist, and political activist.

[15] Żeleński (February 23, 1905 – December 3, 1981) was a Polish actor of stage and screen, son of the famous playwright, poet, critic, and translator Tadeusz Kamil Marcjan Żeleński (better known as Tadeusz Boy-Żeleński, December 21, 1874 – July 4, 1941).

[16] Kotarbiński (March 31, 1886 – October 3, 1981) was a noted Polish philosopher and logician, creator of a philosophical theory called "reism."

[17] Wańkowicz (January 10, 1892 – September 10, 1974) was a Polish writer, journalist and publisher, noted for his reporting and other writings on World War II.

[18] Kieniewicz (September 20, 1907 – May 2, 1992) was an extremely influential Polish historian and university professor, especially known for his work on Poland in the 1800s.

[19] Andrzejewski (August 19, 1909 – April 19, 1983) was a prolific and internationally respected Polish author.

[20] Małcużyński (August 10, 1914 – July 17, 1977) was a noted Polish pianist, especially known for performing Chopin.

[21] Saint Faustina was happy to see her former employer and be able to speak to a sympathetic friend about the difficulties she was experiencing.

[22] The aspiration of a soul in love, rather than an achievable goal. None could love God better than could the Blessed Virgin Mary, for instance.

[23] Dobraczyński was a Polish writer and journalist known for his works on biblical themes, the history of the Church, and the strength of Catholic moral convictions and its effectiveness on people during the war. During World War II, he was a soldier in the Polish Army and later a member of the Polish Underground where he helped hide Jewish children in convents. In 1985, Dobraczyński was awarded the Cross of *Virtuti Militari* and, in 1993, the title of Righteous Among the Nations.

[24] Graduation towers are wooden structures through which salt water is run and allowed to evaporate in order to imitate the "salt air" from the seaside. Believed to offer important health benefits, they are popular forms of therapy in Poland, Austria, and Germany.

[25] Here the complex is described from the side opposite to where its present entrance is located.

[26] It seems that Sr. Borgia "offered" a sister, got home to Vilnius, and then asked for another to be sent to Vilnius (who was Sr. Faustina).

[27] With regard to the sins referred to in the promise, St. Thomas Aquinas refers us to Psalm 19:12-13. "By them your servant is warned; obeying them brings much reward. Who can detect trespasses? Cleanse me from my inadvertent sins."

[28] For, as St. John of the Cross teaches: "The reason for which it is necessary for the soul, in order to attain the Divine union with God, to pass through this dark night of mortification of the desires and denials of pleasures in all things, is because all the affection which it has for creatures are pure darkness in the eyes

of God, and, when the soul is clothed in these affections, it has no capacity for being enlightened and possessed by the pure and simple light of God, if it first cast them not from it; for light cannot agree with darkness; since as St. John says: 'the darkness has not overcome it [the light]'" (*The Ascent of Mt. Carmel*, Book I, Ch. 4:1).

[29] There is a custom, mostly observed in European countries, of marking the doors with the names of the three kings and the year on the feast of Epiphany. This is done with blessed chalk.

[30] In 1913, the eastern part of Poland was still occupied by Russia; therefore, the Russian currency was used.

[31] "Karaites, from the Hebrew word '*kara*' (to read), are members of a sect that adheres to the Torah without the addition of oral laws — distinguished from 'Rabbinic' or 'Talmudic' Judaism. For centuries, Karaites have lived alongside mainstream Jewish communities in various countries. Currently, some 30,000 Karaites live in Israel, with much smaller communities in the United States and Eastern Europe. In Crimea, around 800 Karaites remain, and their houses of worship are distinctive architectural monuments in several cities. Unlike other Karaite groups, the Crimean Karaites (or 'Karaylar,' as they call themselves), do not identify as Jews. Yet they consider the Torah their holy text and keep a religious calendar that includes Rosh Hashanah, Passover, and Shavuot. The oldest evidence of Karaite presence in Crimea dates back to 1278, and Karaite gravestones are scattered around Ukraine, in Crimea in particular." Talia Lavin, "In Crimea, a Karaite community carries on, and welcomes Russia," *Jewish Telegraphic Agency (JTA)*, March 26, 2014, jta.org/2014/03/26/news-opinion/world/in-crimea-a-karaite-carries-on-and-welcomes-russia.

[32] Literally, a stove built using tiles. The tiles serve to retain heat. Traditionally found in certain countries in Europe, including Poland.

[33] Tarnawska, Maria. *St. Maria Faustina Kowalska: Her Life and Mission* (Stockbridge, Massachusetts: Marian Press, 1990), p. 153.

[34] Ibid., pg. 315.

[35] Mickiewicz (December 24, 1798-November 26, 1855), was a principal poet in Polish Romanticism, regarded as the national poet, and one of the "Three Great Bards" of Poland. In his youth, he belonged to a secret college organization that tried to win independence for the country. After his arrest, he was imprisoned by the Tsarist regime in a prison cell in the Basilian Monastery in Vilnius and later sent into exile. He describes that cell in detail in his internationally known drama *Forefathers' Eve* through the eyes of Conrad, the main character, who is portrayed as having wrestled with God there. Later devotees of Mickiewicz's work named the cell "Conrad's prison cell."

[36] Literally, "the shooting out of a sheet anchor."

[37] "It will be a new splendor for the Church, although it has been dormant in it from long ago" (*Diary*, 378).

[38] In 1877 in Poland, two girls reported seeing visions of the Blessed Virgin Mary. She repeatedly asked that they pray the Rosary every day and call others to do so, as well. A spring emerged at the apparition site, which Mary blessed at the request of the visionaries. The apparition site has since become known as the Lourdes of Poland. On Sept. 11, 1977, during the 100th anniversary celebrations led by Cardinal Karol Wojtyła, the apparitions were solemnly approved.

[39] In the early 1800s, a dying Polish soldier, fighting for Napoleon in Germany, saw a vision of Our Lady. She reportedly told him to find an image of her and to display it where it could be venerated by the faithful. Upon his recovery and return to Poland, he found the image of Our Lady and placed it in the woods near his home, close to Licheń. Then, in 1850, a local shepherd had a vision of Our Lady while he was pasturing cattle near the image. A Shrine was built eight years later, and the image's fame grew. The Marians took over the Shrine in 1949. Construction of the new Shrine began in 1994 and was completed in 2004. It is the largest church in Poland and one of the largest in the world. The square in front of the Shrine holds 250,000.

[40] This quote comes directly from the Vatican website, June 26, 2000. vatican.va/roman_curia/

congregations/cfaith/documents/rc_con_cfaith_doc_20000626_message-fatima_en.html

[41] According to Fr. Seraphim Michalenko, MIC, the first public exposition of a television set took place at the New York World's Fair in 1939.

[42] Literally, "Hairs will sooner grow on the palm of my hand than that should happen!"

[43] Kościuszko was a skilled Polish military engineer and a general in the American Revolutionary War who made many significant contributions to the defeat of the British after travelling to the American colonies in 1776. There is a national memorial to him in Philadelphia, one of the bridges in New York City is named after him, and a statue of him stands in Lafayette Square directly opposite the White House (among other memorials). After his return to Poland, he led the failed Kościuszko Uprising against the Russian Imperial forces in 1794.

[44] All three painters of great repute; among their other talents, the men were contemporaries in the mid-to-late 1800s and frequent collaborators.

[45] Tarnawska, p. 325.

[46] She became a "sharer of the divine nature" (2 Pet 1:4).

Part Two

[47] Tokens offered in fulfillment of vows.

[48] See also Cardinal Joseph Ratzinger, *Spirit of the Liturgy* (San Francisco: Ignatius Press, 2000), p. 125, "Art is still ordered to the mystery that becomes present in the liturgy … the heavenly liturgy."

[49] Similar instances of the approval of a portion of the legacy of a mystic leading to the acceptance of the rest of their contributions exist in the history of the Church. As a matter of fact, bringing the Church's attention to the contributions of St. Juliana of Cornillon to the institution of one of the most important liturgical solemnities of the year, that of Corpus Domini or Corpus Christi, Pope Benedict XVI stated that in the decree of the institution of the feast, Pope Urban IV "even referred discreetly to Juliana's mystical experiences, corroborating their authenticity" (Address of Benedict XVI, General Audience, November 17, 2010). This telling observation would confirm Pope John Paul II's foresight regarding the recognition of her sanctity permitting the recognition of the authenticity of Sr. Faustina's mystical experiences.

[50] It was Monsignor Deskur, later a Cardinal, whom Wojtyła met through the clandestine seminary, who had introduced him to the devotion to the Divine Mercy as transmitted through St. Faustina, and told him about her tomb above the Solvay quarry where Wojtyła was working.

[51] Which his friend Fr. Andrew Maria Deskur read to him while he was convalescing after the assassination attempt of May 13, 1981.

[52] John Paul II, Homily, April 18, 1993, [Divine Mercy Sunday] (*L'Osservatore Romano*, April 21, 1993), reprinted on thedivinemercy.org/message/johnpaul/homilies/apr181993.php.

[53] John Paul II, Homily, April 30, 2000: [Divine Mercy Sunday], "Sr. Faustina: God's gift to our time" (*L'Osservatore Romano*, May 3, 2000), reprinted on thedivinemercy.org/message/johnpaul/homilies/apr302000.php, par. 5, 6.

[54] John Paul II, Homily During Mass for Dedication of the International Divine Mercy Shrine, August 17, 2002, reprinted on thedivinemercy.org/message/johnpaul/homilies/aug172002.php, par. 3.

[55] Ibid., par 5.

[56] Fulfilling Faustina's prophecy: "It will be a new splendor for the Church, although it has been dormant in it from long ago" (*Diary*, 378).

[57] Hardly three years later, on April 27, 2014, the Feast of Divine Mercy, then-Blessed John Paul II was declared a saint, thanks to an additional miracle attributed to his intercession.

BIBLIOGRAPHY

Publisher's Note: This Bibliography only includes materials available in English. It does not include the full list of works referenced.

Andrasz, Fr. Joseph. *Divine Mercy… We Trust in You!* Stockbridge: Marian Helpers. 1994.

Boniecki, Fr. Adam. *The Making of the Pope of the Millennium: Kalendarium of the Life of Karol Wojtyła.* Stockbridge: Marian Press, 2000.

Bujak, Adam and Sąsiadek, Jolanta. *The Gospel of Łagiewniki. Life and Work of Saint Sister Faustina.* Kraków: Biały Kruk, 2002.

Grzegorz, Górny and Rosikoń, Janusz. *Trust: In Saint Faustina's Footsteps.* San Francisco: Ignatius Press, 1987.

John of the Cross, St. "Spiritual Canticle" catholictreasury.info/books/spiritual_canticle/index.php.

John of the Cross, St. "Ascent of Mount Carmel" catholictreasury.info/books/ascent/index.php

John Paul II, St. *Dives in Misericordia.* Encyclical of November 30, 1980. vatican.va/holy_father/john_paul_ii/encyclicals/documents/hf_jp-ii_enc_30111980_dives-in-misericordia_en.html

_____. Mass in St. Peter's Square for the Canonization of Sr. Maria Faustina Kowalska. *Homily of the Holy Father John Paul II.* 30 April 2000. vatican.va/holy_father/john_paul_ii/homilies/2000/documents/hf_jp-ii_hom_20000430_faustina_en.html.

_____. Dedication of the Shrine of Divine Mercy. *Homily of the Holy Father John Paul II.* Kraków-Łagiewniki. 17 August 2002. vatican.va/holy_father/john_paul_ii/homilies/2002/documents/ hf_jp-ii_hom_20020817_shrine-divine-mercy_en.html.

Kowalska, St. Maria Faustina. *Diary of Saint Maria Faustina Kowalska: Divine Mercy in My Soul.* Stockbridge: Marian Press, 1987.

Kosicki, Fr. George W. *Thematic Concordance to the Diary of Saint Maria Faustina Kowalska.* Stockbridge: Marian Press, 1996.

Michalenko, Sr. Sophia. *Mercy My Mission: Life of Sister Faustina H. Kowalska C.O.L.M.* Stockbridge: Marian Press, 1987.

Piekut, Sr. Beata (Ed.). *The Letters of Saint Faustina.* Kraków: Wydawnictwo Misericordia Zgromadzenia Sióstr Matki Bożej Miłosierdzia, 2005.

Siepak, Sr. Elizabeth and Bałuk-Ulewiczowa, Teresa. *A Gift from God for Our Times: the Life and Mission of Saint Faustina.* Kraków: Wydawnictwo Misericordia Zgromadzenia Sióstr Matki Bożej Miłosierdzia, 2007.

Siepak, Sr. Elizabeth. *Sister Faustina's New "Congregation": The Apostolic Movement*

of the Divine Mercy. Kraków: Wydawnictwo Misericordia Zgromadzenia Sióstr Matki Bożej Miłosierdzia, 2005.

Siepak, Sr. Elżbieta and Dłubak, Sr. Nazaria *The Spirituality of Saint Faustina: the Road to Union With God.* Dorchester: The Congregation of the Sisters of Our Lady of Mercy, 2000.

Sopoćko, Fr. Michael. *Mercy of God, the Only Hope of Mankind.* Stockbridge: Marian Press, 1950.

Tarnawska, Maria. *St. Maria Faustina Kowalska: Her Life and Mission.* Stockbridge: Marian Press, 2000.

Websites

http://www.faustyna.pl/en
http://www.faustina-message.com/
www.konstancinjeziorna.pl

AUTHOR'S ACKNOWLEDGMENTS
FOR THE POLISH EDITION

I WOULD LIKE TO EXTEND A HEARTFELT THANK YOU TO ALL those who helped me in the writing of this book. First of all, the Sisters of the Congregation of Our Lady of Mercy, and in particular Sr. Elizabeth Siepak, the spokeswoman for the Shrine in Łagiewniki and the author of several books about Sr. Faustina. I am deeply grateful to Sr. Siepak for her support and kindness, as well as for her invaluable pointers and suggestions. I owe the opportunity to visit all the convents where Sr. Faustina lived to the kindness of the Sisters who showed me around: Vaclava Siemienik (Rabka), Senta Krajza (Walendów), Viannea Dąbrowska (Derdy), Joela Ślazyk (Kiekrz), Clavera Wolska (Płock), Tobias Wilkosz (Biała), Seraphina Sałacińska (Częstochowa), Catherine Zakrzewska, and Kordiana Szołtysek (Warsaw). The memories Sr. Amata Strojewska, Sr. Urbana Trybocka, and Camilla Maria Olszewska shared with me in Walendów were especially valuable.

I would also like to express my gratitude to the members of the Congregation of Sisters of the Merciful Jesus: Sr. Dominique Steć of Ostrówek and Sr. Anna Młynarczyk of Vilnius.

The memories of Maria Nowicka proved crucial for establishing the details of Sr. Faustina's stay in Warsaw in 1924. I would like to thank her for hours of fascinating conversation. The ins and outs of life in Ostrówek were explained to me by Grażyna Musiałowska, while Włodzimierz Dudka shared with me the details about Sr. Faustina's life in Głogowiec and Świnice Warckie.

My sincere thanks for their help and kindness must also go to Fr. Jan Bednarczyk, the Director of the Library of the Pontifical University of John Paul II in Kraków; Sr. Gregoria Burlikowska from the library and archives at the

Shrine of Divine Mercy in Łagiewniki; Fr. Jan Machniak, the author of several books about Sr. Faustina's spirituality; Fr. Miecislaus Różański and Sr. Lucyna Witczak from the archives of the Łódź Archdiocese; Petras Marcela of the Prayer and Pilgrimage Center in Vilnius; Grażyna Kaniuk and Alfred Lipnicki of the John Paul II Hospital in Kraków; Fr. Joseph Naumowicz, Fr. Henry Bartuszek, Fr. Thaddaeus Polak, and Fr. Matthew Matuszewski.

I would like to thank the following individuals for their help in solving certain historical riddles and enabling me to learn about the history of the places where Sr. Faustina lived: Thomas Pietras, Christopher Klociński, Richard Bonisławski; and the team of those devoted to the history of Rabka: Joseph Szlaga, Gregory Moskal, Camillus Kowalczyk, and Michael Rapta.

I have warm memories of all the others that I met while working on this book, but whom I do not mention here. A heartfelt thank you to you all.

SAINT FAUSTINA
BIOGRAPHICAL TIMELINE

August 25, 1905
Birth of the third child to Marianne and Stanislaus Kowalski in the village of Głogowiec.

August 27, 1905
Baptism in St. Casimir's Church in Świnice Warckie, administered by Fr. Joseph Chodyński. The Kowalski's child is given the name Helen.

1912
Young Helen experiences God's love and hears His call to a more perfect way of life for the first time in the parish church of Świnice Warckie.

1914
Helen Kowalska receives her First Holy Communion in Świnice Warckie.

1917
Helen Kowalska begins elementary school in Świnice Warckie.

1921
Helen begins work as a domestic servant in the home of Casimir and Leocadia Bryszewski in Aleksandrów.

1922
Helen Kowalska returns from Aleksandrów to Głogowiec and tells her parents about her wish to enter a convent. They oppose the idea firmly.

Fall 1922
Helen Kowalska leaves for Łódź to seek employment. She stays with her uncle Michael Rapacki at 9 Krośnieńska Street and works as a servant for some Franciscan Tertiaries.

February 2, 1923
Helen begins work as a domestic servant for Marcianna Wieczorek (Sadowska), the owner of a store at 29 Abramowski Street, Łódź.

July 1924
- Helen Kowalska travels to Warsaw in order to enter a convent.
- Works as a domestic servant for Aldona and Samuel Lipszyc in Ostrówek, Klembów District.
- First visits a convent of the Congregation of the Sisters of Our Lady of Mercy and conditional acceptance by Mother Michael Moraczewska.

August 1, 1925
Helen Kowalska officially enters the Congregation of the Sisters of Our Lady of Mercy at the convent on Żytnia Street in Warsaw.

August 1925
Postulant Helen Kowalska travels to the Congregation's summer house in Skolimów in order to regain her health.

1925
Postulancy of Helen Kowalska at the Congregation's Warsaw convent under the supervision of Directress Jane Bartkiewicz.

January 23, 1926
Helen Kowalska arrives in Kraków in order to complete her postulancy and the two-year-long novitiate under the supervision of Mother Margaret Gimbutt and Mother Mary Joseph Brzoza.

April 30, 1926
Investiture ceremony where Helen Kowalska receives her habit and religious name: Sister Maria Faustina.

April 30, 1928
Sister Faustina makes her first religious vows (of poverty, chastity, and obedience). These vows are valid for one year and are renewed annually for four years, until the profession of perpetual vows.

October 31, 1928
Sister Faustina leaves for the Warsaw convent where she is to work in the kitchen.

February 21, 1929
Sister Faustina travels to Vilnius to take over for Sister Petronela Basiura who is leaving in order to complete her third probation.

June 11, 1929
Sister Faustina returns from Vilnius to the Warsaw convent on Żytnia Street.

June 1929
Sister Faustina travels to the Congregation's new house on Hetmańska Street in the Grochów district of Warsaw.

July 7, 1929
Sister Faustina travels to Kiekrz to work in the kitchen as a replacement for the ill Sr. Modesta Rzeczkowska.

October 1929
Sister Faustina stays at the Congregation's Mother House on Żytnia Street in Warsaw.

May-June 1930-1932
- Sister Faustina arrives at the convent in Płock and works in the bakery and kitchen.
- Sister Faustina stays briefly in the Płock convent's affiliated house in Biała (around 7 miles from Płock).

February 22, 1931
The beginning of Sr. Faustina's prophetic mission. She has the first vision of the Merciful Jesus and receives instructions on having His image painted.

February, 1931
Jesus gives instructions to establish the Feast of Divine Mercy on the first Sunday after Easter.

November 1932
- Sister Faustina travels to Warsaw for her third probation.
- Retreat in Walendów. Sister Faustina makes a confession with Fr. Edmund Elter, SJ, and receives the first confirmation of the supernatural origin of her visions.

December 1, 1932
Sister Faustina begins her third probation under the direction of Mother Margaret Gimbutt.

April 18, 1933
Sister Faustina arrives in Kraków.

April 21, 1933
Sister Faustina begins an eight-day retreat in the convent in Kraków. She makes a confession with Fr. Joseph Andrasz, SJ, for the first time.

May 1, 1933
Sister Faustina professes her perpetual vows in Kraków.

May 23, 1933
Sister Faustina travels from Kraków to Vilnius. She makes a stop in Częstochowa on the way.

May 24, 1933
Sister Faustina prays in the Chapel of Our Lady of Częstochowa.

May 25, 1933
Sister Faustina arrives at the Vilnius convent where she takes up working in the garden.

June 1933
Sister Faustina's first meeting with Fr. Michael Sopoćko, her confessor and spiritual director in Vilnius.

January 2, 1934
Sister Faustina's first visit to the studio of painter Eugeniusz Kazimirowski. She later visits the studio regularly accompanied by one of her superiors, Mother Irene Krzyżanowska or Mother Borgia Tichy.

March 29, 1934
Sister Faustina writes the act of oblation, offering her life for sinners, especially those who have lost trust in the Divine Mercy.

June 1934
Completion of the image of the Merciful Jesus in Eugene Kazimirowski's studio.

August 12, 1934
Sister Faustina falls ill. Fr. Michael Sopoćko is summoned and administers the Sacrament of the Anointing of the Sick.

February 15, 1935
Sister Faustina makes a visit to her home village of Głogowiec in order to be with her gravely ill mother.

April 26-28, 1935
The first public display of the image of the Merciful Jesus at the Chapel of Our Lady of Ostra Brama in Vilnius.

May 1935
Sister Faustina receives the first revelation concerning the establishing of a new Congregation.

September 13-14, 1935
Sister Faustina receives the words of the Divine Mercy Chaplet in a revelation.

October 19, 1935
Sister Faustina departs to make an eight-day retreat in Kraków.

November 4, 1935
Sister Faustina returns to Vilnius after the retreat in Kraków. On the way, she makes a stop in Częstochowa.

January 8, 1936
Sister Faustina meets with Archbishop Romuald Jałbrzykowski, during which she presents Jesus' instructions to establish a new Congregation.

March 21, 1936
Sister Faustina leaves Vilnius for Warsaw.

March 25, 1936
Sister Faustina arrives in Walendów, and later departs for Derdy.

May 11, 1936
Accompanied by Sr. Edmunda Sękuł, Sr. Faustina leaves Derdy for Kraków, where she will remain until her death.

June 19, 1936
Sister Faustina takes part in a procession in honor of the Sacred Heart of Jesus at the Jesuit Church on Kopernik Street in Kraków.

September 19, 1936
Sister Faustina is examined by a doctor at the hospital in Prądnik, Kraków.

December 9, 1936
Sister Faustina is admitted to the hospital in Prądnik.

December 24, 1936
Sister Faustina returns to the convent for Christmas.

December 27, 1936
Sister Faustina returns to the hospital in Prądnik for further treatment.

March 27, 1937
Sister Faustina is released from the hospital and returns to the convent in Łagiewniki.

April 13, 1937
Sister Faustina's health deteriorates.

May 4, 1937
Sister Faustina receives permission from Mother General Michael Moraczewska to leave the Congregation, but because of great spiritual darkness does not act on this permission, deeming that it is not God's will for her to do so.

July 29, 1937
Sister Faustina travels to Rabka for treatment.

August 10, 1937
Sister Faustina returns from Rabka to Kraków.

August 12, 1937
Sister Faustina meets with Fr. Michael Sopoćko at the convent in Łagiewniki.

September 6, 1937
Sister Faustina is reassigned from her duties in the garden to being a gatekeeper because of the poor state of her health.

September 27, 1937
Sister Faustina, along with Mother Irene Krzyżanowska, visits the J. Cebulski publishing house on 22 Szewska Street to arrange the printing up of holy cards with the image of the Merciful Jesus. Afterwards, she prays at St. Mary's Church in Kraków.

October 1937
Sister Faustina receives a revelation about the Hour of Mercy at the convent in Łagiewniki, Kraków.

April 21, 1938
Sister Faustina is readmitted to the hospital in Prądnik.

July 1938
Mother General Michael Moraczewska pays a visit to Sr. Faustina at the hospital in Prądnik.

August 25, 1938
Father Theodore Czaputa, chaplain at the Congregation's convent in Łagiewniki, administers the Sacrament of the Anointing of the Sick to Sr. Faustina in the hospital in Prądnik.

August 28, 1938
Father Michael Sopoćko travels to Kraków and visits Sr. Faustina several times in the hospital in Prądnik.

September 17, 1938
Sister Faustina returns from the hospital to the convent in Łagiewniki.

September 22, 1938
In accordance with a tradition in the Congregation, Sr. Faustina makes an apology to the other sisters for her unintentional shortcomings.

September 26, 1938
Sister Faustina meets with Fr. Michael Sopoćko for the last time.

October 5, 1938
Sister Faustina departs this life (at 10:45 p.m.).

October 7, 1938
Sister Faustina's funeral takes place on the first Friday of the month on the feast of Our Lady of the Rosary. She is buried in a tomb in the convent cemetery in the Congregation's garden.

March 6, 1959
The Holy See issues a Notification banning the spreading of the devotion to the Divine Mercy in the forms outlined by Sr. Faustina.

October 21, 1965
The diocesan investigation into Sr. Faustina's life and virtues is initiated.

November 25, 1966
Sister Faustina's body is transferred from the tomb in the cemetery to the convent chapel in Łagiewniki, where it is interred in the crypt.

September 20, 1967
Cardinal Karol Wojtyła declares the diocesan investigation completed. The documents are sent to Rome.

April 15, 1978
The Notification banning the spread of the devotion to the Divine Mercy in the forms outlined by Sr. Faustina is lifted (published on June 30, 1978).

1981
The first edition of the *Diary of Sr. Faustina Kowalska* is published.

April 18, 1993
Beatification of Sr. Faustina by Pope John Paul II in St. Peter's Square, Rome. Sister Faustina's relics are placed on public display at the altar below the miraculous image of the Merciful Jesus in the Shrine of Divine Mercy in Łagiewniki, Kraków.

June 7, 1997
Pilgrimage of Pope John Paul II to the Shrine of Divine Mercy in Łagiewniki, Kraków. The Pope prays in front of the miraculous image of the Merciful Jesus and the relics of Blessed Sr. Faustina.

April 30, 2000
Canonization of Sr. Faustina by Pope John Paul II in St. Peter's Square, Rome, which is linked via two-way live video transmission to the Shrine of the Divine Mercy in Łagiewniki, Kraków. The Feast of Divine Mercy is established for the entire Church.

August 17, 2002
The second pilgrimage of Pope John Paul II to the Shrine in Łagiewniki, Kraków, where he entrusts the whole world to the Divine Mercy during the consecration of the Basilica.

May 27, 2006
Pope Benedict XVI prays in front of the miraculous image of the Merciful Jesus and the relics of St. Faustina at the Shrine of Divine Mercy in Łagiewniki, Kraków.

INDEX OF PERSONS

S

T

U

W

Z

Ż

PHOTO CREDITS

PHOTOS IN THE TEXT:
p. 19 — Marian Helpers Center Archives
p. 29, 39, 57, 64, 66, 67, 75, 91, 96, 161, 164, 169, 173, 281, 327 —
Archives of the Congregation of the Sisters of Our Lady of Mercy
p. 42 — Photo taken by Iwona Podgórska
p. 49, 115, 125, 131, 179, 187, 205, 213, 289, 317 — Photos taken by ©
Maciej Talar
p. 203 — Archives of the John Paul II Hospital in Kraków
p. 347 — *L'Osservatore Romano*
p. 355 — Photo taken by © Marie Romagnano

PHOTO INSERT:
Photo 8 — Archival family photo from personal collection of Barbara
Stachlewska-Bernatt
Photo 13 — Archives of the Metropolitan Curia in Białystok
Other photographs courtesy of the Archive of the Congregation of the Sisters
of Our Lady of Mercy
Photos 15, 16, 19, 20, 25, 26 — Archive of the Congregation of the Sisters of
Our Lady of Mercy
Photos 23, 24 — Archives of the John Paul II Hospital in Kraków
Photos 17, 18, 27 — Photos taken by Iwona Podgórska
Photo 21 — Reproduction of the image of the Merciful Jesus by Eugene
Kazimirowski, the Shrine of Divine Mercy in Vilnius
Photo 22 — Reproduction of the image of the Merciful Jesus by Adolf Hyła,
the Shrine of Divine Mercy in Kraków-Łagiewniki
Photo 29 — Photo taken by Iwona Podgórska
Other photographs courtesy of the Archives of the Congregation of the Sisters
of Our Lady of Mercy
Photos 43, 44 — Photos taken by Iwona Podgórska

Other photographs courtesy of the Archive of the Congregation of the Sisters of Our Lady of Mercy

Photos 53, 54, 58 — Photos taken by © Joseph Romagnano

Photo 55 — Photo taken by © Philip Chidell

Photo 56 — Photo taken by Maciej Talar

ABOUT THE AUTHOR

Ewa K. Czaczkowska (pronounced Ava K. Chachkovska) is an award-winning historian, journalist, and biographer. She graduated from the University of Nicolaus Copernicus in Toruń, Poland, with a major in history and completed postgraduate studies in journalism at the University of Warsaw.

Since 1990, Czaczkowska has worked for *Rzeczpospolita* (*The Commonwealth*), one of the most influential newspapers in Poland, specializing mainly in religious and social topics. Beginning in 1991, she reported on St. John Paul II's pilgrimages to Poland and other countries. Czaczkowska's professionalism, zeal for the truth, and talent for research were recognized when she received the prestigious "Ślad" award ("The Trace") in 2002, which is in honor of Bishop Jan Chrapek.

In 2010, Czaczkowska co-founded The Areopagus XXI (The 21st Century Areopagus) foundation; the Areopag21.pl internet portal, which facilitates talks on God, the Catholic faith, and religion; and "Cinema with a Soul" movie festivals.

Since 2012, she has been an adjunct professor at the Institute of Media Education and Journalism, part of the Cardinal Stefan Wyszyński University in Warsaw. Czaczkowska collaborates with several weeklies and has been a guest on various radio and TV programs.

She has written several books, including: *The Church of the 20th Century* (1999); *Father Jerzy Popiełuszko* (with co-author Tomasz Wiścicki: first edition in 2004; second in 2009); *Cardinal Wyszyński* (2009); *St. Faustina: A Biography of the Saint* (2012); *Cardinal Stefan Wyszyński: The Biography* (2013); and *Miracles of St. Faustina* (2014).

Czaczkowska is a three-time recipient of the "Phoenix" award from the Polish Association of Catholic Publishers. The Polish edition of the present volume, published under the title *St. Faustina: Biography of the Saint*, won one of the Phoenixes and has been translated into seven languages: Italian, Spanish, Portuguese, French, Croatian, Slovak, and English.

Czaczkowska holds a Ph.D. in history and lives in Warsaw.

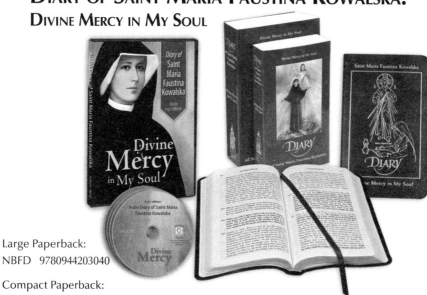

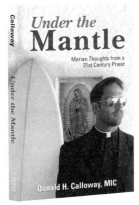

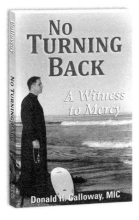
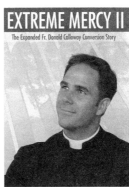

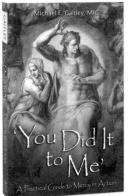

1. Marianne Kowalska née Babel
(sometimes her maiden name is spelled
"Bawej"), mother of St. Faustina Kowalska.

2. Stanislaus Kowalski, father of St. Faustina.

3. Natalia, younger sister of St. Faustina, who
was married twice and went by the names
Natalia Olszyńska and Natalia Grzelak.

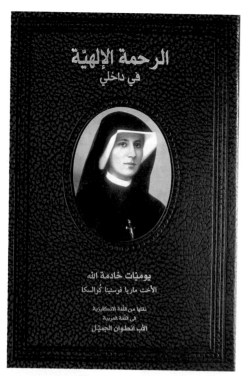

43. The Arabic edition of St. Faustina's *Diary*.

44. The Korean edition of St. Faustina's *Diary*.

45. The Chinese edition of
St. Faustina's *Diary*.

46. The Indonesian edition of
St. Faustina's *Diary*.

47. The beatification of Sr. Faustina on April 18, 1993. Sister Faustina's eldest sister, Josephine, is receiving Communion from Pope John Paul II.

48. Above and below: The Feast of Divine Mercy is being celebrated at the Shrine of Divine Mercy in Kraków-Łagiewniki.

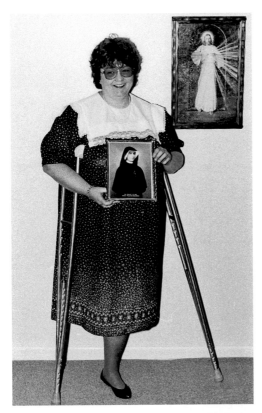

49. Maureen Digan, an American, was healed from lymphedema at the tomb of Sr. Faustina in Kraków-Łagiewniki March 28, 1981. This is the miracle recognized for her beatification.

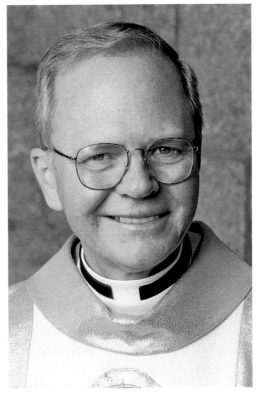

50. Father Ronald Pytel, pastor at the Church of Our Lady of the Rosary in Baltimore, Maryland, was healed from heart disease on Oct. 5, 1995, the miracle recognized for Sr. Faustina's canonization.

51. Canonization of Sr. Faustina, April 30, 2000. During the telecast between St. Peter's Square in Rome and the Shrine of Divine Mercy in Kraków-Łagiewniki.

52. The praying of the Chaplet of Divine Mercy at the convent's chapel at the Shrine in Kraków-Łagiewniki.

53. The crowd waves to Pope Benedict XVI before the beatification of John Paul II on May 1, 2011, Divine Mercy Sunday. More than 1.5 million pilgrims came to Rome, many carrying images of the Divine Mercy.

54. In his homily for John Paul II's beatification, Pope Benedict XVI said:
"Today is the Second Sunday of Easter, which Blessed John Paul II entitled Divine Mercy
Sunday. The date was chosen for today's celebration because, in God's providence,
my predecessor died on the vigil of this feast."

"There was his witness in suffering: the Lord gradually stripped him of everything, yet he
remained ever a 'rock,' as Christ desired. His profound humility, grounded in close union
with Christ, enabled him to continue to lead the Church and to give to the world a message
which became all the more eloquent as his physical strength declined."

55. On March 31, 2013, during the Easter Sunday liturgy in St. Peter's Square, Pope Francis venerates an icon of the Risen Christ. In his Easter *Urbi et Orbi* message, Pope Francis says, "God's mercy can make even the driest land become a garden, can restore life to dry bones (cf. Ez 37:1-14). ... Let us be renewed by God's mercy."

56. In his first Sunday homily as Pope on March 17, 2013, Francis goes so far as to say that "the Lord's most powerful message" is "mercy."

57. In opening Vatican II on October, 11, 1962, Pope John XXIII — who was canonized with John Paul II on April 27, 2014, Divine Mercy Sunday — stressed that "nowadays ... the Spouse of Christ prefers to make use of the medicine of mercy rather than that of severity." This beloved Pope was known for his humility, gentleness, and love toward all.

58. On April 27, 2014, Divine Mercy Sunday, Blessed John Paul II and Blessed John XXIII are canonized together by Pope Francis in St. Peter's Square. The canonization of John Paul II comes only nine years after his death, and the miracle recognized for it involves the instantaneous healing of Floribeth Mora, a Costa Rican woman, from a brain aneurism. She is healed on May 1, 2011, the very day of John Paul's beatification, which is on Divine Mercy Sunday.